D0847410

Velázquez

Painter and Courtier

Velázquez

Painter and Courtier

JONATHAN BROWN

YALE UNIVERSITY PRESS
NEW HAVEN AND LONDON · 1986

Designed by Gillian Malpass
Filmset in Monophoto Baskerville by
Jolly & Barber Ltd, Rugby, Warwickshire
Color originated by
Amilcare Pizzi, s.p.a., Milan
Printed in Spain by Heraclio Fournier, S.A., Vitoria

Library of Congress Cataloging in Publication Data

Brown, Jonathan.
    Velazquez, painter and courtier.

    Bibliography: p.
    Includes index.
    1. Velázquez, Diego, 1599–1660 —— Criticism and
interpretation. I. Title.
ND813.V4B89 1986   759.6[B]   85–14234
ISBN 0–300–03466–0 (cloth)
        0–300–03894–1 (pbk)

Frontispiece: After Velázquez, *Self-Portrait* (Florence, Uffizi), 1.01 × 0.81 m.

A los meninos – Claire, Michael, and Daniel

PREFACE

My interest in Velázquez began in 1958, when I spent a year in Madrid as an undergraduate. I can no longer remember how I came to know of the artist, but what I knew was enough to send me to the Prado to see his pictures. I liked them at once and, thinking that I would like them even more if I had some information about the artist, I started to look for a book to read. By chance, the one that came to hand was entitled *Velázquez. Six Color Reproductions of Paintings in the Prado Museum*, with a short introduction by José Ortega y Gasset (Oxford, 1946). As I now recognize, Ortega took a highly personal approach to Velázquez. But then, his words seemed to be authoritative and definitive. According to Ortega, Velázquez "was probably one of the coolest men in existence. To him, to live meant to keep distance. His art reflects his attitude toward life. It is an art of distance." These words made a staggering impression on me, a still-uncertain youth who was living at a time when emotional detachment — we called it being cool — was counted among the ultimate virtues. At once, Velázquez became my favorite artist and, although for different reasons, he has remained so ever since.

In the intervening time — more than twenty-five years — I have studied Velázquez from the perspective of an art historian and no longer believe him to be the "coolest" artist who ever lived, at least as Ortega used the term. During these years of study, I have pondered both the data of Velázquez' life and works and the variety of ways in which this data has been construed by successive generations of artists, critics, and historians. From this vantage point, I still value the writings of Ortega as valuable examples of the unceasing play between the past and present, between the subjective and the objective, which keeps great art of earlier ages before our eyes. Yet, my faith as an historian makes me skeptical of interpretations which rely more on speculation than investigation. There is what might be called a "wall of fact" against which misguided theories inevitably crash and fall to the ground.

Unfortunately, the wall of fact often has holes and fissures, those parts of the past which have yet to be retrieved and may be lost forever. The study of Velázquez is a case in point. In some ways, his life and career are reasonably well-documented. There are considerable gaps in the period between his birth (1599) and his definitive installation at the court of Philip IV (1623). But from then until the end of his life (1660), there is abundant evidence of his official activities. The documentation, however, is wanting in two crucial respects. First, there is virtually no record of Velázquez as a person or as a thinker on art. Private letters, such as those left behind by Rubens or Poussin, are few in number and never touch on what interests us most, Velázquez' objectives as an artist. Second, the documents seldom help to date his paintings with any degree of precision. After 1640, Velázquez received an annual stipend plus perquisites which was meant to pay for paintings executed for the king. This method of payment implies the absence of commissions or receipts for many pictures, an implication which is borne out by fact. The majority of the documents fall into the category of the administrative or bureaucratic and concern questions such as payments of arrears in salary or the matters of household service in which Velázquez was involved.

It would be reassuring to believe that one day we will discover the missing pieces in the wall of fact about Velázquez, but I am doubtful. Research has been in progress for over a hundred years and has investigated the logical places where documents might be found. Also, I do not believe that many more pictures by Velázquez, a notoriously unproductive artist, will come to light, and certainly no major works. In other words, we now know a high percentage of what there is to be known about the facts of the life and output of this great master. Thus, it must be asked, is there anything new to say about Velázquez? Obviously, my answer is, Yes, as can be seen in the rather lengthy book which follows these prefatory remarks.

As the title implies, this book considers Velázquez from an artistic point of view, on one hand, and from a biographical point of view, on the other. In analyzing the development of Velázquez' art, I have tried to place it in the wider context of seventeenth-century painting and theory. Velázquez, in most respects, is not a representative Spanish painter of the period. His excellent education, his extensive contacts with foreign art and artists, and, above all, his privileged patronage by Philip IV, shaped his career in ways that removed him from the mainstream of Spanish Baroque art. But, as the comparison with the leading painters in other parts of Europe demonstrates, Velázquez was not a typical international Baroque artist either. In fact, despite certain undeniable points of contact with some of his contemporaries, Velázquez really seems to have been attempting to find a new approach to the goals and methods of the art of painting.

The recognition of the revolutionary nature of his artistic enterprise is by now a commonplace in the literature on the master, but many of the definitions of Velázquez' extraordinary achievement presuppose the existence of modern art and are therefore incongruous with his epoch. The issue at the center of Velázquez' art, as I see it, concerns his reevaluation of the importance of nature and the classical ideal of beauty for the process of artistic creation. There is no written proof of this assertion, although the pictures seem to leave little doubt about its validity. However, just over a century after Velázquez' death, the issue was raised explicitly by artists who knew his paintings and still spoke the language of his time. To Anton Raphael Mengs, who spent several years in Spain and looked at Velázquez through the lens of classicism, it was clear that his great strength was his powerful approximation to the appearance of nature. In Mengs' opinion, this quality, although admirable, did not entitle him to a place among the greatest artists such as Raphael and Poussin, who, unlike Velázquez, were guided by standards of ideal beauty which perfected the flaws of an imperfect nature. Therefore, he classified the artist among the naturalists (together with Titian) and assigned him to the second rung on the ladder of great painters.

A younger contemporary of Mengs saw the matter rather differently. For Francisco de Goya, Velázquez' powerful grasp on the appearances of nature was evidence of great art. Thus, he prized Velázquez as a supreme artist and a worthy source of inspiration for others to follow. As reported by his son, Goya "looked with veneration at Velázquez and Rembrandt, but above all he studied and looked at Nature, whom he called his mistress." With his usual prescience, Goya perceived the standards which, by the middle of the nineteenth century, had replaced Raphael and the ancients as the yardsticks by which great art was to be measured.

Indeed, I believe that Goya could have been speaking for Velázquez when, in 1792, he reported to the Academy of San Fernando on the study of art and wrote these words: "What scandal it is to hear nature despised in favor of Greek statues by those who know neither one nor the other and are not conscious of how the smallest part of nature overwhelms and amazes those who know most." These remarks, aimed at servile followers of Mengs, are probably more inflammatory than those which Velázquez would have permitted himself. But the issues and terms of the debate are ones that he must have known and pondered long and hard as he worked his way toward his original, non-classical, style of painting.

A biography of Velázquez, in the conventional sense of the word, is extremely difficult to write because we lack the personal documents which would open his inner life to scrutiny. Without a record of his feelings, thoughts, and reactions to events and personalities, it is hard to know the human side of the artist. Yet this does not mean that the task is entirely hopeless. We shall never know Velázquez as well as we know Picasso or even Goya, to mention the most distinguished Spanish painters to follow him. But by reading between the lines of the copious official documentation of his career at court, it is possible, I believe, to reconstruct certain aspects of Velázquez the man.

Extrapolating personal information from official papers is admittedly perilous. In the case of Velázquez, we are guided in the quest by his long association with the court of Philip IV, which provides a framework for interpreting the seemingly routine information found in the documents. The phenomenon of the court artist is well known in the history of the seventeenth century. Indeed, some of the greatest figures of the age — Rubens, Bernini, Van Dyck, for example — found their *juste milieu* in working for powerful princes of the church and state. Velázquez has long been included in this company, but the full implications of this circumstance, in my opinion, have yet to be drawn. Recent studies by J. H. Elliott and J. E. Varey in particular have provided information on how Philip's court functioned, making it possible to read the Velázquez documentation in a different way. Also valuable are the studies by Julián Gállego and Richard L. Kagan on the social status of the artist in sixteenth- and seventeenth-century Spain, a subject to which I too have devoted attention in the past. With the help of this work, I have attempted to reconstruct Velázquez' career as a courtier and to integrate the resulting personal profile with his artistic development.

I believe that my approach to the documents is informative on several points. First, it helps restore the balance between Velázquez' activities as an artist and as a courtier. Second, it offers a clue to the solution of one of the central mysteries of his career. It has long been noted that the quantity of his artistic production fell substantially after 1640. One explanation for the decline was offered by Palomino: that Velázquez' increasing responsibilities as an official of the royal household usurped the time available for painting. This is undoubtedly correct, but fails to recognize that at least some of the official duties had an artistic dimension. Philip IV, his patron, was one of the greatest picture collectors of the Baroque age, a little-appreciated fact that is now starting to become apparent. From about 1630 at the end of his reign, Philip acquired an extraordinary number of paintings, many of them masterpieces. As the collection grew, the king became interested in its display, a circumstance which decisively affected the direction of Velázquez' career. It emerges from the documents that, especially after 1640, he devoted an increasing part of his attention to work as a court decorator. This aspect of his life is given full attention in the following study. Finally, the evidence offers an explanation of why Velázquez decided to follow a course which led him away from the art of painting. To my mind, it is clear that he knew what he was doing when he sought promotion in the hierarchy of royal service. By analyzing his motives, I hope to reveal the central dilemma of Velázquez' career — his attempt to reconcile the often-contradictory demands of the desire to be considered both a great gentleman and a great artist.

A few remarks about the organization of the book are now in order. In principle, this book is addressed both to specialists on Velázquez and general readers interested in seventeenth-century art. I recognize that the requirements of this dual audience are not always compatible and have tried to solve the problem by confining the detailed consideration of specific scholarly questions to the footnotes and Appendix A. However, my desire to produce a seamless, consecutive narrative is not always consistent with the partial and at times ambiguous nature of the documentation. Within the limits of the possible, I have tried to refrain from using unsupported speculation to fill the gaps and settle the doubts. As a consequence, there are passages in the text where the reader will be asked to follow a consideration of evidence which leads to an uncertain conclusion.

The most frequent occurrence of tentative discussion involves the chronology of Velázquez' works. Dated or firmly datable pictures comprise the minority of the master's oeuvre. Understandably, many scholars have tried to compensate for the uncertainty by establishing a chronology based on circumstantial evidence and stylistic analysis. I cannot claim to have resisted completely the temptation myself. But the fact remains, and is often acknowledged in the literature, that the evolution of Velázquez' style is difficult to plot except in a general way. The recent discovery of evidence which confirms a date of 1650 for the Villa Medici landscapes, instead of 1630 as had been preferred by some recent writers, demonstrates the pitfalls of a purely intuitive approach to chronology. Therefore, I have tended to use approximate dates, sometimes with fairly generous limits, rather than to hypothesize that a problematic picture was done at a specific time.

Over the years, there has been a tendency to reduce the number of authentic works. José López-Rey, author of the most recent catalogue, lists 129 works, of which six are drawings. My list is even somewhat smaller. Although I have not attempted to compile a catalogue raisonné, I have discussed and illustrated every work which I consider to be authentic and appended a list of attributions for the convenience of the reader.

The impetus for writing this book was furnished by the invitation to deliver the Slade Lectures at Oxford University, which I did in January–February 1982. I can only hope that the experience was half as enjoyable for the audience as it was for the lecturer. For this memorable occasion, not to mention the invitation, I am grateful to the members of the Slade Committee, and especially to Francis and Larissa Haskell, who made a visitor from the United States feel at home in the unique world of Oxford. I also appreciate the generous hospitality and good company offered by the Warden and Fellows of All Souls College, where I resided.

During the years of research on Velázquez, I have benefited greatly from discussion with several scholars who shared their information on the artist and his times with exemplary generosity. Thus, it is with heartfelt gratitude that I mention their names: Enriqueta Harris Frankfort; William B. Jordan; Gridley McKim-Smith; Steven N. Orso; and Marcus B. Burke. I owe a special debt of thanks to my friend and collaborator, J. H. Elliott, for a dialogue, now of twelve years' standing, which has enriched my knowledge of seventeenth-century Spain in more ways than I can tell.

As always, I want to acknowledge the contribution of my students at the Institute of Fine Arts, New York University. I offered seminars on Velázquez in 1974, 1980, and 1983, and on each occasion was rewarded with excellent papers and discussion. In some instances, I have made use of the work of specific members of the seminars, which is acknowledged in the appropriate place in the notes.

Like the author of every art-historical study, I have counted on the goodwill and cooperation of colleagues in museums, archives, and libraries and have rarely been disappointed. In particular, I want to thank Allan Braham, Alfonso E. Pérez Sánchez, John Brealey, Erich Schleier, Irene Martín, Mary Schmidt, José M. Calderón, Rocío Arnáez, María Teresa Alcón, and the directors and staff of the Archivo and Biblioteca de Palacio, Madrid; Archivo Histórico de Protocolos, Madrid; and Archivo General de Simancas.

I am very grateful to the trustees of the Robert Lehman Foundation, and particularly to Michael M. Thomas, for a generous subsidy to Yale University Press to help with the publication of this book. I also thank the American Council of Learned Societies for a grant-in-aid which enabled me to go to Spain in 1983 to restudy works by Velázquez in Spanish collections.

In the writing and production stages, I was ably assisted by Cindy Mack, my resourceful research assistant; Lynda Emery, whose skill as a typist has kept me from entering the computer age; Gillian Malpass, who edited the manuscript with unfailing professionalism and good humor; and John Nicoll, whose concern for every aspect of the publication is deeply appreciated. I also thank Sandra Brown for helping with the layout of the illustrations and with the instruction of our "meninos" in the (flexible) *etiqueta* of our household.

Princeton, June 1985

CONTENTS

CHAPTER I

Velázquez in Seville

Diego de Velázquez was born in Seville in 1599, the first of seven children of Juan Rodríguez de Silva and Jerónima Velázquez.[1] Both of Velázquez' parents claimed descent from the lesser nobility, a claim which the painter was to assert and seek to validate later in life. Evidence suggests that this claim was true, although the family credentials were not in perfect order. The little we know of Velázquez' early years indicates that the family, whatever its pretensions, lived a middle-class rather than an aristocratic life. For one thing, the decision to allow his son to become a professional painter shows that Juan Rodríguez was somewhat indifferent to the criteria of a noble life, because painting was considered to be a craft in seventeenth-century Spain, and therefore an unworthy pursuit for the son of a nobleman, especially the first-born son.[2] Yet Juan Rodríguez evidently provided his son with a good grounding in letters, which of itself indicates that the family was not destitute of money or ambition. This education, which can be safely deduced from the contents of Velázquez' library, was a valuable asset in a country where only about twenty percent of the population could read and write.[3]

Evidence replaces inference on 1 December 1610, when Velázquez' father gave the boy over to the painter Francisco Pacheco as an apprentice.[4] The contract of apprenticeship, which was not signed until 17 September of the following year, is standard for the period and stipulated a six-year term, during which Velázquez would reside in Pacheco's house while he learned the techniques of the painter's art. The choice of Pacheco as master was undoubtedly the turning-point in Velázquez' life, although not for the obvious reason.

Pacheco was not a gifted painter, a fact, however, which was no impediment to a successful artistic career in Seville.[5] He and his brother had been orphaned at an early age and taken into custody by his uncle, who was also called Francisco. The elder Pacheco was a canon of the Seville Cathedral and renowned in the city as a scholar and theologian. Canon Pacheco had made friends with other writers and scholars in Seville and with them constituted an informal academy of letters. This academy followed the model created by Italian humanists in the fifteenth century and was comprised of a group of scholars who met occasionally to discuss matters of common interest and to criticize each other's work-in-progress. For the sake of convenience, this group can be called Pacheco's academy,[6] but in fact it had originally been formed in the 1560s by an important Spanish humanist, Juan de Mal Lara, who, like many of his contemporaries, was a follower of Erasmus. After his death in 1571, his work was carried on by three associates, the Canon Pacheco, Francisco Medina, and Fernando de Herrera, the last of whom is now recognized as a major Spanish Renaissance poet.

The members of Pacheco's academy in most respects were typical Renaissance humanists, who focused their studies on classical languages, literature, and history. They wrote scholarly books packed with dense, recondite erudition, composed Latin inscriptions for memorial celebrations, and wrote poetry rich in classical allusions.

Their activities would not be of interest to historians of art except for the accident of fate which brought the painter Francisco Pacheco, and eventually his apprentice, Diego de Velázquez, into their midst.

This accident of fate meant that the painter Pacheco was destined to develop a profound admiration for humanist thought and scholarship and a smattering of knowledge of these subjects. In fact, after the death of his uncle in 1599, Pacheco assumed the mantle of academic leadership and devoted much of his time to perpetuating the association. Documents and contemporary witnesses corroborate Palomino's oft-cited description of Pacheco's house as a site for reunions of the academy: "Pacheco's house was a gilded cage of art and an academy and a school for the greatest minds of Seville."[7] Here Pacheco would gather with the new generation of Seville's scholarly community: with the poet and scholar, Francisco de Rioja; with the antiquarian and local historian, Rodrigo Caro; with the poet and amateur artist, Juan de Jáuregui; and with the Jesuit theologians, Juan de Pineda and Luis de Alcázar. Members of the nobility were also associated with the academy, especially Fernando Enríquez Afán de Ribera, III duke of Alcalá, whose spacious palace was sometimes the site of academic meetings. And intermittently, Gaspar de Guzmán, later known as the count-duke of Olivares, made contact with members of the academy.[8]

From the early days of the academy under the leadership of Juan de Mal Lara, there had been an interest in the visual arts, although admittedly it was not great. Both Mal Lara and the Canon Pacheco had tried their hand as emblemists, and Herrera and Medina had written briefly on art theory. But when the painter Pacheco became a predominant force in the academy, the arts moved closer to the center of attention. Pacheco was encouraged to pursue an interest in art theory by a painter from Córdoba, Pablo de Céspedes, who had received a humanist education at the University of Alcalá and then spent several years in Rome.[9] Céspedes enjoyed a stipend from the Cathedral of Córdoba, and made trips to Seville from time to time on church business, during the course of which he became a close friend of Pacheco.

For Pacheco, Céspedes, with his knowledge of Latin and possibly Greek, was the learned painter incarnate and a productive writer on art whom he was bound to imitate. Thus, beginning around 1600, Pacheco started to write a treatise of art theory and practice which he worked on until just before he died in 1644. This is the famous *Arte de la pintura*, which was published posthumously in 1649.[10] The treatise is a patchwork of personal ideas, technical tricks for the painter, and extensive quotations from earlier sources. Its importance lies not in its originality, which is scant, but in the very fact that Pacheco undertook to write it.

Unlike in Italy, where by 1600 the connection between the arts and letters had become well established, in Spain the two had never been joined. The consequences of this failure were profound, because it was through the identification of painting with poetry that the former gained the status of a liberal art, as opposed to a craft. In practical terms, this meant that painters were regarded by the ruling class of Spanish society as the social equals of blacksmiths, coopers, and carpenters. The reasons for the existence of this attitude are complex, but there can be no doubt that the most important was the deeply-ingrained aristocratic prejudice against commerce and manual labor.[11] Painting in Spain was considered to be a handicraft and painters were therefore artisans whose work was essentially characterized by physical rather than mental activity. The organization of the art world did nothing to discourage the prejudice, although this may have been the consequence of the reigning social attitude rather than the cause. Painters' guilds were still organized as medieval craft unions to which admission was granted only on the basis of a practical test of competence designed, administered, and judged by the painters themselves. Elaborate work rules governed the practice of the profession and were meant to protect the established order.

A third factor which unintentionally contributed to maintaining the low status of painting was the predominance of ecclesiastical patronage. Recent studies of art patronage in Renaissance and Baroque Spain have suggested that secular paintings were collected in greater numbers than has usually been thought.[12] On a quantitative basis this may be true, but it does not alter the fact that the majority of the most prestigious and lucrative commissions came from the Catholic Church. The Spanish Church, as the self-appointed defender of Catholic orthodoxy, was especially sensitive to the accuracy of the representations of Scripture and dogma displayed in cathedrals, parishes, and monasteries. This concern is reflected in contracts with artists, which left the power to formulate and approve the representation of subject matter in the hands of the religious authorities. In this system, the artist's room to maneuver was considerably reduced and must have done something to encourage the conservative development of style in Spanish art of this period.

In practical terms, the result of these circumstances was to define the role of the painter as a practitioner rather than a creator. In Italy, from 1400 onwards, but especially after 1500, the best artists were given charge both of the conception and execution of a work of art and therefore prided themselves on their erudition and mental agility. The acceptance of painting as a liberal art imposed an obligation to study humane letters, although there were always shortcuts around this problem, such as emblem books, for those not inclined to the pursuit of knowledge. But in Spain, the responsibility for intellectual conception was rarely vested in painters. Thus the vicious circle of expectation, performance, and evaluation was closed. Spanish painters, with the few exceptions of those who had spent time in Italy, such as Alonso Berruguete and El Greco, were unlettered because the patronage did not expect, require, or reward a knowledge of letters. And because painters were unlettered, they were doomed to be regarded as craftsmen rather than as artists

After this brief excursus, we can see clearly what an extraordinary thing it was for Pacheco to write his treatise. We can also see why he dedicated almost half of its contents to arguing the case for painting as a liberal art. And, finally, we can see the overwhelming importance for Velázquez of having had the chance to study the art of painting in a milieu in which the union of arts and letters was a living reality. Velázquez, as a precocious artist, could have learned the craft from any experienced painter. But only in the house of Pacheco, where accomplished men of letters frequently came and went, could he have developed his mind as well as his hand. This experience was to prove decisive for Velázquez' future development. Of course it provided him with a grounding in the literary culture of Renaissance humanism and familiarized him with a fairly broad range of textual sources upon which to draw as he conceived his paintings. But this knowledge was secondary to something of far greater importance — the method of critical thought. The ability to analyze, evaluate, and articulate the condition of man and nature is the foundation and fruit of humanistic learning and it was this ability, fostered in the academy of Pacheco, which enabled Velázquez eventually to recast the principles and practice of the art of painting.

Needless to say, Velázquez also spent considerable time in developing his command of the techniques of painting, and with results which are perhaps more spectacular than is usually realized. Not that the paintings which he executed from about 1617 to 1622 are ever dismissed as inconsequential. But frequently they are viewed with hindsight, from the perspective of his later works, and therefore studied as intimations of what was to come. If, however, we look at these paintings in their own terms by comparing them to works by Velázquez' contemporaries, then they strike us in quite another way.

In 1610, when Velázquez became an apprentice painter, the state of the art in Spain was entering the final stages of a profound transformation which had begun about thirty years before. Throughout the first half of the sixteenth century, Spanish painting, with few exceptions, had been both provincial and conservative. The reasons for the failure of Spanish painters to create an important indigenous Renaissance style, as was done in architecture and sculpture, have never been studied. In the broadest terms, the primary reason may have been the lack of significant patronage. The preference of ecclesiastical patrons for sculpture is obvious, and contributed to the rise of the great school of polychrome sculptors in sixteenth-century Spain, personified by Alonso

Berruguete and Juan de Juni. The other major potential sources of patronage, the crown and the aristocracy, were operating in a European theater and therefore dispensing their favors outside Spain. In particular, the itinerant style of kingship practiced by Charles V gave his court an international scope and allowed him to choose his artists from an exceptional range of talent in Italy and Flanders.[13] With a painter like Titian at his beck and call, it is no wonder that the emperor did not look for Spanish painters to employ.

These circumstances were dramatically altered when Philip II ascended the throne and, in 1561, established his residence in Madrid. At last, Spain had a permanent site for the royal court. Philip was a great patron of the arts who had great artistic projects in mind, the most important of which was El Escorial, the gigantic building project begun in 1563.[14] By 1570, the construction of the southern half, which housed a monastery of Hieronymites, was nearly complete and ready to receive its decoration. The king, who supervised every detail of construction, had decided to adorn the endless walls of the building with frescoes, and for this task, he was obliged to import Italian painters, the technique having been little practiced in Spain. Thus, around 1570, the first of what would prove to be two waves of Italian painters arrived in Castile.

The importance of these painters for the history of Spanish art can hardly be over-stressed, despite the fact that they created almost no certifiable masterpieces.[15] All of a sudden, current styles of Italian painting arrived in Spain. The first group of artists included Francesco da Urbino, Romulo Cincinnato, Niccolò Granello, and Patrizio Cagesi. Most of their works are done in a dry, bloodless classical style, which is typified by Urbino's *Judgment of Solomon* (Plate 1), a fresco on the ceiling of the Prior's Chapter Room. No claims of greatness can be made for this painting, but in comparison with the prevailing provincial style of Spanish painting, it has significance. The clarity of composition, the elevated narrative tone, and, above all, the monumental figures would all make an impact on Spanish artists.

4

4. Bartolomé Carducho, *Descent from the Cross* (Madrid, Museo del Prado), 2.63 × 1.81m.

5. Bartolomé Carducho, *Death of St. Francis* (Lisbon, Museu Nacional de Arte Antiga), 1.15 × 1.53m.

1 (facing page top left). Francesco da Urbino, *Judgment of Solomon* (El Escorial, Prior's Chapter Room).

2 (facing page top right). Pellegrino Tibaldi, *Christ Appearing to St. Mary Magdalene* (El Escorial, Imperial Staircase).

3 (facing page bottom). Federico Zuccaro, *Annunciation* (El Escorial, Basilica), 4.91 × 2.90m.

The second group of artists, who began to appear on the scene after 1582, was comprised of more famous names — Luca Cambiaso, Federico Zuccaro, and Pellegrino Tibaldi. In varying degrees, these artists had begun to incorporate effects of light and color learned from the study of Venetian painters into their monumental central Italian manner. Zuccaro's *Annunciation* (Plate 3), painted for an altar of the church in 1585–86, makes dramatic use of light to enhance the narrative, while Tibaldi's *Christ Appearing to St. Mary Magdalene* of *c*. 1590 (Plate 2), which decorates the Imperial Staircase, demonstrates an awareness of the rich, muted colors of Titian's late paintings.

This survey of Italian painters at El Escorial is obviously schematic, but perhaps it is sufficient to suggest the fact that a new, potent source of inspiration had come upon the scene, which thoroughly transformed the development of painting in Spain. We can confirm the validity of this idea simply by noting that many of the exponents of the revival of Spanish painting, usually called Spanish Naturalism, were relatives of the Italians who had worked at El Escorial. Of these, the most important are the Carducho brothers, Bartolomé and Vicente.

Bartolomé, the elder by almost twenty years, had come to Spain as an assistant of Federico Zuccaro, and worked within the style now called reform or counter-Mannerism, which sought to purge the artificiality of Mannerism and return to a more normative, lucid form of narrative exposition.[16] His *Descent from the Cross*, painted in 1595 (Plate 4), and the precocious *Death of St. Francis* of 1593 (Plate 5), describe the limits of the style which he developed and taught to his younger brother, who chose to remain within them for the rest of his career. Vicente Carducho was the most successful painter in Madrid during the first two decades of the seventeenth century and continued to be an important figure until his death in 1638.[17] We see him at the height of his powers in the commission of fifty-six pictures executed in the late 1620s for the Carthusian monastery at El Paular. These two examples (Plates 6, 7) from the series show Carducho's strengths — his gift for narrative, his restrained, somber style, and his ability to individualize the

8. Antonio Mohedano, *Annunciation* (Seville, University Chapel).

actors in the drama. Yet there is a wall of decorum and idealization which he never attempted to breach. By 1620, this style of painting, by progressive Italian standards, was out-of-date. But in Madrid, thanks in large measure to the influence of Vicente Carducho, it continued to prevail for at least another fifteen years. It also became established in Seville, although under somewhat different circumstances.

Around the year 1600, painting in Seville was dominated by a group of painters who, with one exception, have been remembered only by specialists in Spanish art. On the whole, the oblivion into which names like Antonio Mohedano, Alonso Vázquez, Gerolamo Lucente da Correggio, and Pablo de Céspedes have fallen is deserved.[18] These painters were practicing a nearly exhausted manner of the later sixteenth century, comprised partly of the Tuscan-Roman Counter-Maniera style and partly of Flemish interpretations of this style which had been introduced into Seville by the northern artists who worked in the city in the 1540s and 1550s. Among the painters just named, only Mohedano showed an occasional flash of talent. His *Annunciation* of 1604–1606 (Plate 8), painted for the altarpiece of the Jesuit Church in Seville,[19] is admittedly wooden in style, but the clarity and monumentality of the composition and the brittle, sculpturesque modeling constitute a sturdy version of the austere style then being practiced in Madrid by artists such as the Carducho brothers.

The painter of repute who emerged around 1600 was, of course, Francisco Pacheco, the master of Velázquez. Pacheco the artist lacks the conviction of Pacheco the writer, and, in truth, it must be said that nature had not been generous in bestowing her gifts on him. In 1600, he was awarded part of a commission to paint scenes from the life of St. Peter Nolasco by the Seville Order of Mercy (Plate 9).[20] The results are rather jarring pictures, in which simple matters such as scale and perspective seem to cause more difficulty than they should in so practiced a painter. In addition, the drawing of the figures is rather wooden and the choice of colors rather pale and bloodless.

9. Francisco Pacheco, *Mercedarians Redeeming Captives* (Barcelona, Museo de Arte de Catalonia), 2.03 × 2.51m.

6 (facing page top left). Vicente Carducho, *St. Bruno Renounces the Archbishopric of Reggio* (Madrid, Museo del Prado), 3.42 × 3.02m.

7 (facing page top right). Vicente Carducho, *Death of Venerable Odon of Novara* (Madrid, Museo del Prado), 3.45 × 3.15m.

10. Juan de Roelas, *Martyrdom of St. Andrew* (Seville, Museo Provincial de Bellas Artes), 5.20 × 3.46m.

Just after the start of the seventeenth century, there did arrive in Seville a painter of some stature. This is the cleric Juan de Roelas, who is first recorded in Seville around 1605.[21] During the preceding six or seven years, Roelas had been working at the royal court, which in 1601 had left Madrid for Valladolid for a five-year stay. There Roelas came into contact with the new generation of Spanish painters, especially the Carducho brothers, and became familiar with the early naturalist style of Spanish painting. Thus Roelas became the principal agent of transmission of the style from Castile to the region around Seville.

Until 1616, when he left Seville to spend five years in Madrid, Roelas was given numerous important ecclesiastical commissions, of which the monumental *Martyrdom of St. Andrew*, painted around 1610–15, is an excellent example (Plate 10). The composition and facial types are clearly indebted to the early naturalists of Madrid, but Roelas is more adventurous as a colorist and aims for a greater degree of movement and emotional expression. His brushwork is also more textured, which imparts a richness to the surfaces lacking in the work of his contemporaries. Yet for all these qualities which elevate him above the other painters of Seville, Roelas was still creating within the framework of the style brought to Spain in the 1570s and 1580s by the Italian painters at El Escorial. As Velázquez' initial works show, this style was not for him.

The first glimpse we catch of Velázquez during the meagerly documented early years of his life dates from just about the time Roelas left for Madrid. On 14 March 1617, Velázquez was granted a license to practice the art of painting.[22] His examiners were Juan de Uceda, a well-established local painter, and Francisco Pacheco, his master. The relationship with Pacheco, which always remained close, was strengthened in the next year when Velázquez married his daughter, Juana, on 23 April 1618.[23] Soon after, the couple had two daughters, Francisca and Ignacia, who were baptized on 18 May 1619 and 1 January 1621 respectively.[24] By 1620, Velázquez was accepting an apprentice, a youth named Diego Melgar, of whom nothing more is heard.[25] We also know that Velázquez, like many an artist of Seville, had acquired rental properties to supplement his income.[26] Thus, to all appearances he was settling down to a prosperous, predictable life as a local painter, ready to capitalize on his father-in-law's excellent connections. But if his life was moving into a comfortable groove, his art was heading in new and extraordinary directions.

Velázquez' artistic production in Seville can be divided into three categories — scenes of everyday life, religious subjects, and portraits. Only a few of these works are dated and none is documented. Although serious attempts have been made to assign specific dates to the others, it is more prudent to treat them as the creations of a single, short period, extending from about 1617 to 1623, when Velázquez left Seville. Seen as a group, these early works stand apart from the dominant style of Sevillian painting. However, the differences are most dramatically seen in the genre paintings, of which *Three Men at Table* (Plate 11) is a representative example. In the first place is the subject, which is one of the earliest surviving genre scenes painted by a Spanish artist in the seventeenth century.[27] Then there is the rendering of the figures which is much less idealized and more directly rooted in appearances than anything else done at this time in Seville. Finally, there is the obvious fascination with effects of light and color, which comes to the fore in the still-life objects.

One more aspect of the picture claims our attention, and this is what might be called its youthful quality. For all his genius and originality, Velázquez still needed time to master the expression of his new ideas. This youthful quality shows up most clearly in the failure to subordinate the parts of the picture to a unified composition, perhaps from a desire to call attention to the novelty of the style and the brilliant technical execution. For instance, one of the most arresting qualities of the picture involves the treatment of the effects of light on the perception of color and form. The exaggerated attention given to this demonstration leaves the impression that the painting has been composed object by object and figure by figure. Hence the still-life elements on the table and wall are all given equal emphasis, providing the painter with the opportunity

11. Velázquez, *Three Men at Table* (Leningrad, Hermitage), 1.07 × 1.01 m.

12. Velázquez, *Three Musicians* (Berlin, Gemäldegalerie), 0.087 × 1.10m.

to demonstrate his impressive ability to reproduce light, color, and texture. On the
front of the table, there is a glass with water, a round loaf of bread, two pomegranates,
and a knife which partly overhangs the edge. Each of these objects poses a different
problem of imitation — hard versus soft, transparent versus opaque, rectilinear versus
curvilinear. By treating each object separately, Velázquez is able to maximize the visual
impact, but only at the cost of compositional unity. The same type of pondered composition is found in the figures — old man, young man, and young boy; laughing, smiling,
and somber-faced. The painting therefore comes across as a brilliant young artist's
creation — audacious but overreaching, and thus finally unresolved.[28]

These same qualities can also be seen in the *Three Musicians* (Plate 12), where the
players are crowded around a small table set with bread, wine, and cheese. Two of the
musicians play and sing, while the third, a young boy carrying a monkey on his back,
smiles and looks vacantly outward while he holds a glass of wine. A beam of strong light
floods into the space from the left, illuminating the heads and hands, and also the wine
and foodstuff. In the center, a loaf of bread reflects the light off its crusty, pitted surface.
Still unsatisfied with this tour de force of realistic painting, Velázquez has set the small
loaf on a thick, white napkin, which in turn rests on a dull silver plate. As a final touch,

9

13. Velázquez, *Old Woman Cooking* (Edinburgh, National Gallery of Scotland), 0.99 × 1.69m.

14 (facing page). Detail of Plate 13.

a knife is seen to slide between the loaf and napkin, the handle jutting out into the space beyond the circumference of the plate. The central placement of this still-life motif and the brilliance of its handling establish it as an independent focal point in the picture, which competes with the figures for attention. Indeed, the strength and vigor of the highlighted passages so capture the eye that it takes time to see the awkward arrangement of the figures and the almost total absence of ambiant space.[29]

Radiographs of the *Three Musicians* also reveal interesting information about the conception and development of the picture. Underneath the broad collar of the central figure can be seen another of a narrower shape. Overpainting of this kind is not an unusual procedure for artists young or old. However, it was to become a frequent practice for Velázquez, who became accustomed to improvise and revise as he worked, rather than to plan the composition in advance of execution. Pacheco mentions that Velázquez, as a young apprentice, made drawings from life, particularly portrait drawings. But neither in this nor the later periods of his life does he seem to have made much use of preparatory drawings.

21. Velázquez, *Christ in the House of Mary and Martha* (London, National Gallery), 0.60 × 1.035m.

22. Jacob Matham after Pieter Aertsen, *Kitchen Scene with Supper at Emmaus* (New York, Metropolitan Museum of Art, Elisha Whittlesey Fund).

gained by Velázquez from his teacher. Thus, in these works, as in the genre paintings, Velázquez struck out on his own to produce pictures of daring conception but uneven execution.

The painting of *Christ in the House of Mary and Martha* (Plate 21), which bears the date of 1618, was inspired by a composition of the kind shown in an engraving after Pieter Aertsen (Plate 22).[40] In this print, as in Velázquez' picture, the principal part of the narrative is subordinated to an incidental activity. In the distance, Christ and the Apostles at Emmaus break bread while in the foreground a rich meal of seafood is being prepared. Velázquez' sullen cook is working on humbler fare — four small fish, their silvery scales gleaming in the light, and two eggs, to be flavored with red pepper and garlic (Plate 24). As in the genre paintings, infinite care is taken to evoke and contrast the colors and textures of the objects. Indeed, the artist has tipped the tabletop at an impossible angle in order to accommodate the array of food and cooking utensils.

The virtuosity of execution is unfortunately partially compromised by a lack of narrative clarity, which has occasioned numerous attempts to explain exactly what is depicted. All agree that in the background, Velázquez has faithfully represented a passage from the Gospel of Luke, 10:38–42:

> Now it came to pass as they were on this journey that He entered a certain village; and a woman named Martha welcomed Him to her house. And she had a sister called Mary, who also seated herself at the Lord's feet, and listened to His word. But Martha was about much serving. And she came up and said, "Lord, is it no concern of thine that my sister has left me to serve alone? Tell her therefore to help me." But the Lord answered and said to her, "Martha, Martha, thou art anxious and troubled about many things; and yet only one thing is needful. Mary has chosen the best part, and it will not be taken away from her." [Douay-Confraternity Bible]

But where does the scene thus described take place? In an adjacent room seen

16

through a small window in the kitchen? Or is it a picture within a picture, framed and hung on the wall? Or perhaps it is a mirror reflecting an action which occurs in the space in front of the picture. Another question concerns the identity and purpose of the two figures in the foreground.[41] Velázquez has represented these figures as if they were not only his contemporaries, but also specific individuals. As a matter of fact, the old woman reappears as one of the protagonists in the *Old Woman Cooking*, indicating that a real person served as the artist's model. Consequently, it is hard to see how they fit into the story.

The answer to the first of these questions is revealed through the close study of the picture. At the bottom of each side of the opening, where the angles are formed, is a thin, diagonal line which recedes toward the center of background composition. These are perspective lines intended to produce the appearance of an embrasure of some depth. The line at the left is still readily visible to the naked eye, while the one at the right has become faint, although it appears under infrared light (Plate 23). The slight effect of flatness in the lower ledge, which could be seen as the surface of a frame, is the result of a partial failure of foreshortening. The same weakness is seen in the ledge of the window of the *Portrait of Cristóbal Suárez de Ribera* (Plate 38). Thus, it is safe to say that the group of figures in the background occupies an adjacent room revealed through a window in the wall of the kitchen.[42]

The relationship of the foreground to the background, both in form and content, is still somewhat uncertain, but this ambiguity is partly the result of the treatment of space. In the sixteenth-century print (Plate 22), the illusion of deep space is carefully rendered, thus cushioning the shock of seeing the Supper at Emmaus set in a contemporary Flemish kitchen. Velázquez, on the other hand, constructs a close, confining space which partly confounds the attempt to represent the past as present. Furthermore, he has introduced a moralizing note into the picture, symbolized by the pointing, admonitory finger of the older woman, which appears to be addressed to the spectator. The meaning of this gesture is related to the larger significance of the picture which, like the composition, is explained by reference to sixteenth-century Flemish renditions of the theme.

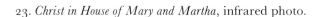

23. *Christ in House of Mary and Martha*, infrared photo.

24 (following pages). Detail of Plate 21.

25. Velázquez, *Supper at Emmaus* (Blessington, Beit Collection), 0.558 × 1.18m.

26. Attributed to Velázquez, *Kitchen Scene* (Chicago, Art Institute), 0.55 × 1.04m.

In the 1550s, Pieter Aertsen made two versions of the scene of Christ in the House of Mary and Martha which have been interpreted as realistic allegories of the active and contemplative life and which point the way to understanding Velázquez' picture.[43] The story of Martha and Mary had long been used to exemplify the two principal aspects of Christian life. Martha, who was occupied with serving, represented the Christian duty to supply bodily sustenance to those in need of it. But this task was regarded as transitory and subordinate to the need to sustain the soul in eternity through Christ. "Mary," as Christ says in the Gospel text, "has chosen the best part, and it will not be taken away from her." Velázquez underscores the message in two ways, one subtle, one blatant. In the foreground, the old woman directs our attention away from the kitchen scene, where the necessary but impermanent act of cooking is shown, to the background, where Mary sits at the feet of Christ. Mary's pose is based on the print by Albrecht Dürer, *Melancholia I*, a famous, familiar symbol of meditation.[44] Echoing the thoughts of St. Augustine, who frequently used the story of Martha and Mary as a metaphor for the two ways of life, Velázquez' picture instructs us that "Martha's part therefore passeth away," a message which the viewer is advised to heed.

The *Supper at Emmaus* (Plate 25) is a comparable if less compelling image.[45] Here Velázquez clarifies the relationship between the foreground and background space by adding a shutter to the window. This element also unmistakably indicates Velázquez' familiarity with sixteenth-century Flemish paintings and prints. As in *Christ in the House of Mary and Martha*, this picture has suggested moralizing interpretations, which in principle make sense even if the precise meaning is yet to be identified. A version of the composition without the scene of Christ and the Apostles also exists, but unfortunately it is damaged beyond the point where authenticity can be judged (Plate 26). On the basis of the composition alone, it is conceivable that the work was done by one of the copyists or pasticheurs who seemed to have capitalized on the success of Velázquez' genre paintings and produced numerous replicas and versions of the originals.[46]

In 1619, Velázquez painted a more conventional religious picture, the *Adoration of the Magi* (Plate 28), which was almost certainly commissioned by the Jesuits for a chapel in the Novitiate of San Luis.[47] Given Pacheco's close contacts with members of the Society of Jesus, it is possible that he was instrumental in obtaining the commission for his son-in-law. Master painters in Seville habitually formed family dynasties, incorporating relatives into their practice and promoting their careers.[48] It is also worth noting that Velázquez' picture, with its uncompromising realism, would have been especially appropriate for devoted practitioners of Loyola's *Spiritual Exercises*, a text which assigns an important role to sensory impressions in actuating the will toward the pursuit of perfection.

In this work, Velázquez moves from the confined, crowded interior spaces of the genre pictures into the open air, a change of scene which is none-too-successful.[49] A tiny patch of distant landscape, lit by a crepuscular light, is like a hasty afterthought; the transition between the monumental figures and the mountain is too rapid because he has neglected to supply the middleground. In fact, the *Adoration of the Magi* is the perfect demonstration of the strengths and weaknesses of the young Velázquez. On the one hand, there is the commanding realism of the faces (Plate 29), each carefully sculpted to the contours of a specific person (none of whom, however, can be identified). Next to a work of a comparable subject by a contemporary painter of Seville (Plate 27), the impact of seeing real people participating in the Epiphany is powerful. But once the shock of the new has subsided, we can begin to see the flaws in the execution. The lap of the seated Virgin, for instance, is shown as if it were flat, although the artist has tried to suggest the bending of the body by laboriously building up the paint in this area. Also, the tiny, swaddled body of the Christ Child appears to be all torso and no legs. And, as frequently occurs in the early paintings, the intervals of space between the massive figures virtually collapse. This forces Velázquez to represent distance by height; the farther back in space a figure stands, the higher his head, in order to accommodate at least part of his upper body. The treatment of the four figures at the left clearly shows this "wedding-cake" effect.

27. Juan de Uceda, *Adoration of Shepherds with St. Benedict* (Carmona, private collection), 2.06 × 1.65m.

28. Velázquez, *Adoration of the Magi* (Madrid, Museo del Prado), 2.04 × 1.26m.

29 (facing page). Detail of Plate 28.

38. Velázquez, *Cristóbal Suárez de Ribera* (Seville, Museo Provincial de Bellas Artes), 2.07 × 1.48m.

church of the Brotherhood of San Hermenegildo. Suárez de Ribera, a priest, had been devoted to the famous saint of Seville and been instrumental in the construction of a new site of worship dedicated in his honor. This church was inaugurated in April 1616, about a year and a half before the priest died at the age of sixty-eight.[58] Suárez de Ribera was connected to Pacheco and had served as godfather to his daughter, Juana (Velázquez' future wife), at her baptism in 1602.[59] Thus Pacheco may have been in a position to help secure the commission for this picture, which is dated 1620.[60]

The fact that Velázquez was painting a posthumous portrait either from memory or from another image of the priest helps to account for the relatively flat characterization of the sitter. Also, the function of the picture as a memorial image may have placed constraints on his approach to the subject. The bulky figure is shown in a kneeling position, pointing toward the main altar which contained a polychrome statue of the

39. Velázquez, *Mother Jerónima de la Fuente* (Madrid, Collection Fernández Araoz), 1.60 × 1.06m.

40 (facing page). Velázquez, *Mother Jerónima de la Fuente* (Madrid, Prado), 1.60 × 1.10m.

patron saint, attributed to Juan Martínéz Montañés. If the special nature of this commission did not permit Velázquez to demonstrate his qualities as a portraitist, the other three portraits of this period are more than promising signs of his future greatness in this genre.

The most ambitious of these works is *Mother Jerónima de la Fuente*, which is known in two autograph versions (Plates 39, 40), both signed and dated 1620.[61] A lengthy inscription, perhaps added by another hand, describes the circumstances of the commission. Mother Jerónima, a Franciscan from Santa Isabel, Toledo, arrived in Seville in June 1620, en route to Manila, where she was going to establish a convent of the order. At the time, she was sixty-six years old.

Both versions of the portrait were discovered in Santa Isabel, where presumably they were sent soon after completion. Although similar in most respects, there are some differences to be seen, notably the position of the Crucifix. It has been suggested that the pose of the figure, and especially the detail of the Crucifix with the phylactery (mistakenly removed from the version in the Prado), was inspired by a print.[62] But even if true, Velázquez took the measure of his sitter by looking her straight in the eye. As portrayed by him, Mother Jerónima is an indomitable person. Wearing the dark brown Franciscan serge like protective armor, and brandishing her cross like a war club, she seems to embody the determined missionary's message inscribed in the flowing white ribbon: "I shall be satisfied as long as He is glorified." Her tight-lipped face with its pouchy cheeks, concisely framed by a black and white cowl, obeys the text of the Latin inscription written above: "It is good to await the salvation of God in silence." It is no surprise to learn that her mission to the Philippines ended in success.

Although the backgrounds of both pictures have suffered from the years of neglect in the convent, it is still possible to see a curious feature of the composition; namely, the ambiguous definition of space. The definition of space is never very elaborate in Veláz-quez' early works. Usually, he employs a dark background, which presses in on the figures, resulting in a characteristic, airless quality. Also, in none of the other paintings of the period do we see a standing figure with its feet on the ground, a type of pose which compels the artist to provide the illusion of a floor. Here, when confronted by this problem for the first time, Velázquez produces an unusual solution. Instead of showing the floor or ground in linear perspective, he seems to tilt it upward, indicating the juncture with the wall simply by darkening the tone of brown. This passage is admittedly hard to read because our usual habits of looking at pictures of this period lead us to expect a conventional illusion of space. But, on further study, it is hard to avoid the feeling that the space in this picture suddenly goes flat. The obvious conclusion to be drawn from this observation is rather alarming — that Velázquez was unschooled in linear perspective, a stock device of European painting of this period. Another possibility is that he knew the trick, but had decided not to use it. But given the evidence of his uncertain handling of spatial relationships in other works, the first conclusion seems more likely. We shall have occasion to return later, and often, to Velázquez' unique conception of pictorial space: here it need only be said that a youthful shortcoming would be turned to a long-term advantage.

The third portrait of this period is much less problematic. This is the small, bust-length *Man with Ruff Collar* (Plate 41).[63] The latest possible date of this portrait is established by a royal decree of 1623, which prohibited the use of the ornate collar. This small picture is modest only in size. Although easily overlooked among the more ambitious pictures of this period, it is full of life and skill. The masterful control of light and shadow on the face intensifies the sitter's expression and deftly reproduces the wrinkles and sagging skin of incipient middle age. The dragging, heavy brushstrokes of the collar and the deliberate build-up of highlights on the face contribute to the forceful projection of this unknown sitter's personality.

The final portrait in this series depicts a famous subject, the poet Luis de Góngora (Plate 42).[64] The circumstances of this commission are known from Pacheco's treatise.[65] In 1622, Velázquez was in Madrid (a trip to be discussed in the next chapter) where, at the request of his father-in-law, he executed this portrait. Pacheco wanted the image of Góngora as a model for one of a series of famous men of letters which he was then making.[66] His request brought the greatest Spanish poet and the greatest Spanish painter of the seventeenth century face to face in a memorable encounter.

When the portrait was painted, Góngora (1561–1627) had been living in Madrid for nearly ten years (he was absent between 1618–20), attempting to ingratiate himself with influential courtiers, whose favor he curried and whose ways he despised. Having succeeded only in antagonizing his friends as well as his rivals, Góngora had become a bitter man. The young Velázquez sensed the sad truth of this great, but isolated genius and recorded it without giving an inch. The skeptical eyes and the dome-like head

41 (above left). Velázquez, *Man with Ruff Collar* (Madrid, Prado), 0.40 × 0.36m.

42 (above right). Velázquez, *Luis de Góngora* (Boston, Museum of Fine Arts, Maria Antoinette Evans Fund), 0.51 × 0.41m.

(originally crowned with a laurel wreath) convey a sense of Góngora's intelligence, while the sharply downturned mouth tells us of his disappointments. Not until 1650, when Velázquez painted the portrait of Pope Innocent X (Plate 227) did he again turn the full force of his merciless eye on another sitter.

As we complete this survey of Velázquez' early career in Seville, we can see how, almost from the first, he was a painter apart from his contemporaries. The apprenticeship with Pacheco had not only equipped him to practice his art, but had also provided him with an experience of the world of letters which no other Spanish painter of his generation enjoyed. Pacheco also must have indoctrinated Velázquez with the sense of the nobility of his profession, a point which is discussed at length in *Arte de la pintura*. But, as for his style of painting, Velázquez seems to have gone his own way, using Pacheco's counsel on technique, but inventing a new style which, if in need of refinement, was still unlike any then practiced in Spain. All that Velázquez needed was the opportunity to put these talents and aspirations to work in a setting where they could bring him fame, honor, and wealth. A painter working in Seville could become rich, but not famous. However, a painter working at court, within sight of the richest, most powerful monarch in Europe, could win it all.

In 1621, a new king had come to the throne as Philip IV and at his side was an influential minister, Gaspar de Guzmán, the count-duke of Olivares. Olivares was a man with connections in Seville, which included members of Pacheco's academy. With friends in high places, it was only natural that Velázquez would see a chance to make a place for himself at the seat of power. And so it was that in 1622, he set off to Madrid to make his fortune at court or, as it was then called, "el teatro de la grandeza," the theater of grandeur, where in time he would become a principal player.

35

CHAPTER II

In the Palace of the Planet King:
The Early Years at Court

IN THE SEVENTEENTH CENTURY, citizens of Madrid often boasted by quoting a popular refrain: "Sólo Madrid es corte," "Only Madrid is the court." These words implicitly recognized the predominance of the prince over culture and society; his presence bestowed distinction on the place where he resided. The statement of civic pride was therefore correct, but, as occurs with self-advertising, it concealed an element of defensiveness. For Madrid was the newest arrival to the ranks of European capitals, and its inhabitants felt the need to proclaim its status.

Until the middle of the sixteenth century, the rulers of Castile had held an itinerant court which moved in an irregular rotation through the major cities of the realm. Over the years, certain towns gradually became royal favorites. Toledo, as the residence of the archbishop primate, was one of the frequent stopping-places, and so were Valladolid and Burgos, the legal and commercial centers. By contrast with these important places, Madrid was a mere village huddled around the massive medieval fortress which had been converted into a royal residence, the Alcázar. Neither man nor nature had seen fit to adorn the town with their works. Set in the midst of the dry Castilian tableland, buffeted by extremes of hot and cold, devoid of natural resources and human industry, Madrid was an unfriendly place for habitation and an unlikely site to establish the court of the most powerful monarch in the world.

Perhaps this is the reason why Philip II never let it be known that his move to the town in 1561 was intended to be permanent.[1] The reasons for the king's choice of Madrid as his capital seem as puzzling today as they did in the sixteenth century. It has been suggested that the king was attracted by Madrid's one noteworthy feature: it was at the geographical center of the Iberian peninsula. As one of Philip's biographers wrote, "It was right that so great a monarchy should have a city fulfilling the function of a heart, located in the middle of the body, to minister equally to all its states in war and peace."[2] This statement seems reasonable until it is remembered that Spain's dominions were far-flung and linked most readily by sea lanes, terminating at ports which were distant from Madrid.

It may be that the very insignificance of the town was the attraction to a king who was addicted to architecture and planning. Madrid, like Brasilia, Canberra, and Islamabad in the twentieth century, offered almost unlimited scope for translating political power into monumental architectural forms. From this point of view, the small size of Madrid — it had only about 12,000 inhabitants in 1561 — and its proximity to forests and granite quarries were ideal prerequisites for grandiose building schemes. In fact, recent studies of Philip's Madrid have shown that he entertained thoughts of realizing such schemes.[3] But only one of these plans ever reached completion: the Segovia Bridge, which was intended as a monumental entranceway to the town.

Without a plan to control growth, Madrid developed by whim and circumstance (Plate 43). Expansion to the west was limited by vast reserves of crown property. Beyond the Alcázar, and running alongside the river Manzanares, was the Casa del

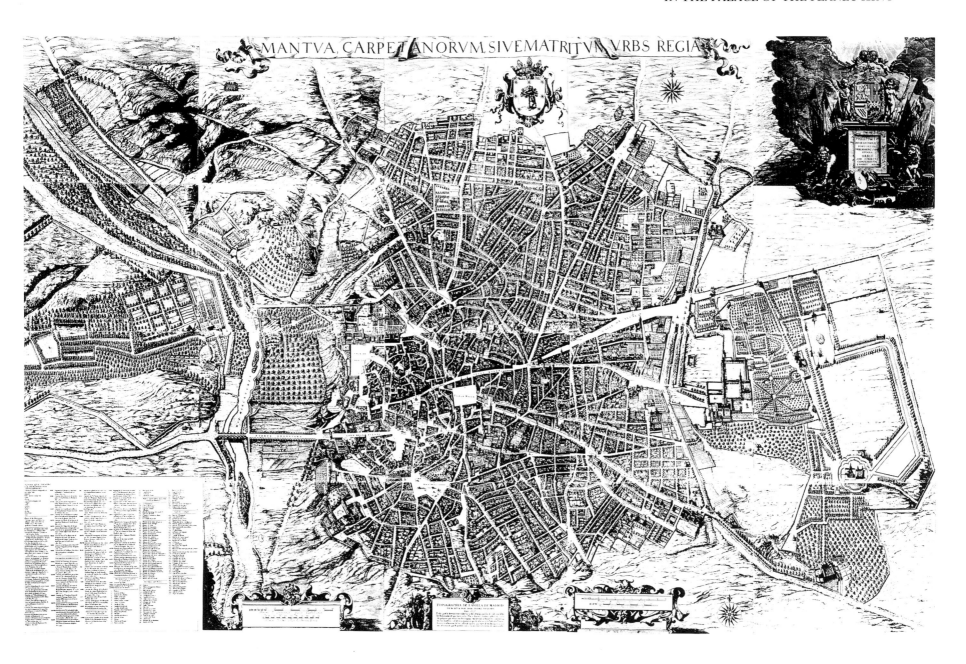

MANTVA CARPETANORVM SIVE MATRITVM VRBS REGIA

43. Pedro de Texeira, Map of Madrid.

Campo, a sprawling parkland which afforded outdoor amusements to the court. Expansion to the east was limited by the monastery and close of San Jerónimo, which was a royal foundation. San Jerónimo played a significant role in the ceremonial life of the court, for it was here that certain state events were held, such as the swearing of the oath of allegiance by the Cortes of Castile to the Prince of Asturias, and the exequies for deceased monarchs. The peripheral situation of the church and monastery near the eastern gate of the town also made it suitable for lodging distinguished visitors, who would rest there before making a solemn entry into Madrid. For this reason, San Jerónimo became the starting point of one of the main thoroughfares, which led across town to the palace. At the foot of the sloping land on which the monastery stood was the Prado, a continuous series of wide, tree-lined avenues where the citizenry took refuge from the crowded, malodorous streets of the city.

Madrid, then, was caught in an east-west pincers of protected land and was forced to grow to the north and south. And grow it did. By 1617, the population had reached a total of around 150,000; that is to say, in fifty-six years, the number of inhabitants had increased by over 1,000 percent! The intense pressure of this influx of people soon caused Madrid to become carpeted with buildings, leaving little room for public spaces within the urban core. The one exception was the Plaza Mayor, a noble, restrained design of Juan Gómez de Mora which consisted of residential apartments and also served as an arena for spectacles.

Only once was the predominance of Madrid challenged. Between 1601 and 1606,

37

44. Anton van der Wyngaerde, *View of Madrid* (Vienna, Nationalbibliothek).

yard (Plate 45).[8] The western half of the building was designated the king's quarters; the eastern contained the queen's quarters. The principal apartments were located on the third of four stories. Above were servants' quarters; below, on the second story were rooms for members of the royal family and certain government officials. Access to the palace was by a monumental staircase set between the two interior courtyards.

The king's quarters were divided rather fluidly between public and private suites, a fact which was at odds with the way the ruler lived. Private rooms and state rooms existed side by side, and certain rooms were used for both state and personal purposes. In the angle formed by the north and west wings were a series of council chambers and audience rooms. Room 6 on the plan illustrated here was used for the weekly meeting of the royal council, while rooms 7 and 8 were the settings for the reception of ambassadors. The two rooms indicated by the number 9 were used as a public dining room, for private audiences with ambassadors, and for administering oaths of office to important government officials. But the logic of the arrangement was defeated by the uses to which the room in the northwest turret and the adjacent long gallery were put; the former was the king's library; the latter was the billiards room.

The private quarters, larger by far than the public ones, were a hodge-podge of different-sized rooms designated for the functions of daily life. The long gallery marked number 10 was a corridor which gave access to the private rooms. At the southern terminus, in a larger tower, was the king's office. To the right of the corridor were rooms used for eating, sleeping, and dressing. The rather untidy division between the public and private life was epitomized by room 12, which was used at different times as a bedroom and audience room. The largest room in the palace, room 23, was entirely public; this was the theater and music room and was also the site of public banquets which were held to celebrate the marriages of ladies-in-waiting.

The intermingling of the public and the private, and especially the feature of mixed usage of several rooms, suggest that court life was dominated by an omnipresent ruler. In fact, the opposite was true. Most of the time the king was in the company of a few gentlemen and servants, who waited upon him with elaborate ritual. Only on special occasions would he appear in public, when an even more elaborate ritual was staged which effectively and intentionally depersonalized the king. For instance, the ambassadorial reception was organized as a procession through several dimly lit rooms, at the end of which was the audience chamber. When the door to this room was opened, the ambassador would see the king standing unaccompanied by any attributes of office. The king would touch his hat as a sign of recognition and listen patiently and motionlessly to the ambassador's address. Then he would utter one or two formulaic remarks in response and again touch his hat as a signal that the interview was concluded. This is but one example of a court etiquette that was constructed like a stepladder of majesty, with the king above all. The closer one came to the top, the more exalted one's position

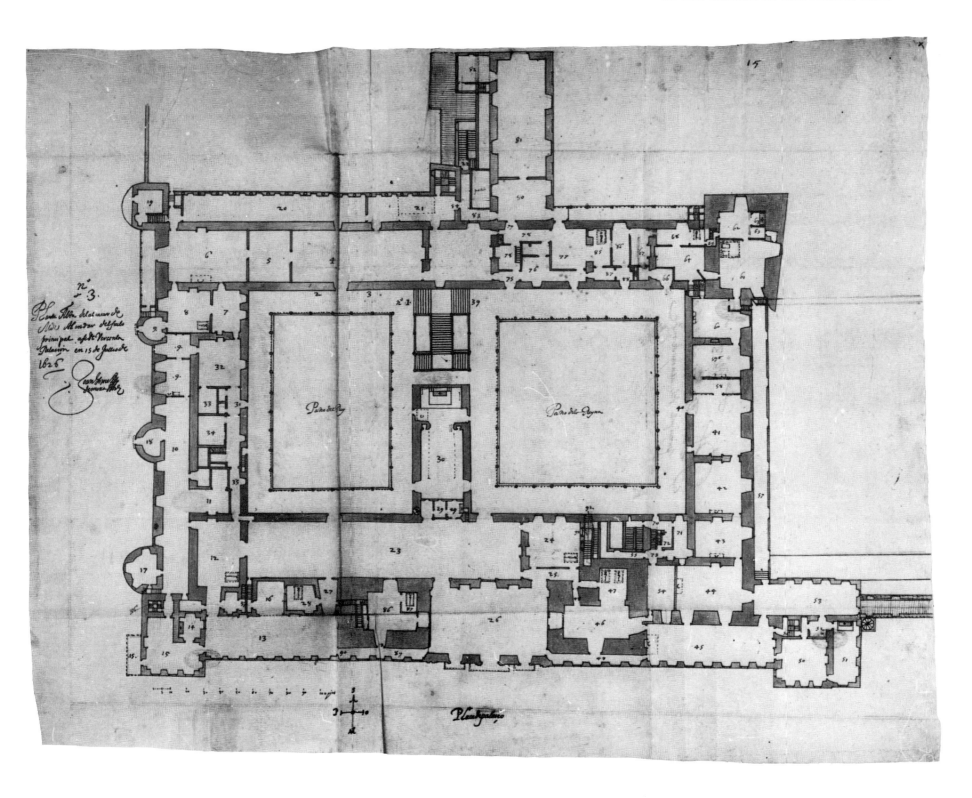

45. Juan Gómez de Mora, Plan of Principal Floor, Alcázar of Madrid (Vatican, Biblioteca Apostolica Vaticana).

and, of course, the steeper the fall if an error was made. A single false step or breach of etiquette could send a person tumbling down into the abyss of disfavor and dishonor.

Fortunately, there were escape hatches from this gilded cage of ceremonial and these were the country houses which were within easy reach of the capital.[9] Nearest to hand was the Palace of the Pardo, some five miles to the north. The Pardo was situated on the southern edge of a vast royal wood which stretched north for miles to the Guadarrama Mountains. This was superb hunting country and the kings of Spain, especially Philip IV, were avid hunters. Almost every year in November or December the king would go to the Pardo for a few weeks of hunting boar and deer. The palace itself was a small, simple building which had been initially constructed by Charles V and then rebuilt by Philip III after a serious fire in 1604. It still survives, although it was much altered and expanded in the eighteenth century.

Further to the north was a building which defies the name of country house. This was El Escorial, the combination of palace, tomb, monastery, and seminary built by

41

46. Rodrigo de Villandrando, *Prince Philip and Soplillo* (Madrid, Museo del Prado), 2.04 × 1.10m.

Philip II as a royal pantheon and monument to the Spanish Habsburgs as defenders of the Catholic faith.[10] The shadow of Philip II hung heavy over El Escorial and discouraged his successors from using the place for any but pious purposes, despite the fact that its mountainous setting provided relief from the hot Castilian summer. However, in the last decades of his reign, Philip IV found El Escorial well suited to his melancholy frame of mind and usually made one or two visits a year.

A more suitable place for idle recreation and amusement was the palace at Aranjuez, located about thirty-five miles south of Madrid in a valley made fertile by the confluence of two rivers. The palace itself was small, but it was surrounded by beautiful gardens and forests which had been laid out by Philip II. Visits to Aranjuez were made in the spring and enlivened by plays, spectacles, and boating excursions. During the course of his reign, Philip IV would make significant additions to the stock of country houses, which will be discussed below.

This, in outline form, was how life was led at the Spanish court during the reign of Philip IV. However, for all the apparent rigidity of routine, the rhythm and variety of court life were not immutable. Above the continuum of etiquette and ceremonial there were changes of direction caused by events and circumstances. One of the most important variables was the evolution of the king's personality during the forty-four years of his reign. The youth who became king in 1621 was very different from the man who was interred with great honors in 1665.

When Philip inherited the crown of the most powerful state of Europe in 1621, he was more a boy than a man (Plate 46).[11] At the time of his father's unexpected and premature death, he was only sixteen years old. Neither heredity nor education had done much to prepare the young king for the immense responsibilities he was now called upon to assume. His father, a lackluster figure, had set a poor example of kingship by assigning the tasks of government to a favorite, the duke of Lerma. Lerma, if not without political talent, had devoted more effort to enriching himself and his family than to matters of state and had fallen from power in 1618, only to be succeeded by his son. Upon his accession, Philip was determined to do better and to rule by himself. But several forces converged to defeat his good intentions.

First, of course, were his youth and lack of experience. But these might have been overcome had it not been for a congenital lack of self-confidence, which plagued him throughout his life. This characteristic was perceived by that most perceptive and experienced observer of European courts, Peter Paul Rubens. Rubens' oft-quoted remark on the king, made during his visit to Madrid in 1628–29, is worth repeating:

> [The king] alone arouses my sympathy. He is endowed by nature with all the gifts of body and spirit, for in my daily intercourse with him I have learned to know him thoroughly. And he would surely be capable of governing under any conditions, were it not that he mistrusts himself and defers too much to others.[12]

Philip's accession also coincided with a critical moment in the history of the Habsburg monarchy, which would have put the most experienced statesman to the test. Observers of the situation shared a growing perception that the power and fortunes of the monarchy were seriously endangered by enemies both from within and without the walls. The revolt of Bohemia in 1618 and the expiration of the truce with the Dutch in 1621 made the possibility of renewed war with Protestant Europe almost a certainty. But there was doubt that the Spanish economy, which was suffering from the accumulated effects of mismanagement and punishing taxation, would be able to support the war effort. In the end, the irresolute king must have felt himself overwhelmed by these problems and decided to call for help. His call was answered by a man who had been waiting to hear it, Gaspar de Guzmán, the count-duke of Olivares.

The count-duke had carefully calculated his rise to power and was ready with a program of reform and action. Olivares' policies and the steps he took to carry them out have been admirably reconstructed by J. H. Elliott and need not be summarized, and inevitably diluted, here.[13] But it is important to insist on one point. Olivares had an

47. Vicente Carducho, *Annunciation* (Madrid, Descalzas Reales), 1.50 × 1.25m.

48. Eugenio Cajés, *Virgin and Child* (Madrid, Museo del Prado), 1.60 × 1.35m.

almost worshipful attitude toward the king and kingship. Philip was styled as the Planet King, so called because the sun was then thought to be the fourth in the hierarchy of planets, as Philip was the fourth of his name. In a royal pageant staged in 1637, Olivares devised for himself the emblem of a sunflower, embodying a metaphor commonly used by royal servants to show that their existence depended on the warming rays of the monarch's favor.[14] The count-duke was therefore eager to mold the object of his admiration into an object of respect, while at the same time keeping the king on a tight rein as far as matters of policy and government were concerned. One solution to this tricky problem was to encourage the king's inherent taste for arts and letters, the pursuit of which on a grand scale would bring glory to the monarchy.

Right from the start, Philip had shown an interest in music, theater, and painting. The first two of these interests were more pronounced in his early years, perhaps because his passion for the theater was at least in part motivated by a passion for the actresses, with whom he frequently had assignations. But his early education had also included lessons in painting from an excellent artist, Fray Juan Bautista Maino.[15] Maino, who was born in 1578, had studied in Rome in the early 1600s, where he had become thoroughly acquainted with the styles of Caravaggio and Annibale Carracci. A few years after his return to Spain, which occurred around 1608, he took holy orders as a Dominican and was called to court as the drawing master of Prince Philip. Maino remained at court for the rest of his long life and, although he rarely painted, seems to have stayed on good terms with the king.

Philip's interest in painting may have been hereditary to some extent. Although his father was not known to have been much of a connoisseur, both his grandfather and great-grandfather, Philip II and Charles V, had been lovers of art.[16] Philip II in particular had been one of the great collectors and patrons of the sixteenth century and had accumulated a large collection of first-rate pictures. As is well known, Philip II was especially attracted to the works of Titian and the Venetian school, which he acquired in great numbers, and was also an important collector of Flemish painting. This great horde of pictures was exhibited primarily in three places — El Escorial, the Alcázar of Madrid, and the Palace of the Pardo. The young prince therefore grew up in a veritable museum of painting and, given his natural disposition toward the art, acquired a profound love of pictures, especially the rich, coloristic manner of the Venetians.

It must therefore have been disheartening for the new king to survey the talents of the six royal painters. The ranking artist in the hierarchy was Santiago Morán, a now-forgotten follower of Juan Pantoja de la Cruz. Morán entered royal service in 1609 and, despite his extremely modest artistic gifts, was given extraordinary status. According to the document of appointment, he was to be attached to the "casa de Su Majestad" instead of to the Committee of Works, as was customary for painters. Thus, he was styled *pintor de cámara*, while the other royal painters were known as *pintores del rey*.[17]

Below him were Vicente Carducho and Eugenio Cajés, who had been in service since 1609 and 1612 respectively.[18] They were competent painters but, as these two examples of their work from around 1620 show (Plates 47, 48), their styles were remarkably similar and remarkably conservative. A fourth royal painter, Bartolomé González, born in 1564, had been in service since 1617 and was, if anything, a less facile painter than either Carducho or Cajés.[19] Much the same could be said of Rodrigo de Villandrando and Francisco López, the fifth and sixth royal painters.[20] Thus, when Velázquez decided to try his luck in Madrid, the prospects for an innovative painter should have been bright. But, curiously, something seems to have gone wrong during his visit to the court in 1622.

The only source of information about this visit is Francisco Pacheco, whose account glides smoothly but honestly over the surface of the unsuccessful sojourn in Madrid:

> Desirous of seeing El Escorial, he left Seville for Madrid around the month of April of 1622. He was warmly welcomed by the brothers Luis and Melchor de Alcázar, and especially by Juan de Fonseca, *sumiller de cortina* of His Majesty (and a lover of

Velázquez' pictures). At my insistence, he did a portrait of Luis de Góngora, which was very celebrated in Madrid. At that time there was not an opportunity to paint the king and queen, although an attempt was made.[21]

The information contained between the lines of this brief account is important, since it establishes that the purpose of the trip was not merely to see the sights of Madrid, but to gain the attention and favor of the king. For this purpose, three friends of Pacheco, all former associates of his academy, were pressed into service. Of these, the most important was Juan de Fonseca, a nobleman-cleric who left Seville in 1609 and who by 1622 held a distinguished position in the royal chapel as *sumiller de cortina*.[22] Fonseca was a keen amateur of painting, the author of a now-lost treatise on antique painting, and the first recorded owner of Velázquez' *Waterseller*. Yet, nothing came of these efforts; Velázquez failed to paint the king's portrait, despite the fact that his *Portrait of Góngora* (Plate 42) was reckoned to be a success. By January 1623, Velázquez was again recorded in Seville, presumably awaiting more favorable circumstances to unfold at the court.[23]

His luck turned at once, perhaps even as he was en route to Seville. In December 1622, Rodrigo de Villandrando, one of the six royal painters, died, thus creating a vacancy in the ranks.[24] According to Pacheco's account, Juan de Fonseca, acting on the orders of the count-duke, summoned Velázquez to Madrid. Clearly, Fonseca had been hard at work on Velázquez' behalf and had managed to bring his name to the attention of the one person who could guarantee the success of his cause, the count-duke of Olivares. During the first years of his regime, Olivares had used his connections in Seville to fill literary and artistic posts at court. In accordance with a time-honored practice of politicians, he wanted to be surrounded with people whom he knew and knew he could count on. Thus was formed what has been called the "Seville Connection," which throughout the Olivares years would bring artists and writers from Seville to Madrid. In due course, not only Velázquez but also Francisco de Zurbarán, Alonso Cano, and the sculptor Juan Martínez Montañés would be the beneficiaries of this special relationship.

Once Velázquez had reached Madrid in August 1623, a well-designed plan was put into action.[25] He immediately painted the portrait of Fonseca (now lost) which was taken to the palace by Gaspar de Bracamonte, fifth son of the count of Peñaranda and an attendant in the household of the king's younger brother, the cardinal infante Ferdinand.[26] With the gears of power now meshing smoothly, the portrait was shown within an hour to the king and his brothers, who approved of it. Velázquez was asked to paint a portrait of the king which, however, because of the visit of the Prince of Wales, could not be executed until 30 August. The portrait was a success and resulted in the hoped-for court appointment. On 6 October 1623, Velázquez was named as royal painter, with a salary of twenty ducats a month to be paid from the account of the royal works.[27] He was also to receive payment for individual paintings as executed. According to a document clarifying the terms of the appointment, this was an advantage which had not been conferred on Bartolomé González, the last painter appointed to the position (1617). Finally, if we are to believe Pacheco, Velázquez was given the exclusive right to paint the portraits of the king.

The evaluation of Velázquez' artistic development between August 1623, when he won his appointment as court painter, and August 1629, when he departed for Italy, is fraught with problems and uncertainties. First, there is the paucity of surviving works; less than a dozen are known to exist. And, unfortunately, the lost works include some of his most important pictures. Then, some of the surviving pictures show signs of having been heavily repainted by the artist himself, which confuses the attempt to evaluate their purpose and significance. Finally, there is the problem of chronology. Only a few of the extant works can be reliably dated by external evidence. Thus, many aspects of this critical period are uncertain and subject to conjecture.

Because Velázquez' entry to the court was obtained by virtue of his skill as a portrait-

49. Velázquez, *Philip IV* (Dallas, Meadows Museum, Southern Methodist University), 0.616 × 0.48m.

ist, it is logical to begin the study of his career in Madrid with a consideration of these works. According to Pacheco, he executed three portraits as soon as he arrived in town. The first was a portrait of his friend, Fonseca, which was quickly followed by portraits of the king and the Prince of Wales. Unfortunately, the portraits of Fonseca and the prince have disappeared without a trace, while the identification of the portrait of the king presents a knotty problem which can best be unravelled by considering a group of related works.

Pacheco notes that the first portrait of the king was executed within the space of one day, 30 August 1623, which suggests that it was probably a small work.[28] Throughout his career, Velázquez (as many a portraitist) began a formal portrait commission by making a bust-length study of the sitter from life, which was taken back to the atelier to serve as a model for the finished work and for copies by members of the workshop.[29] The execution of these studies could be done quickly, as seen in a portrait sketch of Cardinal Francesco Barberini by Juan van der Hamen of 1626. According to the cardinal's secretary, Cassiano dal Pozzo, "in half an hour, or a little more, he did it very well, not, however, having completely finished it."[30]

The best candidate for the life study of the king is a bust-length portrait, now unfortunately much damaged (Plate 49).[31] Using this work, or one like it, Velázquez

45

50. Velázquez, *Philip IV* (Madrid, Museo del Prado),
1.98 × 1.02m.

51 (above left). Workshop of Velázquez, *Philip IV* (New York, Metropolitan Museum of Art), 1.999 × 1.02m.

52 (above center). Workshop of Velázquez, *Philip IV* (Boston, Museum of Fine Arts, Sarah Wyman Whitman Fund), 2.09 × 1.10m.

53 (above right). *Philip IV*, radiograph of Plate 50.

elaborated a full-length portrait, which some years later he extensively repainted (Plate 50). Fortunately, the original composition was twice copied before it was reworked (Plates 51, 52),[32] and with the help of these pictures and a radiograph of the reworked portrait (Plate 53), it is easily reconstructed. The king is depicted in a frontal position, wearing a wide cape which enlarges his figures on both sides. To his left is a table with a hat, the crown of which is at the same height as the king's left hand. Finally, the head is reduced in length by de-emphasizing the protruding jaw, a hallmark of the Spanish Habsburgs.

The decision to revise this portrait seems to have been taken a few years later. Once again the artist made a preparatory sketch (Plates 56, 57) which, to complicate matters, was itself reworked not long after to serve as a model for an equestrian portrait.[33] The relationship of this sketch to the new version of the full-length portrait is obvious, especially in the treatment of the face, which now closely resembles the king's real-life appearance (compare, for example, Plate 74). This change in the proportion of the head necessitated a corresponding change in the proportion of the body. Velázquez altered the pose by turning the body on a slight diagonal, reducing the width of the cape, and moving one leg behind the other. In this version of the portrait, Velázquez accomplishes two aims — greater accuracy of appearance and greater elegance of pose. These changes show a more mature understanding of Philip's taste in portraiture and established the format for royal portraits which was followed from then on.

The next major portrait commission involved Velázquez' benefactor, the count-duke of Olivares. On 4 December 1624, Velázquez received an installment of 800 reales on account for three portraits from a certain Antonia de Ipeñarrieta.[34] The sitters were to be the king, the count-duke, and Doña Antonia's husband, García Pérez de Araciel (died 1624). The portrait of Olivares identified with this commission (Plate 54) is a curious example of court portraiture and may even be a studio replica.[35]

54. Attributed to Velázquez, *Count-Duke of Olivares* (São Paulo, Museo de Arte), 2.012 × 1.111m.

55 (facing page). Velázquez, *Count-Duke of Olivares* (New York, Hispanic Society of America), 2.16 × 1.295m.

56. *Philip IV in Armor*, radiograph.

57. Velázquez, *Philip IV in Armor* (Madrid, Museo del Prado), 0.57 × 0.44m.

58 (facing page). Velázquez, *Infante Don Carlos* (Madrid, Museo del Prado), 2.09 × 1.26m.

Olivares was an imposing but not attractive figure. As represented in this portrait, his powerful personality is asserted almost to a fault. Posed in an uncompromising frontal stance, one hand resting on the hilt of his sword, the other on a table, he looks as if bloated with a sense of his own importance. His mountainous body is blatantly adorned with the symbols of his power — the golden key of the *sumiller de corps* and the golden spur of the *caballerizo mayor*.

In the second full-length *Portrait of Olivares* (Plate 55), executed a year or two later, and undoubtedly by Velázquez, an effort was made to improve the appearance of the subject by placing the body at an angle, thus diminishing the apparent bulk. The artist has also attempted to activate the composition by including a riding crop held in a rigid vertical position, against which the form of the sitter is contrasted.[36]

The last of the court portraits of these years represents the infante don Carlos (Plate 58) and is clearly related to the second full-length portrait of the king. The resemblance was rooted in realities; contemporary observers remarked that the prince fashioned his appearance after that of his brother.[37] Perhaps this is why Velázquez posed the infante

almost exactly as he had posed the king, including the heavy gold chain looped around the shoulder, an adornment which became popular at court in the mid-1620s.[38] This is the most successful of the early royal portraits and displays the first note of courtly elegance in the dainty way the prince holds the glove.

The portrait is also notable for other reasons. On all sides except the top, Velázquez has added a strip of canvas about four centimeters wide. The motive for the addition of the margin appears to be related to his preference for an improvisational mode of creation. It would seem logical that Velázquez added the strips in order to change the balance between the figure and the surrounding space. The effect of the alteration is perceived by comparing this portrait to the full-length *Portrait of Philip IV* (Plate 50). The figure of the prince seems to be placed deeper in space and thus appears less overbearing and more relaxed, as befits the pose. By this simple expedient, which Velázquez was to use occasionally throughout his career, important compositional changes were effected without reworking the canvas.[39]

The expanded space of the portrait also draws attention to another feature common to all the full-length portraits of these years, and this is the singular treatment of perspective. Here, as elsewhere, the floor seems to tilt at an angle to the picture plane, making the figure appear as if it were slightly elevated above the ground. In addition, the brushwork begins to show signs of change toward a looser, more varied stroke (Plate 60). This is especially notable in the handling of the chain, which is rendered by tiny blobs of impasted paint. It can also be seen, although less conspicuously, in the treatment of the prince's tunic, where the effect of the grayish black brocade is obtained by dragging a loaded brush over the underlying layer of black.

These few works are all that remain of Velázquez' early court portraits.[40] There are, however, a few informal portraits of unidentified subjects which should be considered. The first is the small but impressive *Portrait of Young Man* (Plate 61) which sometimes, without much reason, is identified as a self-portrait.[41] In spite of its size, this is a wonderful work, full of the spontaneity and vitality which are absent from the royal portraits. The difference in execution, particularly in the faces, between the portraits of royal and non-royal sitters is a characteristic of Velázquez' art which has often been noted and explained in various ways.[42] The reason for the shift in technique is probably to be found in a mixture of purpose and tradition. Portraits of royalty were not intended to reveal the character of the sitters, but rather their status as rulers. Like the public appearances of the royal family which were intended to glorify and depersonalize its members, Velázquez' images are governed by the spirit and letter of court etiquette. Thus, the full-length portrait shows the king as he appeared when receiving a distinguished visitor — composed, aloof, expressionless. Philip, following the custom of his ancestors, sought grandeur not in magnificent display but in regal reticence. But when painting portraits of friends and other members of the court, Velázquez was free of this restriction and could study appearance and character, and also try out new techniques of painting. In this casual portrait of a young man, Velázquez deftly and economically captures the particular features of the sitter's face — the sad eyes, the pouch-like cheeks, the square jaw.

More ambitious is the half-length *Portrait of Man* (Plate 59), which was left unfinished. From time to time, Velázquez abandoned a portrait in progress,[43] and there are many reasons why he might have done so. But it is worth noting that most of the unfinished portraits which are not preparatory studies (Plates 167, 170, 177, 178) are small in scale and informal in character (none is much over a meter at its largest dimension). Of the half-dozen unfinished portraits,[44] two are known to represent men who were friends or acquaintances of the artist and who were also his social peers. These circumstances suggest that the unfinished works might have been creations of a moment when the artist wanted to make a portrait and pressed a friend into service as a model. Or they may have been executed as tokens of friendship. As such, there was no pressure to complete them either immediately or at all.

In the *Portrait of Man*, Velázquez is attempting a more difficult pose than any en-

59. Velázquez, *Portrait of Man* (Munich, Alte Pinakothek), 0.892 × 0.695m.

60. Detail of Plate 58.

61. Velázquez, *Portrait of Young Man* (Madrid, Museo del Prado), 0.56 × 0.39m.

countered in other works of this period. The figure stands in three-quarter profile facing right, with one hand resting on the hip. The head is turned toward the left, establishing a torsion and movement which differs from the usual stationary compositions of these years. The pose also requires the difficult foreshortening of the bent arm and the fist resting against the waist. Velázquez' resolution of this problem is left in doubt by the lack of finish, but the head, which would normally be executed first, is beautifully modeled with delicate highlights and firmly controlled shadows.

Once outside the realm of portraiture, his production is small. Scenes of religion, mythology, and history constituted a minority of Velázquez' later work, and the same thematic distribution holds true for this period, too. The most important subject picture, the *Feast of Bacchus* (Plate 69), will be discussed shortly, as will the crucial but vanished *Expulsion of the Moriscos*. Otherwise, there are only two works to consider. *Supper at Emmaus* (Plate 62), is one of the four extant religious pictures painted after 1623. This picture is poorly preserved, having suffered abrasion which has destroyed the surface, and therefore is of interest primarily for its composition.

It is a hybrid work, combining the rustic figure types of the Seville religious paintings with an Italianate emphasis on gesture as a means of dramatic expression. Italian paintings, especially by Titian, were well represented in the royal collection, and there is every reason to believe that Velázquez studied them with care. Also, during the 1620s, paintings by important contemporary Italian artists including Domenichino, Guido Reni, and Artemisia Gentileschi, began to arrive in Madrid,[45] and the first works by Rubens appeared at court at the same time. The more dynamic, rhetorical style of these artists lurks in the background of Velázquez' painting, but it has been only imperfectly assimilated. By failing to provide a sufficient illusion of space, Velázquez is forced to crowd the figures together. The expected interval between the two apostles, which should be provided by the table, simply collapses. Thus, the figure in front has to lean backward so as not to interfere with the other apostle, whose body is unduly elevated to keep him in view.

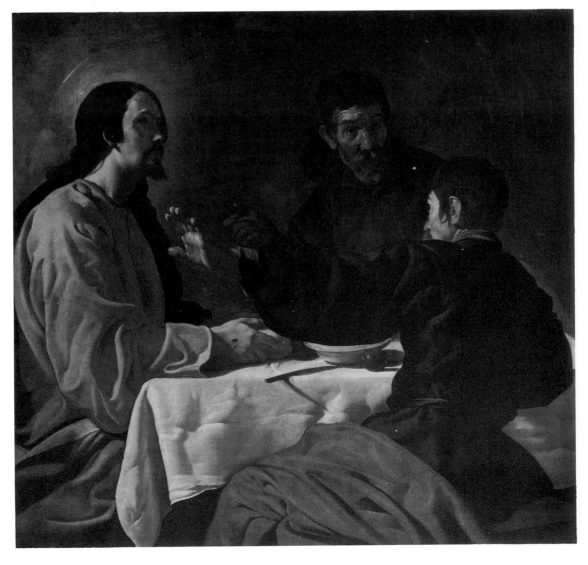

62. Velázquez, *Supper at Emmaus* (New York, Metropolitan Museum of Art), 1.23 × 1.326m.

63. Velázquez, *Democritus* (Rouen, Musée des Beaux-Arts), 1.01 × 0.81m.

64. After Velázquez, *Sense of Taste* (Toledo, Ohio, Museum of Art), 0.762 × 0.635m.

65 (following pages). Detail of Plate 81.

A more modest picture is a single-figured composition which initially represented the Sense of Taste and, years later, was transformed by the artist into *Democritus* (Plate 63). As radiographs show, the figure was originally holding a glass and was copied in this format by an anonymous artist (Plate 64). When Velázquez repainted the face and collar, probably in the late 1630s, he obliterated the hand and glass and replaced it with a table and globe, thus changing the meaning as well.[46]

In assessing the six-year period between Velázquez' court appointment and his departure for Italy, it may not be unfair to say that his career developed more rapidly than his art. Tokens of favor large and small were bestowed on him with extraordinary generosity. His appointment as court painter in 1623 provided not only for a monthly stipend of twenty ducats, but also for separate payment for paintings as executed. He was given lodgings on the calle de Convalecientes which, according to Pacheco's calculations, were worth two hundred ducats a year.[47] In 1626, following the exhibition of an equestrian portrait of the king, Olivares petitioned the nuncio, Monsignore Giovanni Battista Pamphili (later portrayed by Velázquez as Pope Innocent X) for an exemption which would permit the artist to enjoy an ecclesiastical benefice of three hundred ducats a year. The request was forwarded to Rome and eventually granted,

despite the initial reluctance of Pope Urban VIII to accede to it.[48] Olivares also sent his own physician when his protégé fell ill, and later arranged for the artist to execute portraits of himself and the king for the duke of Modena, a commission which had originally been granted to another painter.[49] At a time when the salaries of other court painters were in arrears, Velázquez was being showered with money and favors, and more was soon to come.

Velázquez' success was celebrated by Pacheco, but the other court painters found no cause to rejoice in the meteoric rise of this young rival. Like all who have patiently earned advancement only to see the investment of years surpassed in months by a young upstart, the senior court painters, notably Vicente Carducho and Eugenio Cajés, became embittered and began to criticize Velázquez. The evidence of rivalry is partly indirect, but nonetheless convincing. First is the conspicuous absence of Velázquez' name from Carducho's important art treatise, which was published in 1633. However, it is usually assumed that Velázquez was among those included in Carducho's diatribe against Caravaggio, whom he called an "evil genius," "an anti-Christ," and "this anti-Michelangelo." Caravaggio's cardinal sin, according to Carducho, was "to work naturally, almost without precepts, without doctrine, without study . . . with nothing but nature before him, which he simply copied in his amazing way. . . ." With the barbs of rancor removed from this statement, it could readily describe Velázquez' direct method of painting, which was the antithesis of Carducho's belief in the value of careful study and preparation as a means to achieve an ideal art.

More explicit is Pacheco's brief reference to Velázquez' *Philip IV on Horseback*, which was exhibited in public in March 1626.[50] Although he does not mention names, he states that the picture "won the admiration of all the court and the envy of artists." A younger acquaintance of Velázquez, Jusepe Martínez, also reported years later on the rivalry between the young artist and his senior colleagues, noting that they charged him, perhaps with some reason, with being capable only of painting heads.[51] According to Martínez, this allegation led to a competition between Velázquez and the three other royal painters, Carducho, Cajés, and Angelo Nardi, the last of whom had been appointed without salary in 1625.

This competition occurred in the first months of 1627 and is crucial for understanding the development of taste at the court in this period.[52] The subject for the competition painting was the Expulsion of the Moriscos from Spain by Philip III, and had been chosen to supplement the decoration of the so-called Salón Nuevo of the Alcázar, which was dedicated to extolling the might and virtue of the Spanish Habsburgs as defenders of the faith.[53] According to Pacheco, the judges for the competition were Fray Juan Bautista Maino and Giovanni Battista Crescenzi. Velázquez could only have been pleased with the choice because Maino and Crescenzi were partisans of "modernism," and this was the side on which Velázquez himself had taken a position.

66. Juan Bautista Maino, *Adoration of the Shepherds* (Villanueva y Geltrú, Museo Balaguer), 3.15 × 1.74m.

Maino, as we have seen, had studied painting in the Rome of Caravaggio.[54] As a painting of his of 1612 shows (Plate 66), the artist had made a personal interpretation of Caravaggism that was fully up-to-date with the style of Caravaggio's Roman followers. Giovanni Battista Crescenzi was also an artist, but by no means an ordinary practitioner. He had been born in Rome in 1577 into a famous Roman aristocratic family which had been distinguished by its service to the church.[55] His older brother, Pietro Paolo, was Cardinal Crescenzi. Giovanni Battista had chosen a career as an artist-amateur and had studied painting with Cristoforo Roncalli, il Pomarancio, one of the leading reform painters of late sixteenth-century Rome. In addition, Crescenzi was an architect or, more accurately, an architectural designer, and had been appointed in this capacity to the papal building works.

In 1617, Crescenzi came to Spain, bearing gifts of still-life paintings by his own hand and perhaps a request from his brother for support in the impending papal election. Crescenzi decided to remain at court, where the combination of noble blood and artistic talent made him an arbiter of taste. He easily survived the change in regimes and continually gained favor during the reign of Philip IV. By 1626, he had both a

67. Titian, *Pardo Venus* (Paris, Musée du Louvre), 1.96 × 3.85m.

68. Titian, *Charles V with Hound* (Madrid, Museo del Prado), 1.92 × 1.11m.

Spanish title, marquis of la Torre, and membership in the prestigious military order of Santiago. Four years later, he was simultaneously appointed to the Committee of Works and as Superintendent of the Royal Works, thus placing him in the enviable position of reporting to a committee of which he was himself a member. The outward signs of royal favor are far more conspicuous than Crescenzi's work as an artist, but there is ample reason to believe that the forty years spent in Rome, which included the crucial period of 1590–1610, had made him thoroughly familiar with recent developments in painting styles.

The outcome of the 1627 competition, then, was in the hands of unjust judges, who disposed of the old guard and proclaimed Velázquez as the winner. It is a great misfortune that the prize-winning picture has not survived, for it could have told us much about Velázquez and the taste of the court. Palomino describes it in some detail, but gives no clue to the style.[56] However, it would not be a mistake to interpret the competition as a milestone in Velázquez' career. Shortly after the victory, he received his first household appointment as Usher of the Privy Chamber, which occurred on 7 March 1627.[57] This was a minor position in the royal service, but it created the opportunity for advancement and honors in the household in a way that was not possible for servants in the royal works, who were detached from the main line of the palace hierarchy. It also meant that Velázquez was eligible to draw salary and perquisities from the household budget which, although strained, was considerably larger than the budget of the Committee of Works. The prospect of fame and wealth thus was opened to the artist and was to prove a powerful incentive.

The artistic implications of the 1627 competition were equally great, for it decided this Spanish version of the quarrel between the ancients and moderns in favor of the moderns. Here, however, we must be careful not to limit our consideration of this turning point only to the competition. In the crucial six-year period from August 1623 to August 1629, the court received visits from some of the most enlightened connoisseurs and practitioners of painting of the day, all of whom had a cumulative and decisive impact on the taste of the king and his painter.

In the seventeenth century, Madrid, as the capital of a powerful state with dominions in Europe and America, was a crossroads of the world. Friends and would-be friends, former enemies and future enemies all came or sent ambassadors to treat with the king of Spain in the hopes of winning support or begging money. Thus it was not unusual that, in rapid succession, the court would receive the heir to the throne of England, the nephew of His Holiness the Pope, and the ambassador of the governor of the Netherlands. The extraordinary thing was that they all shared the love of fine painting.

First to arrive were Charles, Prince of Wales, and his companion, the duke of Buckingham, who had travelled incognito from London across France, arriving unannounced in Madrid on 7 March 1623. The Spanish court, momentarily taken by surprise, soon recovered and began plans for a lavish round of receptions and entertainments, beginning with a triumphal entry procession from San Jerónimo to the Alcázar, which took place on 23 March.

The main purpose of the visit was to arrange the marriage of the prince with the king's sister, the infanta María. The tale of the Spanish Match has often been told and need not be repeated here.[58] More to the point of the story is Charles' growing passion for pictures, which lasted long after his passion for the princess had faded. Despite the almost-daily rounds of banquets and bullfights, Charles found time to visit not only the royal collections but private collections as well, making acquisitions as he went. Carducho described the prince's activities in this way: "[Many of the paintings mentioned here] were at great risk when the Prince of Wales (now king of England) was here, because he tried to obtain as many pictures and original drawings as he could, regardless of price."[59]

Charles turned Philip's exquisite courtesy to good advantage by expressing admiration for several pictures by Titian, some of which he was promptly given. Among them were the *Pardo Venus* (Plate 67) and *Charles V with Hound* (Plate 68). He almost succeeded

70 (above). Jan Saenredam, *Feast of Bacchus* (after H. Goltzius) (Amsterdam, Rijksmuseum).

71 (above). *Feast of Bacchus*, radiograph.

69 (top). Velázquez, *Feast of Bacchus* (Madrid, Museo del Prado), 1.65 × 2.27m.

73 (above left). Paulus Pontius, *Count-Duke of Olivares* (Rotterdam, Museum Boymans-van Beuningen), 0.325 × 0.225m.

74 (above center). Rubens, *Philip IV* (Zurich, Kunsthaus).

75 (above right). Attributed to Rubens, *Philip IV* (Genoa, Galleria Durazzo-Pallavicini), 2.21 × 1.48m.

72 (previous page). Detail of Plate 69.

in obtaining the great series of *Poesie* painted by Titian for Philip II. According to Carducho, the paintings had been packed for shipment to England, but were later returned to the royal collection after the definitive cancellation of the match. Charles also had his portrait painted by Velázquez. The now-lost portrait appears to have been a sketch rather than a finished work and Velázquez was paid 100 escudos for it.[60]

The effect on Philip of this remarkable royal collector must have been equal to the effect made on Charles by the remarkable Spanish royal collections. Philip, who was to surpass Charles as a patron and collector, must have been encouraged, if not challenged, by the prince's example to pursue his inherent love of painting. And perhaps it is also fair to suggest that he looked at his patrimonial collection with new eyes after seeing the admiration it aroused in the Prince of Wales.

Two and a half years after the departure of the English prince there was a visit by an important prince of the Roman church, who is known as one of the great art patrons of the seventeenth century. This was Cardinal Francesco Barberini (Plate 225), nephew of Urban VIII. Barberini's greatest days as a patron and collector still lay in the future, but his knowledge of and interest in fine pictures were already well developed. During his short stay in Madrid (24 May–4 August 1626), he took the opportunity to see the royal collections and perhaps had the chance to discuss them with the king.[61] In any event, the visit provided Philip with yet another opportunity to meet a man of his age and status who was an educated connoisseur.

Cardinal Francesco was accompanied by another collector hardly less distinguished than himself; this was the antiquarian and scholar Cassiano dal Pozzo, who was the secretary of the legation. As one of his duties, Cassiano kept a diary in which he recorded the events and sights of the sojourn.[62] The diary is not only an invaluable record of court life of this period, but also contains a comment on a portrait by Velázquez of Cardinal Barberini. The opinion on Velázquez by a cultivated Italian connoisseur was not flattering and tends to corroborate the perception of the artist's early court works as lacking in fluency and polish. Cassiano not only found Velázquez' portrait to be "melancholy and severe," but also preferred the style of Juan van der Hamen, the famous still-life painter, who was commissioned to paint a portrait to replace the one by Velázquez.[63]

The visit of the Italians, then, must have helped both Philip and Velázquez to gain another perspective on taste in pictures, although at some cost to Velázquez' self-esteem. But at least he was able to make the acquaintance of two influential leaders of the Roman art world who would help him when he went to Italy.

The third "artistic visitor" to Madrid in these years was undoubtedly the most important. This was the great Peter Paul Rubens, who arrived in September 1628 as the emissary of Philip's aunt, the infanta Isabella, governor of the Netherlands.[64] Rubens and Velázquez had been in correspondence earlier about a commission of an engraved portrait of Olivares for which, as the inscription states, Velázquez had provided a model. This prototype may be reflected in a drawing (Plate 73) by the engraver, Paulus Pontius, a drawing which Rubens corrected before the plate was cut.[65] The changes by Rubens were intended to improve the modeling and expression, suggesting that they were not to his taste in the original.

The purpose of Rubens' trip was to prepare the ground for a peace treaty with England, but during his seven-month stay he had time for other pursuits, especially painting. Knowing in advance of the king's love of pictures, the artist had brought eight of his works, an assortment of biblical and mythological subjects and hunting scenes.[66] In addition, his appearance in Madrid coincided with the arrival of one of his masterpieces, the magnificent series of tapestries for the royal convent of the Descalzas Reales.[67] Rubens' art, which had been previously represented in Madrid by only a few examples, now became a force to reckon with.

During his stay at court, Rubens added to this stock of pictures in ways which were instructive to the king and his painter. First, he executed a group of royal portraits, thus infringing on Velázquez' monopoly.[68] Rubens' portraits of the king were done in a variety of formats. The bust-length portrait (Plate 74) shows immediately how Rubens was able to infuse movement and a sense of opulence into the stern tradition of Habsburg portraiture. More impressive is the full-length image of the king (Plate 75). Here it seems as if Rubens deliberately made use of a composition by Velázquez (Plate 50), which he then deftly transformed into a model of sophisticated, up-to-date court portraiture. Posing his sitter in a loggia-like setting with a distant landscape, Rubens creates an air of magnificence through the use of a giant column cloaked with luxuriant drapery, which imparts a surging motion to the composition. Next to this confident demonstration of pictorial mastery, Velázquez' portrait lacks space, drama, and finesse.

It is tempting to think that Rubens intended these portraits as a lesson to the young artist, but this may be imagining too much. We do know, however, that a comparison was made in at least one instance and that it was not favorable to Velázquez. In the last months of 1628, Rubens created a monumental equestrian portrait of the king, now known only in a later copy (Plate 76) in which the head has been altered to show Philip as an older man.[69] Upon completion, this portrait was installed in the new gallery of the Alcázar, taking the place of the *Philip IV on Horseback* executed by Velázquez and triumphantly shown in public just three years before.[70]

The lessons which Rubens had to teach Velázquez were not only artistic, for Rubens was no mere painter, but a phenomenal combination of artist, diplomat, courtier, and humanist. While in Madrid, he demonstrated his many talents. Some of his time was spent in negotiations with the king and Olivares, which were his primary business. He also met with men of letters in an attempt to trace manuscripts by Marcus Aurelius for his scholar-friend Jan Caspar Gevaerts, and consorted with noblemen whom he had known in Flanders. The sum of these activities was to bring to life the ideal of the artist-courtier which Velázquez had heard about since his days of apprenticeship, and therefore to provide him with a model to emulate.

Pacheco mentions that Rubens ignored the other court painters and kept only the company of Velázquez. The two went together to El Escorial to look at pictures and undoubtedly talked at length about what they saw. There is of course no written record of this and other encounters, yet there is a painted one which survives in the remarkable series of copies after Titian done by Rubens.[71] These copies are usually understood as an act of homage by a great master to a revered and kindred spirit of the past. But they can also be understood as a kind of lesson from a brilliant, experienced painter to a

76. After Rubens, *Philip IV on Horseback* (Florence, Uffizi), 3.39 × 2.67m.

brilliant, inexperienced painter. Velázquez knew the paintings of Titian by heart, but had not been able to penetrate the secret of their greatness. Rubens, however, had seen and understood. The surviving copies are remarkable works of art which demonstrate almost programatically the continuing vitality of Titian as a source of inspiration and the artistic powers required to turn this inspiration into masterpieces of modern painting.

In some instances, Rubens deliberately kept the compositional changes to a minimum (Plates 77, 78) and concentrated on reworking the color. In others, he made small but telling alterations (Plates 79, 80) to intensify the dramatic and psychological aspects of the painting. The spectacle of seeing one artist recreate the masterpieces of another with such confidence and understanding must have been a stirring, and perhaps somewhat daunting, experience. When we place Velázquez' first major mythological painting, the *Feast of Bacchus*, which was done while Rubens was still at court, alongside Rubens' copy of the *Rape of Europa*, we can see how much Velázquez still had to learn to meet the standards of a great Baroque artist.

The *Feast of Bacchus* (Plate 71) is a nearly brilliant realization of a brilliant conception. Despite attempts to interpret this unconventional painting either as a parody of the Olympian gods or as a sermon on the evils of drink, it seems that Velázquez intended to represent Bacchus as the giver of the gift of wine, which freed man (temporarily) from the harsh, unforgiving struggle of daily life. This interpretation appears in at least two late sixteenth-century sources, which were available to Velázquez. First is an engraving of 1596 by Jan Saenredam after a design by Hendrick Goltzius (Plate 70).[72] A short poem accompanying the print, composed by the Dutch poet Cornelis Schonaeus, is readily applicable to Velázquez' painting:

> O, Father Bacchus, we prostrate our bodies on the ground,
> And humbly beg you to favor us with your gifts,
> Gifts which quiet our sad pains and sorrow
> And free our hearts from troubling concerns.

The same interpretation of Bacchus was proposed in 1585 by the Spanish mythographer, Juan Pérez de Moya, whose influential book, *La philosophía secreta*, was owned by Velázquez.[73] Pérez de Moya's exegesis of the meaning of Bacchus, which is reflected in many features of the picture, ends by praising the god as a "liberator" who frees slaves from servitude when they imbibe the gift of wine.

In the first version of the composition, as seen in the radiograph (Plate 71), Velázquez showed the head of the drinker at the far right in a frontal position rather than in profile, thus isolating the standing beggar behind him from the rest of the company. The change in pose, which links the beggar to the drinkers, adds another dimension of the meaning by suggesting the fleeting effects of the bacchic gift. Deprived of the beneficent liquid, the beggar finds no respite from the hardships which, in sober moments, will be shared by all the company.

Velázquez' way of representing this subject as an earthy genre scene is original and witty. The contrast between the cool, marmoreal figure of the young Bacchus (Plate 72)

66

81. Velázquez, *Christ after the Flagellation Contemplated by the Christian Soul* (London, National Gallery), 1.65 × 2.06m.

and the leathery, weather-beaten faces of the drunkards intensifies the power of the picture. But there are also inescapable flaws. The composition is static and crowded. Once again, Velázquez has failed to resolve the relationship between the foreground and background. The placement of still-life elements in the center is also peculiar; the plate and pitcher look as if they were two-dimensional decals pasted onto the canvas without regard for the surrounding spatial construction. It is hard to believe that this picture was painted during or just after Rubens' stay in Madrid, but the receipt, dated 22 July 1629, indicates that this is so.

The other picture which can provisionally be dated to this period is an imposing representation of *Christ after the Flagellation Contemplated by the Christian Soul* (Plate 81). This rare subject has a few precedents in Spanish art, but appears to have been almost unknown in other parts of Europe.[74] In this rendition of the Flagellation, the narrative elements in the Gospel have been eliminated and substituted by symbolic elements which point to a source in a still-unidentified mystical text. Christ, battered and bloodied, lies on the ground, the weight of His body pulling against the rope which ties Him to the column. From His head a pinpoint of light radiates toward the Soul, symbolizing

82. Domenichino, *Sacrifice of Isaac* (Madrid, Museo del Prado), 1.47 × 1.40m.

the ray of grace which Christ, through His sacrifice, makes available to believers. This heartfelt subject inspired Velázquez to paint one of his most moving pictures, one that is characterized by an expression of emotion rarely found in his work (Plate 65).

The proposed dates for this undocumented picture have straddled Velázquez' first trip to Italy, some writers placing it before his departure, others during his trip or immediately after his return. Much of the uncertainty has been caused by the Italianate figure of Christ, which seems to imply a knowledge of the Bolognese and Roman painters working in Rome after 1600. But, as we have seen, at least a few pictures by these artists had been sent to the king, probably arriving in 1628–29 (Plate 82). The impact of seeing these pictures, and the ones brought by Rubens in the autumn of 1628, may account for the sudden appearance of the more classicizing figure type used here and in the *Feast of Bacchus*. Also, it should be noted that the technique, particularly the use of dense pigments and the weighty treatment of the drapery, are consistent with the works done before the first trip to Italy.[75]

As Rubens came to know Velázquez, he would have seen his promise as a painter, but he also could have seen that it would not be realized in Madrid. Pacheco claims that Rubens "greatly favored Velázquez' paintings for their modesty." Rubens was undoubtedly being polite even as he tactfully showed Velázquez, through his own creations, how much more he had to learn.

Velázquez and his patron were quick to grasp the point. On 28 June 1629, less than two months after Rubens had left for London, Philip granted his painter permission to go to Italy.[76] The purpose of the visit is not stated in the royal license, but it was reported by the ambassadors of Parma and Venice. "It is said that he is going to Italy to perfect his art," wrote the Parmese ambassador, while his Venetian counterpart sent word that "he is going to learn things pertaining to his profession."[77] The second apprenticeship of Velázquez was about to begin.

CHAPTER III

Velázquez and Italy

VELÁZQUEZ' TRIP to Italy in 1629–30 is the turning point of his career as an artist. In reviewing the first thirty years of his life, we have seen how he made a fast start as a painter in Seville and then seemed to develop at a slower pace during the 1620s, as he attempted to master the requirements of a new set of artistic circumstances at court. But during the eighteen months in Italy, his style underwent a revolutionary change, a change which seems to be an exception to the conventional model of progressive artistic development. Although the effect of this important change can be clearly seen in the pictures, the external evidence for the causes is patchy and incomplete.

Our principal source of knowledge is fundamentally reliable. This is the account of Francisco Pacheco, which presumably was based on Velázquez' personal report of the trip.[1] But the promise of complete information is quickly dashed. Upon scrutiny, Pacheco's narrative is merely a chronicle informing us where Velázquez went and how well he was received by important noblemen and ecclesiastics. Not a single name of an artist then living is mentioned; only Count This-and-That, or Cardinal So-and-So. And, unfortunately, the trip is barely documented by other sources. But rather than reproach Pacheco for his reticence, it would be more gracious to accept with gratitude his information and to interpret it as best we can.

The first point to be noted is Pacheco's emphasis on Velázquez' contacts with the well-born and powerful. Since the fifteenth century, artists from all over Europe had been drawn to Italy for the same reason that attracted Velázquez — the desire to perfect their art in the acknowledged center of European painting. But Velázquez was no ordinary artistic pilgrim, hoping to survive as best he could while learning the secrets of the profession. He was the painter of the king of Spain and therefore had entry to places where only the most privileged of his fellow artists could go. Even before he left Madrid, word of the impending trip was being dispatched to Italian cities by the ambassadors at court.

Flavio Atti wrote the news to his ruler, the duchess of Parma, two days before the royal permission was ceded to Velázquez. According to Atti's dispatch, Velázquez' artistic activities were in reality a cover for his true assignment as a spy.[2] The Venetian ambassador, Alvise Mocenigo, was inclined to accept the purpose of the trip at face value and was preparing letters of introduction.[3] Averardo de' Medici, the Tuscan ambassador, was mostly concerned with the problems of protocol posed by the intended visit to Florence. As he saw it, the trick was to pay Velázquez sufficient honor to please the king without, however, giving him more than his due. His haughty advice to the grand duke is an epitome of aristocratic condescension. "I recommend that you commission him to do your portrait and then give him a chain with your medal. Treat him with kingly gravity and treat him well within the compass of his profession, because with these low-class Spaniards [*spagnoli bassi*] you lose the same by esteeming them too little as you do by esteeming them too much."[4] Be this as it may, the fact remains that the grand duke would have received and honored Velázquez, had he chosen to visit the city.

To follow the thread of Pacheco's narrative, Velázquez' journey to Italy began on 10 August 1629, when he sailed from Barcelona in the company of the great Genoese general, Ambrogio Spinola, who was on his way to take command of the Spanish troops engaged in the Mantuan War. Upon arriving, Velázquez made his first important stop in Venice, where he stayed with the Spanish ambassador.[5] He then set out for Rome, pausing on the way at Ferrara where he was received by Cardinal Giulio Sacchetti, whom he had known while Sacchetti was papal nuncio in Madrid from 1624 to 1626. He stayed two nights in Ferrara and on the second spent more than three hours in conversation with the cardinal.

Velázquez lost no more time in making his way to Rome, stopping briefly only in Cento, where perhaps he made the acquaintance of Guercino. In Rome, he was welcomed by Cardinal Francesco Barberini, who was now well-launched on his career as an art patron, and who permitted Velázquez the use of rooms in the Vatican Palace. Pacheco's description is sufficiently precise to allow identification of these quarters, which flank the Nicchione of the Belvedere and are remarkable for their frescoes by Federico Zuccaro and for their remote, isolated location. In effect, Velázquez was living virtually on the outskirts of Rome and, for this reason, he abandoned the lodgings and moved elsewhere. However, before leaving, he was careful to arrange access to the frescoes of Raphael and Michelangelo, in front of which he spent many days making sketches.

When summer came, he used the offices of the Spanish ambassador, the count of Monterrey, to gain permission to move to the Villa Medici.[6] His motive was two-fold: to escape the summer heat and to copy works in the abundant collection of antique statuary. After having spent two months in this delightful setting, Velázquez fell ill and had to move near the house of the ambassador, who took charge of the artist's recuperation. He left Rome in the autumn and returned to Madrid by way of Naples, where he painted a portrait of María of Hungary who was then on her way to meet her new husband, Ferdinand.[7] By early 1631, he was once again in Madrid.

This summary of Velázquez' first Italian trip is a paraphrase of Pacheco's description, which reads rather like the entries in an engagement book. What occurred between these appointments is largely a matter for speculation, but unless the attempt is made to reconstruct his activities, the transformation of Velázquez' style seems like a major miracle when in fact it was only a minor one. The surest way to tread this tricky path is to use as landmarks the persons he met along the way.

First among these is Cardinal Giulio Sacchetti, with whom Velázquez spent over three hours in conversation during his stay in Ferrara. Cardinal Sacchetti and his brother Marcello were enlightened connoisseurs and patrons of painting and were the first protectors of Pietro da Cortona.[8] Their opinions on painting are admirably summarized by Francis Haskell in a way that is relevant for understanding Velázquez' activities in Rome:

> Marcello had decided views on painting and his encouragement of Pietro [da Cortona] to copy Raphael and Titian marks a focal point in the history of seventeenth-century art: that combination of Raphael's freest, most imaginative design with Titian's warmth of color was the foundation stone on which Baroque painting was established. Thereafter every artist was required to undergo similar training.[9]

Having just refreshed his knowledge of Titian in Venice, Velázquez, in fulfillment of this formula, was now ready to make acquaintance of the great works of the High Renaissance in Rome.

Copying the great Vatican frescoes by Raphael and Michelangelo was for a long time considered to be a universal requirement of artistic training. The practice became so common that there is now a temptation to regard it simply as a literary device used by biographers of artists. But the fact is that the *School of Athens* was a real school for painters, who could study in this and in Raphael's other Vatican frescoes the canonical grand manner of Italian painting and hone their skills in harmonious composition and lofty expression. And from Michelangelo's Sistine Ceiling they derived lessons in the subtleties of anatomical draftsmanship and learned how the human figure could be used to reveal ideas and emotions. Thus, we must take Pacheco's information about the days spent by Velázquez copying these masterpieces with the utmost seriousness. None of the drawings he made in the Vatican has survived, but there is no reason to doubt that he made them.

The attentive study of past masters was one part of Velázquez' curriculum. The other was contact with the leading masters of the day, and in this Velázquez was exceptionally fortunate. His arrival in Rome in 1630 coincided with an important moment in the history of Italian art, for it was just then that a new group of young artists was beginning to emerge.[10] The mere mention of their names is sufficient to evoke the extraordinary artistic vitality which surrounded that famous year — Pietro da Cortona, Andrea Sacchi, Nicolas Poussin, Claude Lorrain, and last, but certainly not least, Gianlorenzo Bernini. Most of these men were the exact contemporaries of Velázquez and their names have become synonymous with the age of the Baroque. Nor were the older artists an untalented lot — Giovanni Lanfranco and Domenichino were the leaders of this group.

There is no documentary evidence to connect these men with Velázquez, but the circumstantial evidence is fairly sound because Velázquez was acquainted with some of their patrons. Three of the most influential were already known to him from Spain — Cardinal Giulio Sacchetti, Cardinal Francesco Barberini, and Cassiano dal Pozzo. After his posting to Madrid, Cardinal Sacchetti returned to Rome and a spectacular career as an art patron during the pontificate of Urban VIII. Cardinal Francesco Barberini, a man of great taste and culture, was the most important patron in Rome after the pope.[11] Like the Sacchetti brothers, he was an admirer of Pietro and also patronized Andrea Sacchi and Bernini, two more of the rising stars of the new generation. The cardinal also knew Poussin, to whom he had given the commission for an important altarpiece in St. Peter's (*Martyrdom of St. Erasmus*). But the connection of Poussin to Cassiano was to prove more significant and enduring. Despite Cassiano's reservations about Velázquez' portrait of Cardinal Barberini, he would have treated the Spaniard with courtesy and introduced him to his circle of friends.

The fourth patron with whom Velázquez came into contact was Manuel de Fonseca y Zúñiga, the count of Monterrey and Spanish ambassador to the Holy See from 1628 to 1631.[12] Monterrey was a powerful figure in the Spain of Olivares, to whom he was closely related by marriage (each had married the other's sister). We are less well informed about Monterrey's activities as a patron in Rome than in Naples, where he became viceroy in 1631. But he is known to have been in contact with Domenichino and Lanfranco, both of whom he was to employ during his viceregency. It was also in his embassy that Michelangelo Cerquozzi, one of the bamboccianti, found his earliest support, precisely around the time that Velázquez was in contact with the count.[13]

There is thus every reason to believe that Velázquez' experience of the new in art was an important and extensive as it was of the old. Indeed, common sense is as reliable a guide for his artistic contacts as the reconstruction of his contacts just completed. He had gone to Italy to study painting and would therefore have sought out his Italian colleagues as a matter of course.

The impact of Italian art on Velázquez' style is readily observable in the few paintings which can be dated to this period. Of these, the most important are the *Forge of Vulcan* and *Joseph's Bloodied Coat Presented to Jacob* (Plates 83, 89). The evidence for the date of these pictures is admittedly exiguous, depending only on the statement by Palamino that they were done in Rome. But everything about them suggests that this was so. They are first documented in 1634, when Velázquez sold them to the crown.[14] This document is important because it implies that Velázquez had painted the pictures without a commission and therefore that they were made for his own purposes. His

83 (and facing page detail). Velázquez, *Forge of Vulcan* (Madrid, Museo del Prado), 2.23 × 2.90m.

motivation can be inferred simply by looking at them. In content and style, they aspire to the grand manner of Italian history painting.

Much has been written about the underlying thematic content of these two works, on the assumption that they were intended as a complementary pair. This assumption rests in part on the apparently uniform dimensions and the common use of lofty subjects of a kind regarded by artists and theorists as the true test of a painter's mastery of his art. Also, the fact that they were kept together by Velázquez seems to indicate that they were meant to go together.

However, this idea that they share a common theme does not take account of the fact that the original dimensions were not that much alike. The *Forge of Vulcan* and *Joseph's Coat* now measure 2.23 × 2.90 meters respectively. But the *Forge of Vulcan* was originally around thirty-three centimeters narrower, while *Joseph's Coat* was originally about fifty centimeters wider.[15] In other words, there was once a difference of over eighty centimeters between the width of the two works, a difference which would have implied to viewers that they were looking at two discrete history paintings by a single artist rather than a pair of related works. For this reason, it seems reasonable to regard each painting as a separate, self-contained entity as far as subject is concerned.

84. Antonio Tempesta, *Forge of Vulcan*, from Ovid, *Metamorphoses* (Antwerp, 1606) (New York, Public Library).

In recent years, there have been attempts to interpret the *Forge of Vulcan* as a Christian allegory, despite the fact that the picture offers no explicit clues to this effect.[16] More plausible is the view that Velázquez chose the subject because of its pictorial possibilities.[17] As told by Ovid in the *Metamorphoses*, Apollo came to the workshop of Vulcan to reveal the news of the infidelity of Venus, his wife, with Mars. Ovid's narrative is sparing of details, omitting any mention of Vulcan's assistants, the Cyclops. However, their presence, together with other details in the *Forge of Vulcan*, is found in the visual source which served as Velázquez' point of departure, an engraving in a 1606 edition of Ovid, executed by Antonio Tempesta (Plate 84).[18] By literally fleshing out his composition with the Cyclops, Velázquez adapted the text to his immediate purpose — the representation of emotion through expression and gesture.

Velázquez' choice of scene from the story of Vulcan, Venus, and Mars is admittedly unusual. Painters of the seventeenth century overwhelmingly preferred to illustrate the denouement, when Venus and Mars are trapped in bed by Vulcan's finely woven net of steel. Velázquez chose to avoid this rowdy, burlesque finale in favor of the devastating but psychologically delicate moment when the crippled blacksmith hears from Apollo the news of his wife's infidelity. The impact of the message seems to ripple across the canvas as it reaches the ears of Vulcan and his assistants, who are frozen in mid-action by what they hear. Only the face of the blacksmith is seen in full-view among the figures in front, but the feelings of surprise and concern experienced by the others are impossible to mistake.

Velázquez has cunningly heightened the power of the picture by translating the myth into everyday terms. The realistic setting which makes the picture memorable is already suggested in Tempesta's engraving, but Velázquez intensifies its importance by recreating the dusky atmosphere of the forge, which is littered with the tools of the trade and pieces of work in progress (Plate 83). The figures, although correctly rendered, are common men (Plate 86), not statues come to life, as they would have been in the work of many a contemporary Roman painter. Yet, if certain realistic elements recall the genre paintings of the Seville years (Plate 87), the *Forge of Vulcan* in other respects is clearly a major break from all that had gone before.

85. *Forge of Vulcan*, radiograph.

86 (facing page). Detail of Plate 83.

The departures in style and technique are as important and impressive as the departures in subject.[19] To begin with, there is the convincing treatment of space, where the transition into the background is smoothly handled and where the intervals between figures are properly measured. Another change is in the brushstrokes, which are lighter in touch and more varied in length and breadth. In the earlier works, Velázquez tended to apply several layers of opaque paint, which produce an appearance of density on the surface. Here, even the prime coat has been thinly applied, allowing the grainy texture of the canvas to help modulate the shadows. Thus, when highlights are created with impasto, the play of light and shadow can become dazzling, as it is in the orange robe of Apollo, or in the glowing reddish orange of the molten metal on the forge. Similarly the modeling of the naked forms is now beautifully controled, revealing the structure of muscle and bone beneath the skin.

The artistry of the picture now seems effortless and accomplished, yet beneath the visible layer of pigment another story is told. Radiographs show that, once again, Velázquez improvised as he went, making corrections large and small until the picture looked right (Plate 85).[20] Most important are the changes in the figure of Vulcan. In the first version, Vulcan's head was tilted to the left, not the right, and his arm hung straight down at his side. He wore a moustache, but no beard or kerchief. The pose was therefore static, not dynamic, with the resulting loss of the impression of arrested motion which now adds so much to the drama of the scene. Smaller adjustments to the poses of the Cyclops, which seem to have been made to increase the intervals between the figures, are also visible. The profile of Apollo was also slightly altered. Velázquez' first idea is preserved in one of the rare preparatory sketches from his hand (Plate 88).[21] This pose seems to have been transferred to the canvas and then slightly revised later. More important, Velázquez added a forge in front of Apollo, probably to push him back into the space. He also altered the distribution of light. In the first version, the strongest light was concentrated on the figure of Vulcan and on the fire seen between the first two Cyclops. Later, the painter reduced the importance of the firelight by placing a hammer in the hands of the Cyclops and adding a luminescent aureole around the head of Vulcan and a window behind. Another change concerns the Cyclops in the middle, the one with his mouth gaping wide in astonishment. As first painted, his expression was considerably less animated. The sum of these alterations was to transform a somewhat static composition into the masterpiece of technique and psychology we see today. It is impossible to say when Velázquez revised the picture, but it is intriguing to think that the changes were made after he had become more familiar with the standards of contemporary Roman painting.

Like the *Forge of Vulcan*, *Joseph's Coat* (Plate 89) depicts a moment of revelation. Here, the brothers of Joseph present the fake evidence of his death to his father, who reacts with a broad gesture of surprise and horror. The brothers, who know the truth but must dissimulate, act their parts well, except for the figure at the left, whose extravagant gesture seems unduly theatrical.

Joseph's Coat, a fully and self-consciously Italianate work, is like a catalogue of lessons learned through the study of the great masters. Most conspicuous is the tiled floor, the standard device for creating a convincing illusion of space. It is as if Velázquez wanted to demonstrate his mastery of this trick of the trade. Then there are the carefully posed and modeled figures, in which firm drawing is joined with masterful light effects. As in the *Forge of Vulcan*, Velázquez does not employ idealized figure types; one of the brothers is short and stocky, and has bulging, over-developed calf muscles. But perhaps the most important elements are color and light, aspects of painting in which Velázquez had excelled from the first.

In this picture, we sense that at last Velázquez has grasped the full significance of Titian and the Venetians.[22] Not only is the palette distinctly lighter, but the range of colors has been extended to include brighter tones than any found before. And the shadowing is more refined, used not only to create the illusion of relief by contrast with light, but also to mute and modify colors without obliterating their basic values, as in the two figures huddled together in the middleground.

88. Velázquez, *Head of Apollo* (New York, private collection), 0.363 × 0.252m.

87 (facing page). Detail of Plate 83.

works — *Philip IV in Brown and Silver* (Plate 98). The problem concerns not the attribution, which is beyond all question, but the date. Usually, the picture is dated by relationship to the portrait sent to Vienna in September 1632 (Plate 94), to which it bears some resemblance.[33] But conviction in the usual date of 1631–32 is shaken by two anomalies. The head is identical to *Philip IV as Hunter* (Plate 155), which is datable to around 1636, and the execution of the costume is done in the brilliant, virtuoso manner which does not become fully evident until the middle of the decade.[34] Indeed, were it not for the existence of the portrait of 1632, *Philip IV in Brown and Silver* would be most at home among the works of the mid-1630s. Therefore, it may be worth analyzing this connection with attention.

At first, there seems to be no doubt that the composition of the two portraits is identical. However, there are important differences which become more evident when it is recognized that the portrait of 1632 is a reduced version of a full-length portrait known in a workshop copy (Plate 93). The existence of these two portraits suggests that they derive from a lost prototype by Velázquez which, for the sake of convenience, can be called *Philip IV on a Loggia*. The identification of this as a separate portrait type clarifies the supposed relationship of *Philip IV in Brown and Silver* to the half-length portrait in Vienna.

Philip IV in Brown and Silver is set indoors, while *Philip IV on a Loggia* is set on a terrace. In the first picture, the table is placed to the right and supports a plumed hat, while in the second it is fully behind the king, with a plain, black, wide-brimmed hat on top. In *Philip IV on a Loggia*, the king holds a glove in the left hand (which itself is covered by a glove), while the right is bare; in the *Silver Philip*, both hands are gloved. Smaller points also tell of a difference. In the *Silver Philip*, the king assumes a more frontal pose. The hair along the right side of his face curls back at the level of the ear, not forward. Also, the sword is held almost level to the ground, not at an angle. Last, but unquestionably not least, he wears a brilliantly embroidered costume rather than austere black. For these reasons, it may be permissible to remove the portrait of 1632 as evidence for the date of *Philip IV in Brown and Silver*, and thus to regard the latter as a work of the mid-1630s.[35] In this way, the extraordinary execution of the costume becomes consonant with the noticeable development of a bolder technique which appears at this moment of Velázquez' development.

In fact, it is here for the first time that we see the remarkable and original technique which sets Velázquez apart from almost every other artist of his day. In this portrait, Philip wears a costume comprised of a brown tunic and breeches decorated with silver brocade, under which is an ornate blouse of silvery white and black. On his shoulders there is a black cape also embroidered with silver thread. The challenge of depicting an ornate costume of this kind lies in reproducing the dazzling play of light on the surface without sacrificing the intricacy of the design. The artist who concentrates on the pattern is inevitably forced to imitate the dull geometry of needlework, as dozens of late sixteenth- and early seventeenth-century court portraits show. But Velázquez' approach, which aims at capturing the fleeting effects of light as it glances off the silver threads, is not only difficult, but runs the risk of minimizing the intricate workmanship of the garment and thus displeasing the wearer.[36] His solution to the dilemma is a brushstroke of genius. Realizing that a high degree of finish was fatal to rendering spontaneous effects, he resorted to using a sketch-like technique in a formal, official work of art.

From our perspective, this seems like a logical and not especially innovative idea. But in the context of the seventeenth century, it was virtually unprecedented. A sketchy technique is of course not unknown in the work of other great seventeenth-century painters, but there is a difference of degree which is crucial. In the *Portrait of Philip IV in Brown and Silver*, Velázquez abandons the fluid technique of sketching in oil used, for example, by Rubens, and instead utilizes short, succinct, impastoed strokes of infinite shape and size which are applied so that they appear to hover above the brown ground. Seen at close range (Plate 99), this busy tangle of brushwork appears almost random

97. Velázquez, *Baltasar Carlos* (London, Wallace Collection), 1.18 × 0.955m.

98. Velázquez, *Philip IV in Brown and Silver* (London, National Gallery), 1.995 × 1.130m.

99 (facing page). Detail of Plate 98.

100. Velázquez and assistant, *Isabella of Bourbon* (Switzerland, private collection), 2.03 × 1.14m.

101. Workshop of Velázquez, *Isabella of Bourbon* (Copenhagen, Staatens Museum for Kunst), 2.18 × 1.27m.

and formless. But at a distance, it reproduces the glittering surface of a richly brocaded costume with remarkable fidelity. To keep the technique under control, Velázquez insinuated the sense of a design into the embroidery by the use of an occasional, scattered pinwheel or floral motif which subtly provides the eye with the information it needs to sustain the impression of a regular pattern. This technique appears to be quick and spontaneous, but, upon scrutiny, it is clear that the appearance of rapid execution is entirely deceptive. The placement of every stroke looks like an act of premeditation, not impulse.

The emergence of this technique within a few years of Velázquez' return from Italy is the most surprising part of all. Even in Titian's late canvases, there is nothing to compare to this broken, arhythmic brushstroke, to the sheer daring of a technique which places such implicit trust in the working of the viewer's eye. Velázquez' contemporaries in Italy still operated within the context of classicism, which prized a relatively high degree of finish as a way to honor the sculptural idea of form. Next to their pictures, those of Velázquez look markedly different, less conventional, and more faithful to appearances. The nature and effect of his great innovation was immediately apparent to his contemporaries, who often remarked on it. Much more remains to be said about this technique, but here already we can see the wholly original mind and eye of the painter at work.

It was probably also around 1635 that Velázquez and his workshop produced a full-length portrait of Queen Isabella (Plate 100).[37] The date is established by comparison to the equestrian portrait of the queen (Plate 132), a work completed in 1635, where the head and bust are identical to the standing portrait. This portrait of the queen, like the early portrait of the king (Plate 50), was extensively revised. Radiographs reveal another image in which she wears a lighter-colored dress with a high collar and a string of pearls around her neck. Her hair is also worn in a different style. The first version of the portrait is preserved in a workshop copy (Plate 101), and in other versions, confirming that it was in existence for some time before it was revised. In itself, Velázquez' habit of reworking, even drastically reworking, state portraits seems curious but not especially significant. But, upon reflection, it is strange that he would obliterate the composition of what we assume to be formal portraits. Did not the royal family wish to display them for present glory and to preserve them for eternal posterity? In certain cases, the answer seems unmistakably to be, no. Rather, it would appear that some of the pictures were created as workshop models, which were revised and used until again they were out of date. Then, having outlived their purpose, they were put up on the walls.

The creation of workshop models was the consequence of Velázquez' position as *pintor de cámara*, which entailed the obligation to supply portraits of the royal family. The demand for images of the king and his relatives was great, so great in fact that it was hard to control the production of unauthorized versions. In October 1633, Velázquez and Vicente Carducho were asked to inspect thirty-seven royal portraits for their fidelity to appearances and decorum.[38] As this document shows, anyone competent with a brush could manufacture a portrait of the king, and many did just that to satisfy popular demand. But at least those which came from the royal workshop could be and were controlled by following Velázquez' official models. Above and beyond the commendable desire of loyal subjects to own a picture of the monarch were the requirements of international relations, in which the exchange of portraits was regarded as an important courtesy. There are at least six documented occasions when portraits of the royal family were prepared for shipment to European courts under Velázquez' supervision, and surely there were more. Here again, an authorized model was needed, although sometimes an original by Velázquez was sent abroad. In the interests of efficiency and economy, it made sense to rework an existing portrait-model rather than start anew. Perhaps these circumstances explain why the *Portrait of Isabella of Bourbon* and the early full-length *Portrait of Philip IV* were revised. And when at last they were put on display, they were installed in a private section of the Retiro among other pictures of no particular distinction.

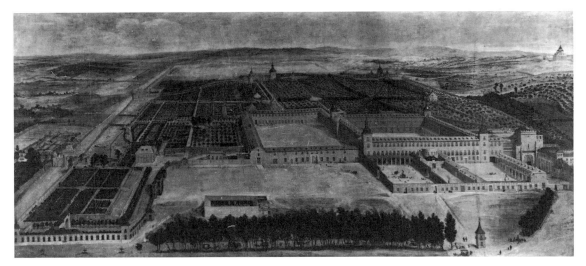

102. Attributed to Jusepe Leonardo, *Palace of the Buen
Retiro* (Madrid, Patrimonio Nacional), 1.30 × 3.05m.

The change in the king's image seen in the *Portrait of Philip IV in Brown and Silver* as
compared to earlier portraits hardly requires comment. In place of the somber sitter of
the 1620s is a radiant, splendid monarch. However, it is important to note that the
change was not entirely the result of Velázquez' new style of painting. During the
1630s, court life acquired an unprecedented degree of magnificence and display.[39] On
the face of it, there was little cause for celebration: the military and economic fortunes
of Spain were to decline throughout the period. But this was also the time when the
count-duke of Olivares sponsored a program of propaganda dedicated to broadcasting
the greatness of his monarch, some of which seems to be reflected in the portrait. The
visible manifestation of the propaganda were projects of new construction and lavish
patronage of the arts. As a setting for this outburst of regal magnificence, a new palace
was constructed, the Palace of the Buen Retiro, which was to be the stage for court
spectacles and also for Velázquez' activities as an artist.

The Palace of the Buen Retiro started life in a very modest way, as a small royal
apartment attached to the monastery of San Jerónimo, on the eastern border of
Madrid.[40] In connection with the swearing of the oath to Prince Baltasar Carlos in
1632, the apartment was somewhat enlarged. But immediately thereafter, it was decided
to expand the building yet again. In July 1632, the count-duke of Olivares and his
descendants were invested with governship of the palace in perpetuity, and from that
point the apartment of San Jerónimo started to become the Palace of the Buen Retiro
(Plate 102).

By January 1633, most of the external construction had been finished and attention
was being directed to completing the interior. Outside the apartment, there had also
been built a formal garden with a large aviary and an artificial pool. In May, just as it
appeared that the work was done, it was suddenly decided to demolish some of what
had been built and to begin a new, much larger structure. Hundreds of workmen
descended on the site and, working without stop, managed in six months to create a
large palace. A royal decree of 1 December gave its name — the Palace of the Buen
Retiro. Four days later, the Buen Retiro was inaugurated with a round of plays, bullfights, and tournaments, the first of the lavish festivities which, in the later 1630s, would
make the name of the Retiro synonymous with court splendor. Over the next seven
years, the palace, and especially the grounds, were continually expanded until the
entire complex covered an area half as large as the existing town of Madrid. Among the
later additions to the palace were a theater, a ballroom, and an arena. In the garden
there were built a series of small hermitage chapels, a large artificial lake, and long
alleys lined with a variety of trees and exotic plantings.

These features indicate the purpose of the Retiro, as indeed does the very name — it
was a retreat equipped as a pleasure palace with every conceivable diversion and
amenity. Its supposed advantage over the existing country houses lay in the proximity
to the Alcázar, from which it was only minutes away. But, in fact, the court retired to
the Retiro at determined periods of the year, usually at Carnival and then for the feast
of St. John, which took place in late June. At these times, all manner of entertainment

114. Albrecht Dürer, *St. Anthony Abbot and St. Paul the Hermit* (New York, Metropolitan Museum of Art).

115. Pietro da Cortona, *Christ and the Samaritan Woman* (detail) (Castelfusano, Chapel of Villa Sacchetti).

This panorama of mediocre talent is worth a mention only to reveal the distance which separates Velázquez from his contemporaries in Spain. He was the quintessential artist of the Spanish court, but he was also the least representative of Spanish painters. Blessed by nature with extraordinary talent, and by the king with extraordinary opportunities, he became the only Spanish painter of his age capable of holding his own with the best works from Flanders and Italy. The validity of this statement can be tested by comparing his numerous contributions to the decoration of the Retiro with other paintings in the palace by foreign artists. There are at least thirteen paintings by Velázquez which were executed at about the time the Retiro was being constructed and which were incorporated into the decoration. First are the six pictures for the Hall of Realms, to be discussed in the following chapter. Second is an altarpiece for the hermitage chapel of San Pablo, which was probably in place by May 1633. Finally, there is a group of six full-length portraits of jesters, the date and placement of which are still matters of controversy.

The *Landscape with St. Anthony and St. Paul the Hermit* (Plate 112) is an inspired creation both for its composition and technique.[50] In plotting the composition, Velázquez hewed closely to the text of the *Golden Legend*, where the encounter of the two hermits is told in detail. The story begins with St. Anthony's desire to find St. Paul, the first Christian anchorite. The start of St. Anthony's quest is depicted in the distant background of the painting, where he asks a centaur the way to St. Paul's dwelling, and then proceeds to the middle ground, where he seeks direction from a satyr. Finally, he arrives at Paul's cave, seen in an opening in the rock to the right; here St. Paul has taken refuge in fear of the arrival of a stranger. In the foreground, the two aged men are seated together, awaiting the delivery of a double ration of daily bread from a crow, who had faithfully fed St. Paul for many years. The concluding episode transpires in the lower left corner, where St. Anthony, having seen Paul's soul being carried to heaven while returning to his own retreat, hastens back to the cave, there to discover the dead body. As he kneels in prayer before the earthly remains of his friend, two lions dig the grave.

The consecutive narration of an episodic story within a single composition is a device rarely used in the seventeenth century, although it was common in earlier art, especially in northern painting of the fifteenth and sixteenth century. Perhaps this is why Velázquez, in planning his picture, referred to examples of northern art for inspiration.[51] The foreground scene, with the seated figures and the descending crow, come from a print by Albrecht Dürer (Plate 114), as does the view of the mountains in the distance. Other elements of the composition, notably the craggy outcropping of rock pierced by a tunnel-like opening, could have been found in paintings by Joachim Patinir, examples of which were in the royal collection.

But, for all these traditional elements, the painting marks an important step forward in Velázquez' evolution. With the thinnest of paints applied over a light beige ground, Velázquez achieves a limpid luminosity unlike anything seen before in his work. Working more like a draftsman with transparent washes than a painter with opaque pigments, he uses the prime coat as an active element in creating the effects of light. He has also thinned the gray and green pigments to the point of translucence, and laid them on the canvas with feathery strokes of the utmost delicacy (Plate 113). Thus, the painting shimmers with a magical light.

The use of this technique is unprecedented in Velázquez' work. Indeed, it would be hard to find it in any oil painting of the period. However, these effects are common to another type of painting, fresco, and suggest that Velázquez may have been attempting to adapt the techniques of the one medium to the other. While in Rome, he could have seen an almost limitless number of landscapes in fresco. As a matter of fact, his arrival there coincided with the completion of an extensive and much-acclaimed cycle of landscape frescoes at the Villa Sacchetti in Castelfusano, executed by Pietro da Cortona and assistants (Plate 115).[52] Given Velázquez' connections with Giulio Sacchetti, the proximity of Castelfusano to Rome (it is on the outskirts of Ostia), and the curious points of similarity in the use of transparent colors on a neutral, sandy ground, it may at least be worth considering the possibility that he had seen Pietro's frescoes and called them to mind when painting this picture.

In the 1701 inventory of the Retiro, there were six portraits of court jesters attributed to Velázquez which were then hanging together in an unspecified part of the palace. Paintings of the court jesters and dwarfs were frequently made by Velázquez in the 1630s and form one of the most intriguing categories of his production. Yet the reason for their appeal is certainly not based on novelty. Buffoons and dwarfs were stock figures of European art.[53] Sometimes they are shown in isolation, sometimes in the company of their masters or employers, sometimes in compositions which serve a moralizing or didactic purpose.[54]

Nowhere was the subject more popular than at the Spanish court, where there was always a sizable number of dwarfs and jesters in residence, who served as playmates to the royal children and as entertainers and figures of fun. There also appears to have been a taste for displaying their portraits in pairs or groups.[55] In fact, most of Velázquez' versions of this subject were conceived as series, too.

Yet the decorative function does not imply that the artist slighted the unusual subject. Some of his most audacious technical experiments occur in the dwarf and jester portraits, perhaps because he knew that the sitters were not free to criticize the results. But technical audacity alone does not explain the attraction of these pictures. They are also important as character studies which provided the opportunity to display psychological nuances often precluded in portraits of friends and associates at court, not to mention the royal family. In the jester portraits for the Retiro, there is humor (Plate 117) and bravura (Plate 121); in the dwarf portraits, there are remarkably perceptive observations of mental deficiency (Plate 175) and a kind of smoldering defiance (Plate 199). Thus, these portraits of unprepossessing subjects offered Velázquez a chance to extend the range of his art, and he made the most of it.

The Retiro jester portraits are famous and, among scholars, controversial as to date and authenticity. The inventory describes the pictures as follows: (1) "a buffoon wearing a *golilla* called Pablillo de Valladolid"; (2) "a buffoon dressed in Turkish costume called Pernia"; (3) "a buffoon called Don Juan de Austria with various pieces of armor"; (4) "Cárdenas, the Buffoon Bullfighter, with a hat in hand, done in Velázquez' first manner"; (5) "Ochoa, the Gatekeeper, holding some petitions"; (6) "Calabacillas with a portrait in one hand and a letter in the other." Documents in the Madrid Palace Archives indicate that the identifications of the sitters are plausible, for each of the names appears on various rosters of the household staff at a time when Velázquez could have painted their portraits.[56]

The information in the inventory is sufficient to identify three of the portraits with certainty: *Pablo de Valladolid* (Plate 121); "*Don Juan de Austria*" (Plate 117); and *Cristóbal Castañeda y Pernia* (Plate 116). *Ochoa the Gatekeeper* is known only in a copy (Plate 118), while *Cárdenas, the Buffoon Bullfighter* has disappeared without a trace. As for *Calabacillas*, there are some who believe that it is identifiable with a portrait in Cleveland (Plate 119), while others remain unconvinced of the authenticity of the attribution.[57]

Uncertainty also prevails about the dates of the known portraits, which have been assigned to a range of time from the late 1620s to the late 1630s. Virtually all the putative dates rest on stylistic analysis and indirect evidence because the pictures were not documented until they were inventoried in 1701. However, a recently discovered document of 11 December 1634, has been related to this group of works.[58] On that date, Velázquez received 797 ducats from Diego Suárez, secretary of the Council of Portugal, "for the paintings which, on the orders of said secretary, he made for the decoration of the living or sleeping quarters (*alcobas*) of the Buen Retiro." Unfortunately, the receipt does not specify the number or subjects of the pictures, but the sizable amount of payment suggests that more than one work was involved. In the inventory of 1701, the buffoon portraits occur about three-quarters of the way down the list, which would have put them somewhere in the southern wing, where the queen's apartments were located. They were also observed hanging together in a staircase in this part of the

CHAPTER IV

Images of Power and Prestige

123. View of Hall of Realms, Buen Retiro Palace.

122. Detail of Plate 135.

THE SECOND HALF of the 1630s were the most productive years of Velázquez' career. This upsurge of activity was related in large part to a concerted effort by the government to glorify the Spanish monarchy and was stimulated by the threat of war with France, which became a reality in 1635. Having become his own master of painting, Velázquez was now required to paint for his masters. Thus, he joined a group of writers, poets, and artists who were enlisted to create works exalting the Habsburg dynasty. These artisans of glory also served the interests of another patron, the count-duke of Olivares, whose interest in personal propaganda increased as his position of power weakened. Under Olivares' direction, two royal houses were expanded and decorated, the Palace of the Buen Retiro and the Torre de la Parada. In creating pictures for these sites, Velázquez was put to the test as a maker of images of power and prestige.

The focal point of the Buen Retiro was the Hall of Realms, or Salón Grande as it was known in the 1630s, which served as the principal state room of the palace (Plate 123).[1] The Hall, which still survives in its original form, is a simple rectangle measuring 34.6 meters long by 10 meters wide by 8.25 meters high. This space is illuminated on both sides by twenty windows, ten large windows on the floor level and, above them, ten smaller windows. On the ceiling is an elaborate decoration of gilt grotteschi, beneath which, on the vaulted zone, are the coats of arms of the twenty-four kingdoms of the Spanish monarchy. From these escutcheons was fashioned the traditional name of the room — the Hall of Realms.

The importance of the Salón required an exceptional decoration, which was executed from late in 1633 to early in 1635. The key elements were three groups of paintings — twelve battle scenes, ten episodes of the life of Hercules, and five royal equestrian portraits. In late November 1633, the carpenter Jerónimo Sánchez was paid 396 reales for "twelve stretchers which he made for the *salón grande de Buen Retiro.*" These stretchers were intended for the large-scale battle paintings which were then being commissioned from a group of court painters as the principal part of the decorative scheme. The largest share of the commission went to the senior court painters and their disciples. Vicente Carducho painted the *Victory of Fleurus*, the *Victory of Constance*, and the *Capture of Rheinfelden.* His long-time friend and collaborator, Eugenio Cajés, was assigned two subjects, the *Recapture of Puerto Rico* and the *Expulsion of the Dutch from St. Martin* (lost). Cajés was able to complete only the second of these before he died on 15 December 1634. The first, which he designed, was executed by two members of his shop.

Both Carducho and Cajés managed to secure commissions for their followers. Félix Castelo, who had been Carducho's apprentice, painted the *Recapture of St. Christopher*, while Jusepe Leonardo, Cajés' assistant, executed the *Surrender of Jülich* (Plate 137) and the *Relief of Breisach*. The remaining four pictures were allotted to four different artists. Juan Bautista Maino, the artist-friar, produced a masterpiece, the *Recapture of Bahía* (Plate 144). A surprising choice was Antonio de Pereda, then only twenty-three years

130. Velázquez and others, *Philip III on Horseback* (Madrid, Museo del Prado), 3.00 × 3.14m.

which commissioned Carducho, Cajés, and González to paint companion pieces to Velázquez' equestrian portrait of Philip IV (lost).[12] This idea seems most applicable to *Margarita of Austria*, which, except for the parts retouched by Velázquez, is executed in the dry, fastidious, out-of-date style of González.[13] However, a careful reading of the document reveals that these three portraits were to be of the same size as Velázquez' lost portrait of the king, or about 3.85 × 3.29 meters.[14] This is about a meter larger in both height and width than the original size of the portraits in the Hall of Realms, which decreases the probability of this idea.

The second explanation rests on a document of 3 September 1628, already mentioned in chapter II.[15] On this occasion, Velázquez was given access to the Royal Armory to use whatever he needed to execute the portraits of Philip III and Philip IV which he then had in hand. It has also been thought that these are the pictures referred to in a payment order of 22 July 1629, by which Velázquez was to be given three hundred ducats on account for paintings being done in the service of the king.[16] None of these documents specifies that the pictures were equestrian portraits. However, just a month after the Royal Armory was opened to Velázquez, a similar order was issued on 10 October 1628 in favor of Rubens, who, as specified in the document, was painting a portrait of the king on horseback (Plate 76). This suggests that equestrian portraits were in demand at the time, but still does not confirm the type of portrait on which Velázquez was working.

The final possibility is that these three problematical paintings were designed by Velázquez for the Hall of Realms, executed by assistants, and finally retouched by the master.[17] In the circumstances, there is no choice but to leave the question open. But it should also be noted that the most original of the portraits are those of Philip IV and Baltasar Carlos, the only two entirely by the hand of Velázquez.

As he was painting the king's portrait (Plate 133), the shadows of the great equestrian portraits by Titian and Rubens in the royal collection must have fallen across his

131. Velázquez and others, *Margarita of Austria on Horseback* (Madrid, Museo del Prado), 2.97 × 3.09m.

132. Velázquez and others, *Isabella of Bourbon on Horseback* (Madrid, Museo del Prado), 3.01 × 3.18m.

133. Velázquez, *Philip IV on Horseback* (Madrid, Museo del Prado), 3.01 × 3.18m.

134 (facing page). Detail of Plate 132.

canvas.[18] To meet the challenge, he found a deceptively simple way to follow these prototypes without blindly copying them — he rejected allegory in favor of a straightforward representation of the king, thus turning fact into symbol. The secret of the success of the king's portrait is the pose in strict profile. Philip, displaying the attributes of the captain-general — red sash, armor, baton — sits on a rearing horse, calmly executing the *haute école* maneuver called the *levade*, using only one hand to control the horse in this difficult exercise. The ease of control combined with the rigidity of the pose

114

convert the horse and rider into a realistic hieroglyph of kingly power and the capacity to rule.[19]

The portrait of the prince (Plate 135) adheres to the same non-allegorical mode of expression, but is less hieratic in the presentation of the sitter. Here, as in the equestrian portrait of the king, the image of the rearing horse and rider was intended to unleash a train of symbolic thought, invoking ideas such as rulership and the education of the prince.[20] Thus, the pose of the horse closely follows a conventional type well known in prints of the sixteenth and seventeenth centuries. (The barrel-chested appearance of the pony is explained by the need to compensate for the height of the original placement.) But Velázquez economically conveys the impression of the prince's energy and vitality by the flowing sash and upraised arm.

Both the portraits of the king and the prince are among Velázquez' masterpieces. The fact that the pictures, and especially that of the prince, were large in size and meant to be seen at some distance from eyelevel encouraged him to loosen and abbreviate his technique, with extraordinary results. These qualities are seen to best advantage in *Baltasar Carlos on Horseback*. As it looks today, the picture appears to have been enlarged by the addition of a border measuring about six or seven centimeters, except at the top where two superimposed strips of canvas can be seen. The first of the upper strips, which run on a line just above the hat, was probably added by Velázquez; without it the frame would appear to rest on the prince's head. However, the second strip, as well as those along the other three sides, was stitched on at a later date, perhaps when the picture was moved from the Retiro to the Royal Palace, where it was recorded in 1772.[21] This expansion of the dimensions considerably alters the presentation of the figure, which is now pushed deeper into space than Velázquez intended, with the resultant diminution of its apparent size and proximity to the viewer. As first conceived, the horse and rider would have seemed almost to be jumping out of the frame.

If the present, lower placement of the picture in the Prado galleries alters the effect, it does in compensation allow us to see the marvelous technique with clarity (Plate 122). Fortunately, the picture is in an excellent state of preservation, with all of the intricate brushwork and deft touches of impasto intact. These stand out especially in the prince's costume and saddle, where the burnished gold highlights swarm over the surface, making the light and texture sparkle and glow. The pink sash is comprised of long, dragging strokes, trailing off at the end into a golden fringe, the threads of which dissolve into the sky. Baltasar Carlos' face is painted smoothly, with a diaphanous touch which softens the still-immature features of the boy.

The prince and his pony are placed in an expansive landscape, with the snow-covered sierra in the distance. Here, as in *Philip IV on Horseback*, there is the wintery light of a pale sun, low in the sky, shielded by high, thin clouds. Seen in this even, cool atmosphere, the trees and foliage take on a greenish gray cast; in the middleground, the presence of short trees and scrubby bushes is suggested by the merest of brushstrokes. By painting over a light ground, parts of which are left exposed near the prince's head, Velázquez obtains the flinty effect of a chilly, overcast day in the mountains, into which the leaping horse and his rider burst like a ray of golden sunshine.

Velázquez' other painting for the Hall of Realms is justly the most famous — the *Surrender of Breda* (Plate 136).[22] Once more, as in the equestrian portraits, he referred to a well-established pictorial type, but here the precedent is adjusted with greater freedom. Scenes of military surrender abounded in Renaissance art and were almost always used to emphasize the power of the king to crush his enemies. An example drawn from the prints of Charles V's victories represents dozens of surrender scenes (Plate 128). The victor is elevated above the vanquished, who approaches the conqueror bereft of arms and men, striking the pose of a humbled petitioner. This is precisely the formula used in the other scene of surrender in the Hall of Realms, the surrender of Jülich to Ambrogio Spinola (Plate 137), the same general who defeated the Dutch at Breda.

Clearly, Velázquez' painting departs from this convention. First and foremost, victor and vanquished meet in an encounter of surprising benevolence. Second, the Dutch

135. Velázquez, *Baltasar Carlos on Horseback* (Madrid, Museo del Prado), 2.10 × 1.75m.

137. Jusepe Leonardo, *Surrender of Jülich* (Madrid, Museo del Prado), 3.07 × 3.81m.

commander, Justin of Nassau, is accompanied by an escort of his own troops, who are seen at the left holding pikes and halberds with orange pennons. The sources of this unprecedented representation of surrender are found partly in fact and partly in fiction.

The year-long siege of the Dutch city of Breda by Spanish and Burgundian troops was brought to a successful conclusion on 2 June 1625. Articles of surrender were drafted which were notably generous and allowed the Dutch to withdraw three days later in good order, with drums beating and colors flying. In 1627, Jacques Callot depicted the retreat as it happened (Plate 138). Spinola, seated on a horse and flanked by his troops, reviews the retreating Dutch column which is led by a coach carrying the Dutch commander and his family.

The clemency shown in Velázquez' painting thus had its origins in the historical record, but the focal point of the ceremony, the delivery of the keys of the fortress, is at variance with the actual event. This motif of surrender commonly appeared in paintings and prints and could have been taken from such a source by Velázquez. However, the

138. Jacques Callot, *Surrender of Breda* (detail) (Princeton University, Art Museum).

139. *Surrender of Breda*, radiograph.

136 (facing page). Velázquez, *Surrender of Breda* (Madrid, Museo del Prado), 3.07 × 3.70m.

idea was put in immediate circulation at the court in a play by Pedro Calderón de la Barca, which was performed in 1625 to commemorate the victory. At the climax of the drama, called *El Sitio de Bredá*, Nassau hands over the keys of the city to Spinola, who receives them with the words embodied in Velázquez' painting: "Justin, I receive them in full awareness of your valor; for the valor of the defeated confers fame upon the victor."

Building on these sources, Velázquez made the surrender of Breda into something more than a military victory. The victory of arms is of course conveyed by the famous motif of the upright Spanish pikes, whose number and prominence form a contrast with the bedraggled Dutch troops at the left. But, in the center of the picture, Spinola gracefully places a restraining hand on the shoulder of Nassau, who is about to kneel and deliver the keys (Plate 140). Behind the Spanish general is his horse, whose hindquarters conspicuously occupy the right-hand side of the picture. The riderless horse in this context acquires great significance, for normally Spinola would be seated astride the animal, looking down at his vanquished enemy, as he does in the *Surrender of Jülich*. In the *Surrender of Breda*, however, the two men meet on equal footing. By means of these subtle touches, Velázquez transformed the scene from a tableau of Spanish military power into a metaphor of Spanish moral superiority, which reflected the glory of the king in whose name Spinola commanded, and glorified the faith which he and his forebears had sworn to defend.

The *Surrender of Breda* is fascinating not only because of its original interpretation of history and tradition, but also because of the way in which Velázquez has captured the reactions of ordinary men as they observe what seemed like a major event in the war with the Dutch. (As it happened, Breda was recaptured just two years after the picture was completed.) Some of the soldiers and officers observe the ceremony with rapt attention, while others appear to be distracted by activities outside the picture or by their thoughts and emotions. The orchestration of this complex picture seems perfectly attuned to its significance; everything and everyone is in the right place. Yet just below the surface, as revealed by radiographs, a remarkable process of trial and error can just be glimpsed.

140 (following pages). Detail of Plate 136.

Initially, the radiograph (Plate 139) looks like a jumble and blur of overlapping

119

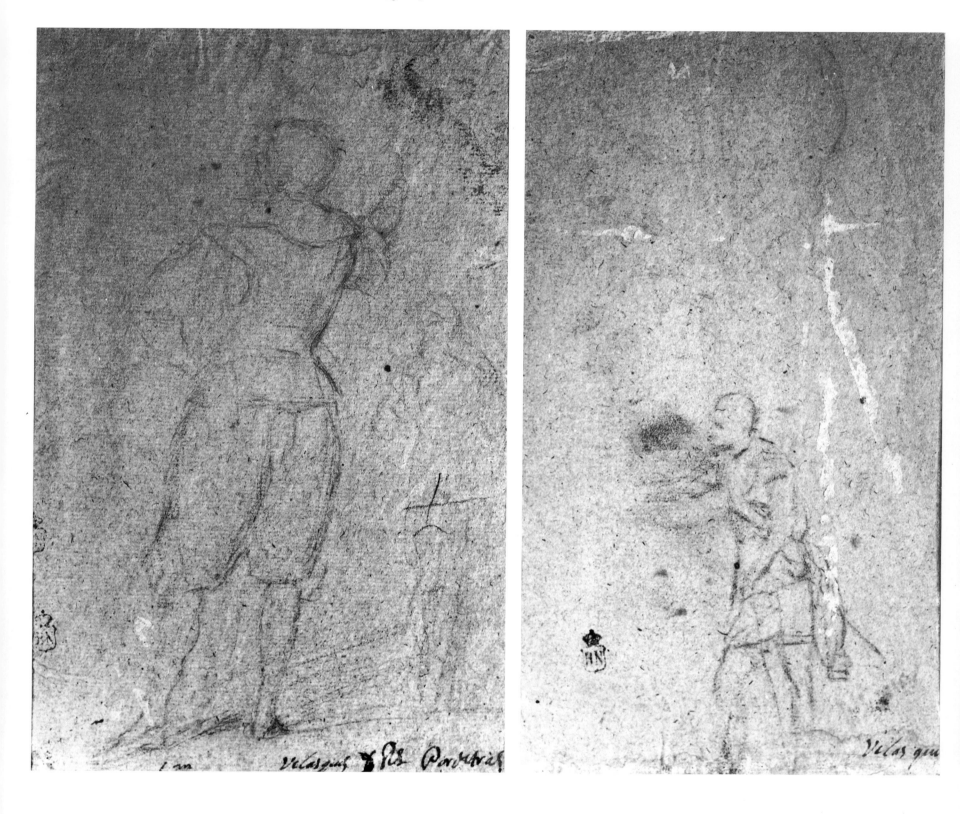

141 (above left). Velázquez, *Study for Surrender of Breda*, recto (Madrid, Biblioteca Nacional), 0.262 × 0.168m.

142 (above right). Velázquez, *Study for Surrender of Breda*, verso (Madrid, Biblioteca Nacional).

images and even with attentive study it is not entirely decipherable.[23] But many small changes in the composition can be detected. Once again, Velázquez experimented while he worked, despite the fact that, contrary to his usual practice, he had made preparatory drawings for the picture (Plates 141, 142). A major change involved the lances, the most famous motif in the painting. In the first draft, these important symbolic elements were shorter and thus would not have been nearly as effective in conveying the might of Spanish arms. Numerous alterations were also made in the groups of Spanish officers at the right. Slowly but surely, Velázquez tried and discarded poses and gestures as he sought, and ultimately found, the right form to express his meaning.

Taken as a group, Velázquez' paintings for the Hall of Realms represent the most forceful and explicit examples of political imagery in his entire career as court painter. Up to a point, they constitute his response to the great works of princely glorification of the Baroque age. But if the underlying concepts find a place in the conventional language

143. Titian, *Charles V* (Munich, Alte Pinakothek), 2.05 × 1.21m.

144. Juan Bautista Maino, *Recapture of Bahía* (detail) (Madrid, Museo del Prado).

of the day, the vocabulary of forms is different from comparable works by Rubens, Pietro da Cortona, and Charles LeBrun, to name other masters of the genre. Reticence and reserve are the words that immediately come to mind when confronting these paintings. The absence of the apparatus of glory is conspicuous. Gone are the putti and the personifications who busily flutter around the hero, proclaiming his virtue in unmistakable allegorical terms. And with them has gone the commotion, the roiling, and the heaving of the full-dress Baroque glorification picture. The artist who comes closest to Velázquez is, of course, Van Dyck. But the utter refinement and self-indulgent beauty of Van Dyck's representations of Charles I and his court are equally removed from Velázquez' unsentimental, understated representations of royalty.

This much is obvious to anyone versed in the history of Baroque art. Less obvious is the reason why Velázquez painted Spanish royalty in what appears to be a matter-of-fact manner. Leaving aside the question of the artist's temperament, it is possible to find a partial answer by looking once again at the history of artistic representations of the Spanish Habsburgs. Beginning with Titian's *Portrait of Charles V* (Plate 143), we see a consistent preference for what might be called resounding understatement. It is almost as if a kind of reverse snobbery was at work — the most powerful could afford to be the most modest. Spanish power was the overwhelming fact of European political life in the sixteenth and part of the seventeenth centuries, and made itself felt by invincible armies and enormous wealth. There was little that a royal portrait could add to these facts and therefore the Spanish kings preferred to be portrayed with simplicity. The late portraits of Philip II, which Velázquez imitated in his early portraits of Philip IV, gained their effect when the viewer compared the reality of almost unlimited power with an image of reticence and restraint. Only the greatest of the great could afford to dispense with the trappings of majesty and feel the confidence to face the world without the aid of rhetoric or theatricality. Thus, in the most explicit display of power of his reign — the Hall of Realms — Philip IV and his painter remained faithful to the ideals of an earlier age.

The subdued expression of royal majesty in Velázquez' paintings of the king becomes more evident if we examine the portraits of Olivares, the man who was second only to the monarch. Olivares' grasp on power was tight but ultimately uncertain, for he depended on royal favor to survive. Furthermore, his rank among the nobility was secondary; he was a member of the cadet branch of the house of Guzmán which was headed by the dukes of Medina Sidonia. Although he quickly improved his status once he came to power, he was always regarded as an upstart by the old-line aristocracy. Thus, the count-duke, unlike his royal master, could not take his position for granted and had to rely on propagandists to help bolster his claims and defend his policies and person.

Velázquez joined the ranks of Olivares' apologists, at least where portraiture was concerned. In a succession of works done between 1624 and 1638, Velázquez expressed Olivares' claims to greatness in pictorial form. In the portrait of 1624 either by or after an original by Velázquez (Plate 54), Olivares displays the outward symbols of his newly won power. The overbearing manner, which made enemies of his fellow aristocrats, is but thinly disguised. In the portrait done about a year later (Plate 55), the ostentation has been toned down. Velázquez has reduced the impression of Olivares' imperiousness by setting him within a larger space, and by treating the symbols of office more discreetly.

The drift toward restraint was dramatically reversed in the 1630s, as opposition to Olivares' increasingly unsuccessful policies grew and, with it, the stridency of his propaganda. Toward the middle of the decade, Olivares twice had himself depicted with members of the royal family. The first image is the one by Juan Bautista Maino in his painting of the *Recapture of Bahía* for the Hall of Realms.[24] In this blatant display of pride, power, and arrogance, Olivares is shown as the co-author of the king's victories, immodestly sharing the honor with Minerva, goddess of war (Plate 144). A year or so later Velázquez also presented the count-duke shaping the destiny of the monarchy

Fuenterrabía proved to be Olivares' final victory, but at the time it seemed a momentous event, and perhaps just the occasion to commission an imposing portrait of the count-duke as warrior. But whatever inspired the portrait, Velázquez responded to the charge with every artistic resource at his disposal. The count-duke is depicted on a rearing chestnut horse as if leading a contingent of troops to join the battle raging in the distance. Before attempting the difficult diagonal pose of the horse, Velázquez made a large-scale study (Plate 148), which remained in his possession for the rest of his life and was used by the workshop over and over again.[31] Nevertheless, small adjustments to the pose were made as Velázquez worked, which are now visible as pentimenti.

Seated astride the horse is the imposing figure of Olivares, clad in glistening, damascened black armor and wearing gold embroidered breeches. Over his shoulder is draped an exceptionally large and showy red sash, the ensign of the captain-general, which is exaggerated in size and importance to commemorate Olivares' role as a victorious commander. The painting of the costume is in Velázquez' freest manner; flecks and daubs of golden pigment, no two alike in shape or size, are scattered helter-skelter over the surface. Only at a distance do they fuse into a convincing illusion of a rich clothstuff reflecting the strong light which is concentrated on the shoulder. The face of Olivares is also splendidly done. Posed in three-quarter profile, with only one

147. Antonio Tempesta, *Julius Caesar on Horseback* (New York, Metropolitan Museum of Art, Harriet Brisbane Dick Fund).

146 (facing page). Velázquez, *Count-Duke of Olivares on Horseback* (Madrid, Museo del Prado), 3.13 × 2.42m.

148 (right). Velázquez, *Rearing Horse* (Madrid, Patrimonio Nacional), 3.10 × 2.45m.

149. Velázquez, *Count-Duke of Olivares* (Leningrad, Hermitage), 0.67 × 0.545m.

eye visible and wearing a cocked hat at a rakish angle, the count-duke appears as a man in charge — cool, decisive, confident, brave.

The truth of the matter was different. Olivares, not the horse, was reaching the end of the tether, as we see in another portrait of 1637–38 (Plate 149).[32] This painting is probably a life study intended for use by the workshop.[33] Thus, the toll taken by years of unremitting labor in a losing cause is but little disguised. Olivares looks subdued and slightly dazed. The end of his regime was now not far away. In January 1643, he was relieved of his responsibilities and two years later, his mind gone mad, he died in exile in Toro, having failed to rehabilitate the power of the Spanish monarchy or his own reputation.

The paintings for the Hall of Realms and the portraits of Olivares thus reveal Velázquez as the complete maker of political imagery. From the traditional equestrian portraits to the imaginative pictures of the surrender and the riding lesson of the prince, he created vivid pictures of his patrons' status and pretensions. For the king, secure in his majesty, he made skillfully nuanced versions of traditional types; for Olivares, struggling to keep his balance on the shifting ground of the favorite, he promoted claims of power and glory which were destroyed by events.

These works, however, do not exhaust his royal commissions during the 1630s. Shortly after the completion of the Buen Retiro, another important, although infinitely smaller, building project was begun — the Torre de la Parada. Unlike the Retiro, which was a center of court life and entertainment, the Torre was a small, private lodge in the hunting reserve of the Pardo Palace[34] and, as the name suggests, was a stopping-place where the king and his party could rest from the rigors of the hunt. In 1635, it was decided to expand an existing tower on the site by enclosing it within a two-story envelope containing a number of small rooms. Construction was completed by the autumn of 1637, and while it was going on, plans were laid for the decoration. Two sets of pictures were ordered in Flanders by the cardinal infante. The first was a series of about sixty paintings with scenes from Ovid's *Metamorphoses* by Rubens and Company, which arrived in Madrid in May 1638. The second consisted of about sixty hunting and animal scenes by Frans Snyders, which were sent from Brussels in December of the same year.[35]

The third contributor to the decoration was Velázquez, several of whose works appear to have been interspersed among those of the northern artists. It is now difficult to reconstruct the original disposition of the pictures because there is no detailed description of the interior before the inventory of 1701. But there is reason to believe that this inventory substantially reflects the original placement of the pictures.[36] If this is so, then we can assess Velázquez' contribution to another commission involving the creation of royal imagery.

The principal public room of the Torre came to be known as the Galería del Rey, or Royal Gallery, in which a tribute to Philip IV's hunting prowess was created.[37] Philip was in fact an avid, skilled hunter, who made regular excursions to the countryside to pursue this favorite recreation. His passion for hunting also allowed him to display the mastery of a skill regarded as proper to kings and as excellent training for war. Philip's hunting master, Juan Mateos (Plate 167), summarized these points in his treatise on hunting, which was dedicated to the king and published in 1634: "The dignity of this noble exercise is easily recognized by the participation of kings and princes. And it is the best instructor for teaching the theory and practice of the military arts."[38] The Galería del Rey, therefore, can be interpreted as a counterpart of the Hall of Realms. In the Retiro, the king was shown as victorious on the battlefield; in the Torre, his conquests on the playing field of royalty, the hunting ground, were commemorated.

150. Peter Snayers, *Philip IV Killing a Wild Boar* (Madrid, Museo del Prado), 1.80 × 1.49m.

The Galería del Rey contained fifteen pictures, of which six were gamepieces. Among the remaining nine works, six showed the royal hunt all its diversity, with Philip IV cast in the role of hunter supreme. All but one of these pictures was executed in Flanders by Peter Snayers, who worked under the supervision of Philip's brother and one-time hunting companion, the cardinal infante Ferdinand. Some of Snayers' paintings are documentary, recording events in the king's career as hunter. For instance, the picture of *Philip IV Killing a Wild Boar* (Plate 150) is based on an incident which was described in a dispatch of the Florentine ambassador in August 1635.[39] The other surviving work by Snayers shows the king shooting deer, a picture which demonstrates Philip's famous skill as a marksman. The third surviving hunting scene is Velázquez' picture known as "*La Tela Real.*"

"*La Tela Real*" (Plate 151) is the only known painting by Velázquez which documents an actual event in the life of Philip's court, and a curious work it is.[40] The hunting exercise known as the *tela* was a kind of boar-baiting which took place in an enormous canvas enclosure into which wild boars were driven. Next, the animals were herded into a small enclosed area known as the counter-tela, where they were engaged by horsemen with *horquillas* (two-pronged blunt forks with long handles). In Velázquez' painting, the hunting party, with the king about to engage a boar, is represented by a small group in the right-hand part of the counter-tela. Looking on from carriages are the queen and other distinguished ladies of the court. The rest of the picture is given over to the incidental activities of onlookers and attendants, who monopolize the composition. The remarkably off-handed quality of the picture becomes even more pro-

151. Velázquez, *"La Tela Real"* (London, National Gallery), 1.82 × 3.02m.

153 (facing page). Detail of Plate 151.

152. Peter Snayers, *Philip IV and his Brothers Hunting* (Madrid, Museo del Prado), 1.81 × 5.76m.

nounced when we compare it to a similar work by Snayers, which hung in another room in the Torre (Plate 152). Although a different type of hunt is shown, the scale and composition are not dissimilar. Snayers leaves no doubt about the identity of the protagonists — Philip IV and his two brothers — who are posed at the juncture of the two canvas fences.

The attribution of *"La Tela Real"* has often been questioned, perhaps because it is of a type almost unique in Velázquez' production. Also, the condition is poor — only the figures in the foreground are reasonably well preserved — which complicates the assessment of quality. Yet these two factors should not disguise the brilliance of conception and the excellent bits of painting in the parts still in good condition. There are also numerous pentimenti which, while no guarantee of authenticity, reveal the kinds of changes in pose and composition often made by Velázquez in the course of execution.

In planning the composition, Velázquez chose an unusually high vantage point from which we look down into the counter-tela and then up again to the hills beyond.

155 (facing page). Velázquez, *Philip IV as Hunter* (Madrid, Museo del Prado), 1.89 × 1.25m.

From this distance, the view resembles what can be seen from the top rows of a large stadium. The players are remote, small, and hard-to-follow, while the members of the crowd, who are nearer at hand, become almost as interesting as the game (Plate 153). By assuming the position of a casual spectator, Velázquez emphatically breaks with the customary procedure for paintings of the royal hunt. Yet this unusual treatment of the event appears to have been a success; a copy of the picture was made for the palace in Madrid, suggesting that the composition was admired.

But, then, the portraits of the king done by Velázquez for the Galería del Rey, and those of his brother Ferdinand and his son Baltasar Carlos, are equally unconventional (Plates 155, 157, 159).[41] Their utter lack of pretension has long and frequently been noted. Only the faces identify these hunters as members of the Spanish royal family. Of course, it must be remembered that the Torre was a private place and that the pictures were hung in a gallery where other works of art broadcast the king's courage and skill as a hunter. Yet even when these considerations are given due weight, the portraits are extraordinarily modest.

Once again, the reason for this unusual presentation of royalty may be found in tradition. The portrait by Titian, *Charles V with Hound* (Plate 68), which was in the royal collection until 1623, when it was given to the Prince of Wales, adopts the same understated attitude to the ruler. From the picture alone, it would be hard to guess that this gentleman was in fact the most feared and powerful ruler of his age. The man is the office and the office is the man; this is the message which these paintings seem to bear. By deliberately situating his portraits within this tradition, Velázquez was excused from the rhetorical excesses of Baroque portraiture.

Nevertheless, the portrait of the king (Plate 155) may not have been originally devoid of symbolic meaning, if we are to believe Palomino's description of the first version. Looking at the picture closely, it can be seen that certain parts have been reworked. For one thing, the lower part of the body, from about the waist down, was located farther to the right. Also, the gunbarrel was a few centimeters longer. And, finally, the king was bare-headed, holding his hat in his hand. A workshop copy (Plate 154), which is based on the first version, shows how the picture looked before it was reworked by Velázquez. The copy is probably the composition seen by Palomino, whose response may reveal something of Velázquez' original idea, or at least the associations it triggered in the minds of contemporary viewers:

> It seems that Velázquez saw them [the writer is also commenting on the portrait of the cardinal infante] at the hottest moment of the day, arriving tired from their exercise of hunting, which is as arduous as it is delightful, in lively disarray, their hair dusty and not as it is worn today by courtiers, their faces bathed in sweat, just as Martial, on a similar occasion, painted Domitian, handsome with sweat and dust.
> "Here, graced by the dust of Northern war, stood Caesar, shedding from his face effulgent light."
> Diego Velázquez could emulate many other poets, who told how much grace can be added to beauty by an effect of fatigue, insouciance, and disarray.[42]

154. Workshop of Velázquez, *Philip IV as Hunter* (Castres, Musée Goya), 2.00 × 2.10m.

Philip IV as Hunter was cleaned in 1983, revealing the original tonality of silvery gray and restoring the subtle interplay of the muted colors. Philip is depicted in a simple costume of dark brown, to which the other tones are keyed. Behind him to the left is a tree with dark green leaves, which sets off his luminous face. The background seems to rush away into the distance where, behind a clump of trees, there is an orange patch of light from the setting sun. At the king's feet is a hunting dog, brushed in with Velázquez' allusive technique of loosely placed strokes, which makes it seem almost alive. This is exactly the technique used to paint an unusual "portrait" (Plate 156) which, although not known to have been associated with the Torre de la Parada, is related to the theme of the hunt.[43] This gentle, almost sentimental picture of the king's favorite quarry is calculated to bring despair to the hearts of animal lovers.

Cardinal Infante Ferdinand as Hunter (Plate 157) appears to have been modeled on an

156. Velázquez, *Head of Stag* (Madrid, Museo del Prado), 0.66 × 0.52m.

earlier image and not the infante himself, who left Madrid for good in the spring of 1632 and by this time had grown a moustache and longer hair. Unlike the portrait of the king, this work was little changed after the original execution; only slight adjustments to the silhouette are now visible to the naked eye. However, Velázquez decided to enlarge the surrounding space by adding a thin strip of canvas to the upper margin. If the pose of the figure is conventional (and somewhat unsteady), there are still marvelous passages of painting to be seen, especially the handling of the dog and the dark green foliage behind (Plate 158). In both these areas, Velázquez used a fluid technique of wet-into-wet painting, which softens the contours and details, as if they were seen out of the corner of the eye.

The final picture of the group, and undoubtedly the most winning, is *Baltasar Carlos as Hunter* (Plate 159). Workshop copies reveal that the portrait was once wider and included an additional dog at the right (Plate 160). An inscription in the lower left indicates the sitter's age as six, thus telling us, if correct, that the portrait was painted between 17 October 1634, and 16 October 1635. Given the prince's diminutive size, Velázquez was able to pay more attention to the background, which is an expansive view of the sierra in slate gray, dark green, and beige. In keeping with the compositional formula used in the other hunting portraits, there is a tree at one side, which spreads a

157. Velázquez, *Cardinal Infante Ferdinand as Hunter* (Madrid, Museo del Prado), 1.91 × 1.09m.

158 (facing page). Detail of Plate 157.

159. Velázquez, *Baltasar Carlos as Hunter* (Madrid, Museo del Prado), 1.90 × 1.03m.

165. Velázquez, *Pedro de Barberana y Aparregui* (Fort Worth, Kimbell Museum of Art), 1.982 × 1.118m.

166. Velázquez, *Francesco d'Este, Duke of Modena* (Modena, Galleria Estense), 0.68 × 0.51m.

February 1638, having made a spectacular flight from the clutches of Cardinal Richelieu, Spain's arch-enemy. On 16 January 1638, a gazetteer noted that Velázquez was working on her portrait, which has not survived.[7]

The duchess of Chevreuse was followed some months later by Francesco d'Este, duke of Modena, who arrived in the capital on 24 September 1638.[8] We are well informed about this state visit through the copious and fascinating correspondence of the Modenese ambassador, the poet Fulvio Testi.[9] By any standard, Testi was a brilliant letterwriter and a clever diplomat, and through his dispatches we can see how he promoted the interests of his master, a feckless, vain princeling, whose lands were essential to Spain in the war against France. Eager to impress, the king and his minister treated Duke Francesco like royalty. On 7 November 1638, three days after the duke had started the journey home, Testi wrote a jubilant letter to Cardinal Guido Bentivoglio in Rome, cataloguing the favors and presents lavished on his ruler.[10] A few days later, he wrote to the duke, announcing yet another precious gift — a jewel in the shape of an eagle, with a portrait miniature of Philip IV by Velázquez on the reverse.[11]

Velázquez had also taken the opportunity to paint a portrait of the duke (Plate 166) during his sojourn at court. This picture can be dated with considerable accuracy because it shows him wearing the insignia of the Order of the Golden Fleece, to which he was admitted on 24 October 1638. Ten days later, he left Madrid. Obviously, in these circumstances, Velázquez had to produce the portrait in some haste, which may account for the sketchy quality often noted in commentaries on the picture. However, it is also possible that this picture was a study from life to be used as a model for a large-scale equestrian portrait. This would account for the military accoutrements worn by the duke, which are signs of the office of Admiral of the Fleet granted him by Philip IV during his visit. It was perhaps this appointment, grandiloquently described by Testi as "generale degli oceani col supremo comando di tutti i vaselli e di tutte le armate che sua maesta tiene en terra nei mari di ponente, d'oriente e di settentrione," which occasioned the commission of the equestrian portrait.

We first hear of such a portrait in a letter written by the duke from Cadaqués on 21 November 1638, that is to say about two weeks after his departure from Madrid.[12] Addressing himself to Testi, he asked that a copy of his equestrian portrait be made "by the hand of the painter who is making the original." The name of the painter is not given, but in a letter from Testi to the duke, dated 12 March 1639, we learn that it was Velázquez:

> Velázquez is making the portrait of your highness, which will be marvelous. However, like other men of talent, he has the defect of never finishing and of not telling the truth. I have given him 150 pieces of eight on account, and Marquis Virgilio (Malvezzi) has arranged a price of one hundred doubloons. It is expensive but he does good work. And I can assure you that I hold his portraits in no less esteem than those of any other famous painter, either ancient or modern.[13]

Testi was right about the price. One hundred gold doubloons was a great sum of money, probably too great for the small picture now in Modena (.68 × .51 m.), the dimensions of which roughly coincide with the other portraits here identified as oil studies made from life. Testi was also right about Velázquez' slowness in finishing his paintings, a complaint made more than once by his patrons. In fact, the picture is never heard of again and may not have been brought to completion. One detail suggests that this was the case. In Velázquez' death inventory, we find an entry which could refer to this portrait — "un capitán a cavallo, dibujado en pintura."[14] It may be that, in the end, Velázquez delivered the study from life to the duke as partial satisfaction for the more ambitious, but never-completed work, which remained in his possession until he died.

Nevertheless, there is no reason to believe that the duke of Modena, or, more accurately, his ambassadors in Madrid, continued to collect paintings by Velázquez. In an inventory of the ducal estate, dated 16 June 1685, three portraits attributed to Velázquez are to be found.[15] One is a portrait of the count-duke of Olivares and is possibly the picture now in Dresden in the Staatsgemäldegalerie, which is a product of the workshop. The other two belong to the category of informal portrait and include the *Portrait of Juan Mateos* (Plate 167) and *Portrait of a Knight of Santiago* (Plate 201). The acquisition of these paintings and other works was motivated by more than mere love of art. As Testi's successor in Madrid, Padre Ippolito Camillo Guidi, makes clear, the purchase of art works was a way to protect the value of the several pensions given to the duke during the visit of 1638.[16] These stipends were paid in *vellón*, a copper currency which fluctuated, often dramatically, in value, and could be used only for internal payments in Castile. By investing the payments in paintings and tapestries, a local, unstable currency could be transformed into a medium of international exchange.

Guidi was actively involved in these transactions during his tenure as ambassador (1641–43) and, on one occasion, asked Velázquez to assist him in negotiations.[17] It is

167. Velázquez, *Juan Mateos* (Dresden, Gemälde-sammlungen), 1.08 × 0.895m.

168. Pedro Perret, *Juan Mateos*, from *Origen y dignidad de la caza*, 1634.

pure supposition, of course, but Juan Mateos died on 15 August 1643, just when Guidi was purchasing works of art. In the evaluation of Mateos' estate, there were listed, without author, portraits of himself and his wife.[18] Perhaps this was the occasion when the striking image of the royal huntsman moved from Madrid to Modena.

However that may be, the *Portrait of Juan Mateos* (Plate 167) brings us to the second type of Velázquez' portraiture as practiced in the 1630s. As a matter of fact, informal portraits are known from the 1620s as well (Plates 41, 59, 61) and are a logical component of the production of any portrait painter. Generally speaking, these portraits show the sitters in bust- or three-quarter-length against a dark or neutral background. The subjects often are not identifiable, but those whose names are known prove to be people like Velázquez himself — servants in the royal household or fellow artists and writers.[19] Also, the jester portraits might be said to fall into this group. Presumably done on a casual basis, and with no great pressure to present the portrait to a public audience, the informal works were often used by Velázquez as a kind of experimental laboratory and thus contain some of his most audacious painting.

Juan Mateos had come to court with his father, also a huntsman, in 1603, and succeeded to the position of Master of the Hunt under Philip IV. Like many a royal servant, he had married within his metier, choosing as a wife Mariana Marcuarte, the

170 (facing page). Velázquez, *Juan Martínez Montañés* (Madrid, Museo del Prado), 1.09 × 0.835m.

granddaughter of a famous German arquebusier who arrived in Spain during the reign of Charles V.[20] As Master of the Hunt, Mateos was responsible for staging the often-elaborate hunting expeditions, such as the one depicted in *"La Tela Real"* (Plate 151). In addition, Mateos was the author of an important treatise entitled *Origen y dignidad de la caza* (Madrid, 1634). Thus, he was a person of some standing and importance in the household and was remembered fondly by the cardinal infante Ferdinand, who wrote to the king from Flanders lamenting that he now had to do without the services of a first-class huntsman like Juan Mateos.

Velázquez' depiction of this burly man is suitably grave and dignified. Indeed, the apparent absence of identifying attributes gives the impression that the sitter is a gentleman of the court. However, it seems clear that Velázquez intended to indicate Mateos' vocation by showing a pistol in his right hand. Although this part of the painting was left unfinished, the position of the two extended fingers makes sense if we imagine them as wrapped around the handle of a sidearm, with the thumb resting on the hammer.

The genius of Velázquez' portrait is most efficiently revealed by a comparison with the engraving of Mateos which appears on the title page of his book (Plate 168). This small-scale print by Pedro Perret has no ambition other than to present a more or less faithful image of the sitter, who looks a modest, rather meek man of advanced age. In Velázquez' portrait, probably done around the same time, Mateos personifies the "dignidad de la caza." Standing fully erect and in a three-quarter pose, Mateos is a man worthy of respect. Velázquez has minimized the effects of age and also reduced the corpulence by redefining the right-hand contour of the body (the original outline has now become visible with the deterioration of the overpaint). Attention is concentrated on the head and hands, the only parts of the painting which reflect the beam of light illuminating the composition. Also to be noted is how the light strikes the right background with greater intensity than the left. This subtle distortion of natural light, which is commonly employed in the portraits, is all that is needed to bring the figure forward in space.

Much the same approach is taken in the splendid portrait of the great Sevillian sculptor, Juan Martínez Montañés (Plate 170). Montañés was known to Velázquez from the painter's early age, for he had collaborated from time to time with Pacheco in the production of the polychromed wood sculpture for which he was famous. In June 1635, Montañés, at the time sixty-seven years old, was called to Madrid to produce a portrait bust for the Florentine sculptor, Pietro Tacca, who was executing a life-size equestrian statue of Philip IV.[21] Montañés arrived at court in June 1635 and returned to Seville in January of the following year, thus allowing the portrait to be dated securely. Once again, we have another, although earlier, portrait of the sitter to use as a comparison with Velázquez' work — the drawing by Francisco Pacheco for his *Libro de retratos* (Plate 169).[22] Pacheco's portrait is undoubtedly an accurate representation of the sculptor's physiognomy, but it lacks the sense of quickness and refinement which radiates from Velázquez' version. It is logical that Velázquez would have taken great care in painting the portrait of a fellow artist. Correctly recognizing that painters and sculptors had to make common cause in the struggle to elevate the stature of the visual arts, Velázquez pointedly shows Montañés dressed as a gentleman-artist, serenely modeling the bust of the king. Thus, he tacitly rejects the validity of the long-standing dispute between painters and sculptors about the superiority of their respective arts, a dispute in which the painters impugned the dignity of their rivals by emphasizing the "dirty work" involved in sculpture. And, in a gesture which presages his own self-portrait in *Las Meninas* (Plate 323), Velázquez shows Montañés in the moment of thought and reflection which precedes execution. The hand is the servant of the mind, and it is by the workings of the mind that sculpture attains the status of a liberal art.

The *Portrait of Martínez Montañés*, like the *Portrait of Juan Mateos*, was never finished, a fact which, together with its excellent state of preservation, permits us to study Velázquez' technique in detail. Looking at the unfinished passage, we see how he first

169. Francisco Pacheco, *Juan Martínez Montañés*, from *Libro de retratos* (Madrid, Fundación Lázaro Galdiano).

laid a ground of medium gray over a finely woven linen canvas. With a few deft strokes, he then sketched the outline of the bust of the king. The quickness and sureness of touch show why Velázquez seldom made preparatory drawings; with his superb sense of design, he was able to put his ideas directly onto canvas.

However, he was willing to work and rework and then rework again any and every part of the painting until it looked as he wished. In the *Portrait of Martínez Montañés*, as in other paintings of the 1630s, Velázquez constantly retouched and remodeled the canvas to soften contours and details and to prevent a regular pattern from developing in his brushstroke. Thus, when viewed at close range, this portrait, and all of the informal portraits, reveal a remarkable variety of techniques. Some of the procedures are additive, for instance the use of short, choppy, irregular impasted highlights. Other procedures are subtractive, as when it seems that Velázquez scraped or wiped away pigment to expose the grain of the canvas and to use the nap as a way of adding texture to the surface, thus softening it (Plate 171). Painting wet-into-wet, as is done in the eyes, allowed the creation of a filmy effect, one of the hallmarks of the artist's style. In these and other ways, Velázquez achieved two seemingly contradictory aims — one is a heightened realism, the other is a richness and variety of surface that insistently calls itself to our attention.

Toward the end of the decade and into the next, the use of these procedures becomes more confident and bold, as seen in the memorable portrait of the jester, *Calabazas* (Plate 172). Calabazas died in October 1639, thus establishing the latest possible date of execution.[23] Velázquez' vision of this misbegotten man is subtle, haunting, and strangely moving, uncompromisingly realistic but tinged with feeling. Calabazas' eyes are crossed, his head lolls to one side, the fingers of one hand grind into the palm of the other while he smiles a vacant smile. On either side are the gourds which have given him a mocking name. The composition is unusually complex for a single-figure portrait. The jester is seated on a low wooden stool, one leg tucked under the other. Thus, we are required to look down upon his curiously bent figure. Behind him, the ground rises up at the right, meeting what may be a door or window, while at the left, the space dissolves into formlessness. As a result, Calabazas seems almost trapped in a narrow, confining room which crowds in upon him. The laws of nature, which have played a cruel trick on this mindless fool, have also ceased to function normally in the world around him.

The technique of the portrait shows Velázquez at the height of his powers (Plate 173). From a distance, the face seems to be bathed in a pearly light which envelops the distorted features in a haze. Even at close range, it is hard to see how Velázquez obtained this effect, for the individual touches are small and irregular, the result of using the brush like a sculptor's modeling tool. Highlights are concentrated on the forehead, the right cheek, and the nose. Over the rest of the surface, the paint thins away to the weave of the canvas, which softens the light and forms. Below the head, a broad lace collar is rendered by strokes of the loaded brush that dart and pulsate over the surface in seemingly erratic paths. Miraculously, every daub of paint has fallen into just the right place.

Also to be dated to the later years of this decade are two portraits of dwarfs, *"El Primo"* (Plate 174) and *"Francisco Lezcano"* (Plate 175). These important paintings are usually dated to the mid-1640s, principally because *"El Primo"* is considered to be a documented work of 1644. But there is some reason to believe that they were executed *c.* 1636–38 for the Torre de la Parada, and were installed there as overdoor or over-window paintings.[24] These circumstances would account for the reference to the Sierra de Guadarrama in the background in both portraits (also used in the royal hunting portraits in the Torre), and, more importantly, the low vantage point from which the subjects are viewed. The summary execution of the pictures would also be explained if the pictures were designed to be seen at some distance above the floor.

The high placement and the informal subject presented Velázquez with the opportunity to display his virtuosity in unalloyed fashion. "El Primo's" mood seems to be

171 (facing page). Detail of Plate 170.

172 (page 150). Velázquez, *Calabazas* (Madrid, Museo del Prado), 1.06 × 0.835m.

173 (page 151). Detail of Plate 172.

pensive, as he absently turns the pages of the large book which is a counterpoint to his own diminutive stature. Radiographs have shown that, in the first version of the portrait, Velázquez painted the dwarf as bare-headed and wearing a falling collar. The addition of the hat, perched on his head at a sharply raking angle, adds dignity and stature to the little man, and perhaps was done to distinguish him, a member of the royal bureaucracy, from the dwarfs employed for frivolous purposes.

In tone, the painting is somber (although the badly discolored varnish now exaggerates this effect); the black costume is complemented by the tan-colored terrain and set off against what was once a silvery gray sky. Yet despite Velázquez' characteristic preference for muted colors, the portrait has tremendous power. In part, this is a result of the psychological perception of the sitter, who is regarded by the painter as an individual and not simply an ornament of the court. Also, the low vantage point makes the figure seem to loom large against the landscape.

As a result of the elevated placement, the painting is executed with extraordinary freedom. The hands are rendered as a blur of brushstrokes which define fingers, knuckles, and bones only in a summary way. The execution of the face is also masterful: small patches of exposed ground are juxtaposed to irregular blobs of thicker paint, especially on the forehead, under the left eye, and along the contour of the jaw at the left. These highlights anchor the tenuous web of shadow on the sitter's face. Finally, there is a summary treatment of the landscape, in which the illusion of snow-covered mountain peaks is created by just a few dragging strokes of a brush loaded with thick white paint. (The technique is identical to the handling of the mountains in the *Baltasar Carlos on Horseback* [Plate 135], a painting of similar date also installed high in a room.)

The companion-piece to *"El Primo"* is the portrait of a dwarf thought to be Francisco Lezcano (Plate 175). Although the identification has not been firmly established, there was a dwarf of this name who served at court from 1634 to 1649, except for an absence of three years between 1645 and 1648. According to the Torre de la Parada inventory of 1701, he holds in his hand a deck of cards, a time-honored symbol of idleness, which may refer to his function as playmate of Baltasar Carlos, or more generally to his function as an entertainer.

"Francisco Lezcano" fully deserves its fame. Velázquez' analysis of the sitter's mentality is keen and telling. The dwarf sits on a rock, with his right leg daringly extended toward the viewer. His hands idly finger the cards, a mindless activity which is all that is needed to enliven the pose and establish a psychological atmosphere. He wears a costume of forest green and is posed against a dark escarpment of rock. In the midst of these woodsy colors, his face is the irresistible focal point of the composition. The head is slightly thrown back and tilted just enough to one side to upset the equilibrium of the pose. The imbalance is gently asserted by the white blotch of his shirt, fully visible on one side, nearly invisible on the other. Although his features are painted with the filmy technique of the informal portraits, the bridgeless, upturned nose, the crooked, half-unconscious smile, and the veiled but vacant expression of the eyes make a telling portrayal of a creature seemingly as deformed in mind as in body.

The technique of *"Francisco Lezcano"* is even sketchier than that of *"El Primo."* Taking full advantage of the fact that the picture would not be seen at close range, Velázquez was emboldened to take daring shortcuts in execution. One brilliant passage among many can be noted — the summary description of the hands, where the fingers are seen to emerge from shadow by means of two short, irregular strokes of reddish orange pigment.

Informal portraits of female sitters are rare in the catalogue of Velázquez' work, for reasons which are unknown. Also uncertain is why most of them appear to have been done in the 1630s and early 1640s, although there is nothing to suggest that this is due to anything but chance. The most impressive of these is the *Woman with a Fan* (Plate 176), one of the artist's most appealing portraits.[25] The air of veiled sensuality that clings to the subject has prompted various hypotheses about the identity of the sitter, none of which can be confirmed.[26] However, the simple, low-cut dress, otherwise unknown in

174 (page 152). Velázquez, *Diego de Acedo, "El Primo"* (Madrid, Museo del Prado), 1.07 × 0.84m.

175 (page 153). Velázquez, *"Francisco Lezcano"* (Madrid, Museo del Prado), 1.07 × 0.83m.

176 (facing page). Velázquez, *Woman with a Fan* (London, Wallace Collection), 0.93 × 0.685m.

177. Velázquez, *Young Girl* (New York, Hispanic Society of America), 0.515 × 0.41mm.

178. Velázquez, *Woman Doing Needlework* (Washington, National Gallery of Art, Andrew W. Mellon Collection), 0.74 × 0.6om.

Velázquez' portraits, does offer a clue about the date. This fashion was French in origin and was popularized in Madrid by the duchess of Chevreuse. Two years after her departure from court it was decided, in one of those misguided efforts to improve public morality, that low-necked bodices would henceforth be prohibited to all women except prostitutes. The pragmatic was published on 13 April 1639, which establishes the latest date for the execution of the portrait. Despite the physical attractions of the sitter, the portrait appears to have been chaste in intention. This handsome woman wears a golden rosary chain with cross looped around her wrist, while a blue ribbon hanging at her side holds the somewhat faded remains of a religious medal. Thus, beauty and piety are discreetly conjoined in this masterful portrait.[27]

One of Velázquez' most captivating female portraits is the *Young Girl* (Plate 177), an unfinished work in a small-scale format (0.515 × 0.41 m.). This solemn, but beautiful little girl, the only portrait by him of a child who was not a member of the royal family, has a freshness and a simplicity which have suggested to some that she was a granddaughter of the artist. This shall probably never be known. But whoever the person may be, her fetching portrait, executed with remarkable spontaneity and economy of color, shows Velázquez in a rare moment of unguarded, if restrained feeling.

The final work in this group is another small, but fascinating work, the *Woman Doing Needlework* (Plate 178), which seems to be halfway between genre painting and portraiture. Once again, there are no clues about the identity of the sitter,[28] and the picture is another of those which pose an unsolvable dating problem, although the consensus now seems to be that it was done around the year 1640. It has been plausibly suggested that this picture is identical to one described in Velázquez' death inventory as follows: "Otra caveça de una mujer aciendo labor" ("another head of a woman doing needlework"), which was hanging in a room of Velázquez' apartment known as the "bobedilla."[29]

The *Woman Doing Needlework* is obviously unfinished; only the head seems near completion. The rest is sketched in to varying degrees, with the hands only blocked out in a summary manner. Because of its incomplete state, the picture offers us another opportunity to study Velázquez' method of working. First, he laid down a gray-green prime coat and then quickly sketched the outline of the figure. After establishing the larger color areas, he must have stepped back to judge the balance of the composition. Here, as in many of his works, he apparently did not like what he saw and made certain adjustments. The most noticeable of these is the reduction of the width of the left side of the body, which was motivated by a desire to change the position from a frontal to slightly diagonal view, thus enlivening the composition. Once this correction was made, Velázquez concentrated on bringing the head nearly to completion. This was no easy matter because of the extreme difficulty of foreshortening the facial features and then modeling them with light and shadow to produce an impression of the intense concentration of a woman doing painstaking work. Having reached this point, Velázquez put the painting aside and never returned to complete it.

There are only a few subject paintings of the 1630s besides the ones discussed in chapter IV, but these works are of enormous interest because they offer interpretations of themes rarely treated by Velázquez. *Christ on the Cross* (Plate 179), for example, is one of two religious paintings after 1630, an extraordinary point, given the fact that he worked in a society where a high percentage of all pictures were devoted to religious subjects. This imposing picture is hard to date precisely. Palomino, who is often correct about the details of Velázquez' life, believed the painting was done around the time of the duke of Modena's visit in 1638. In its present condition, coated with thick, discolored varnish which imparts an unpleasant greenish hue to the colors, the style is difficult to analyze. But the smooth handling of the body seems to favor a date early rather than late in the decade. There are other indicators that point in the same direction.

Christ on the Cross is first mentioned by Palomino, who saw it in the cloister of the convent of the Benedictine nuns of San Plácido, Madrid, for which it was presumably commissioned. The connection with this establishment may show the way to identifying the patron, the notorious Jerónimo de Villanueva, one of the most powerful men in the Olivares regime.[30] Although of Aragonese descent, Villanueva was born in Madrid on 24 March 1594, the son of a royal official. While still a young man, he attracted the attention of Olivares, who elevated him, in Villanueva's own words, to "the second place in the monarchy," that is, second to Olivares himself. In 1626, he was appointed as one of the secretaries of state, and became the intermediary between the king and the count-duke, and a party to all the official business. After the fall of Olivares in 1643, Villanueva was made to pay the price of his and his master's sins. In 1644, he was accused by the Inquisition and spent the rest of his life defending himself against the charges.

The process of 1644 was not Villanueva's first brush with the Holy Office. In 1628, he was a central figure in the curious case involving the nuns of the convent of San Plácido, which had been founded by Villanueva in 1623. In 1628, the Inquisition began to investigate the head of the convent, Sor Teresa Valle de la Cerda, its chaplain, and some of the religious on charges of hysterical and heterodoxical religious practices. Villanueva, who had been engaged to marry Sor Teresa before she took vows, and who

179. Velázquez, *Christ on the Cross* (Madrid, Museo del Prado), 2.48 × 1.69m.

181. Francisco Pacheco, *Christ on the Cross* (Granada, Fundación Rodríguez Acosta), 0.58 × 0.38m.

180. Detail of Plate 179.

had personally appointed the suspect chaplain, was also brought before the tribunal. In the end, he was saved by his powerful position at court and, in 1632, was ordered to perform a token act of penitence as the only punishment for his suspected involvement.

This occasion would have been a suitable one on which to commission a picture of Christ on the Cross, as a kind of votive piece and proof of good faith, and Velázquez, an artist with whom he was frequently in contact at this time, would have been the logical choice of painter. Villanueva administered the *gastos secretos* (Privy Purse), from which disbursements were made to Velázquez in 1634 and 1635.[31] There is also evidence that he was interested in adorning San Plácido with important works of art. While Rubens was in Madrid in 1628–29, Villanueva appears to have commissioned him to make a sketch for the picture in the main altar.[32] The argument for the date and occasion of Velázquez' painting is admittedly circumstantial, but it is possible that the commission came from Villanueva, whose name has always been linked with the convent.[33]

It is often noted that the composition of *Christ on the Cross* follows the recommendations in *Arte de la pintura*.[34] Pacheco had developed a lengthy proof that Christ had been crucified with four nails rather than three, and painters of Seville unquestioningly accepted this prescription throughout the first half of the seventeenth century. Indeed, Velázquez' painting is an adaptation of a composition used by Pacheco, which presents the strongly lit figure of Christ against an obscure background (Plate 181). Yet the result can hardly be called conventional. The exquisite draftsmanship of the body, the beautiful motif of the hair falling over the right half of the face (Plate 180), the subdued glow of the halo around the head impart elegance and dignity to the subject. With great artistry and restrained feeling, Velázquez has captured the redemptive power of Christ's martyrdom, the benefits of which are offered to the faithful through the ineffable beauty and perfection of His body.

Forming a transition between Christianity and antiquity is the small, underrated *Sibyl* (Plate 182). Although the identification of the subject has repeatedly been questioned,[35] the iconography leaves no doubt that it is correct. According to Christian tradition, the sibyls were the antique prophets of Christ, who had preached His coming to the Gentiles. For a long time, the number of sibyls varied, but during the late Middle Ages it settled at a canonical twelve, each of whom was given a specific attribute.[36] This iconography was popularized in the late fifteenth century first in a series of prints by an anonymous Florentine artist (Baccio Baldini?), and then in an influential book, *Duodecim Sibyllarium vaticinia* by Filippo Barbieri, which was published in 1481. The Florentine prints established certain conventions for the pictorial representation of sibyls: they were depicted as young women wearing exotic, heavily draped costumes which symbolized their missions to the distant corners of the globe (Plate 183).[37] In several of Baldini's prints, the sibyls are shown wearing flamboyant, flowing headdresses.

This convention was almost immediately broken by the most famous images of sibyls ever made, the ones in Michelangelo's Sistine Ceiling fresco, which are shorn of specific attributes and exotic costumes and identified by inscriptions. During the seventeenth century, however, a compromise was struck, at least by Italian artists. The colorful, heavily draped costumes were retained, but the attributes were minimized or eliminated. Especially important for this development was Domenichino's painting of 1617, often but not certainly identified as the *Cumaean Sibyl* (Rome, Galleria Borghese).[38] As seen in other versions of the subject by Guido Reni and Guercino, the type could be reduced further to a woman wearing a turban and contemplating a book (Plate 184). Without the inscription, Guercino's *Libyan Sibyl* would be impossible to identify.[39]

With this compressed history of the image in mind, it can be seen that Velázquez followed the seventeenth-century version of the subject faithfully. The headdress, the drapery, and the tablet are standard attributes of the sibyls. What is more, the pose in strict profile, otherwise rare in Velázquez' work (Plate 204), also indicates the theme. Sibyls were sometimes represented in this way, looking out of the picture to something unseen by the viewer, which implied their gift of prophecy (see, for example, the Libyan sibyl on the Sistine Ceiling).

not applied to the right half or perhaps the artist was comparing two possible ways of treating this section of the dress. Also, the row of inset pearls is handled summarily, as seen by the way the upper strand does not carry smoothly across the bodice, but rather changes level slightly at the center. The loop of free-hanging pearls, which is supposed to spring from the rosette and continue across to the shoulder (Plate 258), is also indicated in a shorthand way. This method of treating the costume is consistent with a sketch from life, in which the essential, the sitter's face, is the only part to be carefully studied.

Velázquez appears to have painted only one portrait of the king in the 1640s, but fortunately it is an impressive work about which we are well informed. This is the picture known as the "*Fraga Philip*" (Plate 196), so called because it was painted in the town of that name during the Aragonese campaign of 1644. Following the rebellion in Catalonia, the French army had invaded the region, pushing as far south as Lérida. In February 1644, Philip set out for Aragon to lead his troops in the reconquest of the territory.[5] Among the five-hundred members of the royal retinue was Velázquez, who was in attendance as *ayuda de cámara* and also to record the expected triumphs of the king. The court first stopped in Zaragoza for two months, while the army was gathered. On 2 May, the soldiers passed in review before the king at nearby Berbegal and, two days later, started to move north. The first objective was the town of Fraga, which would serve as headquarters for the king during the successful seige of Lérida. It was here, during a three-month stay, that Velázquez was ordered to paint the portrait of the king. Expense accounts in the royal archive contain a wealth of detail about how the work was executed under difficult campaign conditions.[6]

During the month of May, the king issued orders for two windows to be cut into the wall of his lodgings and for a carpenter to make an easel for Velázquez. At the same time, the house where Velázquez was billeted was repaired and a window opened "so that he could work and paint." On 1 June, the room or alcove in the royal dwelling was ordered to be restored. According to the entry in the accounts, the walls were collapsing and the floor was unpaved. Once this was done, the king sat for Velázquez at three different times. Presumably after the sittings, the artist returned to his quarters and worked on the picture. At the same time, Velázquez was executing a portrait of the dwarf "El Primo" which was ready for shipment by the end of June. In July, further repairs were made on Velázquez' house which, from the description, was in an advanced state of decay: "it was without a door and in such poor condition that you could not enter into it." Later that month, the king's portrait was ready to be shipped to the queen. It arrived in Madrid and, at the urgent request of the resident Catalan community, was displayed in the church of San Martín on their national day (10 August).[7]

In the portrait, the king is set in a conventional pose, remarkable only for the absence of articles of glory or attributes of military prowess.[8] Velázquez seems to have based his work on Van Dyck's *Portrait of Cardinal Infante Ferdinand* (Plate 197),[9] which had been in Madrid since 1636, although he further simplified the image. In addition, he was remarkably faithful to details of costume, which is the one worn by the king when he reviewed the troops at Berbegal. As described by a contemporary source, it consisted of "tight-fitting breeches embroidered with heavy silver, sleeves of the same material, a waistcoat of smooth buckskin, a red sash embroidered with silver, a small short sword and silver spurs, a falling Flemish collar, and a black hat with crimson feathers."[10]

The "*Fraga Philip*" immediately dispels any thought that the decline in the numbers of paintings in the 1640s implies a decline in the level of quality. As usual, the head of the king is meticulously painted with a smooth, seamless technique. By contrast, the rose-colored baldric and cloak shimmer with silvery highlights. As in the *Portrait of Philip IV in Brown and Silver* (Plate 98), Velázquez applies innumerable blobs of impasto to convey the impression of silver braid twinkling under a powerful light. By loosely following the pattern of an embroidered design, these short, thick blobs of paint evoke the impression of needlework. Yet the illusion of a varied, almost kaleidoscopic play of

197. Van Dyck, *Cardinal Infante Ferdinand* (Madrid, Museo del Prado), 1.07 × 1.06m.

196. Velázquez, *Philip IV at Fraga* (New York, Frick Collection), 1.335 × 0.985m.

light is virtually perfect. Once again, Velázquez has struck the delicate balance between order and accident required to bridge the distance between artifice and appearance.

There is only one more formal portrait thought to have been done in this period, although it no longer survives. This is the *Portrait of Cardinal Borja*. Gaspar de Borja y Velasco, who was born in 1582, had followed an important career in the church and spent considerable time in Rome. He returned to Madrid in January 1636, and soon was appointed as president of the Council of Aragon, where he became one of the chief supporters of the disastrous Catalan policy which provoked the revolt of 1640. According to testimony given by the painter Carreño de Miranda in December 1658, Velázquez had executed the portrait while Borja was archbishop of Toledo, a position which he held from 3 January 1643 until his death on 28 December 1645.[11]

Numerous versions of this portrait are in existence, but all appear to be replicas by assistants, followers, or copyists.[12] However, a drawing of the sitter still survives, one of the handful of drawings which has a secure claim to authenticity (Plate 198).[13] This drawing, small in size (0.186 × 0.117m.) and executed in soft black chalk, proves that Velázquez was an accomplished draftsman, despite the fact that he seems to have made but few drawings after leaving Seville. His sense of form, sometimes overlooked in the paintings where the brushwork is compellingly attractive, is sure and solid. In fact, in the drawing we see how Velázquez uses transparent shadows both to model form and animate the surface. By varying the pressure on the chalk, he is able to create filmy passages suggesting the play of soft light over the face, which contrasts with the darker, more concentrated passages of shadow reinforcing the contours.

198. Velázquez, *Cardinal Gaspar de Borja* (Madrid, Academia de San Fernando), 0.186 × 0.117m.

199. Velázquez, *Sebastián de Morra* (Madrid, Museo del Prado), 1.07 × 0.82m.

The number of surviving informal portraits from the 1640s is also very small. Although Velázquez is known to have done two portraits of dwarfs, *"El Primo"* and *Sebastián de Morra*, only the latter is still in existence (Plate 199).[14] Before 1643, Sebastián de Morra had been in Flanders with the household of the cardinal infante. He first appears at the court of Spain in August of that year, serving the prince, Baltasar Carlos. Morra outlived the prince only by three years, dying in October 1649. Thus, the portrait can securely be dated to this six-year period.[15]

As we see it today, *Sebastián de Morra* is somewhat smaller than it was originally. In the seventeenth-century inventories of the Alcázar, the dimensions were given as roughly 1.25 × 1.25 meters; they are now reduced to 1.07 × 0.82 meters. These rather substantial losses appear to have occurred when the picture was reframed in an oval format early in the eighteenth century, a procedure which involved first cutting the picture into a smaller square or rectangle and then folding the corners to fit the new frame. Later, the picture was reframed to its present shape. All this cutting, folding, and unfolding have taken their toll on the surface of the picture and disturbed the balance of the composition. An idea of the original is preserved in a somewhat scaled-down copy which, if faithful, shows that there was once an earthenware jug in the right-hand corner.[16] The removal of this lateral strip of canvas centralizes a composition which Velázquez wanted to be slightly out-of-balance.

Sebastián de Morra is the most forceful of all the dwarf portraits. By setting the figure against a dark, undefined background (an effect which is dissipated in the copy by the indecisive representation of a window or alcove), Velázquez permits no distractions from the direct confrontation of viewer and subject. Unlike *"Francisco Lezcano"*, who, in his portrait looks dim-witted, this dwarf seems to be in full possession of his mental faculties. His expression is compounded of intelligent curiosity and thinly veiled intensity. The note of assertiveness is subtly conveyed by his red, gold-trimmed smock and by the strong highlight on his forehead. His hands, rolled into tight, ball-like fists, are clenched around his belt, making him seem defiant. Velázquez' technique is almost notational in places, adding to the air of bravura. A splotch of red defines the lips; the right ear is little more than a crusty deposit of orangish pigment with two small, quick parallel strokes defining the lobe.

Two more portraits complete the meager list of Velázquez' production in this genre during the 1640s. The names of the sitters in these half-length portraits are not known,

200. Velázquez, *Portrait of a Man* (London, Wellington, Museum), 0.76 × 0.648m.

although several suggestions have been made for each one. The *Portrait of a Man* (Plate 200) recently has been provisionally identified as José de Nieto, like Velázquez an upper-level servant in the palace, who is seen dimly portrayed in the door in *Las Meninas*.[17] There is undoubtedly a resemblance between the two images, but the indistinctness of the features of the person in *Las Meninas* makes it difficult to be certain that the two men are one and the same. Whoever the person may be, he clearly inspired one of Velázquez' most commanding portraits. The darkness of the black costume and the brown background provides a foil for the dramatically lit head, which appears to be turning abruptly, as if reacting to an intruder, fixing him with an inquisitive, penetrating glance. The psychological power is multiplied by the audacious technique. The impasted highlight on the forehead quickly falls away almost to bare canvas along the hairline; the ear, sunken in shadow, is somehow defined without exact detail; the stiff collar, seen from the side and foreshortened, is made up of two dragging brushstrokes which disappear for a moment into darkness. Velázquez "turns the corner" of the throat by means of a cup-shaped blob of paint.

The *Knight of Santiago* (Plate 201) is a dignified, restrained portrait of an older sitter. Difficult to date with any degree of exactness, it is generally thought to be a work of the 1640s.[18] In contrast to the almost fiery demeanor of the *Portrait of a Man*, this sitter

201. Velázquez, *Knight of Santiago* (Dresden, Gemälde-galerie), 0.665 × 0.56m.

seems somewhat withdrawn and reticent, with a tinge of sadness around the eyes. The contrast in personalities of two portraits which are close in style and technique provides an opportunity to see Velázquez' power to express a wide range of human feeling and expression.

During the 1640s, his production of pictures other than portraits seems to have been exceedingly small. There is the large *Coronation of the Virgin* (Plate 202), painted for the oratory of Queen Isabella in the Alcázar, where it was inventoried and appraised three years after her death.[19] The inventory reveals that the *Coronation* was incorporated into a series of nine paintings of the feasts of the Virgin, which had been brought from Rome by Cardinal Borja. In a later inventory (1735), these paintings were attributed to the Neapolitan Andrea Vaccaro. Vaccaro was born in 1604 and thus would have been too young to have painted the pictures during Borja's first stay in Rome (1612–20). Presumably, they were commissioned during Borja's second Roman sojourn (1631–35) and arrived in Madrid more or less simultaneously with the cardinal on 28 January 1636. These facts establish the boundaries for the date of execution of Velázquez' picture — between 1636 and 1644.

It is at moments like this that the pitfalls of dating Velázquez' pictures on the basis of style are mercilessly exposed. His style evolved slowly during this eight-year period, making it difficult to be very confident about assigning a specific date to an undocumented picture. Recently, students of Velázquez have dated the *Coronation* over a wide range of time, depending on the point of comparison chosen. One writer has proposed a date of around 1635 on the basis of perceived similarities to *St. Anthony Abbot and St. Paul the Hermit* (Plate 112), a picture thought by him to have been done *c.*1635–40 (although it is more likely to have been completed in the spring of 1633).[20] Yet the author of another catalogue of Velázquez' works favors a date in the mid- to late 1640s, basing his opinion on the similarities he sees to the *Fable of Arachne* (Plate 314), a work usually dated to the late 1650s, but thought by him to have been done *c.*1644–48, and to the "*Rokeby Venus*" (Plate 206), which was almost certainly in existence by 1648.[21] The desire to date undocumented works is strong and intuition has a rightful place in the study of any artist. But paintings like the *Coronation of the Virgin* could in fact be dated on style over the entire range of *c.*1636–48. Instinctively, a date in the early 1640s seems plausible, but there is really no evidence to verify this opinion.

It is immediately apparent that the *Coronation of the Virgin* is an atypical work. The balance and symmetry of the composition, the ponderous monumentality of the figures, and the carefully studied poses and gestures make the picture seem more appropriate for an Italian Baroque church than a Spanish oratory. It may be that Velázquez felt obliged to make a concession to the nine paintings by Vaccaro among which his would hang. It has also been suggested that Velázquez was inspired by an engraving after a painting by Rubens of the same subject.[22] It is possible that Velázquez was acquainted with the print, but the differences between the two compositions are as impressive as the similarities, especially the sense of equilibrium which pervades the *Coronation* and distinguishes it from the twisting movement of Rubens' composition.

Velázquez also makes some important changes in the iconography. His Christ, for instance, is fully clothed whereas often in this period He is shown wearing drapery that exposes the wound in His side. Indeed, the heavy robes worn by all three persons suggest that heaven may be a colder place than imagined. The depiction of Christ as fully gowned, however, is traditional to Spain and was probably motivated by the excessive concern for decorum which characterizes much official Spanish religious art of the seventeenth century.

But what most distinguishes the painting from any putative models is the realistic conception of the figures and the amazing brushwork. To be sure, Velázquez has idealized Mary, Christ, and God the Father, but they still seem to be specific people. Although Mary is rendered as an exceptionally beautiful woman, it is hard to escape the feeling that she was studied from a live model. Similarly, God the Father, with His bald head and long, gray, flowing locks, looks like a dignified old man once observed by the painter. The sense of disjunction between the exalted subject matter and the veristic treatment of the figures accounts for much of the considerable impact still made by the picture. Also the unusually bright palette, based on shades of red, maroon, purple, rose, and blue, makes the picture vibrate with color. As for the brushwork, the painting is almost an encyclopedia of Velázquez' technique. Every trick in his book — and there were many — is here on display. Thanks to the superb state of preservation and the use of thick pigments, the surface has a freshness unsurpassed in any other work by the master. Here we can almost see the brush in action, bringing the forms into being with matchless skill and confidence (Plate 203).

A mere two works of mythological or allegorical subject can plausibly be assigned to the 1640s; one is a masterpiece in which a traditional theme is given an unconventional treatment, the other is a small but sparkling picture of uncertain subject. The ambiguous theme of the second picture (Plate 204) is unusual even in the work of a painter who preferred to use an allusive approach to traditional subject matter. At first, the picture seems to be related to the *Sibyl* (Plate 182): both show half-length female figures in strict profile, facing to the right, and holding a tablet. But it seems unlikely that the later picture was in fact meant to be understood in this way, principally because the figure lacks the flowing robes and headdress essential to representations of a sibyl.[23] It has also

202. Velázquez, *Coronation of the Virgin* (Madrid, Museo del Prado), 1.79 × 1.35m.

203 (facing page). Detail of Plate 202.

204. Velázquez, *Female Figure* (Dallas, Meadows Museum of Art, Southern Methodist University), 0.64 × 0.58m.

205. Hendrik Goltzius, *Clio* (New York, Metropolitan Museum of Art).

been suggested that the picture is an allegory of the power of the painter to recreate the world through the exercise of his imagination, but the absence of a brush and canvas seems to rule out that possibility, too.[24] Thus, we are left with no choice but to make what we can of the few elusive clues in the composition — a young woman with disheveled hair and clothes holding a small tablet to which she points. Some but not all of these features are to be found in representations of Clio, the muse of history (Plate 205). Most important is the small tablet, an attribute commonly associated with this subject.[25] There is also a certain similarity in the figure type, although the hair and dress of Velázquez' young woman are in greater disarray than is usual for the subject. But the principal obstacle to this identification is the absence of a pen, the necessary implement for writers of history (or of anything else). For the present, there seems little choice but to apply a purely descriptive title to this excellent picture.

As for the date, this is also a question without a clearcut answer.[26] On style alone, it could be placed almost anywhere in the last two decades of Velázquez' life. However, the firm modeling of the figure and the well defined silhouette perhaps argue for a date in the 1640s rather than in the 1650s, when Velázquez' technique became exceptionally loose and liquid.

Venus and Cupid, also called the *"Rokeby Venus"* (Plates 206, 209), Velázquez' only mythological painting of this decade, is rightly counted among his major works. It has

most prolific painters of the age. Its use on that occasion suggests that the word could be employed by disgruntled patrons as an expression of impatience, and probably resulted from the conviction that painters, as a class, took more time than was thought necessary to finish a picture. We can also be sure that Velázquez could work rapidly when required to do so. As we saw, the "*Fraga Philip*" was executed in difficult conditions in about a month's time. It is clear that Velázquez was able to paint with the utmost facility if time was of the essence. Still, it is probably true to say that Velázquez' talent for painting was great but not fecund. Unlike two of his famous contemporaries, Rubens and Rembrandt, who created torrents of paintings and drawings, Velázquez measured out his genius by the thimbleful. Thus, the decline in production in his later years did not cost us dozens upon dozens of masterpieces. Yet it is a phenomenon to be reckoned with, and a complex phenomenon at that.

The search for an explanation begins with the purely circumstantial. There is some reason to believe that Velázquez spent a considerable amount of time away from Madrid in the 1640s, even before he left for Italy in November 1648. In 1640, for example, he and Alonso Cano, who had come to court in 1638 as part of a new team of painters formed by Velázquez following the deaths of Eugenio Cajés in 1634 and Vicente Carducho in 1638, went to Valladolid to find paintings to replace the ones lost in a fire at the Buen Retiro.[37] Then there is the question of his trips to Aragon as part of the royal retinue.

In every year from 1642 to 1646, Philip journeyed to Aragon for periods of time varying from six to ten months.[38] The first trip lasted from April to September 1642 and was undertaken to lead the troops against the French. On this occasion, Velázquez stayed behind in Madrid where, on 29 May, he was present as the godfather at the baptism of his grandson, Diego.[39] The king went again to Aragon in late August 1643, returning to Madrid in mid-December. Velázquez' presence on this trip is theoretically possible because on 6 January 1643 he had sworn the oath of office of *ayuda de cámara*, or assistant in the privy chamber, which in principle required him to be in attendance on the king.

There is no doubt that Velázquez was in Aragon from February to October 1646; this was the occasion when he painted the king's portrait at Fraga. In 1645, the court was absent from Madrid for almost ten months, between March and December, so that the prince could receive the oath of allegiance from the Cortes of Aragon, an event which occurred on 20 September.[40] Thereafter, the court went to Valencia before returning to Madrid. The presence of Velázquez is not documented, although his son-in-law Mazo was in the royal party as painter to Baltasar Carlos.

A final trip to the north was begun in March 1646 and came to a disastrous conclusion on 9 October when Baltasar Carlos died in Zaragoza. On this occasion, Velázquez apparently stayed in Madrid, where he was documented on 27 July.[41] In any case, the regular and prolonged absences of the king from Madrid interrupted the normal rhythms and routines of court life and would presumably have had an effect on Velázquez among others. Here, then, is one possible explanation why Velázquez painted so few pictures in the 1640s.

Beyond these accidental causes, however, is something more fundamental and enduring. This is Velázquez' ambition for wealth and, above all, status and prestige. As noted before, Velázquez worked in a society which regarded painters as craftsmen, not artists, and treated them accordingly. The painters themselves must shoulder part of the blame for this state of affairs because they were unwilling to break free of the artisan mentality. Vicente Carducho, who fought long and hard to establish the legitimacy of his art, specifically indicts his colleagues for refusing to form an academy under the protection of the count-duke of Olivares.[42] Obviously they were afraid that a new order would disturb their long-established ways of doing business. But the reluctance and ultimate failure to provide intellectual underpinnings for the practice of painting left the artists open to charges of being merely craftsmen.

Indeed, if we look at the community of painters in seventeenth-century Madrid without prejudice, we see a pattern of life which resembles late medieval practice. Numerous painters and sculptors lived together in a certain section of the city, near the church of San Sebastián, whose registers are a rich mine of documents recording their coming into and going out of this world.[43] Many had open shops where they sold their wares and paintings by others as well, often at prices which were extremely low. In addition to painting and selling pictures, they also were available for repairing damaged canvases and acting as estate evaluators. Even at the court, painters were employed for all sorts of menial tasks, a point that is illustrated by the career of a minor artist named Julio César Semín.

Semín was the son of an Italian painter, Alessandro Semini, who came to Spain late in the sixteenth century.[44] Julio César entered royal service under Philip III and continued almost to the end of the reign of Philip IV, although he never received a court appointment. Because of his employment by the king, his activities are abundantly documented in the royal archives. Here is a small sample of the jobs he was given to do. In 1618, he gilded picture frames; in 1619, he painted fountains for a garden of the Alcázar. In 1620, he worked at painting imitation stone in one of the galleries. Later in his career, he gilded handrails on balusters, painted a portrait of the pope, restored pictures, covered ironwork with protective paint, working in this way until he died at an advanced age in 1662.

Semín, of course, was an artisan-painter, but the distinction between him and the painters to the king was blurred by the fact that the royal painters were sometimes commissioned to do similar tasks. In 1621, for instance, we see Vicente Carducho called upon to restore a fresco in the king's private dining room and to "make other repairs in the pedestals of the west gallery." In the next year, he made copies of battle paintings for the queen's apartments.[45] Velázquez appears to have been spared such menial tasks, but nonetheless could not help but suffer a certain amount of guilt by association.

Years ago, José Ortega y Gasset asserted that the principal motivating force in Velázquez' life was the desire to be a nobleman.[46] Ortega over-emphasized this hypothesis in his interpretation of the artist, but the events of Velázquez' life in the 1640s and 1650s corroborate that this was a burning ambition. Given this fact, Velázquez might have come to believe that his gifts as a painter were a drawback as far as his social aspirations were concerned. We know, for instance, that in 1638, his name appeared on a list of Madrid painters who were being prosecuted by an agent of the Council of Finance for payment of back taxes in the sale of their works.[47] It was bad enough to have paintings taxed as if they were manufactured goods; but then to be lumped together with some very second-rate artists would have been insulting to one who had consorted with kings and cardinals. Velázquez might have become convinced that, as a painter, he had gone as far as possible along the upward path of honors and glory. Now it was time to advance his career at court by seeking higher office in the royal household where, through the exercise of patience, skill, and good connections, a clever person could go far. Velázquez was one of those who knew how to play the game. Using the artistic patronage of the king as the foundation of his career, he gradually piled up an impressive list of offices and emoluments.

First was his appointment in 1623 as *pintor del rey*, which brought in a monthly salary of twenty ducats, plus payments for individual paintings. In 1626, he received the ecclesiastical pension worth 300 ducats per year. The appointment as Usher of the Chamber in 1627 not only paid an additional 350 ducats (and a clothing allowance of ninety), but also incorporated Velázquez into the royal household, which opened new vistas of opportunity.[48] At some point between 1633 and 1637, he was also given the use of a house on the calle de la Concepción Jerónima, a perquisite valued at 500 ducats a year.[49] On 28 July 1636, it was reported that he had moved another step up the ladder by swearing the oath of office as Assistant in the Wardrobe (*ayuda de guardarropa*).[50] This was followed seven years later by a significant promotion to Assistant in the Privy

Chamber (*ayuda de cámara*). The oath of office was administered by the count-duke himself on 6 January 1643,[51] and was among the last of his official acts, for only eleven days later he was given leave by the king to retire.

Offices and honors also brought financial rewards, and from the surviving documentation we can see that Velázquez was doing very well in this respect, too. By March 1640, he could count on at least 1,550 ducats per year in salary and allowances in addition to the value of his house, 500 ducats, and free medical care (which was probably worth what it cost). Additional grants were made periodically to cover the price of paintings commissioned by the king. A document of 1642 records that Velázquez collected about 3,500 ducats between 1633 and 1642 in various forms as payment for his pictures. In 1640, an annual amount of 500 ducats was granted to cover the cost of any and all pictures executed for the king. This allowance was increased by 200 ducats a year in 1648. (These all-inclusive stipends explain why there is little hope of discovering the documents on individual pictures painted for the king after 1640.) An additional grant of sixty ducats a month (720 per year) was made as an *ayuda de costa* in 1644, and on 12 May 1643 an extraordinary grant was ordered by the king to be paid to the artist to the amount of 2,000 ducats. Finally, the appointment to *superintendente de obras particulares* (discussed below) provided yet another 720 ducats a year. Thus, by 1648, the grand total of Velázquez' annual income from the crown (both salary and perquisites) reached the formidable amount of about 3,300 ducats, exclusive of occasional grants like the one of 1643.[52]

The rewards afforded by household service were obviously a great temptation and Velázquez, like any courtier, succumbed. And there was yet another advantage to royal employment because, in certain circumstances, it was possible to transfer offices to relatives. The roll of household servants included the names of many who were the third and fourth generations of their family to work for the king. Velázquez himself transferred the position of Usher of the Chamber to his son-in-law Mazo in 1634,[53] thus initiating a succession of royal employment from which his descendants were still profiting in the early years of the reign of Philip V, over seventy years later.[54]

This recitation of Velázquez' quest for wealth and position makes him appear like a brazen opportunist, who forsook a great talent to pursue the vain and ephemeral rewards of royal service. But this retrospective judgment is unfair. In his time, his success at court would have been viewed with admiration and envy not only by other painters, but also by poets, playwrights, scholars, indeed by virtually the entire society. Also, there is no reason to believe that he lost interest or faith in the art of painting; the masterpieces of the 1640s and 1650s prove this point decisively. But clearly he was willing to devote the necessary time to advancing his position at court, even if it meant painting fewer pictures than he had painted earlier in his career. One more important point should be made; namely, that a major aspect of his employment as a high-ranking court official was by no means incompatible with his talents as an artist. For one of the principal reasons why he curtailed his activity as a painter was the growing interest of his patron, Philip IV, in collecting and exhibiting fine pictures.

During the 1630s, the king had been refining his taste for pictures and sharpening his appetite for collecting. The change was noted by the English ambassador, Sir Arthur Hopton, in a letter to Lord Cottington, dated 5 August 1638:

> They are now become more judicious in and affectioned unto the art of painting than they have been or than the world imagines. And the king within this 12 month had gotten an incredible number of ancient and of the best modern hands, and over with the Conde de Monte Rey came the best of Italy, particularly the Baccanalian of Titian. And in this town is not a piece worth anything but the king takes and pays very well for them.[55]

The paintings mentioned by Hopton can easily be identified. Titian's "Baccanalian" is the famous *Bacchanal of the Andrians* (Plate 307) which was accompanied by another great masterpiece of Titian, the *Worship of Venus* (Plate 306), both of which were gifts to the king from Niccolò Ludovisi, the prince of Piombino. As for the "incredible number of the best modern hands," it seems likely that Hopton was referring to the shipment of Rubens' paintings for the Torre de la Parada and the Retiro, which had arrived in Madrid in May 1638.

In fact, beginning in 1636 with the commisssion for the Torre, the king had become almost obsessed with collecting paintings by Rubens and was in constant contact with his brother, the cardinal infante, who was in charge of shepherding the orders through the master's studio. After the Torre paintings had been received in Madrid, another commission was sent to Flanders, which was acknowledged in a letter from Ferdinand. On 27 February 1639, this lot was dispatched and may have comprised works for the Retiro. Only one picture is mentioned by name in the correspondence, the ravishing *Judgment of Paris* (Plate 109).[56] Once this group had been sent, still another was ordered – eighteen paintings for the *bóvedas de palacio*.[57] The *bóvedas*, or vaulted rooms, was the name for a set of apartments which had been created in the early 1630s in the basement of the northern wing of the Alcázar and used by the royal family during the summer. These pictures have been identified as a group of hunting scenes done by Rubens in collaboration with Snyders.[58] Although only one or two of the pictures seem to exist, others are known through Rubens' oil sketches. By May 1640, these pictures were in the hands of the cardinal infante awaiting shipment to Madrid.

A final commission arrived in Flanders in September 1639 which included four new pictures for the Salón Nuevo.[59] These were to be installed alongside the ten works by Rubens already hanging in the room. Unfortunately, Rubens never lived to complete the order. According to the cardinal infante's letter of 10 June 1640, the painter at his death had almost managed to finish one of the pictures and sketched in the other three. In September, Ferdinand tried to persuade another artist to finish the work. When he refused, the commission was assigned to Jordaens, who was able to deliver three of the paintings by March 1641 and the fourth probably in early autumn. Two of the paintings, the *Rape of the Sabines* and the *Reconciliation of the Sabines and Romans*,[60] were destroyed in the great fire at the Alcázar on Christmas Eve of 1734, along with numerous other works by Rubens and other masters. The companion pieces were *Perseus and Andromeda* (Madrid, Prado) and *Hercules*, which also was consumed in the blaze.

Thus, between 1636 and May 1640, when Rubens died, Philip ordered at least eighty-two paintings from him, and the number may have been considerably higher if as yet unidentified paintings for the Retiro and the Casa de la Zarzuela are included in the total. These works joined a least twenty paintings by Rubens which had previously entered the royal collection through a variety of gifts, purchases, and earlier commissions. If this count is correct, then by 1640, Philip owned a minimum of 102 paintings by the Rubens atelier.

But the king's appetite for Rubens' art was still not satisfied. On 23 September 1640, Ferdinand wrote from Flanders that Rubens' personal art collection would be coming on the market and suggested that the king consider making purchases.[61] To assist the selection, he sent a memorandum listing the works for sale. Some months later, the printed catalogue of the collection was published which the cardinal infante also forwarded to Madrid. Presumably the king made his wishes known because he was represented at the sale by Francisco Rojas (called Rochas in the annotated inventory of the sale), who was the *guardajoyas*, or keeper of precious objects, for the cardinal infante. In the king's name, Rojas bought thirty-two pictures, fourteen by Rubens and eighteen by other masters.[62]

Almost without exception, the paintings of Rubens purchased for Philip have survived and are now in the Prado. It was by any measure an extraordinary haul, including many of his finest easel paintings. Two of the pictures were known at first hand to the king: these were the copies of Titian's *Adam and Eve* and the *Rape of Europa* (Plates 78, 79), which Rubens had painted under the royal gaze in 1628–29. Among the paintings

210 (above left). Rubens, *Diana and Her Nymphs Surprised by Satyrs* (Madrid, Museo del Prado), 1.28 × 3.14m.

211 (above right). Rubens, *Rest on the Flight with Saints* (Madrid, Museo del Prado), 0.87 × 1.25m.

212. Tintoretto, *Portrait of Man with Fur Robe* (San Francisco, DeYoung Museum. Gift of Dr. and Mrs. Rudolf J. Heinemann), 0.99 × 0.74m.

of secular subjects were the *Three Graces* and *Diana and Her Nymphs Surprised by Satyrs* (Plate 210). The religious pictures included such masterpieces as the *Rest on the Flight with Saints* (Plate 211) and *St. George Slaying the Dragon*.

The group of paintings by other masters does not seem to have been quite up to this level, but this is hard to judge accurately because eight of the eighteen pictures have yet to be traced. Philip's acquisitions fell into two groups, which denote permanent characteristics of his taste — sixteenth-century Venetian and seventeenth-century Flemish. In the first category, he bought the moving late *Self-Portrait* by Titian (Madrid, Prado) and Tintoretto's *Portrait of Man with Fur Robe* (Plate 212). Among the Flemish paintings he acquired were Van Dyck's *Arrest of Christ* (Plate 213) and Elsheimer's *Judith and Holofernes* (London, Wellington Museum).

The final major acquisition of works by Rubens occurred in 1649, when Philip managed to prise most of the cartoons for the Eucharist tapestries from the grip of another avid collector, Archduke Leopold William. Six of these monumental pictures, executed mostly by the studio, were subsequently given to Luis de Haro, who installed them in the church of the Dominican convent of Loeches, outside Madrid.[63]

The stalking and bagging of great pictures by wealthy, discerning collectors is usually an interesting story. But in the case of Philip IV, the tale has some important ramifications. While it is generally known that he was a collector of art, principally of paintings by Velázquez and Rubens, it is not generally recognized that he was among the greatest picture collectors of the Baroque era and an exceptionally discerning connoisseur. The reason for the failure to appreciate his achievements in this field is simple — they have never been studied. And yet, without this knowledge, it is virtually impossible to understand Velázquez' activities during the last two decades of his life.

Philip's interests as a collector and connoisseur were somewhat slow to develop. Until he reached the age of around thirty-five, he seems to have been more of a passive than active collector, allowing his agents abroad to select and acquire pictures. Starting in the late 1630s, however, the king's tastes appear to have matured and he started to play the game himself. An immediate consequence was a shift in emphasis from quantity to quality. In the earlier part of the decade, paintings were often commissioned and purchased in wholesale lots. If the works obtained for the Retiro are added to those commissioned for other royal sites, the total is probably in excess of a thousand. Obviously, these were not all masterpieces; in fact, the majority probably fell into the category of space-fillers. By contrast, many fewer paintings were acquired in the 1640s and 1650s, but the level of quality seems to have risen significantly. The acquisitions from the Rubens sale may be taken as a turning point in the royal taste, completing the development first noted by Sir Arthur Hopton in 1638.

Along with the king's growing discernment as a collector came the natural desire to display the pictures in harmonious groups. Most great collectors are exhibitionists, and Philip was no exception. Once again, signs of this developing interest can be seen in the 1630s, notably in the ever-changing array of the pictures which were hung in the Salón Nuevo of the Alcázar.[64] When Cassiano dal Pozzo described the room in 1626, it contained, at least to his eye, very few points of interest. Of the thirteen paintings he

THE START OF A NEW CAREER

213. Van Dyck, *Arrest of Christ* (Madrid, Museo del Prado), 3.44 × 2.49m.

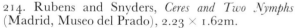

214. Rubens and Snyders, *Ceres and Two Nymphs* (Madrid, Museo del Prado), 2.23 × 1.62m.

mentioned, eight were by or after Titian and one was by Rubens. But in 1636, when an inventory of the room was made by a palace official, it held all kind of treasures. There were still six works by Titian, including the *Charles V on Horseback* and the *Allegorical Portrait of Philip II* (or the *Allegory of the Victory of Lepanto*). To these had been added nine pictures by Rubens, the principal survivor of which is *Ceres and Two Nymphs* (Plate 214), a collaborative work with Snyders. Van Dyck's *Portrait of Cardinal Infante Ferdinand* (Plate 197) rounded out the Flemish contingent.

A group of pictures by contemporary Italian and Italianate artists were also among the new acquisitions. The fire of 1734 unfortunately claimed paintings by Ribera, Domenichino, Guido Reni, and Artemisia Gentileschi. But Orazio Gentileschi's excellent work, the *Finding of Moses* (Plate 215), which entered the collection in 1633, still survives. The only Spanish painters represented in this room were the three court painters, Velázquez, Carducho, and Cajés, each by a work that has since disappeared.

In other rooms of the palace, too, there are signs of a growing interest in the systematic display of the collection. Between 1626 and 1636, the summer quarters were decorated by rearranging several great paintings by Titian which previously had been scattered throughout these apartments.[65] In 1636, the Retiring Room, where the king reposed after his meal, provided a visual dessert of extraordinary richness — the complete set of Titian's *Poesie* for Philip II plus three more pictures by the master, including *Adam and Eve* (Plate 79), *Tarquin and Lucretia* (Cambridge, Fitzwilliam Museum), and *Venus and Cupid with Organist* (Plate 216). In the adjacent dining room, the main course was comprised of works by painters of the Antwerp School, especially Rubens. By this master were *Diana as Huntress* (Plate 217) and *Ceres and Pan* (with the assistance of Snyders) (Madrid, Prado). Also on the walls were Jan Brueghel's *Five Senses* (Madrid, Prado), with figures by Rubens.

Another room to be redecorated in the 1630s was the Salón Dorado, or Gilded Hall, which was used principally for theatrical representations. From 1636 to 1640, this room was renovated first by gilding the ceiling, giving rise to the name of Salón Dorado.[66] Then the Tunis tapestries were installed on the walls, and finally, a gallery of portraits of the thirty-two kings of Castile was commissioned from local painters, here represented by a fine painting by Alonso Cano (Plate 218). These were eventually hung in the space just above the tapestries on the long lateral walls. A drawing of *c.*1672 by Francisco de Herrera the Younger, with a partial view of the hall, is the only visual record of the appearance (Plate 219). Here it can be seen that the decoration was another example of a Spanish Hall of Princely Virtue.

These two impulses of the king — to collect and then display great works of painting — determined the new course of Velázquez' career after 1640. Although continuing to serve as court painter, he was now to spend a greater portion of his time in the remodeling and redecoration of important rooms of the Alcázar and, later, El Escorial. Evidence of this fact is not hard to find. One of his friends, the court musician Lázaro Díaz, writing four years before the artist's death, explicitly describes this activity:

His Majesty put him in charge of the arrangement and adornment of his imperial palace, for which purpose, on His Majesty's orders, he twice went to Rome and other places, from where he brought back paintings, statues, and models made by the most famous artists in the world. And in this present year of 1656, thanks to his careful concern, solicitude, and excellent arrangement and work, the palace is so illustrious and grandiose that it augments the number of the wonders of the world.[67]

The words of Velázquez himself tell the same story. In a document of 1652 regarding the appointment of a new *aposentador mayor de palacio*, the writer, paraphrasing a memorandum from the artist, referred to the "many years in which he has been occupied with the adornment and arrangement of His Majesty's quarters, with the care and skill which is known to His Majesty."[68] Some of the duties of the *aposentador* concerned the arrangement of the palace interior, which is why the document concluded with these

215. Orazio Gentileschi, *Finding of Moses* (Madrid, Museo del Prado), 2.42 × 2.81m.

216. Titian, *Venus and Cupid with Organist* (Madrid, Museo del Prado), 1.48 × 2.17m.

217. Rubens, *Diana as Huntress* (Madrid, Museo del Prado), 1.82 × 1.94m.

words: "He petitions Your Majesty to grant him the favor of this office because it is so fitting to his talent and occupation."

The involvement of Velázquez in these activities is by no means a fresh discovery. Palomino devotes considerable space to describing them, and more recent writers have also discussed certain aspects of the question.[69] But what have been lacking are an appreciation of the full extent of this work and a recognition of its significance as an artistic activity instead of a wholesale diversion of Velázquez' talent to a tiresome round of household chores. To put the matter in sharp focus, it can be said that after 1640 Velázquez became the designer and decorator to the court of Philip IV. In certain ways, the role he played was analogous to that of Inigo Jones at the court of Charles I, Bernini at the court of Urban VIII, or LeBrun at the court of Louis XIV. In each instance, a great patron employed a great artist to design a suitable setting to display his wealth, power, and taste. In the case of Philip IV and Velázquez, the nature of the partnership was determined by the fact that the prince was a great lover of painting while the artist was a great practitioner of the art. As a result of this collaboration, somewhat akin to a museum director and his curator of paintings, the court of Philip IV achieved a distinctive visual character and appearance.

The first certain manifestation of Velázquez' new career appears in a document of 9 June 1643 in which the king appointed the artist as an assistant in the superintendency of private works (*obras particulares*), under the direction of the marquis of Malpica.[70] There is no evidence of Velázquez' work in this capacity until 1645, probably because of the displacement of the court to Aragon.

But once back in Madrid, Velázquez turned to his work in *obras particulares*. From about 1645 to 1648, a major campaign of remodeling and renovation was started in certain state and private rooms in the Alcázar in which Velázquez was to be heavily involved. The documentation of the work establishes the fact that the king participated in the approval of the plans, which were being drafted by Velázquez and the court architect, Juan Gómez de Mora. A good deal of discussion has been generated about the division of responsibility between these two artists. At first glance, the documentation is contradictory and ambiguous. We know, for instance, that Velázquez was eventually given administrative authority over the remodeling of a room in the south wing of the palace, later to be known as the Octagonal Room. A document of 13 March 1645 specifically states that Velázquez was fully in charge of the work, and his authority was reinforced in January and March 1647 when he was successively appointed as overseer and accountant of the Octagonal Room.[71] On the other hand, except in one instance, Gómez de Mora clearly emerges as the person in charge of the substantial work of demolition and reconstruction involved in the creation of the Octagonal Room.

The answer to the question of Velázquez' part in these extensive renovations to the palace lies in the finished product rather than in the process by which it was achieved. In the years between 1645 and 1648, the king had decided to undertake the modernization of the palace interior with the intention of making it conform to Italian models. The motive was to create opulent picture galleries for display of the ever-growing royal collection, complete with complementary furnishings and accessory decorative objects. During this period, three areas of the palace were selected for improvement (Plate 45). First was the main floor of the king's quarters in the south wing, comprised of what would be known as the Hall of Mirrors, the Octagonal Room, and the South Gallery. Second were the quarters of Prince Baltasar Carlos, which became vacant in 1646. The third area was the long, narrow gallery on the main floor in the northern part of the king's quarters, known as the North Gallery.

Once we understand the overall program, we can understand the division of responsibility. At the top, of course, was the king, who set the goals and made final decisions about design and cost on the basis of plans and estimates sent to him by the superintendent, the marquis of Malpica. Malpica emerges from the documents looking like a shuttlecock, being batted back and forth between the king and the artists, without always understanding what was happening. At the design level were Veláz-

218. Alonso Cano, *King of Castile* (Madrid, Museo del Prado), 1.65 × 1.25m.

219. Francisco de Herrera the Younger, *Salón Dorado of the Alcázar, Madrid* (Vienna, Nationalbibliothek), c.0.208 × 0.155m.

quez and Gómez de Mora, who had separate but inevitably overlapping responsibilities.[72] Velázquez was given charge of the decoration of rooms which were to be structurally redesigned by Gómez de Mora, who was also the supervisor of the construction work.

The first room to be completed was the smallest in size but the largest in terms of the remodeling. This was known initially as the *alcoba*, or alcove of the South Gallery, and then as the Octagonal Room, reflecting its shape after the transformation.[73] The *alcoba* was an irregular space which had been created from one of the thick-walled towers of the medieval Alcázar. In order to enlarge the space and regularize the design, the old walls had to be demolished, a difficult undertaking because it risked weakening the fabric of the structure. As the dismantling of the old walls was progressing, an unforeseen problem arose, which became the subject of a memorandum from Malpica to the king. This document, dated 13–14 March 1645, is revealing both of the chain of command and of the personalities involved.[74]

As soon as the problem had been discovered, Malpica consulted with Velázquez, who suggested that the matter be referred to the king. Malpica took this advice, but first asked for a report from Gómez de Mora, which indicated that a change in plan was advisable in order to ensure the stability of the structure. This change must have posed a potential conflict with Velázquez, which Malpica was eager to avoid. In his memorandum, therefore, Malpica requested a royal decision on the architectural question and instructions on how to deal with Velázquez because, "knowing him as I do, I always try to avoid debating with him." The king's reply to Malpica was suitably autocratic: "Velázquez is your subordinate and thus will obey you in everything." And then he communicated his decision about the architectural problem, ordering that the work be carried out according to the plan of yet a third person.

Malpica's timorous attitude toward Velázquez reveals a side of the artist's personality that is otherwise not in evidence. Without knowing more of the temperaments of both men, it would be unwise to draw conclusions. And, in any event, Velázquez and Gómez de Mora appear to have worked together without further difficulty until the architect's death in 1648, the same year in which the reconstruction of the Octagonal Room was finished. It may be that once overruled on matters architectural, Velázquez decided to confine his intervention to the decoration.

The documents of the decorative work are reasonably abundant and informative.[75] First, a small-scale wooden model of the room was prepared, which was painted by the ever-ready Julio César Semín late in 1646. On at least one other occasion in the 1650s, a preliminary plan was made to decorate a room in El Escorial (Plate 289), suggesting that the procedure may have been habitual. In fact, given the king's interest in these projects, it would have been logical for some sort of model or drawing to be made for his inspection and approval. It may even be that an oil sketch of the Salón Dorado attributed to Velázquez in a palace inventory of 1694 was some sort of preliminary design for a decorative project.[76] During the first six months of 1647, marble work and decorative painting were accomplished. On 28 May, a major element of the decoration arrived in the room. These were seven over-life-size bronze statues of the Seven Planets, executed by Jacques Jonghelinck, which had been sent to the Retiro in 1637 by the cardinal infante from Flanders (Plate 220).[77] Also in the shipment from the Retiro were life-size bronzes of Charles V, Philip II, and the queen of Hungary, almost certainly the works by Leone Leoni now in the Prado.

During the latter part of the year, twenty frames were made for the pictures to be hung in the room; the end of the project was then in sight and must have occurred early in 1648. It is difficult to be certain about the identification of the pictures which were first installed in the Octagonal Room.[78] The earliest inventory of the contents was not made until 1666, at which time new works of sculpture had been added to the collection while others had been removed. But there is a good chance that most of the paintings listed in 1666 were also there in 1648. If this is so, then the Octagonal Room was to some extent a memorial gallery dedicated to Peter Paul Rubens, eight and

220. Jacques Jonghelinck, *The Planet Saturn* (Madrid, Palacio de Oriente).

221. Juan del Mazo, *Mariana of Austria* (London, National Gallery). 1.97 × 1.46m.

possibly ten of whose pictures were in the room. Virtually all these paintings were hunting scenes, reflecting the king's passion for the sport and his belief in the pursuit as a mark of royal distinction. But the programmatic aspect of this and most of the other rooms should not be insisted on. The primary aim of the redecoration, as we shall see, was aesthetic, not ideological.

Sad to say, knowledge of the appearance of this and the other galleries in the Alcázar decorated by Velázquez and the king is scanty. The disastrous fire of 1734 and subsequent demolition of the Alcázar spared none of the original palace, and artists at the court were not given to making paintings of interior views. Would that David Teniers had worked in Madrid as well as Brussels! Thus, all that can be seen of the Octagonal Room is the thin slice that appears in the background of Mazo's *Portrait of Mariana of Austria* painted in 1666 (Plate 221), which shows one of the planetary statues set on a pedestal high above the floor.[79] This detail, plus the entries in the 1666 inventory, however, inform us that the Spaniards favored the combination of painting and sculpture which is typical of Italian palaces of the seventeenth century.

As a matter of fact, it has been pointed out that a similarity exists between the famous Tribuna of the Uffizi and the Octagonal Room.[80] However, there are important differences beyond the common shape of the rooms and their similar function as art galleries. The Uffizi Tribuna in 1648 still retained the appearance of a sixteenth-century *Kunstkammer*, and was filled not only with pictures but with a multitude of small-scale works of sculpture and decorative art.[81] The combination of large-scale sculpture and important pictures found in the Octagonal Room actually anticipates the re-installation of the Tribuna that occurred during the reign of Cosimo III de' Medici in the late 1670s. In this connection, it is perhaps worth remembering that Cosimo visited Madrid in 1668–69, when he had a chance to see the Octagonal Room of the Alcázar.[82] By then, casts and copies of antique works had been added to the Planets and the statues of the Habsburg rulers, making the connection somewhat more plausible.

The Octagonal Room was the first component of the extensive program for the redecoration of the palace, and it was accomplished with uncharacteristic speed. The other rooms were only slowly brought to completion, as money and objects became available. Nevertheless, the campaign of redecoration was well under way in the later 1640s. For instance, in August and September 1646, the old-fashioned Moorish-style wooden ceiling in the North Gallery was removed to make way for a plain vault.[83] During the months of January and February 1648, the installation of pictures in the summer quarters in the northern sector of the palace began to be revised.[84] This is probably also the time when plans were being laid to complete the conversion of the Salón Nuevo, the room first described by Cassiano dal Pozzo in 1626, into the Salón de Espejos, or Hall of Mirrors, the ceremonial center of the Alcázar. As early as 1640, the sculptor Antonio de Herrera had produced models for the mirror frames in the shape of double eagles which would give the name to the room. From August 1641 to October 1646, the foundry of Pedro de la Sota made bronze casts from Herrera's molds as a kind of preamble to the final stage of a decorative scheme not to be completed until 1659.[85]

Small wonder, then, that Velázquez' paintings were few and far between in his later years. The king's desire for enlarging his collection of pictures and displaying both old and new acquisitions in impressive groupings placed a prior claim on the artist's time. And, eventually, it led to the decision to send him once more to Italy to acquire objects that were needed to give the state rooms and galleries the desired effect of Baroque splendor.[86] The assignment of Velázquez to this mission was of course logical, given his overall responsibility for arranging the new galleries. But the trip to Italy can also be interpreted as the confirmation of the artist in his new career as court designer and decorator. Hereafter, painting was to become a sideline to the main work of assisting the king to form and display one of the greatest collections of pictures the world has ever known.

CHAPTER VII

The King Collects

IN LATE NOVEMBER 1648, Velázquez left Madrid en route to Italy, beginning a journey from which he would not return until 23 June 1651, two years and eight months later. Velázquez had two missions to perform in Italy, one official, the other personal. The official mission was to obtain works of sculpture and painting to install in the new rooms of the Alcázar. The personal mission, on the other hand, concerned the attainment of a long-standing ambition: a knighthood in one of Spain's elite military orders. For an artist-courtier, the knighthood spelled social acceptance which was denied to painters by a status-conscious aristocratic society. Not surprisingly, the official mission was more easily accomplished than the personal mission.

Velázquez traveled to Italy in the party of the duke of Nájera, which had been dispatched to meet Mariana of Austria, the intended bride of the king, her uncle.[1] The escort sailed from Málaga late in January 1649 and arrived in Genoa in early March. At this point, Velázquez separated from the group and made his way to Venice, which he reached in mid-April. On 24 April 1649, the first of numerous letters which record the artist's activities was dispatched to Madrid by the Spanish ambassador, the marquis de la Fuente.[2] De la Fuente, who had earlier been sent royal instructions to assist Velázquez in his quest for paintings, reported that he had received the artist three days before and was now doing everything possible to help him find pictures. He also reported that Velázquez was soon to leave for Modena, where he expected to acquire additional paintings. Velázquez appears to have left Venice empty-handed, but would return two years later to follow up with success on his initial inquiries. According to Palomino, the route south to Rome, his principal destination, was punctuated by stop-overs in Modena, Parma, and Florence. Only a stay in Modena is recorded, the first of two, but it would be safe to assume that he also broke his journey in the other places.

By 24 April 1649, he had reached Rome, as reported in a letter from Cardinal de la Cueva to his brother, the marquis of Bedmar, in Milan. The letter establishes the fact that the official purpose of Velázquez' trip was widely known and widely censured:

> A certain Velázquez, *ayuda de cámara* of the king, has arrived here and, it is said, with a commission to travel through Italy looking at statues and paintings and attempting to buy the best to adorn the palace in Madrid. And this court [the papal court], which assumes for itself the prerogative to judge freely and keenly on all matters, and in particular on the actions of princes, is very much against this, saying that it is not appropriate to a time in which all sorts of losses and calamities are happening to spend time and money in something of such little substance. . . .[3]

In another letter of 10 July, the cardinal added his voice to the chorus of critics: "These are the enterprises with which we try to emulate those who conquered the world [i.e., the king's ancestors]; they went forward, we go backward."[4] Velázquez, of course, was deaf to public opinion and, after a trip to Naples to collect money still owed him from the grant of 1643, he settled down to business.[5]

222. Fountain of the Four Corners of the World, Aranjuez, Jardín de la Isla.

224 (above). Giuliano Finelli, *Nymph with Conch Shell* (after the antique) (Madrid, Museo del Prado), height 0.61m.

223 (center). Matteo Bonarelli, *Hermaphrodite* (after the antique) (Madrid, Museo del Prado), length 1.55m.

The documentation of his activities in Rome continues until the end of November 1650. Much of this time was spent in arranging for the casting of antique sculpture and in commissioning ornamental bronzes which were to be installed in the palace galleries. Palomino gives a full account of the project, much of which has been confirmed by recent scholarship.[6] From these sources it is evident that Velázquez had a huge job on his hands. First and foremost was the making of the casts and molds. Just ten years before going to Italy, he had had his first experience with this ever-growing passion of princely collectors. In 1639, the English ambassador in Madrid, Sir Arthur Hopton, had received an order from London to have casts made of some antique heads at Aranjuez.[7] Hopton sought the assistance of Velázquez in fulfilling the request and the molds were dispatched in November 1639. Seven months later, a letter arrived from London complaining that two of the busts were of the wrong subjects, a charge rejected by Hopton who claimed that, "the heads I sent by His Majesty's order were certified to be right by Diego Velázquez, the king's painter, a man of great judgment."

Making the selection of works to be copied thus posed the first problem, and presupposes that Velázquez had familiarized himself with the prevailing taste for classical statuary. Then came the task of securing the owners' permissions to make the molds, which was not always freely given because of the risk of damage to the originals.[8] As the representative of the king of Spain, Velázquez had an easier entry to collections than many a would-be copyist, but the path was not always smooth. By March 1650, he still had not been able to gain access to the greatest collection of all, the papal collection housed in the Belvedere of the Vatican. It required two letters from the viceroy of Naples, the count of Oñate, the second more obsequious in tone than the first, to persuade Cardinal Panciroli to open the doors of this essential storehouse of antiquities to Velázquez.[9]

Some collectors were more kindly disposed to the project.[10] Cardinal Peretti, then the owner of the Villa Montalto, is specifically mentioned by Palomino as a friend who allowed casts to be made of the works in his collection. Velázquez also eventually obtained permission to copy sculpture in most of the other famous Roman collections, including the Borghese, Farnese, Medici, and Ludovisi. But simply as a practical matter, the obtaining of permissions, the visiting of collections, and the supervising of the work must have been a time-consuming business. The artist also had to administer the financial accounts, which meant at least one trip to Gaeta to obtain funds from the viceroy.[11]

Then, of course, he had to recruit the workforce of sculptors, for which he turned to Alessandro Algardi, then nearing the end of his distinguished career. Although Algardi did not help with the casts himself, he did make original works for the king, of which survives only a set of four large andirons with figures of Jupiter, Juno, Neptune, and Cybele. These sculptures were probably brought to Spain in February 1654 by the new nuncio, Camillo Massimi, and eventually installed in a fountain in the gardens of Aranjuez where they are still to be seen (Plate 222).[12]

Most of the work of making casts was assigned to Algardi's principal assistant, Giuliano Finelli, who had worked for many years in Naples and was thus known to Spanish collectors. He in turn employed Domenico Guidi, Matteo Bonarelli, Pietro del Duca, and Cesare Sebastiani, all of whom produced both bronze and plaster casts. By Bonarelli and Finelli are the *Hermaphrodite* and the *Nymph with Conch Shell* (Plates 223, 224), respectively, from originals in the Villa Borghese; while Sebastiani and del Duca produced the *Orator* and *Germanicus* (Madrid, Palacio de Oriente), after marbles in the Peretti-Montalto collection.

In addition to the collection of casts, Velázquez was also commissioning original works of decorative sculpture from Finelli and his group. Most important was a set of twelve bronze lions designed to support six marble console tables in the Hall of Mirrors. These were designed by Finelli and cast in 1651 by Matteo Bonarelli, and still survive in the Prado and the Royal Palace, where they are now put to different uses.[13] Finally, Velázquez spent time scouting for original statues and decorative objects. Years later,

225. Andrea Sacchi, *Cardinal Francesco Barberini* (Cologne, Wallraf-Richartz Museum), 1.29 × 0.955m.

226. Andrea Sacchi, *Francesco Albani* (Madrid, Museo del Prado), 0.73 × 0.54m.

his work was still paying dividends. In a letter of 10 March 1657, the Roman ambassador, the duke of Terranova, wrote to the minister, Luis de Haro, that a collection of statues and vases seen by Velázquez while in Rome was about to become available and asked for instructions concerning the purchase.[14]

Even from the partial documentation, we can see that Velázquez was assiduously accomplishing his mission. But from Madrid, it looked as if he was dragging his feet. The king must have assumed that he would be gone for about a year: thus, by February 1650, he started to grow impatient for his return, and to send letters to the duke of Infantado, his ambassador in Rome, urging him to hasten the artist's departure. These letters, some written by the king, some by his secretary, Fernando Ruiz de Contreras, arrived at intervals up to March 1651, and on two occasions were accompanied by enclosures addressed directly to Velázquez, which regrettably have not been found.[15] It is remarkable that, despite this incessant pressure, Velázquez remained in Rome until the end of November 1650.

Of course, it must be admitted that Velázquez did permit himself some distractions from the official business of the mission, one of which produced an illegitimate son, called Antonio.[16] He also painted pictures, which met with great success. In fact, his stay in Rome has the hallmark of a personal artistic triumph. During his first trip, he was still a student; now he was a master, and a master of a genre in which he had no serious rivals among the painters in the Eternal City, portraiture. In fact, portraiture in Rome around 1650 was at a low ebb, if we consider only painting and leave Bernini out of the discussion. Next to the conventional images, for example, of Andrea Sacchi (Plates 225, 226), Velázquez' portraits must have seemed not only great but matchless, and they were soon much in demand.[17] This must account for the spate of portraits executed during the seventeen-month residence in Rome. The exact number is hard to calculate, but it was considerable. Five of them are extant and Palomino mentions others.[18] Cassiano dal Pozzo also owned an unfinished portrait of himself by Velázquez which might have been done at this time, if not during the first trip.[19]

Whatever the number, the Roman portraits include some of Velázquez' greatest works in the genre, beginning with the incisive *Portrait of Innocent X* (Plate 227), which was probably done soon after Velázquez arrived in Rome in May 1649.[20] Innocent X (Giovanni Battista Pamphili), who knew Velázquez from his years in Spain as nuncio (1626–30), had ascended the papal throne in 1644 and reversed the strong anti-Spanish policy of his predecessor, Urban VIII. Thus, Velázquez, through the Spanish ambassador, could have had immediate access to the pope and might have asked permission to paint his portrait as a token of esteem and to help obtain support for his artistic mission. (It was probably also through the papal court that Velázquez was introduced to Algardi, whom Innocent X had chosen to replace Bernini as the favorite sculptor.) There is some evidence to indicate that the portrait was finished by January 1650, the date when Velázquez became a member of the Academy of St. Luke, Rome. In an ambiguous reference by his friend and would-be biographer, Lázaro Díaz del Valle, it is said that the pope "le offreció poner su retrato en el número de los famosos pintores de Roma insignes académicos . . ."[21] Papal intervention in Velázquez' election to this organization is perhaps reflected in the records of the Academy itself.[22]

Innocent was in his seventy-sixth year when he sat for Velázquez, a fact which is in no way apparent in the portrait. The pope, however, was renowned for his vitality. In 1649, the probable year of the portrait, he was described by an eyewitness as having the "voice, complexion, and bearing of an adolescent." He was also famous for his ugliness which, in the minds of some, disqualified him for election to the papacy. This quality is softened in the painting, but is plain to see in two exceptional drawings which have been cautiously ascribed to Velázquez.

These drawings (Plates 228, 229) are executed with pen and brown ink in a remarkable shorthand style.[23] The lack of any comparable drawing surely attributable to the master poses a serious obstacle to establishing the authenticity. Yet, intuitively, the attribution seems to deserve consideration. The very quality of the drawings and the

228 (above left). Attributed to Velázquez, *Study for Portrait of Innocent X* (Toronto, Theodore Allen Heinrich), 0.203 × 0.156m.

229 (above right). Attributed to Velázquez, *Study for Portrait of Innocent X* (Toronto, Theodore Allen Heinrich), 0.26 × 0.194m.

uniqueness of their style speak in their favor. From the skein of broken lines, the form and features of the pope emerge with impressive force. The variety of poses and views also accords with the notion of drawings executed in the short space of time that might have been granted to Velázquez for a sitting. Looking at the five sketches of the seated figure as presented on the two sheets, there is an uncanny sense of the restless movement of an energetic sitter who allows a painter to work in his presence while he transacts the business of the day. Finally, there are important differences in the poses essayed in the drawings and the painting, which seem to be characteristic of the impromptu process of the preparatory sketch. In particular, it should be noted that in the lower right-hand sketch in Plate 228, the pope holds the letter in his right hand, whereas in the painting it appears in the other hand.

The finished portrait is another demonstration of Velázquez' genius for combining elements of artistic tradition with keen powers of observation and original technique. It has often been noted that the pose depends on a convention of papal portraiture which was given definitive form in Raphael's *Portrait of Julius II* (London, National Gallery), and used thereafter by many other artists. But despite the constraints of this format, Velázquez seems to have gone to the very heart of his subject, producing a portrait which, to judge from the numerous copies, was recognized as definitive. Innocent had gained the reputation of a watchful, waitful man who was mistrustful of others and tenacious and indefatigable in the conduct of office. This is whom we meet in the portrait. In his left hand, he holds a piece of paper which Velázquez has used both to identify himself as the author of the picture and to serve as a petition to the pope: "Alla Sant^ta di Nro.Sig^re Innocencio X°. Per Diego de Silva Velazquez dela Camera de S. M^ta Catt.^co." It is easy to imagine that we are seeing the pope

227. Velázquez, *Innocent X* (Rome, Galleria Doria-Pamphili), 1.40 × 1.20m.

230. Velázquez, *Innocent X* (London, Wellington Museum), 0.78 × 0.68m.

as he gives an audience to the painter of the king of Spain. The petition has been read and now the pontiff gazes at the writer with an expectant but challenging glance. By means of this dramatic device, the portrait becomes the man rather than a mere image or record of his appearance. As the nuncio in Madrid reported in 1651, after seeing the autograph copy of the bust which Velázquez had brought, it is "a very lifelike portrait of His Holiness [Plate 230], with which His Majesty has taken great pleasure."[24]

The traditional requirements of the papal portrait went far to establish not only the pose but also the color harmonies. As usual, the pope wears the red cap (*camauro*) and manteletta and the white rochetta. The red drapery behind the pope, while not required, was frequently used in portraits of important ecclesiastics. And, as if there were not enough of the mandatory red, the pope also had an unusually ruddy complexion, which Velázquez chose to emphasize. Red and white, with the touches of gold on the chair, thus comprise the tonality of the picture. But Velázquez takes the color red through an astonishing variety of changes, from the shiny crimson of the manteletta, scored by brilliant highlights, to the muted maroon of the backdrop. Equally impressive is the handling of the creamy rochetta, made up of dragging brushstrokes which give it a convincing texture and feel.

The success of the *Portrait of Innocent X* can be measured not only in the copies but also by the numerous portraits commissioned by members of the papal court. According to Palomino, Velázquez executed nine portraits (exclusive of the pope's), of which only two can be identified with certainty. The most impressive of these is *Monsignor Camillo Massimi* (Plate 232), an important art patron of mid-century Rome.[25] Massimi was a cultivated man with discerning taste. He was a great admirer of Poussin, whom Velázquez probably knew as well, either through the prelate or through Algardi, one of the Frenchman's close friends. Monsignor Massimi was also a devoted student and collector of classical antiquity and could have been of help in guiding Velázquez' choice of works to copy in the collections of ancient statuary. The two men evidently formed a cordial relationship, a trace of which appears in the letter written by Velázquez to Massimi in 1654. When Velázquez met him in 1649–50, he was a young man (b. 1620), but already well advanced in a career at the papal court. His status is manifested by the unusual costume of *cameriere segreto* or *d'onore*, to which he was appointed in 1646. The holder of this office wore peacock blue, represented by Velázquez in the costly pigment of ultramarine. The unusual choice of color and brilliant brushwork confer great distinction on the portrait of one of Velázquez' most urbane sitters.

Smaller in size but as lively in character is the portrait of Cardinal Camillo Astalli, also known as Cardinal Pamphili (Plate 233).[26] Camillo Astalli, as he was called at birth (1611 or 1619), had a short, spectacular career at the court of Innocent X. The pope was known to be capricious, but nothing had prepared the courtiers for the honors heaped upon this obscure figure on 19 September 1650, when, all at once, he was raised to the purple and given the use of the name and arms of the Pamphili, as well as the family palace in the Piazza Navona. Cardinal Pamphili, as he was thenceforth to be known, was a distant relative of the pope's tyrannical and corrupt sister-in-law, Olimpia Maidalchini (also portrayed by Velázquez), and was made cardinal-nephew in the hope that he would be skillful in administering the business of the papacy.[27] As it turned out, Camillo Pamphili was incompetent and, in a reversal of fortune no less dizzying than his rise, he was stripped on 4 February 1654 of all that he had been given three-and-a-half years before.

Velázquez' portrait must have been made shortly after Astalli had been raised to the purple and promoted to the ranks of the Pamphili. For sheer economy of means, it is unsurpassed in Velázquez' oeuvre. Painted on a finely woven canvas of horizontal weave, lightly primed with white, the portrait has a wispy quality, the result of using thin pigments which barely cover the texture of the grainy surface. The effect is magical; the play of light and shadow is suggested by the perfect control of the brush. The strokes are so sparingly applied that they can almost be counted, yet the image is complete and

231. Velázquez, *Portrait of Man* (New York, private collection), 0.483 × 0.444m.

convincing. And the characterization of this vain, feckless man, who wears his biretta at a rakish angle (deliberately tilted to one side after first having been painted as level), is nicely understated.

One other work has been associated with the series of portraits of members of the papal court (Plate 231), although the absence of any specific attribute or trait makes certain identification impossible.[28] A date to the second Italian trip is, however, plausible, as suggested by a comparison to the *Portrait of Cardinal Astalli-Pamphili*.

The last of the Roman portraits known to survive is *Juan de Pareja* (Plate 234), the slave of Moslem descent who accompanied Velázquez to Italy. Pareja, who had been born in Antequera at an unknown date, served as Velázquez' slave until 1654 when, by virtue of an act signed by the artist in Rome on 23 November 1650, he was granted freedom.[29] Thereafter, until his death in 1670, he worked as an independent painter, which suggests that he had served Velázquez, at least part of the time, as a shop assistant. The principal source of knowledge of the portrait is a section in Palomino's biography, which the author claimed was based on the eyewitness account of a Flemish painter, Andrea Schmidt, who later worked in Spain. By Schmidt's account, the painting was displayed at the annual exhibition of the Congregazione dei Virtuosi al Pantheon, which occurred every year on 19 March in the portico of the famous Roman monument. Velázquez had been admitted to the Congregation, an artists' confraternity, on 13 February 1650, just a month before the portrait was exhibited.[30] Palomino also states, on his own authority, that the portrait had been painted before the pope sat for Velázquez, an observation usually cited to establish the relative dates of both works in

232 (above left). Velázquez, *Monsignor Camillo Massimi* (Kingston Lacy, The National Trust), 0.736 × 0.585m.

233 (above right). Velázquez, *Cardinal Camillo Astalli-Pamphili* (New York, Hispanic Society of America), 0.61 × 0.485m.

234. Velázquez, *Juan de Pareja* (New York, Metropolitan Museum of Art), 0.813 × 0.699m.

the early months of 1650. But even if true, there is no reason to make a close connection between the date of the exhibition and the date of execution of the portraits. For one thing, to state the obvious, Velázquez had already been in Rome for about seven months in 1649, leaving ample time to have painted both portraits in that year. In any case, the exact date of this portrait is not a burning question, for only a matter of months is involved.

Of far greater interest is the technique of the painting and the characterization of the sitter.[31] *Juan de Pareja* is a challenging picture, as implied by its display in public. By placing the portrait alongside the works of other painters in Rome, Velázquez invited criticism, comment, and comparison, all of which appear to have been favorable. According to Palomino, the picture "gained such universal applause that in the opinion of all the painters of the different nations everything else seemed like painting but this alone like truth." It is easy to dismiss this remark as the hyperbole of a reverent biographer, but it deserves serious consideration because *Juan de Pareja* is an understated but unmistakable manifesto of Velázquez' way of painting.

In contrast to the Italian preference for a smooth, unified finish, Velázquez' portrait is painted with an understanding of how to obtain convincing optical effects through variations of the surface. First is the subtle relationship between the ground color, a medium-light brown, and the colors of the flesh and costume. Pareja's costume is gray, but the color subtly changes from the warmer to the cooler tones. The warmer tones are obtained by applying the paint thinly over the ground, so that the priming mixes with the upper layers of pigment. Cool grays are achieved by laying on thicker layers, which effectively cover the prime coat beneath. In the sleeve of the right arm, Velázquez allows the ground to show through in broken patches and suggests the play of light over the creases in the cloth by means of touches of light gray impasto. From a distance, all

the colors combine to produce a velvety illusion. As a further refinement, occasional deposits of pink serve to relate the cool grays to the warmer ground, thus intensifying the tone. On the bodice and cloak, which are meant to be of a different, coarser material, the brushstrokes are applied more closely together, thereby reflecting the light. By using the technique of scumbling in these parts, Velázquez produces different effects with the same colors.

The conspicuous interplay between layers of paint is a technique developed by Venetian painters of the sixteenth century, notably Titian, who were Velázquez' principal source of inspiration. By simplifying this technique, and then applying it with unprecedented directness, Velázquez heightened the sense of the sitter's presence. At the same time, he carefully avoided the virtuoso brushwork used by painters like Rubens and Hals, whose show of skill sometimes distracts the viewer from the effect of "truth." *Juan de Pareja*, with its firm, self-confident pose, is a demonstration of a way to paint which the artists of Rome could admire, but did not care, or perhaps dare, to imitate.

In addition to the portraits, Velázquez also created two of his most unusual pictures — the Villa Medici landscapes (Plates 238, 239). Until recently, the date assigned to these works fluctuated between the two Italian sojourns: 1629–30 or 1649–50.[32]. The earlier date, it must be said, seems to imply that by the time Velázquez was thirty or so, he had completed his evolution as an artist, for these are paintings of great sophistication and maturity. Fortunately, it has now been established through indirect evidence that they were done during the artist's second stay in Rome.[33] Yet even as works of this date, they are extraordinary.

These small landscapes have no apparent subject but the play of light over identifiable but inconsequential settings in the gardens of the Villa Medici. The artist has focused on a single motif, the "Palladian" arch, which changes appearance under varying atmospheric conditions. In the *Pavilion of Cleopatra-Ariadne* (Plate 238), the sun shines through the trees, the rays fractured by the leafy branches, creating a dappled effect on the surface which seems to dematerialize substance. The sketchy figures in the foreground are depersonalized by the flickering light; the ground beneath their feet is a brilliantly observed patchwork of broken shadow. In the *Grotto-Loggia Façade* (Plate 239), the sun is filtered through thin, gray clouds, producing a flinty, even light. As a result, the colors are subdued and lack the vibrancy of the pendant picture. Nevertheless, this understated picture shows a profound understanding of nature.

The novelty of the Villa Medici landscapes lies not so much in the subject, however, as in the execution. Beginning in the 1620s, Dutch artists like Breenburgh, Poelenburgh, and Swanevelt began to make drawings of sights in Rome and the Campagna. These studies seem to have been regarded as independent works of art rather than as preparatory models for paintings.[34] A drawing by Breenburgh of an unidentified Roman ruin (Plate 235), datable to around 1625, is a good example of the type, which shows the same informal treatment of figures in an architectural setting as used by Velázquez in the Villa Medici landscapes.[35] During Velázquez' stay in Rome, an even greater practitioner of the nature study was at work, Claude Lorrain. A chalk and wash drawing of

235 (below left). Bartolomeus Breenburgh, *Unidentified Roman Ruin* (London, British Museum), 0.221 × 0.379m.

236 (below right). Claude Lorrain, *Fountain of Egeria* (London, British Museum), 0.214 × 0.313m.

the *Fountain of Egeria* (Plate 236), datable to 1640–45, sensitively records the effects of light washing over monumental architectural forms.[36] The figures standing at the table provide an anecdotal accent to the composition, but are not a center of attention. Claude made numerous drawings from nature during the 1640s, drawings which experiment with representing an endless variety of attractive places and atmospheric conditions.

However, unlike Claude's nature drawings, Velázquez' landscapes are executed in oil paint, a crucial distinction the importance of which at first may not be obvious. Drawing from nature was commonplace by 1649, but painting in the open air seems to have been done infrequently. In fact, Velázquez' Villa Medici landscapes are among the first known paintings that, to judge by their size and technique, appear to have been made directly from nature, although it may be that landscape studies in oil were painted *en plein air* in the 1630s by Joachim Sandrart and Claude Lorrain, if Sandrart's account, published some forty years later, is to be believed.[37] In any event, by mid-century the practice was starting to spread, as shown by the rough sketch (Plate 237) of a painter's box designed for working out-of-doors, drawn in Rome around 1650–52 by the English traveler, Richard Symonds.[38] Still, the idea was a novelty when Velázquez decided to paint his on-the-spot views of the Villa Medici gardens.

By choosing the opaque, less manageable medium of oil paint, Velázquez was denied the considerable powers of allusion available to the landscape draftsman, who could achieve and modulate luminosity with relative ease by exploiting the whiteness of the paper and the transparency of the drawing medium. He also sacrificed the principal advantage of drawing as a means to depict casual or informal views. Drawing, almost by definition, is a notational art, allowing the artist to capitalize on the viewer's predisposition to accept abbreviated, incomplete forms. By painting rather than drawing the Villa Medici gardens, Velázquez dispensed with the inherent informality which the draftsman needs to work in his allusive, cryptic manner. As Claude's nature studies show, or Rembrandt's landscape drawings for that matter, a great draftsman brings the scenery to life through suggestive touches of the pen. He also tries to render what he sees, unlike painters of landscape who were expected to produce elaborate works of art in which the parts of the composition were manipulated to serve a preconceived idea of nature.

To some extent, Velázquez emulates the draftsman's technique by using a light ground which controls the overall luminosity of the compositions. Glimpses of the ground are revealed here and there, particularly in the passages of the architecture and sky. In fact, in the *Grotto-Loggia Façade* (Plate 239), he scrapes away small areas of pigment on the surfaces flanking the arch, suddenly incorporating the weave of the primed canvas into an illusion of rough brick exposed under a worn layer of stucco. He also employs the suggestive treatment of details used in nature studies; almost none of the forms, animate or inanimate, is finished. But the chief device of the draftsman — the easy sweep and breadth of handling made possible by the water-based medium — was incompatible with the viscous, resistant substance of paint. So Velázquez devised a painterly solution. He created both forms and highlights by daubing and superimposing innumerable, fractured brushstrokes which dissolve outlines and contours. In this way, he was able to retain the spontaneity of a drawing while adding the one essential element missing in graphic nature studies — color. The greens, grays, beiges, and yellows are closely related in tone and keyed to the dark foliage. It is this subtle range of related colors which makes the scenes so authentically evocative of Rome on a summer day. The Villa Medici landscapes are small in size, but the penetrating powers of observation and originality of technique are enormous.

In both the landscapes and the portraits, Velázquez gave convincing demonstrations of his mastery and maturity as an artist. It would be fascinating to know how the artists of Rome regarded these original works of art, but there is not much to show what they thought. The admission to the Academy of St. Luke and the Congregazione del Virtuosi, if not arranged solely by the pope, suggests that he was well received by his fellow

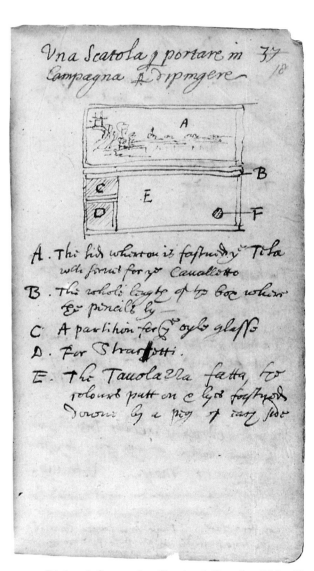

237. Richard Symonds, *Sketch of Box for Plein-Air Painting* (London, British Library).

238. Velázquez, *Villa Medici, Pavilion of Cleopatra-Ariadne* (Madrid, Museo del Prado), 0.44 × 0.38m.

239. Velázquez, *Villa Medici, Grotto-Loggia Façade* (Madrid, Museo del Prado), 0.48 × 0.42m.

240. Angelo Michele Colonna and Agostino Mitelli, Salone, Sassuolo, Palazzo d'Este.

241. Paolo Veronese, *Venus and Adonis* (Madrid, Museo del Prado), 2.12 × 1.91m.

242. Paolo Veronese, *Cephalus and Procris* (Strasbourg, Musée des Beaux-Arts), 1.62 × 1.90m.

artists. But otherwise, silence reigns. And, however the pictures were judged, there is no evidence that they made a lasting impression on the international community of painters of Rome.[39] His appearance was like a comet in the summer sky, attracting notice while visible and then disappearing at once into the darkness from which it came.

Of greater immediate consequence was the pursuit of a more prosaic goal, namely to gain the support of the Vatican for his ambition to become a knight of a Spanish military order. Given his profession of painter, his desire for this honor is significant because the three military orders — Alcántara, Calatrava, and Santiago — were bastions of aristocratic privilege. Despite the expansion of noble titles under Philip IV, and the consequent dilution of the once-impeccable standards for admission, membership in these orders was still regarded as a mark of high status and prestige. Velázquez' desire to belong indicates his lofty personal ambitions and the beginnings of a major effort to enter the upper echelons of a society normally closed to artists. The Vatican was prepared to support his ambition to the fullest extent, as made clear by the letter written on 17 December 1650, by Cardinal Panciroli to the nuncio in Madrid.[40] Velázquez, he says, has demonstrated his extraordinary merit in the portrait of His Holiness. He is therefore writing to express his support of the artist's pretension to the habit of a military order. He concludes the brief letter by affirming his personal interest in the matter. It is worth noting that Panciroli supported Velázquez for precisely the reason that he was rejected in Spain — his talent as an artist.

By late November, Velázquez must have believed that sufficient progress had been made in Rome to permit him to return to Spain.[41] But there was still one more task to be performed — namely, to acquire pictures. On 12 December he stopped in Modena to pay his respects to the duke and to inspect the picture collection. The duke was absent but was informed of Velázquez' arrival in a letter from a nervous servant named Gemignano Poggi.[42] Poggi saw it as his duty to defend the ducal picture collection and refused to let Velázquez view it, claiming that he did not have the key to the rooms where it was housed. As compensation, he arranged for him to see the country house at Sassuolo (Plate 240), which had been recently decorated by Michele Colonna and Angelo Mitelli, two fresco painters, as Velázquez informed Poggi, whom he was bringing back with him to Spain.

Despite Poggi's transparent ploy to keep Velázquez from viewing the picture collection, the artist found a way to see it (or perhaps had already seen it on a previous visit). On 13 January 1652, the Modenese ambassador in Madrid reported that Velázquez had just spoken to him about one of the duke's masterpieces, Correggio's *Adoration of the Shepherds*, known as *La Notte*.[43] Velázquez had approached the ambassador with the suggestion that this picture would make a welcome gift to the king, who was now more inclined than ever to great pictures. According to Velázquez, this had been talked about when he and the ambassador were in Genoa about to embark for Spain. The ambassador expressed doubt that he had ever discussed the possibility of giving this picture to the king because he knew that the duke had put it in deposit, so to speak, for his descendants. Velázquez, he was pleased to report, seemed to be satisfied with this explanation, thus concluding a pretty feeble attempt to acquire a great picture.

Velázquez acted more decisively upon his return to Venice, where he bought several works, including two superb paintings by Veronese, *Venus and Adonis* (Plate 241) and *Cephalus and Procris* (Plate 242).[44] In addition, he acquired a ceiling decoration by Tintoretto, consisting of seven canvases, which are now in the Prado (nos. 386, 388–9, 393–6). We also know that he left a list of pictures which the ambassador was to purchase if they became available. On 11 July 1653, in compliance with these instructions, the ambassador wrote to Madrid, advising that a *Gloria* by Tintoretto was now up for sale, which he would buy if it corresponded to the one on Velázquez' list.[45] Don Luis de Haro, to whom the letter was addressed, consulted with Velázquez and then apparently ordered the picture to be bought. Unfortunately, it is not now identifiable.

After Venice, Velázquez went to Genoa where he expected to meet Colonna and Mitelli; but they did not appear. He sailed for Spain without them toward the end of

May, arriving in Valencia on 13 June.[46] Ten days later, he was at last once more in Madrid. Just behind him, arriving from Naples, was the first shipment of the works commissioned in Rome, which slowly trickled into Madrid over the next twelve months. The collecting phase of this mission was over; the installation phase now lay ahead.

But before considering the eventual placement of the objects in the palace, there is another important development in the history of the royal collection to discuss. For even as Velázquez was criss-crossing Italy on his collecting mission, the king's ambassador in London was preparing to participate in the greatest art sale of the century — the sale of the collection of Charles I of England. Philip's interest in acquiring the pictures of a brother monarch showed itself at an almost indecently early moment. On 30 June 1645, while Charles was still at large, Philip wrote to his man in London, the resourceful Alonso de Cárdenas, ordering him to buy pictures from the royal collection, which he mistakenly thought was about to come on the market.[47] In fact, it was the duke of Buckingham's collection which was being talked about, as Cárdenas soon informed the king. In 1646, the Council of State noted Cárdenas' news about the sale of this collection but, as it was ultimately restored to the heirs and sold in Flanders, there was nothing for the king to buy.[48] But when the disposal of Charles' collection finally commenced in October 1649, Cárdenas was ready. Now, however, the campaign of acquisitions was being managed in Madrid not by the king, but by his minister, Luis de Haro.

Luis de Haro was the son of the eldest sister of the count-duke of Olivares and the marquis of Carpio. Olivares always claimed to be a disinterested servant of the king. But if it is true that his personal gains from power were modest compared to the standard set by his predecessor, the duke of Lerma, it cannot be denied that he bestowed enormous wealth on the members of his family. Thus was created what contemporaries called the "clan," a network of relatives by blood and marriage who became the new-rich of the reign of Philip IV. In addition to money, the clan also possessed the taste for picture collecting, which they were able to indulge by dint of postings in Italy and Flanders, where good pictures were available to be bought.

The most prodigious collector of the clan was Diego Messía Felípez de Guzmán, the marquis of Leganés, Olivares' first cousin and perhaps his favorite relative.[49] After having made an excellent marriage in 1627 to Policena Spinola, daughter of the Genoese general, and having acquired wealth through royal grants of land, offices, and money, Leganés spent much of the 1630s commanding Spanish armies in Flanders and Milan, where he amassed a fabulous collection of pictures. In 1630, an inventory of his collection listed a mere eighteen pictures. Twelve years later, he owned 1,132, which were primarily composed of Flemish and Italian works, following both the fashion of the day and the route of his foreign assignments. Like other members of the Olivares clan, Leganés made a point of currying royal favor by occasional gifts of paintings to the king, among them two works by Rubens, a beautiful painting of the *Immaculate Conception* (Plate 243) and the *Devotion of Rudolph I of Habsburg to the Eucharist* (Prado no. 1645). It was also Leganés who presented the king with Van Dyck's *Portrait of Cardinal Ferdinand Infante* (Plate 197). Leganés shared one other characteristic with his relatives — he was a patron of Velázquez and owned some of his works at his death in 1655, none of which has been traced.[50] The relationship with Velázquez seems to have been friendly, because Leganés made the painter a gift of a picture by Ribera.[51]

Another senior member of the Olivares group was Manuel de Fonseca y Zúñiga, count of Monterrey and the count-duke's brother-in-law. Short in stature but long on greed, Monterrey took advantage of a ten-year stay in Italy, first as ambassador to the Holy See, then as viceroy of Naples, to amass a small but choice collection of pictures, most of which have proved difficult to trace, although *St. Catherine*, attributed to Titian (Boston, Museum of Fine Arts), was surely among them.[52] Monterrey owned other works attributed to Titian, the old master most sought-after by Spanish collectors, but he was also a discerning patron of contemporary artists, especially in Naples. In addition to commissioning works for the Retiro by Lanfranco, Domenichino, Stanzione, and Artemesia Gentileschi, he also ordered a number of altarpieces and paintings to decorate

243. Rubens, *Virgin of the Immaculate Conception* (Madrid, Museo del Prado), 1.98 × 1.34m.

244. Interior, Church of the Agustinas Recoletas, Salamanca.

245. Raphael, *Madonna of the Fish* (Madrid, Museo del Prado), 2.15 × 1.58m.

the church of Agustinas Recoletas, Salamanca, of which he became patron in 1634 (Plate 244).[53] With its altarpieces by Cosimo Fanzago, funerary effigies by Giuliano Finelli, and paintings by Ribera, Lanfranco, Stanzione, and others, the church even today is an excellent example of the arts in Naples around 1635. Monterrey also came into contact with Velázquez, first in 1630 when he arranged the permission for the painter to spend the summer at the Villa Medici, Rome. At some point he acquired a pair of royal portraits by him, which are listed in his death inventory of 1653. Another point of contact is recorded in a letter of 1652, in which the countess of Monterrey mentions a large portrait of herself done by Velázquez at the urging of her brother, the count-duke.[54]

Briefer mention can be made of the count-duke's son-in-law, the duke of Medina de las Torres.[55] Medina began life as an obscure member of an old noble family, but rocketed to prominence when he was selected to marry Olivares' daughter María in 1624. The premature death of María in 1626 in no way impeded his rise to wealth and power. In addition to winning important government and household appointments, Medina had a knack for choosing wealthy wives. In 1637, he married Anna de Caraffa, princess of Stigliano, and later, in 1660, the countess of Oñate. After the death of Luis de Haro in 1661, Medina became the first among the king's advisers. Having started with so little and ended with so much, Medina was at pains to show his gratitude to his sovereign by gifts of pictures. Before 1636, he had given the king a series of Five Scenes by Jan Brueghel (Prado nos. 1394–8), which he had received as a gift from the cardinal infante. During his tenure as viceroy of Naples (1638–45), Medina wrested Raphael's *Madonna of the Fish* (Plate 245) from the hands of the prior of S. Domenico.[56] An inventory of Medina's possessions has not yet come to light, leaving in suspense the question of whether he formed a picture collection of his own.

This resumé of the collecting patterns and proclivities of the Olivares clan suggests that Luis de Haro was running to form when he decided to become a picture collector.[57] Haro appears, however, to have started slowly. In 1647, when his wife Catalina died, the usual inventory was made of her possessions, including a picture collection.[58] There is some reason to believe that the pictures listed in this inventory were owned jointly with her husband. In any event, the collection was not a large one; it contained 241 pictures, most of which were not attributed. There was, however, at least one important work by Velázquez, *Baltasar Carlos in the Riding School* (Plate 145), possibly inherited from the count-duke.

As a matter of fact, the collection of Haro's young son, the notorious Gaspar, marquis of Eliche, was already larger than his own. According to an inventory of 1651, it contained 331 pictures.[59] Gaspar de Haro would one day become famous as an art collector, but even at the age of twenty-two, he had paintings attributed to all the right masters: Titian, Veronese, and Tintoretto; Rubens, Van Dyck, and Bril; Raphael, Claude, and Ribera. The marquis of Eliche also owned paintings by Velázquez, the best of which was of course *Venus and Cupid* (Plate 206). Obviously, the patronage of Velázquez by the Olivares clan was second only to that of the king.

In 1651, Gaspar's great age of collecting still lay in the future. Now it was his father's turn. The event that turned Luis de Haro from an ordinary to an extraordinary collector was the Commonwealth sale.[60] For reasons which are not entirely clear, Philip stepped aside in favor of his minister at this, the greatest opportunity of the century for picture collectors. However, documentation of Luis de Haro's collecting activities implies that the minister saw an excellent opportunity to please the king by making him presents of important paintings. The choice of works destined for the king's collection was made on the advice of Velázquez and other royal painters, some of whose opinions are recorded in Haro's letters to Cárdenas.[61]

Haro's participation in the sale was motivated by another consideration, which is referred to in the papers of the Council of State — the desire to shield the king from charges that he was financing treason by purchasing pictures from the rebels. And then, of course, there was the concern about future claims in the event of the English

246. Andrea del Sarto, *Madonna and Child with a Saint and Angel* (Madrid, Museo del Prado), 1.77 × 1.35m.

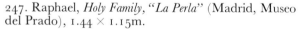

247. Raphael, *Holy Family, "La Perla"* (Madrid, Museo del Prado), 1.44 × 1.15m.

monarchy being restored. When that day finally arrived, Philip was clearly not prepared to give up his beloved pictures. On 3 June 1662, the Council of State gave instructions in this regard to the new representative in London:

> If anyone proposes the restitution of the pictures and tapestries . . ., excuse yourself from answering by saying that you have no notice of this matter. If nevertheless they insist that you take it up, you will say that you will write to your correspondent without entering into further discussion and without entering into any other undertaking. . . .[62]

The Spaniards unquestionably had much to hide, because no one bought more at the Commonwealth sale than did Haro and Cárdenas. However, few, if any, pictures were acquired directly from the state.[63] Many excellent pieces were given to creditors of the crown in lieu of cash payment of debts, and then sold to the agents of continental collectors. Thus, Cárdenas was able to buy works from John Emery, the King's Plumber (Titian's *St. Margaret*) and Edmund Harrison, the Royal Embroiderer (Titian's *Marquis del Vasto Addressing His Troops*, Prado no. 417).

While Cárdenas had some leeway in choosing works to buy, he kept in close touch with Don Luis throughout the sale, advising him of the availability of pictures and asking him to make selections from lists which were periodically sent. Haro's side of the correspondence was published almost a hundred years ago, but the letters from Cárdenas to Haro, which are possibly of greater interest, have only recently been studied.[64] From this source, it is possible to derive more precise information on the Spanish participation in the sale.

Although Cárdenas started to make purchases in 1650, the surviving correspondence does not begin until 1651, when he wrote frequently to Don Luis regarding the sale and shipment of pictures and tapestries. The first extant letter, dated 23 January 1651, concerns the shipment of a set of Raphael's tapestries of the Acts of the Apostles which had been acquired during the previous year for 14,236 escudos (£3,599).[65] However, Cárdenas also had been on the trail of paintings and sculpture. On 8 August 1651, he sent a report of works purchased and prices paid.[66] Don Luis had sent 26,839 escudos to Cárdenas, all but 2,000 of which was spent on art objects plus shipping costs and bribes to customs agents. The works in this lot, which were sent to Spain between 18 August and 13 September, were kept for the most part by Haro in his personal collection and are now hard to trace, especially because of the uncertainty of the attributions. They included, however, paintings said to be by Correggio, Titian, Giorgione, Parmigianino, and Perugino, plus the set of Raphael tapestries and six statues by Gianbologna. One picture from this group was given to the king, Andrea del Sarto's *Madonna and Child with a Saint and Angel* (Plate 246).

On 24 November 1651, Cárdenas wrote again, announcing the shipment of a *Madonna and Child* by Titian and two portraits by Van Dyck.[67] He also mentioned that the Pembroke Collection was coming on the market, but was not enthusiastic because the best works had been claimed by the son. Consequently, he advised Don Luis to refrain from making purchases. Of greater interest were the Twelve Caesars from the royal collection, attributed to Titian, which had been sold to Captain John Stone at the value of £1,200. Although Cárdenas accepted only eight of them as works by Titian, and attributed one of the remaining four to Van Dyck, he recommended the purchase. Eventually this set (now lost) was acquired and given to the king.[68]

The next letter of consequence, dated 11 August 1653, was intercepted by the French at Bayonne and sent to Paris.[69] Presumably a copy eventually found its way to Madrid because it mentions purchases which were consummated. First, Cárdenas mentioned new acquisitions, including three works given to Raphael — the *Portrait of the Medici Cardinals*, a small *Madonna and Child with St. John*, and the *Holy Family*, known as "*La Perla*" (Plate 247), which, as he reported, was considered to be the finest picture in Charles' collection. Having thus purchased the best paintings by Raphael, he was now planning to buy works by Correggio — the *Education of Cupid* (Plate 248) and *Venus and*

248. Correggio, *Education of Cupid* (London, National Gallery), 1.55 × 0.915m.

249. Raphael, *Madonna of the Rose* (Madrid, Museo del Prado), 1.03 × 0.84m.

the Satyr (Paris, Louvre). The second picture escaped from Cárdenas' grasp and was purchased by M. de Bordeaux for Cardinal Mazarin. The *Education of Cupid* was acquired for Don Luis and sent to Madrid where a curious fate awaited it.

Two other purchases were on Cárdenas' mind — Mantegna's *Death of the Virgin* and the *Virgin and Child with St. John and Other Saints*. In the event, he obtained them both for Haro, who gave one to the king (Prado no. 248) and kept the other, which eventually came into the collection of the National Gallery, London. He also promised to try to buy Raphael's *Madonna of the Rose* (Plate 249) and succeeded in doing so. The last item of business covered in this letter concerns purchases from the collection of the deceased earl of Arundel, about which Cárdenas was seeking information.

The next ten or eleven months were busy ones for the ambassador. On 25 May 1654, he submitted an account of his purchases, which listed the works just mentioned and others of equal importance, a total of twenty-four in all.[70] First was Tintoretto's magnificent *Christ Washing the Feet of the Apostles* (Plate 250), which was given to the king. He also bought two works by Dürer, the famous *Self-Portrait* and the *Portrait of an Unknown Man* (Prado nos. 2179–80), which had been presented to Charles by the city of Nuremberg and bought at the sale by the agent of a German collector. There were also two paintings by Palma Giovane — the *Conversion of St. Paul* (Plate 251), and *David with Head of Goliath* (Plate 252), both given by Haro to the king, and other paintings by Gentileschi, Guido, and Rubens.

This group of pictures was quickly sent off to Madrid, where it arrived toward the end of the year. In a letter of 1654, Haro wrote to Cárdenas acknowledging receipt and recording his impressions of the pictures, and those of a local connoisseur, Diego de Velázquez.[71] The minister was very pleased by what he saw emerge from the packing crates:

> And I assure you that all of them, as regards the quality, have seemed to me to be very good, and were bought at very reasonable prices, particularly the *Portrait of the Medici Cardinals* by Raphael . . . the *Venus and Mercury* by Correggio and the *Lavatorio* by Tintoretto. I therefore believe that His Majesty will be very pleased to receive them as will I to be able to give them to him, although they are things of little importance, because he has such a very particular liking for pictures.

Haro subsequently informed Cárdenas that he planned to install the large *Holy Family* by Raphael in the king's bedroom. But first he had shown it and the others to Velázquez: "Velázquez has already seen it and it seemed a very great thing to him, as it does to everyone."[72] A few weeks later, on 22 January 1655, he could report that Tintoretto's *Christ Washing the Feet of the Apostles* had also met with approval. "The other one which I have given to His Majesty these days is the large *Lavatorio* by Tintoretto, and Velázquez as well as Nardi have not only taken it to be a great work but also . . ." (here a break in the document occurs).[73] Nardi, of course, was the Italian painter to the king who had been at court for over thirty years.

Two of the pictures in the 1654 shipment fared less well at the hands of the artist-connoisseur. The *Portrait of the Medici Cardinals* ascribed to Raphael was the subject of an art-historical discussion. Evidently it has been assumed from Cárdenas' earlier description that he had bought either the famous picture of *Leo X with Two Cardinals* or the equally famous copy by Andrea del Sarto, mentioned by Vasari as being indistinguishable from the original. The picture that arrived in Madrid, which had been the property of the earl of Arundel, was clearly neither by Raphael nor del Sarto, as Velázquez was able to attest. Haro wrote to Cárdenas that the artist had seen one of the versions in Rome four or five years before (Velázquez was not sure whether it was the one by Raphael or del Sarto), and knew that the picture from London was neither of those. It now appears that he was correct and that the work sent by Cárdenas was probably yet another copy by Giulio Bugiardini (now in Rome, Galleria Nazionale d'Arte Antica).[74]

But the other attribution questioned by Velázquez proves that not even great painters

250 (right). Tintoretto, *Christ Washing the Feet of the Apostles* (Madrid, Museo del Prado), 2.10 × 5.33m.

251 (below). Palma Giovane, *Conversion of St. Paul* (Madrid, Museo del Prado), 2.07 × 3.35m.

are infallible judges of great paintings. The work in question was Correggio's *Education of Cupid* (Plate 248) which, Haro wrote, had been rejected by an unnamed expert: "And with this [opinion] it seems that Velázquez was in accord, and Angelo Nardi was also called . . . ,"[75] and apparently agreed with the others. Don Luis was content to keep it for himself, trusting that the painters in England who had approved it knew more than the painters in Spain.

In 1655, the partnership of Haro and Cárdenas was forced to close down its English operations. Cárdenas was first imprisoned by Cromwell's government and then expelled from the country. He went to Flanders, where he continued his indefatigable work as a buying agent, this time arranging the purchase of a sizable lot of pictures from the countess of Arundel, including Veronese's *Christ in the House of the Centurion* (Plate 253).[76]

The collecting activities of Luis de Haro, however important, are secondary to and wholly dependent on the passion of Philip IV for pictures. As numerous sources observed, including Don Luis himself, the king "had a very particular inclination to painting." In fact, as the affairs of state worsened, the king's interest in his collection seemed to grow, almost as if it was a source of solace and diversion from the melancholy drift of events. Thus, the king required his *pintor de cámara* to put his brushes aside and to assist in arranging the treasures of the royal collection. Working simultaneously at the Alcázar and El Escorial, Philip and Velázquez conceived and realized a style of court decoration which may justly claim a place as one of the wonders of the Baroque age. At the same time, this collaboration strengthened the relationship between the two men and provided Velázquez with his chance to attain recognition as a nobleman as well as a noble artist.

252 (above). Palma Giovane, *David with Head of Goliath* (Madrid, Museo del Prado), 2.07 × 2.35m.

253 (right). Paolo Veronese, *Christ in the House of the Centurion* (Madrid, Museo del Prado), 1.92 × 2.97m.

CHAPTER VIII

Velázquez and the Decoration of El Escorial

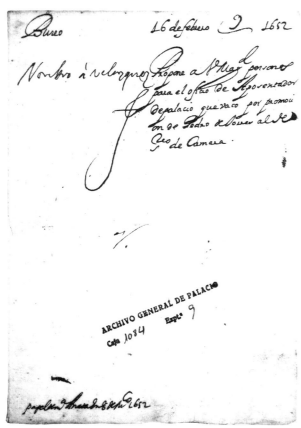

255. Document appointing Velázquez to office of *aposentador*.

254. Detail of Plate 263.

ON 16 February 1652, the committee for the governance of the royal household met to consider the vacancy in the office of *aposentador mayor de palacio*.[1] The names of four candidates had been proposed for the post, Velázquez among them. Each member of the committee sent a recommendation to the king, listing his preferences in rank order, one through four. No clear favorite emerged; Gaspar de Fuensalida, a member of a dynasty of household servants, and Francisco de Rojas, the man who had made the king's purchases at the Rubens sale, each had three first-place votes. Velázquez, on the other hand, fared poorly in the balloting. He was mentioned once for second place and twice for third and fourth. Fortunately, the one decisive vote was in his favor. "Nombro a Velázquez," reads the terse marginal note written by the king: "I appoint Velázquez" (Plate 255).

In making his choice, Philip must have given weight to Velázquez' work on the decoration of the palace, because the other applicants had records of distinguished service. Indeed, Velázquez made a point of emphasizing this qualification in his petition to the committee, where he noted that he had been involved for many years in the adornment of the royal quarters, "with the care and skill which is known to Your Majesty." However, the position of *aposentador* entailed many additional responsibilities.[2] The most onerous of these was the maintenance of the *oposento del rey*, or the king's quarters, which imposed some rather mundane tasks on Velázquez. For instance, he was in charge of cleaning the part of the palace used by the king, for which purpose he commanded an army of sweepers and scrubbers. He was also responsible for the supply of firewood in the winter months (the official "heating season" lasted from 15 November to 24 May). Another aspect of the job was to arrange the accommodations for the king and his retinue when they traveled. Many of these duties put heavy demands on Velázquez' time and negligible demands on his artistic talents.

The palace records for the period from 1652 to 1660 reveal many a notice of these joyless, petty tasks, some of which were needlessly complicated by minor disputes between household servants.[3] In documents of October 1655 and October 1657, Velázquez was concerned with the replacement of rush mats, which were used to cover the floors of the palace in winter;[4] in May 1654, he was occupied with bed linen for the servants.[5] A major responsibility occurred whenever the king left Madrid, as he did with predictable regularity. Each trip required the mobilization of servants in the *furriera*, the section of the household directed by Velázquez, and the transport and arranging of appropriate furnishings.[6]

On the other hand, the office carried numerous responsibilities which made use of Velázquez' capacities as a designer and increased his prestige at court. For instance, the *aposentador* was in charge of the arrangements for such important ceremonial acts as audiences with cardinals, the swearing of oaths of office by viceroys and council presidents, and the swearing of the oath of allegiance to the prince by the Cortes of Castile. He was also ordered to consult with the king about the staging of plays, masques,

257. Velázquez, *Infanta María Teresa* (New York, Metropolitan Museum of Art, Jules Bache Collection), 0.444 × 0.40m.

infanta which was reproduced in varying sizes and formats. This composition is recorded in two versions, one by the master (Plate 258), the other by the workshop, which were dispatched to Vienna and Brussels respectively in December 1653.[22] An inventory of the archduke's collection made in Brussels in 1659 indicates that the picture of the infanta received by him was then considerably taller, and so presumably was the one sent to the emperor. In their present condition, both versions lack not only the lower part of the figure, but also a few centimeters of canvas above. Nevertheless, the brilliant display of technique, characteristic of all the finished portraits of the 1650s, compensates for the loss of a certain grandeur in the composition as a result of the reduction of size. The striking color harmonies are established by the pearl white dress, while accents are provided by the rose-colored collar and cuffs and by the two ribbons which hang over the ample *guardainfante*, holding two small clocks at the end. The same pink and white tones are used in the face, which is covered with the customary heavy make-up. Behind the figure is a flowing curtain of deep blue-green, emphasizing the silvery tones of the costume.

The brushwork now reaches a maximum point of virtuosity. Except for the face, which is smoothly finished, the surface is comprised of innumerable touches of impasto which have been flecked on top of the bold, unblended strokes of the costume. The tightly knit wig, with the curious ringlets at the ends, adorned by a rosette and surmounted by an ostrich feather, is little more than a jumble of amorphous touches which miraculously fuse into a perfect composition as one recedes from the canvas. With the characteristic combination of premeditation and intuition acquired through years of thought and practice, Velázquez achieves profound insights into the reality of appearances and the essence of his medium.

Philip's new queen, Mariana, was only fourteen when she married her uncle and came to Madrid. In fact, she was only four years older than her step-daughter, María Teresa, whom she closely resembled, at least until after the difficult birth of her first child, Margarita, in July 1651. For some time following her confinement, the queen was ill and therefore was probably not portrayed by Velázquez until the following year.[23] (He had been in Italy during her first years at court.) The result is an impressive

258. Velázquez, *Infanta María Teresa* (Vienna, Kunsthistorisches Museum), 1.27 × 0.985m.

259. Velázquez, *Mariana of Austria*
(Madrid, Museo del Prado),
2.31 × 1.31 m.

260. Workshop of Velázquez, *Mariana of Austria* (Vienna, Kunsthistorisches Museum), 2.04 × 1.261m.

full-length, formal portrait (Plate 259), the only one of her in this format done by Velázquez. As we see it today, the picture has been considerably enlarged by a heavy-handed painter who added a strip of canvas at the top, measuring about twenty centimeters. The appearance of the composition before alteration is preserved in workshop versions in Paris and Vienna (Plate 260), the latter of which is probably the picture sent to the imperial court on 22 February 1653, thus establishing the latest possible date for the creation of the original.

Like the other full-length portraits of the 1650s, *Mariana of Austria* offers the contrast of a stiffly posed sitter with an impassive expression who is painted with a display of technical virtuosity. It may be that Velázquez was assisted in the execution of the costume; some of the touches in the silver embroidery along the hem of the dress lack the spontaneity and lightness of the master's touch. But the upper half of the figure, especially the wig and bodice, is alive with the seemingly casual but perfectly controled brushwork of the mature artist. With an economy of means unsurpassed by any painter of his day, Velázquez makes each touch of pigment play a part in creating the illusion of a brilliant costume glittering under a radiant light.

Some years later, Velázquez had to revise the image of the queen to take account of

261. Velázquez, *Mariana of Austria* (Dallas, Meadows Museum, Southern Methodist University), 0.465 × 0.43m.

262. Workshop of Velázquez, *Mariana of Austria* (Sarasota, Ringling Museum), 1.46 × 1.145m.

the introduction of a new style of wig in which the hair is worn in waves rather than ringlets and surmounted by an ostrich feather laying close to the surface. The revision was carried out in a small bust-length portrait (Plate 261; 0.465 × 0.43 m.), of which only the head was painted by him.[24] Judging from a workshop picture (Plate 262), the new appearance of the queen was meant to be grafted onto the earlier composition, thus efficiently saving Velázquez the trouble of inventing a fresh image.

The birth of Margarita, the first child of Philip and Mariana, occurred on 12 July 1651, and afforded Velázquez the opportunity to paint a series of captivating portraits, which show her growing to maturity. None is dated, but the changing appearance of the princess seems to indicate that they were done in intervals of two or three years. Once completed, the pictures were dispatched to the imperial court in Vienna, where her cousin Leopold, to whom the princess had been promised at birth, could observe her progress. (They were married in 1666.)

In her earliest years, Margarita was described as being exceptionally beautiful and thus she appears in the portraits. The first of the series, probably painted in 1653 when she was two years old, is undoubtedly the masterpiece of the group (Plate 263).[25] Solemn in expression, erect in bearing, the little princess is presented as a very important person. But the glorious color harmonies — the salmon pink dress with its soft, silvery brocade, the richly patterned oriental carpet, the deep blue cloth on the table, and the blue-green curtain behind — soften the image and make it irresistibly attractive. Velázquez has lightened the formality by placing a bunch of flowers in a transparent vase at the left. A single rose has fallen to the tabletop, a small touch which adds a note of casual grace to the ceremonial mood of the portrait (Plate 254).

264. Velázquez, *Infanta Margarita* (Vienna, Kunsthistorisches Museum), 1.05 × 0.88m.

265. Velázquez, *Infanta Margarita* (Vienna, Kunsthistorisches Museum), 1.27 × 1.07m.

266 and 267 (following pages). Velázquez, *Infante Felipe Próspero* (Vienna, Kunsthistorisches Museum), 1.285 × 0.995, and detail.

268. Velázquez, *Philip IV* (Madrid, Museo del Prado), 0.69 × 0.56m.

269. Workshop of Velázquez, *Philip IV in Armor* (Madrid, Museo del Prado, 2.31 × 1.31m.

The second portrait (Plate 264) is generally thought to show the infanta at around five years, or just slightly younger than she appears in *Las Meninas* (Plate 323).[26] Here, her blonde hair hangs loosely over her shoulders and her face has become longer and less full. The final autograph portrait (Plate 265) is probably the one mentioned by Palomino as having been sent to Vienna in 1659.[27] Although the background is much damaged and the canvas reduced in size, the figure remains in good condition and shows the supremely confident technique of Velázquez' last years. Laying and over-laying broad, dragging strokes of the heavily loaded brush, he creates the brilliant, shimmering surface of the blue satin dress. Specks of high-keyed pigments are deposited almost as if at random on the gold and enameled chain worn over the left shoulder. By means of this magical freedom of execution, Velázquez glorifies the medium as much as the subject.

Also sent to Vienna in 1659 was a portrait of Prince Felipe Próspero (Plate 266), the frail heir to the throne who lived but four years (28 November 1657–1 November 1661).[28] It may be that the knowledge of the imminent demise of the little prince influences our perception of the portrait, yet a comparison with the *Portrait of Baltasar Carlos and a Dwarf* (Plate 96) suggests that the artist, too, was acknowledging the dynastic crisis facing Philip IV. Felipe Próspero wears amulets against the evil eye and is accompanied by a small, watery-eyed lapdog (Plate 267). Not even the incomparable execution of the picture can dispel the faint but unshakable atmosphere of gloom which pervades it.

The late portraits of Philip IV are also sometimes interpreted as psychological records of a defeated and dispirited monarch. But this idea seems to be contradicted by the large number of copies based on two prototype portraits created in the 1650s, which suggests that they were intended as official images and not as the artist's subjective impression of his monarch's state of mind and body.[29] The effect is probably the result of an uncompromising depiction of Philip's advancing age and of the austere composition of the pictures. When the head is incorporated into a state portrait of the king in armor, as once was done by the workshop (Plate 269), the cloud of melancholy dissipates.[30]

The first of the prototype portraits is a small, unfinished life study (Plate 268), in which the head is fully modeled while the chest and shoulders are only summarily indicated. The approximate date of execution is indicated by the fact that the picture served as the model for a print of 1655 by the court engraver, Pedro de Villafranca.

A second portrait in the same format (Plate 270) has proved to be a much-debated attribution. Some writers have dismissed the work as a copy of Plate 268, while others believe that it was done by Velázquez a few years later.[31] A partial compromise solution has also been proposed — that the head alone was painted by Velázquez, while the costume was executed by another hand.[32] (There is no doubt that the image was approved by the king because it was copied over and over again; in fact, no portrait of Philip ever generated so many imitations.) On the whole, it can be accepted that the king looks older in this portrait; the incipient sagging of the skin, especially around the eyes, has now become a visible reality. Thus, the picture should be considered as an independent work which was done to satisfy the king's preference for true-to-life portraits. Another engraving by Villafranca, this one of 1657, indicates that the model was executed before that date.

Yet these extrinsic considerations are not conclusive about the authenticity of the portrait, which thus becomes a matter of individual judgment of style. On this basis, it can be said that the painting of the costume and chain is decidedly inferior to Velázquez' other royal portraits of the period. But this still leaves room for a compromise solution; namely, that he merely outlined this part of the figure, much as he did in the earlier version, which was then completed by another painter. As for the head, this seems to be painted in a smoother, less focused manner than in Plate 268, although the abrasion of the surface is partly responsible for the effect. This manner of painting heads is not unknown in the very late works of Velázquez' life. For instance, a comparable treatment is found in the 1659 *Portrait of the Infanta Margarita* (Plate 265). It is therefore probable

270. Velázquez, *Philip IV* (London, National Gallery),
0.641 × 0.537m.

that the first as well as the second late portrait of Philip IV was executed by the master.

These portraits, plus a small group of subject pictures to be discussed in the final chapter, constitute the known production of the artist between his return from Italy in June 1651 and his death in August 1660. But they do not constitute all of his artistic activity. As suggested above, a substantial part of Velázquez' energies was devoted to his work as a designer and decorator. Immediately upon arriving in Madrid, he began the task of refurbishing the Alcázar. But it might be more convenient to postpone the discussion of this project, even at the risk of disturbing chronological order, to consider the other important focus of Velázquez' work as court decorator, El Escorial. In this way, we are afforded a more coherent view of the major decorations executed under his supervision.

During the first four decades of his reign, Philip IV seems to have made little use of the royal quarters of El Escorial. We can only speculate on the reasons for this fact, but certainly the speculations would take into account that the building constructed by Philip II, the king's grandfather, was not an ideal place to indulge in the delights of the senses favored by the youthful monarch. Not only did the daunting spirit of the Prudent King hang heavy over the place, but El Escorial was a religious retreat little suited to an urban creature like Philip IV.

But during the 1640s, Philip began to put El Escorial on his itinerary of country

271. Pantheon, El Escorial.

seats. One reason for this decision was the emergence of his latent religiosity, which is documented in the extraordinary letters written to Sor María de Ágreda, a member of a convent of Discalced Nuns of the Order of the Immaculate Conception, with whom the king faithfully corresponded from 1643 to the end of his life.[33] Historians of Philip's reign have often noted the profound differences between the first and second half, drawing the dividing line at the year 1643, when Olivares left the government. The fall of Olivares meant the end of a vigorous if unsuccessful policy to restore Spain to its former greatness and power. Thereafter, the king attempted to prevent further loss of territory or prestige, an attempt which, in the end, was also doomed to fail. In the correspondence with Sor María, we can see how adverse circumstances, both personal and political, encouraged the development of a morbid fatalism which, among its consequences, would have made El Escorial seem a more congenial place. In addition, El Escorial housed the Royal Pantheon (Plate 271), a crypt located beneath the high altar of the church, which had been designated by Philip II the burial place for his father, himself, and all future rulers of Spain. As Philip's religiosity intensified, so must his thoughts have turned to the last things and thence to El Escorial and its Pantheon.

Although Philip II and his architect, Juan de Herrera, had included the crypt in their plans for El Escorial, the construction was not begun until late in the reign of Philip III.[34] Work commenced in 1618–19, when plans were drawn and contracts let. The design was prepared by the court architect, Juan Gómez de Mora, and the interior decoration, which was to consist of gilt bronze ornament over marble revetment, was assigned to the Italian artist-courtier, Giovanni Battista Crescenzi. Slow but continual progress was made during the early years of Philip IV's reign, but in 1630, the work inexplicably came to a halt. Perhaps the building and decoration of the Retiro and the Torre de la Parada diverted interest and money from the Pantheon. Whatever the reason, workers returned to the site in 1638, but little was done except to pave the floor.

It was not until 1645 that Philip turned his full attention to the project.[35] By then, the waters of an underground spring had invaded the site, necessitating the removal of the pavement and a good deal of repair work. It was also decided to improve the illumination of the airless chamber by opening windows in the lunettes of the cupola. Overseeing the work at the site was an enterprising friar, Nicolás de Madrid, who found a way to staunch the flow of water and who directed construction according to the designs provided by a new architect, Alonso Carbonel. Above the team of artists and supervisors was the king, who considered and approved every detail of the work, much as his grandfather had done during the building of El Escorial itself.

231

278 (facing page top left). Titian, *Virgin and Child with Sts. Anthony and Roch* (Madrid, Museo del Prado), 0.92 × 1.3m.

279 (facing page top right). Titian, *Virgin and Child with Sts. Dorothy and George* (Madrid, Museo del Prado), 0.86 × 0.130m.

275. Sacristy, El Escorial.

276. Veronese, *Crucifixion* (Madrid, Museo del Prado).

made [for all the pictures]."[47] When Philip paid a visit to El Escorial on 17 October to see what had been done, he could only have been well-pleased.

The sacristy is comprised of two parts — the long, narrow space with cupboards for vestments (Plate 275), and the ante-sacristy, which is immediately adjacent and links the basilica to the sacristy proper. Before Velázquez began to work, the rooms were filled with an eclectic, uneven group of pictures.[48] In the ante-sacristy were two canvases by Titian, *St. Margaret* (El Escorial) and the *Agony in the Garden* (Prado no. 436), and a Flemish painting, *St. Jerome* (Prado no. 2099), given variously to Quentin and Jan Massys.[49] All of these, even the works by Titian, were removed and replaced by a superb array of canvases by sixteenth-century Venetian painters and their artistic descendants. By Titian was the *Rest on the Flight into Egypt* (Plate 277).[50] Veronese was represented by four pictures, of which survive the *Adoration of the Magi* (El Escorial, Nuevos Museos) and the *Crucifixion* (Plate 276). Rubens and Van Dyck, who were considered the legitimate heirs of the Venetians, were also present. Rubens' *Supper at Emmaus* (Prado no. 1643), acquired by the king from the painter's estate, was accompanied by a now-lost painting of the *Virgin and Child Adored by St. Mary Magdalene and Two Saints* by Van Dyck.[51]

After this introduction came the collection of the sacristy — thirty-two paintings which covered almost all the available wallspace. When Velázquez began the re-

277. Titian, *Rest on the Flight into Egypt* (El Escorial, Nuevos Museos).

234

280. Van Dyck, *Christ and the Adulterous Woman* (Madrid, Hospital de la Venerable Orden Tercera), 2.00 × 2.35m.

281. Titian, *Christ Mocked* (Madrid, Museo del Prado), 0.99 × 0.98m.

installation, the room contained just over twenty pictures. Four of these were attributed to Titian, including the *Virgin and Child* (Munich, Alte Pinakothek) and *St. Catherine*, now given to Palma the Younger (Prado no. 447).[52] A painting by Luini of the *Holy Family* (Prado no. 242) rounded out the Italian contingent. Then there was a group of Flemish primitives, the best of which were the famous paintings by Roger van der Weyden, the *Descent from the Cross* (Prado no. 2825) and the *Crucifixion* (El Escorial). Finally, there were six paintings by Juan Pantoja de la Cruz, court painter to Philip III, depicting the statues of the royal family by Leone Leoni which flanked the main altar of the church.[53]

Velázquez' conception for the new decoration was based first on consistency of taste, (omitting the obvious consideration of religious subject matter), which meant the removal of the works by the Flemish primitives and the Spaniard. Instead, he concentrated on making the room into a gallery of great Italian masters of the sixteenth and seventeenth century. An exception was made only for Van Dyck, but even this exception was not inconsistent with the general stylistic preference. The star of the show, as always, was Titian, who was represented by ten pictures. Then there were three apiece by Tintoretto and Raphael, two apiece by Reni, Veronese, Van Dyck, and Sebastiano del Piombo, and one each by Correggio, Giorgione, Annibale Carracci, Andrea del Sarto, Schiavone, Palma Giovane, Serodine, and Cambiaso. By a stroke of good luck, all but three or four of these pictures have survived, although the ensemble was dismantled long ago. But armed with de los Santos' text, we can partly revive the appearance of this treasurehouse of painting.

The sacristy was entered through a door at the north, above which hung three paintings; in the center was Van Dyck's *Christ and the Adulterous Woman*[54] (Plate 280), flanked by Titian's *Virgin and Child with Sts. Catherine and John* (London, National Gallery), a picture given to Philip by Niccolò Ludovisi, and a painting then attributed to Giorgione but now thought to be by Titian, the *Virgin and Child with Sts. Anthony and Roch* (Plate 278), a present to the king from the duke of Medina de las Torres.[55] On the opposite wall, above the altar, was the *Holy Family* (Prado no. 308), attributed variously to Raphael and Giulio Romano (Plate 247), which had come from the collection of Charles I.[56] On either side were paintings by Titian, *Christ Mocked* (Plate 281), and the *Virgin and Child with Sts. Dorothy and George* (Plate 279), both of which had been at El Escorial since the reign of Philip II.[57]

The east and west walls were crowded with masterpieces, too, of which a selection must necessarily be made. In the center of the west wall, in the lower zone, was Tintoretto's large-scale picture of *Christ Washing the Feet of the Apostles* (Plate 250), one of the gems of Charles I's collection. Paintings by Titian were abundant: there were five by his hand, including the *Tribute Money* (London, National Gallery) and the *Agony in the Garden* (Prado no. 436), both commissioned by Philip II.[58] The High Renaissance

282 (above left). Raphael, *Visitation* (Madrid, Museo del Prado), 2.00 × 1.45m.

283 (above center). Correggio, *Noli me Tangere* (Madrid, Museo del Prado), 1.30 × 1.03m.

284 (above right). Annibale Carracci, *Assumption of the Virgin* (Madrid, Museo del Prado), 1.30 × 0.97m.

285. Guido Reni, *Virgin and Child* (Raleigh, North Carolina Museum of Art), 1.14 × 0.92m.

was represented by Raphael's *Visitation* (Plate 282), of uncertain provenance; Andrea del Sarto's *Madonna della Scala* (Plate 246), acquired at the Commonwealth sale; and Correggio's *Noli Me Tangere* (Plate 283).[59] also a Ludovisi picture which had been brought to the king by Monterrey. Finally, there was a sampling of Italian Baroque classicism, with Annibale Carracci's *Assumption of the Virgin* (Plate 284)[60] thought to have been purchased for the king by the count of Monterrey, and two works by Guido Reni, the *Virgin and Child* (Plate 285), probably purchased from the admiral of Castile, and *St. Joseph and the Christ Child* (Leningrad, Hermitage).

On the facing wall, the pictures were fewer in number but no less distinguished in quality. Among the works by Titian were *St. John in the Desert* (El Escorial), of uncertain provenance, and the *Christ on the Cross* (El Escorial), acquired by Philip II.[61] Raphael's *Madonna della Tenda* (Plate 286), purchased by Cárdenas in London, hung beneath a picture by the one non-Italian master represented in the room, Van Dyck's *St. Jerome* (Rotterdam, Boymans Museum), an acquisition from the estate of Peter Paul Rubens.[62]

The pictures are now widely scattered, many of them having left Spain in the tumultuous years of the early nineteenth century, when French generals and English picture dealers took advantage of unsettled conditions to enrich their collections and pocketbooks.[63] The only visual record of the appearance of the room in the seventeenth century is found in the background of a picture famous in its own right, Claudio Coello's *Charles II Adoring the Host* (*La Sagrada Forma*) (Plate 287) executed around 1690, which is set in the sacristy and shows the north wall as it looked in 1656. Titian's painting of the *Virgin and Child with Sts. Anthony and Roch* and most of Van Dyck's *Christ and the Adulterous Woman* are just visible on the rear wall. But already by this time, the installation had been altered, because the view of the east wall no longer conforms to the description of de los Santos. And, of course, the reconstruction of the south wall in a late Baroque style further destroyed the harmony of Velázquez' installation.

The selection of pictures for the sacristy made by the artist and the king proves that they were keen connoisseurs. It also underscores the conservative characteristic of their taste, which was biased toward Venetian painting. As far as they were concerned, the history of the art concluded with the work of artists born before 1600. Philip collected pictures by what might be called the younger contemporaries, but usually they were not installed in the masterpiece galleries of El Escorial and the Alcázar. The reasons for this prejudice can only be surmised, but perhaps it concerned the still-prevailing opinion that the ownership of works by the acknowledged old masters confers prestige on the owner and calls attention to his exalted position.

236

The next room to be redecorated at El Escorial was the so-called Chapter Room of the Prior, another long narrow space located on the south wing of the main cloister (Plate 288). The date of the new installation is uncertain, but it probably occurred after the sacristy was completed because it is absent from the first edition of de los Santos' description of El Escorial (1657) but included in the second edition (1667).

Velázquez' participation in the project is established by de los Santos. There is also a fascinating but problematic drawing in the Library of the Royal Palace, Madrid, representing a schematic plan of the Prior's Chapter Room (Plate 289). The sheet, which measures 0.455 × 0.75m., shows the main architectural features of the room, all duly labeled in brown ink. The walls, however, have been ruled into squares, and inside the squares are inscriptions in a different ink and a different hand, which give the title of a picture and the author. All the subjects thus identified coincide with the ones mentioned by de los Santos. When this drawing was discovered, a similarity was noted between the handwriting within the squares and the handwriting of Velázquez.[64] Thus, it was suggested that it was an autograph plan for the re-installation of the Chapter Room.

This hypothesis is attractive, for it would entitle the drawing to a place among the important documents of Velázquez' life. But it is difficult to substantiate. There can be

286 (above). Raphael, *Madonna della Tenda* (Munich, Alte Pinakothek), 0.66 × 0.51m.

288 (top right). Chapter Room of the Prior, El Escorial.

289 (bottom right). Plan of the Chapter Room of the Prior, El Escorial (Madrid, Palacio de Oriente, Biblioteca), 0.455 × 0.75m.

287 (below). Claudio Coello, *La Sagrada Forma* (El Escorial Sacristy), 5.00 × 3.00m.

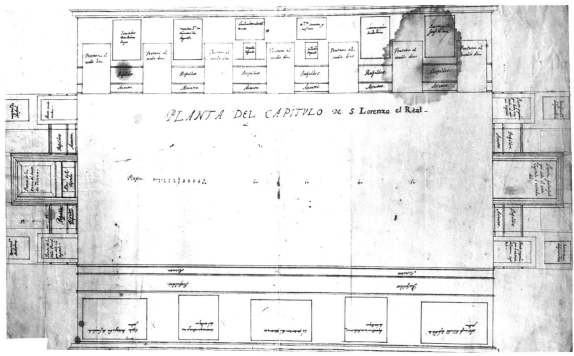

PLANTA DEL CAPITVLO de S. Lorenzo el Real.

290 (right). Van Dyck, *Christ Crowned with Thorns* (Madrid, Museo del Prado), 2.23 × 1.71m.

291 (far right). Van Dyck, *Pietà* (Madrid, Museo del Prado), 2.01 × 1.71m.

292. Guido Reni, *Madonna of the Chair* (Madrid, Museo del Prado), 2.12 × 1.37m.

293. Ribera, *St. Alexis* (Madrid, Museo del Prado), 2.02 × 1.46m.

no doubt that the handwriting style belongs to the seventeenth century. And it does seem logical that a diagram of this sort would have been used to plan the installation and review it with the king. Furthermore, on the part of the drawing corresponding to the east wall, there are faint traces in chalk or pencil of two squares flanking the altar, which are accompanied by dimensions of the height from the cornice to the top of the benches and the width from the frame surrounding the altar to the lintel of the door. These markings suggest that the plan really was a working drawing rather than a record made after the fact.

But the authorship of the plan is still not proved. Comparisons with Velázquez' handwriting, although difficult to make because of the fragmentary nature of the inscriptions, do not favor the attribution. Also, one of the artists is wrongly identified. On the north wall is a label which reads "el centurión del Tintoreto," which refers to the painting of *Christ and the Centurion*, a characteristic work of Paolo Veronese (Plate 253). Velázquez, as we have seen, was not a flawless connoisseur of old pictures, and could therefore conceivably have erred in naming the author of this work. It is also possible that the writer made a careless error. But, on balance, it seems prudent to regard the drawing as a type which Velázquez could have made to plan the installation of a picture gallery rather than a drawing surely made by him for this purpose.

The Chapter Room was hung with eighteen pictures by Italian and Flemish masters, with seventeenth-century artists somewhat better represented here than in the sacristy.[65] Above the altar was Titian's *Agony in the Garden* (El Escorial), the only picture by this master in the room.[66] To the right and left were Raphael's *Madonna of the Rose* (Plate 249), another acquisition from the collection of Charles I, and Rubens' *Holy Family with St. Anne* (Prado no. 1639). Opposite, on the west wall, were two small paintings by Guercino, *St. Jerome* (lost) and *St. Thomas* (El Escorial). Along the north wall was a series of five large paintings, two by Van Dyck and two by Palma Giovane flanking a picture by Veronese in the center. The pictures by Palma, which were yet again English acquisitions, were placed at either end of the wall; these were the *Conversion of St. Paul* and the *David with Head of Goliath* (Plates 251, 252). Next to each of them was a painting by Van Dyck, *Christ Crowned with Thorns* (Plate 290), a purchase from the Rubens sale, and the *Pietà* (Plate 291), of unknown provenance.[67] Veronese's splendid *Christ in the House of the Centurion* (Plate 253), formerly the possession of the earl of Arundel, provided a fitting climax to the composition of this wall.

The pictures on the south wall were more heterogeneous, although the level of quality was by no means inferior. Undoubtedly the most spectacular was Rubens' *Virgin of the Immaculate Conception* (Plate 243), a gift to the king from the marquis of Leganés.[68] Another excellent picture by a seventeenth-century painter was Guido's *Madonna of the Chair* (Plate 292). Also by Guido were two small heads of St. Peter and

238

294. Titian, *Gloria* (Madrid, Museo del Prado), 3.46 × 2.40m.

St. Paul (Prado nos. 219–220), which were placed beneath a lost picture by Veronese and another questionable work by the same artist, *Christ and the Adulterous Woman* (Prado no. 495). The only canvas by a Spanish artist chosen to hang in this company was by Jusepe de Ribera, who qualified because his style was thoroughly Italianate. We know, however, that Ribera was genuinely admired by Philip and Velázquez because they installed his paintings in places of honor in the Alcázar. Ribera's painting in the Chapter Room represents St. Alexis (Plate 293), although it is usually misnamed *St. James Major*.[69]

Adjacent to the Chapter Room of the Prior was the Chapter Room of the Vicar. De los Santos mentions that this, too, was redecorated during the last years of Philip's reign. However, he goes on to say that the king died just at the moment when some of the pictures were being gathered at the Alcázar, and that the installation was carried out under the regency of his widow, Queen Mariana. The selection of pictures described by de los Santos, many of which are still in existence, seems to conform to canons of Philip's taste, but given the fact that neither he nor Velázquez was alive to supervise the final selection and installation, it seems prudent to exclude this room from the discussion.

Finally, de los Santos mentions one more room which was decorated by Velázquez. This is the Aula de Escritura, or Aullila, a small reading room in the confines of the monastery used by the friars for the study of theology. The decoration is described in the first edition of de los Santos' book, indicating that the installation had been completed by 1657.[70] Given the small dimensions of the space, only twelve paintings could fit on the walls. According to de los Santos, seven had been transferred from other parts of El Escorial, the others being gifts of Philip IV. In the decoration of the Aullila, the pro-Venetian taste of Philip and Velázquez once more shines forth like a beacon. There were four works by Titian, three by Veronese, and one apiece by Tintoretto, Palma, Cambiaso, Raphael, and the Spaniard, Navarrete el Mudo, whose picture, however, is essentially a free version of Titian's *Martyrdom of St. Lawrence* (El Escorial).

The paintings by Titian included the famous *Gloria* (Plate 294), painted for Charles V, and the *Entombment* (Plate 295), a donation of Philip IV.[71] Veronese was represented by the *Martyrdom of St. Menas* (Plate 296), which had come into the royal collection as a gift of the admiral of Castile, a former viceroy of Naples, and the *Annunciation* (Plate 297), a painting commissioned by Philip II as a trial piece for the high altar of

295. Titian, *Entombment* (Madrid, Museo del Prado), 1.30 × 1.68m.

296 (right). Veronese, *Martyrdom of St. Menas* (Madrid, Museo del Prado), 2.48 × 1.82m.

297 (far right). Veronese, *Annunciation* (El Escorial, Nuevos Museos), 4.40 × 1.90m.

298. Tintoretto, *Nativity* (El Escorial, Nuevos Museos), 4.32 × 1.89m.

the church of El Escorial. Tintoretto's eccentric *Nativity* (Plate 298) had also been acquired in this way. Finally, there was the obligatory Raphael, the *Madonna of the Fish* (Plate 245), the painting forcibly acquired by Medina de las Torres from the Dominican church in Naples.[72] The effect of seeing so many masterpieces in a small room must have been overwhelming, suggesting that de los Santos was not exaggerating when he wrote, "All these pictures are in measured correspondence with each other, adorning the walls of the study so that it is as much a place to learn about painting as about Scripture."[73]

From the perspective of the late twentieth century, it may seem a pity that Velázquez spent so much time, effort, and thought in organizing these spectacular displays of pictures. Inevitably, as fashions and circumstances changed, the ensembles were first altered and then dispersed, leaving us entirely at the mercy of reproductions and reconstructions to recreate one of the major enterprises of his last years. How much better it would have been had the artist stayed at his easel, where he belonged, and created great masterpieces to delight the eye!

No one could disagree with this melancholy thought. But we must try to understand Velázquez' decision to employ his talents as a decorator, and to respect what he achieved in this endeavour. First, as the loyal servant of a king who had become a passionate, almost obsessive collector, he had little choice about how he would spend the hours of his workday. There is also good reason to believe that by the 1650s the relationship between the two men had evolved into something like a friendship, although the word is admittedly hard to use for a person like Philip IV. The collaboration between this great painter and this great collector must have been a source of enjoyment and satisfaction to them both. It is also worth remembering that decorative projects did bring a set of artistic talents into play. Velázquez had to be a connoisseur, deciding important questions of attribution. He also had to be able to compose (the word often used by de los Santos) combinations of pictures which would be right for the place and right in relationship to each other.

But most importantly, he was given responsibility for creating a splendid setting for the royal majesty of Philip IV. This point emerges repeatedly in the writings of contemporaries who commented on his work as court decorator. Lázaro Díaz, writing in 1656, claimed that he had transformed the Alcázar into the ninth wonder of the world: "Undoubtedly, no other prince in this world has a palace so [beautifully] adorned with such precious and admirable paintings and statues of bronze and marble, or with such curious, elegant, and luxurious objects."[74] Eleven years later, de los Santos also praised Velázquez for making the palace one of the greatest monarchical dwellings. The decorative projects at El Escorial and the Alcázar were perceived as a great achievement in a society which revolved around the figure and authority of the monarch, and indeed they were. Velázquez had designed a stage for the theater of life, upon which even a failing monarch looked grand and powerful. In a way, it was a masterpiece of Baroque illusionism, in which substance was subsumed into image. And like all Baroque illusions, the result was transient and fleeting, serving to mask reality but not to change it and thus itself subject to the vicissitudes of time and fate.

CHAPTER IX

Velázquez and Philip IV

THE REFURBISHING of the Alcázar, like that of El Escorial, reached a peak in the 1650s, as Philip IV and Velázquez worked to refine and arrange the masterpieces of the royal collection. The king's growing interest in his collection in these years was noted by the Modenese ambassador, who wrote in a letter of 1 January 1652 that "nowadays nothing pleases the king as much as the gift of notable pictures, because his inclination for the art of painting is greater than before."[1] Once in a while, we can catch brief glimpses of Philip's involvement in the decorative projects which slowly transformed the Alcázar into a seat of unsurpassed artistic splendor. On 18 February 1658, the nuncio, Camillo Massimi, wrote that the king was suffering from a fever which he had caught "by having spent a long time on the previous day watching pictures being hung in the summer apartments."[2] On another occasion, the king can be seen discussing the attribution of a painting in the royal chapel with the Italian fresco painter, Angelo Colonna. According to the king's advisors, Rubens and Velázquez, the picture was the work of Annibale Carracci. Colonna thought otherwise and, in what may have been a calculated attempt to demonstrate his superior knowledge of Italian painting, suggested an attribution to Giacomo Cavedone.[3]

These anecdotes show that fine pictures were the principal avocation of the aging monarch. It is of course possible to understand the king's dedication to his collection as a form of escapism, and no doubt this played a part in his growing interest in art. But it would be unfair to say this and no more, because Philip's love of painting was famous among those who observed him at close range. It must also be remembered that the spectacular displays of masterpieces were a statement of royal majesty. As de los Santos observed, writing in 1667, "only the power of such great rulers [he refers also to Mariana] could achieve the collecting of these pictures, gathering them from every part of the world, without heed for the great cost and expense. . . ."[4]

Velázquez' work as a court decorator thus had two aspects. First, and most obvious, was what might be called the curatorial function, which involved him in matters of connoisseurship, selection, and restoration. Second was the design function, which involved him in arranging the pictures in groups that suited their settings and, above all, inspired admiration for their owner, his patron.

The assessment of the methods employed and the results obtained in the Alcázar is unfortunately handicapped by the nearly total lack of contemporary views of the interior. In fact, the best evidence comes from an unexpected source, *Las Meninas* (Plate 323), a painting about which more will soon be said. Although it may seem irreverent to put Velázquez' masterpiece to such a prosaic use, nevertheless, the picture contains one of the few representations of the interior of the Alcázar in the seventeenth century. The room depicted in *Las Meninas* is in the prince's quarters. Following the death of Baltasar Carlos in 1646, his apartment was redecorated and partially allocated to Velázquez for use as an atelier.[5] The room shown in the picture, called the Galería de Cuarto del Príncipe, was adjacent to the atelier and was decorated mostly with copies after Rubens by Juan del Mazo, Velázquez' son-in-law.

299. Titian, *Federico Gonzaga* (Madrid, Museo del Prado), 1.25 × 0.99m.

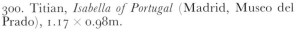

300. Titian, *Isabella of Portugal* (Madrid, Museo del Prado), 1.17 × 0.98m.

Comparison of the identifiable paintings seen in *Las Meninas* with the palace inventory of 1686 has established that Velázquez faithfully reproduced the appearance of the gallery as it looked in the 1650s.[6] The first thing to notice is the uniform frames. Payments to carpenters and eyewitness descriptions show that this discreet type of frame, painted either gold or black, was used to unify the decor of a given room. The second point is the clever combination of pictures of diverse sizes. The rear wall contains two large canvases symmetrically disposed, and two smaller paintings to the left and right of each door. On the side wall, the pictures are accommodated in a three-tier arrangement, in which the small canvases are hung progressively higher, culminating in a cornice-like group of Flemish landscapes at the top.

Las Meninas also represents another feature of the palace — the cavernous, sparsely furnished spaces. The resulting impression of austere chambers decorated with magnificent hangings and pictures was indelible in the minds of visitors to the Alcázar. A French observer of 1659 can speak for many others:

> The king's palace is large. All the apartments are dimly lit. There are hardly any ornaments in the apartments, except in the salon where the king receives ambassadors. But what is admirable are the pictures of which all the rooms are full, and the superb tapestries, which are much more beautiful than those of the crown of France. . . .[7]

The contrast of opulence and gravity, of luxury and austerity, of wealth and modesty, lies at the heart of Philip's court style. It was, by any measure, as grand a style of kingship as existed anywhere in Europe at this time. And yet the contrast with other princely courts is striking. The ostentation, color, brilliance, and theatricality usually associated with the Baroque court was conspicuously lacking in Spain. To some extent, the *estilo Felipe IV*, as it may be called, can be characterized as the style of the "old rich," and was based on an outward modesty which lightly concealed the unlimited confidence in God-given status. For all the military and economic catastrophes which befell the monarchy during his reign, Philip IV was the proud heir of the greatest rulers of early modern Europe — Ferdinand and Isabella, the emperor Charles V, and Philip II. And, despite the undoubted decline in Spanish power, the king of Spain still ruled over a world-wide domain. Velázquez captured the essence of the *estilo Felipe IV* in his last portraits of the king (Plates 268, 270), executed in the early 1650s. These pictures embody the king's magnificent reticence, which he so carefully cultivated all his life long, and it is this quality which the king and his artist-decorator transmitted to the decoration of the royal palace in the 1650s.

The redecoration of the Alcázar happened simultaneously in several rooms, because the transfer of pictures and sculpture necessitated a constant reshuffling of the decorative ensembles.[8] Thus in 1652, documents refer to work in progress in three different sectors. One of these, the Galería del Mediodía, or South Gallery, which was the largest room on the main floor of the south façade, was designed essentially as a portrait gallery.[9] It contained sixty-nine pictures, fifty-seven of which were portraits. Unlike many royal portrait galleries, however, the South Gallery was not exclusively dedicated to family pictures, although some were included. Rather the emphasis seems to have been on great examples of portraiture, as seen by the fact that almost two-thirds of the works were by or attributed to Titian and Tintoretto.

Among the works by Titian were the twelve portraits of Roman Emperors, which had been acquired at Charles I's sale.[10] (These pictures, along with many of those in the south wing, were victims of the disastrous fire of 1734, which did more damage here than in any other part of the palace.) Also by Titian were the *Portrait of Federico Gonzaga* (Plate 299), a gift from the marquis of Leganés, *Philip II in Armor* (Prado no. 411), *Charles V with Hound* (Plate 68), given by Philip to Prince Charles and then reacquired from his estate, and *Isabella of Portugal* (Plate 300).[11] Most of the other portraits have been lost, but the room also contained the two paintings by Veronese which Velázquez had acquired in Venice in 1651 (Plates 241, 242).

Better preserved are the paintings in the Galería del Cierzo, or North Gallery, which

301 (above left). Rubens, *Judgment of Paris* (Madrid, Museo del Prado), 0.91 × 1.14m.

302 (above right). Rubens, *Diana and Callisto* (Madrid, Museo del Prado), 2.02 × 3.23m.

was dedicated to the works of masters of the seventeenth century, with a sprinkling of earlier pictures.[12] Flemish paintings were in the majority, with Rubens leading the contingent. Among his works were the early *Judgment of Paris* (Plate 301), *Diana and Callisto* (Plate 302), the *Portrait of Anne of Austria* (Prado no. 1689) and the *Portrait of Marie de' Medici* (Prado no. 1685), both acquired at the estate sale. Seventeenth-century Italian paintings were fewer in number, but there were at least two authentic masterpieces — Reni's *Atalanta and Hippomenes* (Plate 303) and Annibale Carracci's *Venus and Adonis* (Plate 304). Last but not least was a small group of Spanish paintings, which tend to be conspicuous by their absence from the principal rooms of the Alcázar. (Except for Velázquez and Ribera, Philip tended to shun the paintings of his Spanish subjects.) These included three portraits by El Greco, and Velázquez' first major mythological painting, the *Feast of Bacchus* (Plate 69).

The North Gallery was adorned also with sculpture, specifically ten plaster casts of antique statues which had been commissioned by Velázquez during his second Italian trip. These pieces were placed between the eleven windows which looked out to the north and, in conjunction with the paintings, produced an imitation of the typical

303 (below left). Guido Reni, *Atalanta and Hippomenes* (Madrid, Museo del Prado), 2.06 × 2.97m.

304 (below right). Annibale Carracci, *Venus and Adonis* (Madrid, Museo del Prado), 2.12 × 2.68m.

305. Galleria Colonna, Rome, Palazzo Colonna.

306. Titian, *Worship of Venus* (Madrid, Museo del Prado), 1.72 × 1.75m.

307. Titian, *Bacchanal of the Andrians* (Madrid, Museo del Prado), 1.75 × 1.93m.

311 (facing page bottom left). Tintoretto, *Judith and Holofernes* (Madrid, Museo del Prado), 0.98 × 3.25m.

312 (facing page bottom right). Veronese, *Christ Disputing with the Doctors* (Madrid, Museo del Prado), 2.36 × 4.30m.

seventeenth-century Italian *galleria*.[13] In fact, the effect can be visualized by looking at the Galleria Colonna in the Palazzo Colonna, Rome (Plate 305), which is somewhat later in date than the North Gallery in the Alcázar. Nowhere in the palace does the Italian influence on Velázquez' decorative work appear as evident as it does here.

A third area which underwent redecoration in the early 1650s was the one known as Bóvedas del Tiziano, or the Titian Vaults,[14] which were located on the groundfloor of the south wing. During the life of Baltasar Carlos, this section had been used as the kitchen of the prince's quarters. Shortly after his death in 1646, the room was remodeled and eventually became the site of a dazzling array of pictures dedicated to the representation of the female figure. As was fitting, eighteen pictures by Titian were the focal point of the arrangement, which comprised thirty-eight paintings in all. In the first instance, the *Poesie* were removed from the summer quarters in the north wing and placed here, along with *Adam and Eve* (Plate 80), *Tarquin and Lucretia* (Cambridge, Fitzwilliam Museum), and *Venus and Cupid with Organist* (Plate 216). To these were added the *Worship of Venus* and the *Bacchanal of the Andrians* (Plates 306, 307), and *Venus and an Organist* (Prado no. 420), which had been purchased at the sale of Charles I.[15] Most of the other paintings in this room attributed to Titian were casualties of the 1734 fire.

Among the companions of the works by Titian were other masterpieces in the same lush, sensuous vein; for instance, Rubens' *Three Graces* (Plate 308) and Jordaens' *Nymphs Bathing* (Plate 309). Philip and Velázquez even managed to find a painting by Albrecht Dürer which would fit the requirements of this room (Plate 310), a present to the king from Christina of Sweden. In addition, there were pictures by Veronese, Cambiaso, Zuccaro, and Ribera, all devoted to representing paragons of feminine beauty. It would be tempting to speculate on the king's motives for assembling this gallery of beauties, but we must now turn our attention to a sterner subject.

The final phase of Velázquez' work as a court decorator revolves around a political event of great significance — the arrangement of peace between Spain and France. The two countries had been at war since 1635, a war that had inexorably turned against Spain, especially after the alliance of England and France in 1654. In May 1659, an armistice was at last arranged, followed by the negotiations for a peace treaty, known as the Peace of the Pyrenees, which was concluded on the French–Spanish border in June 1660. In the space of the year between the armistice and the treaty, two important

244

308 (right). Rubens, *Three Graces* (Madrid, Museo del Prado), 2.21 × 1.81m.

309 (far right). Jacob Jordaens, *Nymphs Bathing* (Madrid, Museo del Prado), 1.31 × 1.27m.

310 (below). Albrecht Dürer, *Eve* (Madrid, Museo del Prado), 2.09 × 0.80m.

state events took place which required Velázquez to design settings for the king. A close look at these ceremonies helps us to see the unusual alliance of art and etiquette which formed the essence of the *estilo Felipe IV*.

As part of the negotiation between the two nations, which was conducted by Luis de Haro and Cardinal Mazarin, a marriage was arranged between Philip's daughter, the infanta María Teresa, and his nephew, the young king of France, Louis XIV. In the autumn of 1659, a delegation of Frenchmen, led by the marshal-duke of Gramont, departed for Spain to petition the king for the princess' hand in marriage.[16] Preparations for the reception of the embassy appear to have begun soon after the armistice was declared and were centered on the decoration of a room already discussed — the Hall of Mirrors.

The appearance of this chamber is partly recorded in a series of royal portraits done by Carreño de Miranda, which are set within its walls. For example, a portrait of the dowager queen Mariana (Plate 314) shows the eagle-framed mirrors which were executed in the 1640s, and the console tables with lion supports, made in Rome at Velázquez' command in 1650–51. Finally, there is also a glimpse of the pictorial decoration, which had been continually undergoing revision since the 1620s. This was the room where the king decided to receive the French delegation. In anticipation of the event, several changes were effected.

First, attention was paid to the picture collection.[17] By 1658, seven works had been retired from what might be called the "gallery of galleries." These included four by Rubens and one apiece by Domenichino, Van Dyck, and an anonymous artist. In their stead were placed four paintings by Tintoretto, including *Judith and Holofernes* (Plate 311) and the *Battle of Turks and Christians* (Prado no. 399), two by Veronese (Plate 312), and Leandro Bassano's *Forge of Vulcan*, which constituted the Venetian Renaissance contingent. Rubens was in a class by himself as the author of ten pictures. Other seventeenth-century masters included Ribera and Orazio Gentileschi (Plate 215).

313. Velázquez, *Mercury and Argus* (Madrid, Museo del Prado), *c.*0.90 × 2.50m (original size).

314. Juan Carreño de Miranda, *Mariana of Austria* (Madrid, Museo del Prado), 2.11 × 1.25m.

315 (facing page). Detail of Plate 313.

And, finally, there was Velázquez, already represented by the *Expulsion of the Moriscos*. In addition, he created four new mythological paintings for the room — *Apollo and Marsyas*, *Venus and Adonis*, *Cupid and Psyche*, and *Mercury and Argus*, the sole survivor of the group. The mere fact that Velázquez painted these four pictures for the Hall of Mirrors deserves comment. By installing his pictures alongside those of Titian, Veronese, Tintoretto, and Rubens, he was purposefully associating himself with a famous artistic tradition and inviting comparison to the works of its greatest proponents. His invitation deserves to be accepted.

The appraisal of *Mercury and Argus* (Plate 313) must begin by referring to certain facts about the original placement and the subsequent changes in its dimensions.[18] According to the palace inventory of 1686, the picture measured about 0.835 meters high by 2.50 meters wide in comparison to its present size of 1.27 × 2.50 meters. The addition to the vertical dimension was made in the late eighteenth century and is clearly visible on the surface of the picture today. Minus the added strip of canvas, the picture is markedly low and horizontal in form, a shape which was determined by the original placement between two windows. Thus situated, the picture could only be seen against the light.[19]

This difficult circumstance encouraged Velázquez to relax his technique. In the picture, the power of painting is equated with the power of suggestion. The sleeping figure of Argus is highlighted while the rest of the composition edges from half-shadow toward darkness. When seen from a distance, the soft gradations of light help to produce convincing, rounded forms which are solidly established in space, but at close range, the canvas is a jumble of inchoate brushstrokes which lie on the surface, at times barely covering the light priming layer. The extraordinary freedom of execution was undoubtedly abetted by the original placement of the picture, but this in itself cannot account for the shortcuts taken by Velázquez. Rather, and especially to eyes conditioned by the experience of modern art, he seems to have arrived intuitively at the understanding of the dual nature of the art of painting, namely its ability simultaneously to create form and to express its own essence. Looking, for instance, at the treatment of the left sleeve of Argus (Plate 315), a typical passage in the painting, we see three or four broad horizontal strokes of a brush loaded with thick, gray-white pigment, which are placed on a layer of darker gray. The purpose of these strokes is to define the folds or creases in the loosely fitting garment, which they do effectively. The marvelous economy of this passage soon draws our attention to the brushstrokes, which become objects of contemplation in their own right. We wonder how Velázquez managed to put the correct amount of pigment on the brush, how he knew where to begin and end the lines, how

317. After Charles LeBrun, *Meeting of Philip IV and Louis XIV at the Isle of Pheasants* (Paris, Mobilier Nationale).

unintentionally said it all. To adorn their side of the room, the French chose four tapestry panels representing Scipio and Hannibal; the Spaniards, intending to represent their ruler as defender of the faith, chose four scenes from the Apocalypse.

This momentous event in the history of Europe was recorded in a tapestry designed by Charles LeBrun (Plate 317), in which the contrast between the French and Spanish styles of kingship is vividly recorded. It was also noticed by Louis himself in a remark he supposedly made to criticize LeBrun's depiction of the king of Spain, which he felt failed to capture Philip's famous dignity and sobriety: "Vous avez peché contre la vérité de l'histoire et sacrifié la gravité espagnole à la civilité française."[29]

It is sometimes said that Velázquez is among the Spanish noblemen portrayed in the tapestry, but this is not true. Yet, if Palomino is to be believed (and much of his account of the sojourn is confirmed by the documents), Velázquez participated in the ceremony, receiving from Louis XIV the watch encrusted with diamonds intended as a gift to Philip IV. Palomino also states that Velázquez was indistinguishable from the members of the high nobility and furnishes this remarkable description of Velázquez' presence at the occasion:

> Don Diego Velázquez was not the one who showed that day least consideration for the adornment, gallantry, and finery of his person; for in addition to his gentlemanly bearing and comportment, which were courtly, not to mention his natural grace and composure, he was distinguished in dress by many diamonds and precious stones. It is not surprising that in the color of his cloth he was superior to many, for he had a better understanding of such things, in which he always showed very good taste. His whole costume was trimmed with rich Milanese silver point lace. On his cloak he wore the red insignia [of Santiago]. At his side was a very fine rapier with silver guard and chape, with exquisitely chased designs in relief made in Italy. Round his neck was a heavy gold chain with a pendant badge adorned with many diamonds, on which was enameled the insignia of Santiago, and the rest of his apparel was worthy of such a precious decoration.[30]

This account is probably richer in poetic truth than in fact, but it is nonetheless suggestive. It indicates that, at least on this occasion, the artist had become his own work of art. More seriously, it reveals that Velázquez' ambition to be recognized as a nobleman

250

318. Velázquez, *Fable of Arachne* (Madrid, Museo del Prado), *c.* 1.70 × 1.90m (original size).

had been crowned with success. The red cross of Santiago proudly displayed on his cape and at his breast was an advertisement of his noble status.

As seen through Palomino's eyes, the final years of Velázquez' life are marked by one personal triumph after another, a progression to fame and fortune ended only by death, just a month after the return from the border, on 6 August 1660. But the documents tell a different story. We have already seen how, in his later years, he turned away from painting and toward the personal service of the king as a way to elevate his status at court. As far as the monarch was concerned, this strategy was a success. But the noblemen of the court were not convinced by his claim to parity, as can be seen in the fascinating documentation of his attempt to gain admission to the Order of Santiago.[31]

Although Velázquez' desire to join a military order first surfaced in 1650, when he sought to enlist the support of the papal secretary of state, the requisite royal nomination was not made until 6 June 1658. Nominations for membership were reviewed by the Council of Military Orders and were subject to an investigation of the candidate's genealogy and social condition. The rules explicitly proscribed "those who themselves, or whose parents or grandparents, have practiced any of the manual or base occupations here described. . . . By manual or base occupation is meant silversmith or painter, if he paints for a living, embroiderer, stonecutter, mason, innkeeper, scribe, except for royal secretaries. . . ." This regulation speaks tellingly about the social status of painting in seventeenth-century Spain and shows why Velázquez, eager as he was for noble status, encountered a conflict between his God-given talents and the man-made hierarchy of the court.

The investigation of Velázquez' credentials began in November 1658 and was concluded on 14 February 1659. During this time, depositions were taken in Madrid, Seville, and in several towns along the Spanish–Portuguese border near the place where Velázquez' ancestors had lived. A total of 148 witnesses gave evidence that he descended from noble stock, which appears to have been a fact, and that he had never accepted money for his paintings, which was patently false. Two weeks later, after considering the testimony, the Council rejected the application on the grounds of unproven nobility. This verdict must have been a shock to Velázquez; the attempt to enhance his prestige had dealt him a humiliating blow. He could only fight on, and fight on he did.

According to the rules, a papal dispensation was now required to excuse the unproven nobility. This was obtained by the king and submitted to the Council which, firm in its determination to exclude a painter from the ranks of noblemen, discovered a new flaw in the genealogy. Once again papal intervention was required, after which Velázquez was redundantly ennobled by the king and admitted to the Order of Santiago on 28 November 1659.

This fascinating episode of pride and prejudice provides a bittersweet conclusion to Velázquez' career as a courtier. And it also furnishes a background for understanding certain aspects of the two masterpieces of his later years, which are arguably his two greatest paintings — the *Fable of Arachne* (*"The Spinners"*) and *Las Meninas*. Although of different subjects, these pictures have certain things in common. First is their position within the trajectory of Velázquez' career: they are the largest, most complicated compositions executed between 1640 and 1660, a period during which Velázquez painted mostly portraits of single figures. Also, they are works of Velázquez' later years: *Las Meninas* cannot have been done much before 1656, while the *Fable of Arachne* is generally, and rightly, dated to the same time.[32] These circumstances, not to mention the incomparable artistry, suggest that Velázquez created the two pictures with a special purpose in mind.

The *Fable of Arachne* (Plate 318) is identical with a work painted for a private client, a court official named Pedro de Arce.[33] Arce was married for a second time in 1664, when an inventory was made of his household. Among his goods was a collection of paintings, which was evaluated by the court engraver, Pedro de Villafranca (the same man who had made prints after Velázquez' late portraits of the king and who therefore was acquainted with the painter). In the inventory, Villafranca identified a painting as the *Fable of Arachne* by Velázquez. The dimensions of this picture are smaller than the work now in the Prado (the discrepancy measures about forty-eight by nineteen centimeters), but even with the naked eye it can be seen that the Prado canvas has been enlarged on all four sides.[34] The original size was approximately the same as that of the work owned by Pedro de Arce.[35] Thus the painting represents the scene of the myth of Arachne described in Book VI of Ovid's *Metamorphoses*.[36]

Once the subject is known, the narrative becomes legible, especially if account is taken of the distortions of scale caused by the additions to the canvas, which diminish the importance of the background scene. In this part of the composition, Velázquez has represented an episode in the contest between Minerva and the mortal weaver, Arachne.[37] Arachne presumptuously had challenged Minerva to a competition to show that she could weave like a goddess. Although the contest ended in a draw, it was in fact a victory for Arachne because her tapestry was judged to be the equal of the one woven by Minerva. To make matters worse, Arachne had been so bold as to insult Minerva by weaving tapestries showing the amorous adventures of Jupiter with mortal women. One of these tapestries, representing the Rape of Europa, decorates the rear wall of the room in the background.

Velázquez' depiction of Ovid's text is unique because it eschews the conclusion of the story, when Minerva converts Arachne into a spider.[38] Instead, the action is stopped at the end of the competition, when the skills of goddess and mortal are declared equal. It is at this critical juncture of the narrative that we find a clue to the interpretation — the scene on the tapestry, which is based on Titian's *Rape of Europa* (Plate 78), a painting then in the Titian Vaults of the Alcázar.[39] In the context of the myth, the choice of model is significant. Arachne's tapestry, which is in fact Titian's painting, has equaled the creation of Minerva. By inserting a quotation of this famous work into the composition, Velázquez implies his belief in the nobility and transcendental value of the art of painting.[40] Titian is equated with Arachne, and Arachne could "paint" like a god.

Velázquez' homage to Titian has another dimension because Titian was the favorite painter of Charles V and Philip II, by whom he had been rewarded with honors and presents.[41] Charles had made Titian a knight of the Golden Spur and Philip II had given him a liberal pension. Therefore, Titian provided an artistic and social paradigm for the elevated status of painting at the court of Spain. By paying tribute to this distinguished predecessor in a style that is profoundly Titianesque, Velázquez claimed a place in the succession of the Venetian master, just as he had done by installing his paintings in the Hall of Mirrors.

The programmatic intention, however, is only part of a picture which is neither a derivative work nor merely a calculated petition for social recognition by an ambitious artist. Rather, it is one of the greatest demonstrations of the art of painting ever achieved. In the *Fable of Arachne*, Velázquez seeks to reconcile the artificial world of the myth with the palpable world of visual reality without sacrificing the decorum required by the one, or the verisimilitude, by the other. This intention must lie behind the decision to depict a casual genre scene in the foreground, while placing the narrative subject at the rear, in a flagrant disregard of the conventional requirement to subordinate secondary incidents to the primary action. The five women who labor at the menial chores of a tapestry workshop bring the picture to life.[42] With unprecedented brilliance of technique, Velázquez depicts the restless work required to transform bundles of wool into threads for weaving. In the softly lit space, the women card, spin, and wind the threads with the absent-minded industry induced by the performance of a routine task. Yet this humble activity is magically transformed into a brilliant artistic illusion. At the left, a woman works at a whirring wheel, the spokes of which fuse into a blur of motion. Velázquez nurtures this sublime effect by placing soft, vaporous highlights within the circumference to suggest the play of fugitive reflections on the nearly transparent surface. On the right, a second woman winds the spun thread into balls. Her fingers are a flurry of brushstrokes which convey the impression of a rapid, fluttering motion (Plate 319). In the center, there is a third figure, sunk in half-shadow, who bends to reach for scraps of wool to supply her carding tool. At her feet, a watchful cat sits, seeming to stare ahead.

Behind this group, in a room flooded with a light from a high window at the left, are the protagonists of the story. This is Arachne's studio, and Velázquez represents the weaver as an elegant artist, visited by women dressed in fine clothing. In imitation of Titian, she works to the sound of musical instruments. The contrast between the foreground, where sturdy women toil at burdensome tasks, and the refined atmosphere of the artist's atelier is perhaps Velázquez' way of implying his conviction about the distinction between craft and art. In this section of the picture, Velázquez uses a sketchy technique which suggests hazy effects of distance and light without sacrificing a sense of corporeality. Despite the damaged state of the canvas, the success of the technique is unmistakable. The contours are softened and the details are blurred by short, impasted strokes. Yet no touch of the brush is wasted or misdirected; every stroke and daub goes instinctively to the right place and confirms the true mastery of the artist. Thus, in the end, the incomparable artistry of the *Fable of Arachne* becomes the most compelling argument for the exalted station of its creator.

Velázquez' claims for himself and his art are even more emphatically advanced in *Las Meninas* (Plate 323).[43] Few paintings in the history of art have generated so many and varied interpretations as this, Velázquez' culminating work. While it is obvious that no single interpretation will ever satisfy every point of view, it is also true that there are certain facts which deserve to be considered by anyone who wishes to understand the picture.

The principal source of information is the well-known description by Antonio Palomino which occurs in Part Three of *El museo pictórico y escala óptica*, published in

319 (following pages). Detail of Plate 318.

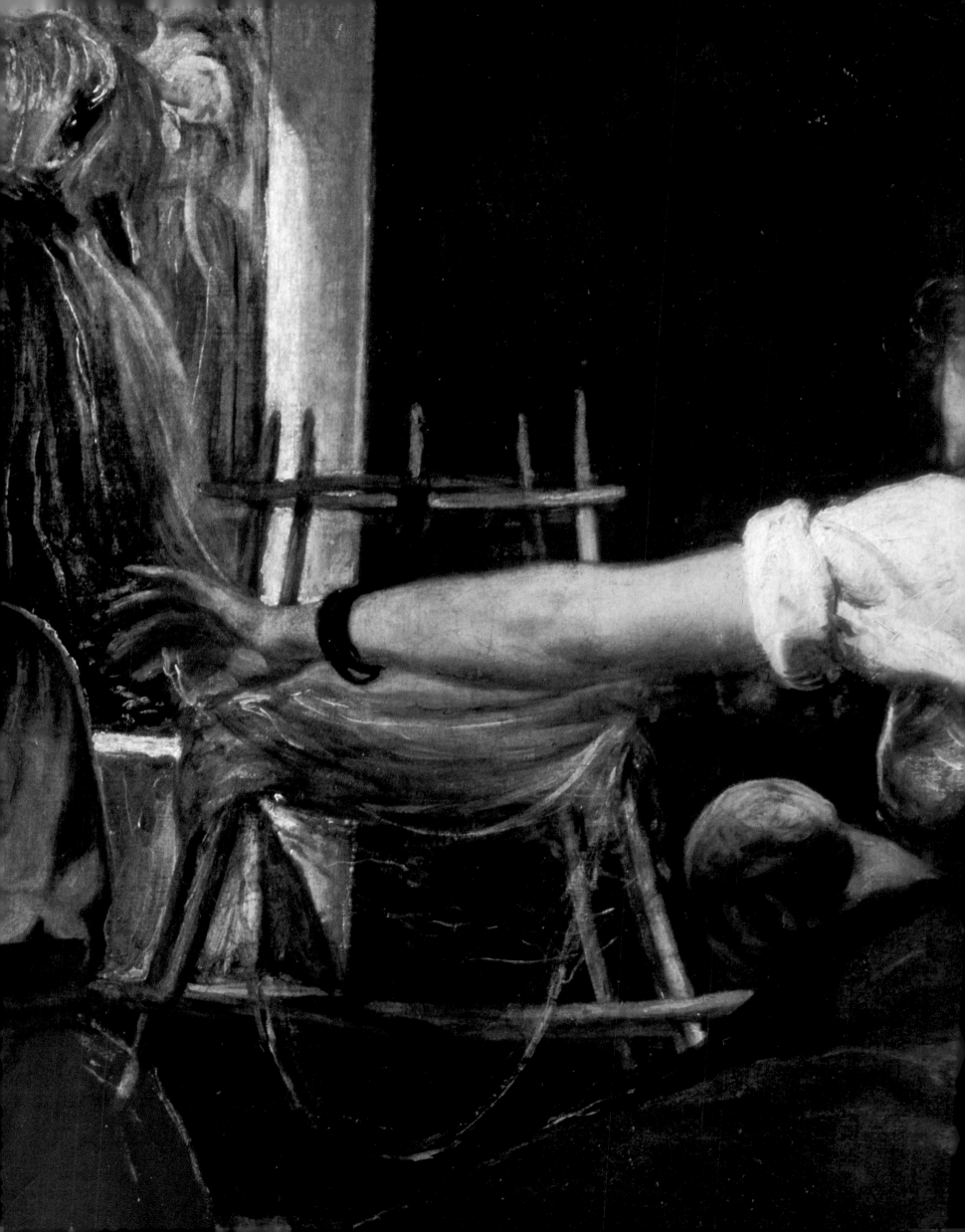

Madrid in 1724. The first thing to note is that the date of publication, sixty-four years after Velázquez' death, is misleading about Palomino's claims to credibility. Palomino died in 1725; thus Part Three, separately entitled *El Parnaso español pintoresco laureado*, narrowly missed becoming a posthumous work. More to the point is the date of his birth, 1655, and of his arrival in Madrid from his native Cordoba, 1678.[44] Palomino came to court just eighteen years after Velázquez died and thus was in a position to talk with people who had known and worked with him. In fact, in the brief introduction to *El Parnaso español*, he states that he had done just that. Recounting the sources of information for his biography of Velázquez, he mentions certain manuscripts and says parenthetically that he added things which "I heard from Carreño and other old men."[45] Carreño, of course, is Juan Carreño de Miranda, who collaborated with Velázquez in the Hall of Mirrors and who testified on the artist's behalf in the investigation of the Council of Military Orders.[46] Carreño survived until 1685 and thus overlapped Palomino's stay at court by seven years. His biography of Carreño establishes that the two men became good friends; indeed, Palomino was present at his deathbed.[47] Carreño is therefore an important link between Velázquez and his biographer.

A second source of information about Velázquez was Juan de Alfaro. Alfaro is today a little-known artist, the first of whose works has only recently been identified.[48] But he played an important part in Palomino's life and thus was given a substantial biography in *El Parnaso español*,[49] where we learn that Alfaro was born in Cordoba and had worked in Velázquez' atelier from about 1650 to 1660. Alfaro died in Madrid in 1680, leaving a set of notes for a planned biography of his master which Palomino was able to use. As Palomino writes, "he [Alfaro] left behind some notes on the life of Velázquez, his master, of Pablo de Céspedes, and of Becerra, which have been of great utility for this work."[50]

Thus, Palomino could rely on two excellent contemporary sources for his information on *Las Meninas*. Furthermore, he would have been able to talk with four of the nine people portrayed in the picture.[51] María Agustina Sarmiento, the *menina* at the left, lived until 1690; Nicolás Pertusato, the male dwarf, until 1710; José Nieto, who stands at the door, until 1684; while the female dwarf, Maribárbola, resided at court until 1700, when she returned to her native Germany. With these participants at his disposal, Palomino was in a position to furnish a reliable account of the picture.

And, indeed, much of what he says can be corroborated by independent evidence. Palomino identifies the setting of the picture as the "prince's chamber, where in fact it was painted. Several paintings can be seen, although not clearly. They are known to be by Rubens and to represent subjects from the Metamorphoses of Ovid." The confirmation of this statement is a simple matter. In the 1686 inventory of the Alcázar there is a description of part of the palace called the "Cuarto bajo que llaman del príncipe que cae a la plazuela de palacio" (the lower quarters called the prince's quarters which face the large square of the palace).[52] As we have seen, following the death of Prince Baltasar Carlos in 1646, part of his apartment was converted to use as the court painter's atelier. According to the inventory, the principal decoration of the gallery of the prince's quarters, known as the "pieza principal," was a series of copies by Juan del Mazo after some of Rubens' pictures for the Torre de la Parada. It has been pointed out that all the pictures reproduced in *Las Meninas* correspond in subject and relative size to the installation described in the 1686 inventory.[53] It has also been possible to identify the room in the plan of the palace made in 1626 by Juan Gómez de Mora (Plate 321), the only differences being a non-load-bearing wall which was removed after the death of the prince, and a second door. Except for the mistaken attribution of the author of the paintings seen in the room, Palomino is correct on these points, too.

Next is the identity of the figures: Palomino names everyone but the man dressed in black standing in the middleground, who is referred to only as a *guardadamas*. All the others were historical personages who lived at the time the picture was painted and occupied the positions in the household to which they are assigned by Palomino.[54]

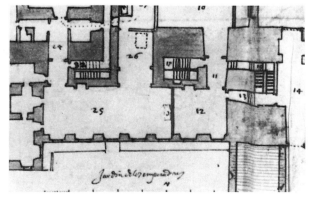

320. Gallery of Prince's Quarters, Alcázar of Madrid, from Juan Gómez de Mora's plan of Alcázar, 1626.

321 (above left). Detail of Plate 323.

322 (above right). Detail of Plate 323.

Therefore, in addition to the infanta and the artist, there is every reason to believe that the *meninas* are María Agustina Sarmiento and Isabel de Velasco; that the dwarfs are Maribárbola and Pertusato; that the *aposentador*, seen in the door, is José Nieto, and that the woman in widow's weeds is Marcela Ulloa. As far as can be told from independent evidence, Palomino is right about the setting and sitters of *Las Meninas*.

On the question of the date Palomino is straightforward: "Don Diego Velázquez finished it in the year 1656." This seems reasonable if we take into account that the infanta, who was born on 12 July 1651, looks to be around five years old. He also says that when "Velázquez painted this picture the king had not yet bestowed on him the honor of a knighthood." This occurred in 1658. Mention of this fact raises another point: Palomino claims that the king ordered the cross of Santiago to be added to Velázquez' portrait after the death of the artist: "Some say that His Majesty himself painted it to encourage practitioners of this most noble art. . . ." It is impossible to test the validity of this statement without technical examination, and even then it might be a hopeless task because only four years had passed between the supposed date of completion and the death of the artist. Examination of the canvas after the recent cleaning (May–June 1984) seems to indicate that the brushwork of the cross is uniform with the rest of the surface (Plate 321). If this is so, and Palomino is correct about the subsequent addition of the cross, then this motif could have been added by Velázquez himself two or three years after the picture was painted. One final point concerns the source of the reflection in the mirror, a much-debated problem. Palomino is confident that the mirror-image reflects the large canvas on which the artist is working. This point is soon to be considered, but first there is one more question to be asked of Palomino's text — how did he interpret the meaning of the picture?

257

Most of Palomino's section on the painting is descriptive. But at one point he interrupts the narrative to explain the significance as he understood it:

I consider this portrait of Velázquez [he speaks of the self-portrait] to be no lesser work of artifice than that of Phidias, the renowned sculptor and painter, who placed his portrait on the shield of the statue he made of the goddess Minerva, executing it with such artifice that if it were removed the statue itself would be completely ruined. Titian made his name no less eternal by portraying himself holding in his hands another portrait with the image of King Philip II. Thus, just as the name of Phidias was never effaced so long as his statue of Minerva remained whole, and Titian's as long as that of Philip II survived, so too the name of Velázquez will live from century to century, as long as that of the most excellent and beautiful Margarita, in whose shadow his image is immortalized.[55]

In short, for Palomino, *Las Meninas* was Velázquez' claim to immortality, a claim based not only on the fact that it was the greatest of paintings, but also, and perhaps principally, on the fact that it showed the artist in the company of the royal princess. As such, the picture epitomized the immutable credence of courtiers that access to the royal family could guarantee nothing less than eternal fame.[56]

Palomino's interpretation reflects the temper of his times,[57] although it does not exclude other points of view. It is also interesting that he regarded the infanta as the protagonist of the picture. Yet it is hard to accept that she is the only subject of the composition. The frozen gestures and outward glances seem to imply another focal point of the action which lies outside the frame.[58] The attempts to identify the source and location of this focal point have occasioned a substantial literature, much of which is concerned with finding the answer by reconstructing the perspective of the picture. The problem concerns the question of whether the mirror reflects the image on the canvas or the imaginary presence of the monarchs outside the picture frame (Plate 322). Unfortunately, despite many valiant attempts, this problem cannot be resolved by measurement alone because it is now clear that Velázquez tempered geometry with intuition when he composed the picture.[59] As the recent cleaning has revealed, there is a pentimento which runs along the entire length of the right-hand wall at the level of the cornice. At one point, this wall was a few centimeters higher than in the final version. The change in this crucial dimension should have forced Velázquez to rework the entire perspective if he had been following a fixed scheme.[60] Instead, however, he made only this one adjustment. This alteration suggests that the composition was guided both by instinct and geometry. By creating numerous focal points within the composition, Velázquez sought to imitate the restless movement of the eye as it scans a large space inhabited by several people and illuminated by light of variable intensity. There is also reason to think that the perspective was deliberately left ambiguous in order to accommodate more than one reading of the composition.

Recent studies of *Las Meninas*, inspired by the ideas of Michel Foucault, have paid considerable attention to the seemingly novel relationship between the scene on the canvas and the spectator. These ideas tacitly assume that the picture was meant to be seen by the public-at-large, as if it were hanging in an important museum, as it is today. (They also exaggerate the novelty of the way in which the spectator is involved in the picture.) However, the original placement indicates that this is not the case. In 1666, the year after the death of Philip IV, *Las Meninas* was inventoried in a room known as the "pieza del despacho de verano," or the office in the summer quarters,[61] in the northern section of the Alcázar. The placement of the painting in this setting implies some important information because the *pieza del despacho* was a room destined for the personal use of the king. Despite its size, *Las Meninas* was regarded at the time of its creation as a private picture addressed to an audience of one, Philip IV. Others who entered the room could have seen it of course, but only the king had a part to play in the composition.[62]

If this conclusion is correct, then it follows that the focal point of the picture was the

323. Velázquez, *Las Meninas* (Madrid, Museo del Prado), 3.21 × 2.81m.

king, who "interrupted" the figures in *Las Meninas* whenever he entered his summer office. The implicit assumption of his presence is recorded not only in the poses and expressions of the characters in the picture, but also in the mirror reflection. Some diagrams of the perspective locate the source of the reflection outside the picture while others identify it with the large canvas standing before the artist. This discrepancy can probably be attributed to the fact that Velázquez' instinctive use of perspective deliberately accommodates both possibilities. The purpose of the mirror is to insinuate the presence of the king (and queen) in the atelier. If the king were present in person before the picture, he could see, as it were, his own reflection in the mirror.[63] If absent, the picture would be understood as a portrait of the infanta and her retinue, while the mirror-image would be attributed to the reflection from the easel, as did Palomino. In either case, the presence of the king proved once and for all that painting was the noblest of arts.

This interpretation of the relationship of the king to the canvas can also be understood to imply that *Las Meninas* is in part a meditation on the nature of representation and reality. This is so, but the ideas expressed in the picture have to be defined with care to avoid imputing to the artist a set of concerns which, however important to twentieth-century thought about the nature of art, were unknown to Velázquez and his times. *Las Meninas* is the culmination of a lifelong examination of the relationship between art and nature. Velázquez seems to have tried to create art without apparent artifice and thus to reduce the gap between what the eye sees in nature and what the eye sees in art. The desire to attain greater naturalism in painting was widely felt in the seventeenth century, but no one went further in achieving it than Velázquez. The proof of his success is *Las Meninas*, a painting in which his new type of artistry is used to produce an intense encounter with reality.

In planning the calculated approximation of art to nature, Velázquez had to redefine the traditional relationship between painting and reality.[64] Renaissance theory placed the intellect at the center of artistic activity; the painter's mind was required to mediate between the haphazard world of appearances and the ordered, harmonious world of art. If the idea of beauty changed according to time and circumstances, the value of an accepted canon of beauty was never challenged. Works of painting which merely recorded natural appearances, such as still life and portraiture, were assigned a lower place in the hierarchy of art than were those which aspired to express universal truths about man, nature, and the divine in an ideal style. In *Las Meninas*, however, the illusion, not the improvement, of everyday reality is given primacy. For whatever the picture may be, it is a brilliant tour de force of illusionistic painting.

On the one hand, this is self-evident and always has been so. But the full impact of the picture is inevitably dulled when it is placed in the gallery of a public museum. The exact dimensions of the *pieza del despacho de verano* are unknown, but given its private function, it was probably not large. Thus, the encounter with the painting by those who saw it in place was overwhelming, as these words by Palomino show: "There is no praise too high for the taste and skill of this work; for it is truth, not painting."[65] Palomino also provides a vivid report of the encounter of Luca Giordano with the painting. Luca, who knew every trick in the painter's book, was taken by King Charles II to the *pieza del despacho* to see the picture. (This would have occurred between 1692, when Luca arrived in Madrid, and 1700, when the king died.) "And when in recent times Luca Giordano came and happened to see it, he was asked by Charles II, who saw his look of astonishment: 'What do you think of it?' And he replied: 'Sire, this is the Theology of Painting,' by which he meant to convey that just as theology is superior to all other branches of knowledge, so is this picture the greatest example of painting."[66]

Even now when seen under different conditions and circumstances, the realism of the picture, if diminished, is still astonishing. In creating the illusion, Velázquez first of all used a real setting with real people which automatically triggered the response of recognition in his contemporaries. A strong residue of this verism still clings to the picture and prepares the viewer to regard it as a true happening, not as an illustration of an imaginary or fictional event. Then, Velázquez brilliantly exploited the contrast between the colorful, strongly lit foreground, peopled with solid figures in a variety of interesting poses, and the vast, shadowy space which envelops them. This powerful contrast simultaneously strengthens the corporeality of the figures and heightens the sense of the vast emptiness of the gallery; the princess and her court are projected forward under the light, while the space seems to flow around, above, and behind them. Furthermore, as the light invades the room, it is unevenly diffused over a variety of surfaces. The mirror shimmers with a silvery glow and provides a more distinct image than the large, matte canvases above. A patch of light escapes from the partly shuttered window in the last bay, forming a pool of luminosity around the lamphook at the rear of the ceiling. And, then, in the background, another source of light is introduced, which illuminates the figure in the doorway and sends a pencil-thin ray shooting across the floor beneath the mirror. Thus, the illusion of space and volume becomes compellingly palpable.

In painting the figures, Velázquez is equally responsive to the requirements of instantaneity and veracity (Plate 324). The six figures in the foreground react to the entrance of the king in varying ways. Some stare at the intrusion, others only begin to react, others still ignore it completely. As the light from the open window strikes the figures, the richly embroidered costumes glitter and twinkle. The illusion of the play of light over deep, satin colors and silver threads is obtained through the final refinement of Velázquez' blotch-and-blob technique. *Las Meninas* could be called the largest oil-sketch ever made. Irregular deposits of pigment float on the surface of rich colors — the sea green dress of María Agustina Sarmiento, the burnished silver of Isabel Velasco, the deep blue of Maribárbola, which is flecked with small bits of the plum-and-orange-colored suit of Nicolás Pertusato. At close range, nothing is defined, no details are resolved. The hands of all the figures are mere blotches of flesh colored pigment. And in the middleground, the two shadowy figures of Marcela Ulloa and the anonymous *guardadamas* almost sink into the weave of the canvas. Yet the impassive expression of the *guardadamas* and the weighty clasp of his hands at his waist are entirely legible. "For it is truth, not painting."

Yet it would be a mistake to admire *Las Meninas* as if it were a photograph, for, as Luca Giordano rightly observed, it is also the "theology of painting." However, the intellectual dimension is not to be found solely, or even primarily, in its allegorical or metaphorical significance. In obtaining the miraculous effects of illusion, Velázquez demonstrates what he had learned in a lifetime of painting. His use of the audacious, short-hand technique rests on the assumption that the eye, or more exactly the power of vision, is not to be disdained. It may be that Velázquez had acquainted himself with the science of optics, or intuitively grasped the importance of the physiological partnership between eye and mind. Whatever the case, his technique, based on the implication rather than the elaboration of detail, was the result of years of meditation and experimentation. At the same time, Velázquez was not ignorant of, or even indifferent to, the precepts of classical art theory. For all the brilliance of its visual effects, the drama of *Las Meninas* is as carefully structured as a mythological or religious painting by Poussin. Gestures, expression, and poses are calculated for maximum effect. The play of compositional forces is exquisitely balanced. Palomino was therefore able to describe the picture using the language of classical theory: "The figures are set off by aerial perspective; their disposition is superb; the invention is new; in short there is no praise too high for the taste and skill of this work...." It is the unprecedented representation and reconciliation of the veristic and the abstract which lies at the heart of *Las Meninas* and has made it among the most admired and discussed paintings of our time.

Las Meninas is also a summation of another kind. Here we see the painter's ambitions as an artist and courtier displayed side-by-side. Executed when Velázquez was nearing sixty years of age, *Las Meninas* is a monument to painting as a noble art. Yet, as we know, the picture was created just at the time when Velázquez' aspirations for personal nobility were being put to a hard test. It is difficult to avoid feeling that the case so

324 (following pages). Detail of Plate 323.

eloquently argued in *Las Meninas* is really a counter-argument; that the defense of the art, by its very nature, acknowledges the existence of a credible attack on its pretensions to a lofty status.

Velázquez' career revolves around this problem. He seems to have habored two enormous, but mutually exclusive ambitions. One was to be regarded as a great painter; the other was to be regarded as a great gentleman. In the rigid, hierarchical court of Philip IV, where painters were assigned a low rank, the realization of these ambitions came into deadly conflict. In the end, Velázquez found the only way out of this quandary: he devoted himself to the service of the king, the one person who had the power both to advance and reconcile his artistic and social aspirations. This solution was not without its penalties. It meant the diversion of Velázquez' energies from painting to the duties of the household. But we cannot be sure that he regretted the change simply because we may disapprove of this use of his talents, some of which, in any case, were required to redesign and redecorate the houses of the king. If our informal age has lost the taste for princely ceremonial and display, the court of Philip IV regarded it as a staple of existence. In helping the king to care for his collections and assisting him with the decoration of his palaces, Velázquez found a way to be an artist and a gentleman. Naturally a compromise was involved, but is this not the essence of royal service — the deference to authority, the exercise of restraint, and the faithful execution of duty as the means to obtain honors, privileges, and wealth? All these rewards eventually came to Velázquez, and it must be accepted that he considered the price of fame and fortune to be worth the sacrifice of time for painting. But time was all that he sacrificed to his ambitions. Required by the consequences of his choice to paint but few pictures in the last decades of his life, he made every picture count in his quest to redefine the medium of which he was the unsurpassed master.

CHAPTER X

*From Painter of Princes
to Prince of Painters*

VELÁZQUEZ RETURNED to Madrid from the Isle of Pheasants at dawn on 26 June 1660. In a letter to a friend in Valladolid, one of the few personal documents which is known, he noted that he had arrived "tired from traveling by night and working by day, but in good health."[1] He settled once more into the routine of his duties at the palace. On 5 July he received a letter from the Italian sculptor, Giovanni Battista Morelli, a pupil of Algardi whom he had known in Rome.[2] In a discreet but obsequious message, Morelli made it known that his services were available to the king. Velázquez seems to have supported the petition because Morelli came to Madrid in the following year and was appointed as royal sculptor in 1664.[3]

Little now remained of Velázquez' life. According to the detailed account of Palomino, Velázquez suddenly fell ill on 31 July, "troubled by a burning sensation that obliged him to retire . . . to his apartments. He began to suffer great anguish and pains in the stomach and heart." Physicians were sent by the king. They were followed, ominously, by the archbishop of Tyre, Patriarch of the Indies, who preached a long sermon to comfort the artist's spirit. At two o'clock in the afternoon of Friday, 6 August, Velázquez died at the age of sixty-one.

His funeral occurred on the following day and, as described by his pupil, Juan de Alfaro, it was a solemn event.[4] Velázquez, who had aspired to be a nobleman, was interred like a nobleman. Dressed in the habit of the Order of Santiago, his body lay at rest in his bedroom until the evening of the next day. Then it was carried to the church of San Juan and buried, as members of the court and servants of the king looked on.

Three days later, Velázquez' executors, his son-in-law Mazo and his close friend, Gaspar de Fuensalida, made an inventory of his atelier in the prince's quarters, accompanied by Francisco de Rojas, newly appointed as *aposentador* in place of the deceased artist.[5] There they found Velázquez' account books of his offices of *aposentador* and *superintendente de obras particulares*. The three men also identified an assortment of objects belonging to the king. Among the numerous pictures was a famous work by Titian, *Spain Coming to the Aid of Religion*. Its presence in the workshop is probably to be explained by the need to restore it, although whether the job was to be done by the master or an assistant is unknown. In addition, there were three portraits by El Greco, one by Velázquez, two works by Ribera, and several anonymous pictures. The workshop also contained vestiges of Velázquez' interest in architecture: one was a large book of building plans, another was a wooden model of a Greek-cross church. An assortment of small-scale sculpture, decorative pieces, and large quantities of frames and stretchers completed the list. From the jumble of objects, scattered throughout half-a-dozen rooms, emerges a kind of catalogue in three dimensions of Velázquez' activities as painter and designer.

On 11 August, the executors began to make an inventory of the contents of the artist's apartments in the Casa del Tesoro.[6] They had scarcely begun the task when Velázquez' widow, Juana Pacheco, died, following her husband to the grave by a mere eight days.[7] On the seventeenth, the lugubrious task of making the inventory was resumed. During the next two and a half weeks, the two men made their way room by room through the apartment, carefully listing well over 400 belongings of Velázquez and his wife. The painter had lived in solid comfort,[8] surrounded by pictures, sculpture, precious objects, carpets, and hangings, which he had been acquiring at least since 1636 and probably before.[9]

In due course, Mazo and Fuensalida came to Velázquez' collection of books. Veláz-quez owned 154 titles, a fair-sized library for a private person in seventeenth-century Spain.[10] A good portion of the contents was devoted to mathematics, geometry, geography, mechanics, anatomy, and architecture. Numerous books on art and art theory were also found, as well as a smattering of emblematic and mythographic treatises. Conspicuously absent were works of fiction, poetry, and religion. Without knowing the name of the owner, it could be supposed that he was either an artist with an interest in science, or a scientist with an interest in art.

In recent times, scholars have exploited Velázquez' library in an effort to refashion our understanding of the artist, especially by focusing on the small percentage of emblem books it contained. This approach is probably doomed to fail, not because it overestimates Velázquez' ingenuity, or even because it unduly emphasizes one of his minor interests, but rather because it underestimates the high purpose of his art. Renaissance theorists never tired of saying that painting was a form of knowledge distinct from, if at times dependent upon, the written word. As we have seen, Velázquez was an original interpreter of traditional subjects and well versed in the history of art. His grasp of a wide variety of source material, both literary and artistic, was also great. But there is more to his painting than the inspired reworking of conventional themes and compositions. Velázquez' career as an artist was in large measure dedicated to reconsidering the relationship between the art of painting and nature, to studying and representing the world with a respect for the inherent expressive possibilities of certain natural phenomena, especially color and light. This goal required him to understand the structure of the visible world, which is why he read books on scientific subjects. Nowadays, science and art are considered (wrongly) to be at opposite ends of the spectrum of human activity, one serving the dictates of reason, the other of emotion. But in the seventeenth century, the scientific revolution was just beginning and it was still possible, as it had been in the Renaissance, for an artist to understand the writings of scientists, if he were so inclined. It is not necessary to transform Velázquez into a physicist or mathematician to see that he instinctively shared the growing interest of the age in understanding the natural order.[11] Similarly, the mastery of art theory was a necessary step in the process of analyzing the limitations of existing pictorial conventions in order to transcend them.

However, Velázquez never attempted to use his knowledge to dismantle the existing structure of art, as painters would do in the nineteenth century. Underlying his study of nature is a continuing respect for certain accepted ideas of Renaissance theory and practice. Thus, the tension between surface and space, between volume and plane, between the significant and the incidental, which is deliberately heightened in modern art, is more latent than explicit in Velázquez' mature paintings. Yet its presence can be sensed and helps to understand the ever-increasing interest in his work which began just over a century ago. Modern painters were also fascinated by the unusual technique which Velázquez devised to express his artistic vision. The shorthand, sketch-like manner of painting which he developed opened a new world of possibilities by showing how fractured touches of pigment could produce the most subtle, complete illusions of light and color. The sheer brilliance of Velázquez' control of the brush has never failed to astound even the most confident painters.

Given the sophistication of his art, it is not surprising that he left no immediate followers. Except in the realm of court portraiture, there is scarcely a trace of his impact on the painters who succeeded him.[12] The School of Velázquez, to use that antiquated but still expressive term, had no pupils. His successors at court and the other painters in Madrid turned to other models, notably Rubens, and painted almost as if Velázquez had never lived. Within the history of seventeenth-century Spanish art, he stands alone; the greatest of Spanish painters seems to have been the least typical representative of Spanish art.

This phenomenon has several explanations, which have been touched on above. Velázquez traveled to Italy while his colleagues stayed at home. He had a broad education while most of his colleagues had learned only to read and write. He began to redefine the purpose and function of his art while his colleagues were content to work within established formulas. He painted portraits and secular themes while his colleagues interpreted religious subjects. He was a gentleman and knight of Santiago while his colleagues lived as artisans, finding work where they could.

Many of the differences can be explained by the connection to the royal court. The circumstances which in 1623 brought Velázquez to the attention of the count-duke of Olivares and Philip IV proved to be decisive for his development. The patronage of Philip IV, a discerning, passionate admirer of painting, gave him the freedom he needed to paint as he chose and to test his mettle against the masterpieces of the royal collection. And it provided the opportunity to encounter the leading artists of Italy and Flanders, and thus to absorb the current ideas and practices of his art. The favor of the king also served to validate his pretensions to nobility. Unfortunately, that goal could be attained only by winning appointment to positions in the household which kept him from painting. But this consequence seems to have been acceptable to Velázquez, who was never hesitant about applying for higher posts and honors. If nothing else, it is clear that the most original artist of his time was also the most conventional of men. In serving the connoisseur-king, he was able to satisfy his lifelong desire for artistic and personal fame. He was not, of course, the first artist to be driven by these ambitions.

The recognition of posterity took longer to arrive. Anyone who scans the literature of art between 1660 and the early nineteenth century will seldom find Velázquez' name mentioned alongside those artists considered to be great.[13] Had it not been for the influential biography of Palomino, it is doubtful whether the painter would have been known outside the Iberian Peninsula until after 1800.[14] Also contributing to the eclipse was the fact that his production was small and mostly confined to collections in Madrid, especially the royal collection. Furthermore, to foreign travelers in search of art, Spain was a difficult and joyless trip with few masterpieces of antiquity and the Renaissance to reward the sacrifices.

Those partisans of the grand manner who found their way to Madrid, like Anton Mengs, admired Velázquez but only with reservations. Mengs' appreciation of Velázquez is extraordinarily keen and perceptive. In 1797, his remarks were published by his friend and patron, Joseph Nicolás Azara. (Mengs had been in Madrid for two stays: 1761–69 and 1774–76.) As a distinguished painter himself, Mengs was able to admire Velázquez' artistic vision and technique with genuine enthusiasm and to plot accurately the evolution of his style:

> What truth and intelligent chiaroscuro can be observed in the paintings of Velázquez! How well he understood the effects which occur when atmosphere is interposed between objects, to make it seem that they are distant from one another. . . . The *Waterseller of Seville* allows you to see how, in his beginnings, he subjected his art to the imitation of the natural, finishing all the parts and giving them that force that he seems to have seen in the model, considering the essential difference which exists in the parts that receive light and shadow. However, this very imitation of the natural made him paint somewhat hard and dry.
>
> . . . But where, without doubt, he gave the most accurate idea of the natural is in the painting of *Las Hilanderas*, which is of his last style, and done in such a way that it seems as if the hand played no part in the execution, but that he painted it only as an act of will.

Nevertheless, Mengs found Velázquez' art less than perfect because he did not attempt to "improve" what he saw:

However, despite these [qualities], Velázquez, not to mention the other painters of the Spanish school, did not have an exact idea of the merit of Greek things, nor of beauty or the ideal; they went on imitating each other. The most talented of them imitated the truth, but without selection, thus remaining pure naturalists.[15]

To a large extent, Velázquez' critical fortunes were involved with the gradual reversal of the aesthetic criteria articulated by Mengs, which occurred during the course of the nineteenth century. Also important was the increasing accessibility of the pictures during the same period of time.

Velázquez' works entered into wider circulation as foreign travelers began to visit Spain, especially during the Romantic era when the country and its culture were discovered by seekers of the exotic. With the opening of the Museo del Prado in 1819, it became possible for visitors to see the most important collection of Velázquez' works without the special permission needed to enter the royal palaces where they had always been kept. Also important was the dispersal of his pictures to major centers of artistic culture, principally Paris and London. Works by Velázquez arrived in France and England as the result of plundering by soldiers and art dealers. Among the first to arrive on the scene were Jean Baptiste Pierre LeBrun, a French dealer, and George Augustus Wallis, a minor English painter in the employ of the Scottish art merchant, William Buchanan.[16] Then came the French army. During the Peninsular War (1808–12), French commanders, notably General Soult, absconded with important collections of Spanish painting. English diplomats also obtained major works by Velázquez, as did the duke of Wellington, who captured from Joseph Bonaparte a cargo of important pictures, including several by Velázquez, which he was allowed to keep by Ferdinand VII.[17] Finally, there was the huge collection made by Baron Isidore Taylor for Louis-Philippe.[18] Although poor in paintings by Velázquez, this collection, displayed at the Galerie Espagnole of the Louvre from 1838 to 1848, stimulated the growing interest in Spanish art.

Artists and critics soon began to take note of Velázquez and spread the word of his greatness to the public at large. A letter of 1808 from Wallis to Buchanan reveals his enthusiasm for the little-known works of Spanish masters in general:

This school is rich beyond idea, and its painters are all great colorists: some of their colossal works are surprising. If you had time and could bear the horrors of traveling in Spain, it would be worthwhile to visit this country. After all, I must own I have, as an artist, learned a great deal this admirable school.[19]

A perceptive appraisal of Velázquez in particular came from David Wilkie, one of the leading British artists of the time. He made the acquaintance of Velázquez' art during a visit to Madrid in 1827 and communicated his impressions to friends in England in a series of letters published in 1843:

Velázquez, however, may be said to be the origin of what is now doing in England. His feeling they [the English painters] have caught without seeing his works. . . . Perhaps there is this difference: he does at once what we do by repeated and repeated touches. It may truly be said, that wheresoever Velázquez is admired, the paintings of England must be acknowledged and admired with him.[20]

On the other side of the Channel, French artists were also starting to awaken to the virtues of Velázquez. In 1824, Delacroix copied a work attributed, if incorrectly, to Velázquez, and noted in his journal that "if I take the palette right now, and I am dying to do so, the beautiful Velázquez would work on me. I would like to spread out a canvas of brown or red, of good, rich, thick pigment."[21] Lesser artists who made the trip to Spain also contributed to the growing enthusiasm for Velázquez. Pharamond Blanchard produced a lithograph after *St. Anthony Abbot and St. Paul the Hermit* (Plate 112) which formed part of a suite of prints of paintings in the Prado, organized by its director, José de Madrazo.[22] And Alfred Dehodenq, who spent thirteen years in Spain, wrote a letter in 1855 which shows how far the reputation of Velázquez had advanced in little more than fifty years. It also shows that naturalism had finally supplanted classicism as the dominant artistic idea:

> My dear friend, what a painter! Nothing can give you an idea. It is nature done on the spot. The finest observation, the truest types, delicious color harmonies; everything is there, thrown in profusion on the canvas. His manner, live and facile, his way of treating costume from the point of view of the shape and character, leaving all the details out, the hands barely indicated, [all this] demonstrates a continual preoccupation with the ensemble, with the general effect. And this is what really hits you and throws you to the ground when you see his works.[23]

The enthusiasm of painters was shared by critics. Writers such as Louis Viardot, Théophile Gautier and, later, Théophile Thoré in France,[24] and Richard Ford in England[25] did much to transform the status of Velázquez from a forgotten to a memorable master. The publication of Sir William Stirling-Maxwell's *Velázquez and His Works* (London, 1855; translated into French in 1865) is a landmark in the rediscovery of the artist. Stirling's carefully researched biography, the first modern study of Velázquez' life and work, conferred the final measure of respectability on the artist.

The revision of Velázquez' reputation and importance took place against the background of a transcendental change in the history of art. Indeed, as we have seen, the rise of his fame is linked to that revolution of artistic sensibility called modernism. Therefore, it is fitting that the most famous remark ever made about Velázquez came from one of its founders, Edouard Manet. Manet undertook his famous journey of discovery to Madrid in 1865, several years after the fame of Velázquez had been secured, so he was not a pioneer among the artist's admirers. But no one was more enthralled by Velázquez nor did more to advance the understanding and appreciation of his art, especially through the example of his own pictures. Writing from his hotel in the Puerta del Sol to his friend, Henri Fantin-Latour, Manet could scarcely contain his enthusiasm for Velázquez and, in the heat of the moment, he coined that memorable lapidary phrase: "C'est le peintre des peintres":

> What a joy it would have been for you to see Velázquez, which for him alone is worth the trip. The painters of every school who surround him in the museum of Madrid, and who are all very well represented, seem completely like fakers. He is the painter of painters. He has astonished me, he has ravished me.[26]

Thus Velázquez was reborn and rebaptized in the modern era. However, the essence of his art is rather more complex than Manet's spontaneous remark would seem to suggest. The painter of painters he was and is and will remain. But Velázquez was also a creature of a certain time and place — the court of Philip IV. Like every great artist, he was shaped by the world around him, even if in the end he transcended it. The style of quiet dignity and restrained majesty set by Philip IV seems to have permeated the spirit of Velázquez. His are reticent masterpieces — "grave, authoritative, harmonious," to use the king's own words. In addition, the king launched him on a career as a great international artist and freed him from the tyranny of a marketplace which limited the possibilities of many an important Spanish painter. Perhaps servitude of another kind was exacted from the artist, but at least it was dignified by honors and emoluments. Thus secure in his protected position, Velázquez nurtured his genius and discovered a way to transmute images of kings and queens and princes and princesses into a new form of art which continues to grow in power long after the memory of his protectors has faded nearly into oblivion.

APPENDIX A

Various Velázquez Problems

THIS SECTION is devoted to the discussion of five paintings which present problems too intricate to be considered in the text or notes.

Calabazas with a Portrait and a Pinwheel

The authenticity of this jester portrait (Plate 119) has been accepted by many, but not all, writers on Velázquez. One of the early doubters was Antonio Ponz (*Viage de España*, VI [Madrid, 1793], p. 119) who described it as "del gusto de Velázquez." Trapier (*Velázquez*, p. 115) rejected the attribution on the grounds that the painting did not conform to the description in the Retiro inventory of 1701, where the jester is described as holding a "billete," or letter, instead of a pinwheel. Steinberg ("Review," pp. 282–3) repeated this point and also argued that the quality did not support an attribution to Velázquez. He proposed Alonso Cano as the author. Finally, John F. Moffitt ("Velázquez, Fools, Calabacillas and Ripa") accepted and amplified Steinberg's criticism of the quality and further established that the picture is largely based on Ripa's emblem for Madness, a procedure which, in his opinion, is at variance with Velázquez' individualized and sympathetic approach to subjects of this type.

The most resourceful defender of the authenticity is José López-Rey ("Velázquez' Calabazas" [summarized in the subsequent editions of his book]). In reviewing the eighteenth-century inventories of the Retiro, he discovered an entry in the inventory completed on 7 September 1789, which reads as follows: "178 — Otra de Velázquez, Retrato de Velasquillo el Bufón, y el inventario antiguo dice ser de Calavacillas, con un retrato en la mano y un reguilete, de dos varas y media de alto y vara y tercia de ancho, con marco dorado." (The "inventario antiguo" is presumably the one of 1701.) López-Rey argues that the writer of the 1701 inventory wrote "billete" for the like-sounding "reguilete," thus explaining the discrepancy between the pinwheel held by the jester and the "letter" which appears in the inventory. As for the name Velasquillo, he believes that this was the result of the scribe's confusion of the name of the painter and of the sitter. Thus, he accepts the authenticity of the portrait, dating it "about 1628–9."

This evidence is not entirely conclusive. First, as Moffitt notes, the dimensions of the painting described in 1701 and 1789 (*c.*2.09 × 1.12 m.) are almost thirty-five centimeters taller than the picture in Cleveland (1.755 × 1.067 m.). (This is a discrepancy of about one foot, not two feet, as stated by Moffitt in note 21.) Second, a document of 15 October 1637, mentions among the household servants a certain Cristóbal Velázquez. The document concerns the clothing allowance to personnel of the royal household, including the painter Velázquez. The name of Cristóbal Velázquez follows those of other court jesters and dwarfs, including Calabazas, Lezcano, "Juan de Austria", and Ochoa, all of whom were painted by Velázquez. Thus, it is not impossible that there was a jester named Velázquez, who might have been called Velasquillo (Cruzada assumes that this was so), and who might have been painted by the artist of the same name. But on balance it is reasonable to suppose that the portrait mentioned in the 1789 inventory was the same one recorded in 1701. This of course does not confirm the attribution to Velázquez.

A more important objection concerns the date of 1628–29 proposed by López-Rey. Calabazas is documented in royal service from 1630 to 1639, when he died. López-Rey implicitly recognizes the difficulties in dating the picture after Velázquez' return from Italy. The style is not sufficiently advanced and the appearance of the sitter is too youthful to have been painted just seven or eight years before Velázquez' *Portrait of Calabazas* of the later 1630s (Plate 172). The difficulty is resolved by assuming that Calabazas "might have occasionally performed as a jester at court before being admitted into regular service." In arguing the dates of other portraits of dwarfs and jesters, however, López-Rey accepts the limits of the terms of service as documented by Moreno Villa, which seems a sound principle to follow without exception.

It seems to me that the stylistic arguments against the attribution to Velázquez advanced by Steinberg and Moffitt are convincing. The picture is uninspired in execution and conception, although the brushwork is somewhat difficult to judge because of the flattening of the surface in an earlier relining. In my view, the picture is by another artist. The artist could not be Cano, who did not arrive in Madrid until 1638, unless, of course, the picture is thought to be a copy by Cano after the work of Velázquez or some other painter.

It should also be pointed out that there is nothing to support López-Rey's assumption that the painting was originally in the Alcázar, from where it was moved to the Retiro.

Temptation of St. Thomas Aquinas

The *Temptation of St. Thomas Aquinas* (Plate 325) has had a history of uncertain attribution to Velázquez. The picture was first published in 1906 by Elías Tormo in "Un Van Dyck, un Zurbarán, un Villacis y un cuatrocentista florentino inéditos" (*Cultura española* [1906], pp. 1142–8) where it was attributed to Nicolás Villacis, an obscure follower of Velázquez from Murcia (an opinion repeated in his article, "Villacis: una incógnita de nuestra historia artística," *BSEE*, 18 [1910], pp. 244–52). Later, Tormo changed his mind and attributed the painting to Velázquez (*Guías Regionales Calpe. III, Levante* [Madrid, 1923], pp. 304–5). However, he also detected significant elements of the style of Alonso Cano: "Pudo la composición deberse a diseño de Alonso Cano, de quien puede ser parte, mínima, de la ejecución." This "minimal" part was actually quite significant — the group of angels, the saint, and the chimney. In 1925, the picture was included without qualification by J. Allende-Salazar in his edition of the Velázquez volume of the *Klassiker der Kunst* (p. 47) and dated *c.*1631–32. Thereafter it was accepted as authentic by most authorities (i.e., Mayer, 1939, no. 44; Lafuente Ferrari, 1943, no. 42; López-Rey, 1963, no. 423; Gudiol, 1973, no. 57).

Still, doubts about Velázquez' execution, or exclusive execution, were voiced from time to time. For Trapier (*Velázquez*, pp. 181–2), the painting seemed "to have more in common with the works of the School of Madrid. The over-sweet, almost sickly sentimentality [!] of the subject is foreign to Velázquez' taste and is in strange contrast to his other religious works." Manuel Gómez-Moreno ("'Los Borrachos,' y otras notas velazqueñas"), like Tormo in 1923, perceived traces of Cano's hand, attributing to him the composition and execution of all the foreground figures except the angel with the girdle and the fleeing temptress seen in the rear. He believed that the painting had been started by Cano and finished by Velázquez after Cano's flight to Valencia in 1644. The most recent challenge to the attribution occurs in the 1979 edition of López-Rey's catalogue (p. 153, note 6), where, reversing his earlier opinion, he excludes it as an authentic work.

In my opinion, the doubters are correct, as are those who have perceived the hand of Alonso Cano in the picture. In design and execution alike, the work is a typical, if

325. Attributed to Alonso Cano, *Temptation of St. Thomas Aquinas* (Orihuela, Museo Diocesano), 2.44 × 2.03m.

outstanding, work by the only artist of Velázquez' generation capable of imitating his style. Cano worked with Velázquez at court from 1638 to 1644, when he left for Valencia following the tragic murder of his wife. During this period, he studied and mastered the elements of Velázquez' mature style without, however, sacrificing his own distinctive manner. The *Temptation of St. Thomas* is an excellent example of this synthesis.

The precise modeling of the musculature of the angel's arms and shoulders is closely comparable to that of the angel in *St. John the Evangelist's Vision of the Heavenly Jerusalem* (London, Wallace Collection), while the careful delineation of the ostentatious chimneypiece, so foreign to the art of Velázquez, is compatible with Cano's experience as an architectural draftsman. The one part of the composition which has always suggested the name of Velázquez is the fleeing temptress in the background. The execution with broken strokes, characteristic of the mature Velázquez, was absorbed by Cano and is evident in *St. Isidoro and the Miracle of the Well* (Madrid, Museo del Prado), his most overt imitation of his companion's style. In general, the crisp, delicate draftsmanship, the chiseled, nervous handling of the drapery, the confident treatment of anatomy, and the facial types all seem to point to Cano as the author of this excellent picture. The only paintings by Velázquez which are comparable are the two done in Rome in 1629–30 (Plates 83, 88) and *Christ after the Flagellation* (Plate 81).

326. After Velázquez, *Archbishop Fernando de Valdés*
(London, National Gallery), 0.698 × 0.584m.

In the Roman paintings, however, there are much subtler effects of light and shadow, which flicker over the surface of the figures, and a more varied and spontaneous brush-stroke with greater use of impasto. In *Christ after the Flagellation*, the forms are more solid and ponderous, the movements of the figures less delicate, the facial types less idealized, and the colors deeper and more saturated in tone. The similarities in the soft handling of the contours of the figures are the result of Cano's ability to imitate aspects of Velázquez' technique.

If this attribution is correct, then a logical date of execution would be the period when Cano was in Valencia (1644–5), a city in the same region as Orihuela. Tormo discovered the picture in the former Dominican college at Orihuela, still in its seventeenth-century frame, and supposed that the picture had been there from the first, a logical assumption given the subject.

Portrait of Archbishop Fernando de Valdés

This portrait in the National Gallery, London (Plate 326) has been attributed to Velázquez, but not universally accepted. Crombie ("Archbishop Fernando de Valdés by Velázquez") believed that the London portrait was part of the same canvas to which belonged the fragment of the hand with Velázquez' signature (Plate 163) and was therefore by Velázquez. This dismembered portrait was the model for a version in the Toreno collection (Plate 164). Ainaud ("Velázquez y los retratos de Don Fernando de Valdés"), while accepting the authenticity of the London head, believed that it came from an autograph replica of the portrait. He based this assumption on the belief that the sitter appears to be older in the London portrait than in the full-length copy and in a second copy in three-quarter format in the Archbishop's Palace, Granada. Ainaud also accepted that the London portrait was not a fragment of a larger work, but was executed in approxmately its present size. A copy of the work in this format is in the Museo de Arte de Cataluña, Barcelona.

MacLaren and Braham (*The Spanish School*, pp. 133–7) defend the attribution to Velázquez, but believe that the format makes it impossible to accept as a self-standing work. They suggest that Velázquez was commissioned to make an up-dated portrait of the archbishop and used the full-length portrait in the Toreno collection (or a version of it) as his point of departure. Both the Madrid fragment and the London portrait would have belonged to Velázquez' replica of the conde de Toreno original.

This thesis is vigorously attacked by López-Rey (*Velázquez* [1979], no. 56, pp. 327–8) who, however, seems to attribute certain arguments to MacLaren and Braham which in fact they reject. López-Rey seeks to refute their principal thesis primarily on the grounds that "it would be implausible to fancy Velázquez making a copy after the mediocre portrait at the Toreno collection and signing his name to it." Although admirable in its loyalty to Velázquez, this assertion is a matter of supposition. More worthy of consideration in his observation that the execution of the two fragments is different, suggesting that the two canvases were done by two different artists.

In the circumstances, it is hard to arrive at a definitive conclusion about the authenticity and original size of the London portrait. It can be observed, however, that the perceived difference in the age of the sitter in the Toreno portrait and London portrait may be the result of the significant difference in quality between the two images. I can imagine that the slightly younger appearance in the Toreno portrait was the result of the changes made by a mediocre artist copying an excellent original, changes which destroy the nuances of modeling and shadow, thus altering the apparent age of the sitter. Second, it is not entirely clear that the London portrait need be a fragment. The existence of a seventeenth-century copy in an identical format (Barcelona) suggests that a version of this composition was in existence at an early date, although of course it is possible that the Barcelona picture was made from the London portrait after it had been excised from a full-length work. Therefore, it is theoretically possible that the London portrait is a copy of an original by Velázquez executed by a painter of talent. I raise this possibility because I find it difficult to accept, on stylistic grounds, that the London portrait was done by Velázquez.

Who might this "painter of talent" have been? A suggestion made in passing by Enriqueta Harris Frankfort during a conversation has been gaining plausibility as I think about it — namely, Alonso Cano. For a more specific point of comparison, see the head of St. Bernard in Cano's *Vision of St. Bernard* (Madrid, Museo del Prado), a work dated by Wethey to *c*.1658–60. Cano was a pensioner at the cathedral of Granada, Valdés' former see, from 1652 to his death in 1667, and therefore would theoretically have had a pretext for having to execute a portrait of the archbishop.

Portrait of "El Primo" and Portrait of "Francisco Lezcano"

The revised dating proposed in chapter V for these portraits is based principally on the interpretation of information in parts of several royal inventories published by López-Rey (*Velázquez* [1979], pp. 436–8, 445–6) who uses it to question the identifications of the sitters in the portraits known as "*El Primo*" and *Sebastián de Morra* (Plate 199).

Either portrait, he argues, could represent either dwarf. As stated below, his doubts appear unwarranted. More importantly, some information not considered by López-Rey throws new light on the date and purpose of the paintings (Plate 174, 175).

The crux of the matter lies in the portrait usually known as *Diego de Acedo, "El Primo"* (Plate 174). In June 1644, while with the king on campaign against the French in Aragon, Velázquez completed a portrait of "El Primo" which was sent to Madrid. (For the documentation, see A. de Beruete, *El Velázquez de Parma*, p. 14, which provides a more accurate transcription than found in Cruzada Villaamil, *Anales*, pp. 145–6.) This portrait has almost always been associated with the picture now under discussion, which is assumed to have been one of four works described in the 1701 Torre de la Parada inventory as "quatro retratos de diferentes sugetos y enanos originales de Velázquez."

It is generally agreed that two of these pictures were the portraits of "El Primo" and Francisco Lezcano. However, it has also been said that the portrait of "El Primo" was first in the Alcázar and later transferred to the Torre (see, for example, *Museo del Prado. Catálogo de las pinturas* [Madrid, 1972], no. 1202, pp. 742–3). López-Rey rightly points out that there were in fact two portraits of "El Primo" inventoried after the death of Charles II in 1700 – one in the Torre, the second in the Alcazár, Madrid. Citing various eighteenth-century inventories of the Pardo, he establishes that the painting at the Torre is identical to the one now in the Museo del Prado. Especially important is a memorandum (for which see below) dated 17 and 28 July 1714, where the dwarf pictures are described for the first time, as follows: "un bufón rebestido de Philosopho estudiando," and "otro bufón con una baraja de naipes." There is little room to doubt, despite the use of "bufón" instead of "enano," that these descriptions apply to the dwarf portraits. (However, López-Rey's association of *Aesop* and *Menippus* as the other works referred to in the 1701 inventory as among the "quatro retratos de diferentes sugetos y enanos" seems to be erroneous. These pictures are specifically mentioned in this inventory in another room. Therefore, the identification of the other two works known as "diferentes sugetos" remains a mystery.) The dwarf paintings were still together in 1747, when they were inventoried in the Pardo. On this occasion, the dimensions of the two pictures were given for the first time – "vara y quarto de alto y vara de ancho" (*c.*1.04 × 0.835 m.), approximately the same size as the paintings now in the Museo del Prado. After this listing, the pictures passed to the Royal Palace in Madrid and eventually to the Prado. López-Rey's reconstruction of the provenance reconfirms that these two dwarf portraits were certainly two of the "retratos de diferentes sugetos etc." at the Torre in 1701; presumably they were there from the start. As López-Rey notes elsewhere (p. 395), there is no evidence that the *Portrait of Calabazas* (Plate 172) was at the Torre before 1747, if it was ever there at all. Finally, López-Rey observes that none of the eighteenth-century inventories gives the name of either dwarf.

As we have seen, there was a second portrait of "El Primo" listed in the Alcázar. In the partial inventory of 1666, drawn up by Juan Bautista del Mazo, a picture in the staircase leading to the Galería del Cierzo is recorded as "otra pintura del Primo enano mano de Diego Belazquez." It hung alongside the portrait of another dwarf called Sebastián de Morra (Plate 199), which measured a "bara y medio de alto casi en quadro" (*c.*1.25 × 1.25 m.). The assumption is that "*El Primo*" was roughly the same size because the dimensions for the next work on the list are duly recorded. It was therefore significantly larger than the portrait of this sitter in the Torre. These two portraits were listed in sequence in the inventories of 1686 and 1700. However, only the picture known as *Sebastián de Morra* appears to have survived the fire of 1734 and its aftermath. Nothing again is heard of "*El Primo*", which, since *Sebastián de Morra* escaped unscathed, may have been lost or stolen rather than burned. (The fire did relatively little damage to the northernmost quarter of the palace, where these pictures were hanging.) Thus, according to López-Rey, if we recognize that the portrait now considered to be "*El Primo*" which came from the Torre was never so named, then there is no basis for determining whether the survivor from the Alcázar (Plate 199) represented

"El Primo" or Sebastián de Morra. It is even possible that the portrait we know as "*El Primo*" is in reality *Sebastián de Morra* and vice-versa.

In my view, this argument does not cast serious doubt on the identification of the portrait traditionally known as "*El Primo*" (Plate 174). According to the researches of José Moreno Villa (*Locos, enanos*, pp. 55–8), Diego de Acedo was in royal service from 1635 to his death in 1660. Although malformed in body, "El Primo" did not usually serve as a playmate of the royal children or as an entertainer (although see Moreno Villa, p. 57 for one occasion when he was involved in a frivolous pursuit). Some evidence suggests that he was of a noble family, and it may be that his nickname was coined in recognition of relationship with a certain Juan de Acedo y Velázquez, knight of Malta, who was *contador mayor* of the cardinal infante. In the royal accounts, his name sometimes figures with the title "don," suggesting that he was an *hidalgo*, or of the lesser nobility. Whether or not any of this is true, "El Primo" was a member of the royal bureaucracy, attached to the secretariat (*secretaría de la cámara*), and was an assistant in the Office of the Stamp, which kept the facsimile signature of the king which was applied to copies of royal orders and decrees. "El Primo's" status at court is suggested in the portrait by the fact that he wears the clothing of a gentleman and not the informal costumes of the other dwarfs depicted by Velázquez, and by the inkwell and books which accompany him, attributes of his function in the household. The fact that he is not named in the 1701 Torre inventory is inconsequential. By then, "El Primo" had been dead for over forty years and probably neither he nor his companion was recognizable to the compilers of the inventory. For the sake of convenience, the makers of the inventory simply entered a description of the painting. (Mazo had worked in the Alcázar with both "El Primo" and Sebastián de Morra and was able therefore to identify them when compiling the Alcázar inventory of 1666.) If we accept that the subject of the painting once at the Torre and now at the Prado is "El Primo," then the picture now known as *Sebastián de Morra* must indeed represent this person because he bears no resemblance to the sitter in the other portrait.

As the inventories make clear, there were two portraits of "El Primo" in existence, one in the Alcázar, now vanished, the other in the Torre de la Parada, now in the Prado. Can it be said which of these was done at Fraga in 1644? Several pieces of indirect evidence suggest that it is the Fraga portrait which was lost and also help to bolster the case that the Prado portrait usually called "*El Primo*" does in fact depict "El Primo." First, the *Portrait of "El Primo"* in the Alcázar was paired with *Sebastián de Morra*, a dwarf who did not come to court until 1643; therefore Morra's portrait could not have been done much before the Fraga version of "*El Primo*." As has been seen, both had the same dimensions and were kept together in the Alcázar for at least sixty-eight years, indicating that perhaps they were a complementary pair. (If this assumption is correct, then the missing portrait of "El Primo" would be set against a neutral background like *Sebastián de Morra*.) It should also be remembered that the Alcázar *Portrait of "El Primo"* was larger than the portrait of this dwarf in the Torre (*c*. 1.25 × 1.25 m. versus *c*. 1.04 × 0.835 m.). (*Sebastián de Morra* has been reduced from its original dimensions; see López-Rey, *Velázquez* [1979], no. 103, pp. 440–1.)

Then there is the matter of certain formal and compositional features of the two dwarf portraits from the Torre. In addition to being virtually the same size, both are set against a background of the snow-covered Sierra de Guadarrama, an appropriate reference for the Torre de la Parada which lies within sight of this mountain range. This topography would be out of place in a picture set in Fraga, which is located on the River Cinca and surrounded by rolling countryside of a terracotta color. In addition, the two dwarfs are painted as if seen from a low vantage point which is compatible with the original placement of the pictures either over doors or over windows.

The evidence for this placement comes first from the above-mentioned memorandum relative to paintings in the Pardo and the Torre, dated 17 and 28 July 1714, which is filed with the 1701 inventory of the Pardo (where the inventory of the Torre, as a dependency of the Pardo, is also kept; see López-Rey, *Velázquez* [1979], pp. 436–7, for this information). Following the description of *"Francisco Lezcano"* are the words, *"sobre puertas."* Later, in the 1747 inventory of the Pardo, this laconic reference is clarified. After the description of the two dwarf portraits follows the phrase: *"ambas son sobrepuertas."*

Once removed from the Torre, the pictures could have been hung anywhere. But a reference in the 1747 inventory of the Torre points to the fact that they were indeed painted to be seen well above eye level. In the preface of this inventory (see Alpers, *Torre de la Parada*, p. 315), the keeper of the Torre notes that he is not to be held responsible for "las quarenta y dos pinturas de sobre ventanas y puertas cargadas por aumento de cargo al Conserje del Pardo, a cuyo Palacio se llevaron de este, en el año passado de mil setecientos y catorce de orden del Rey difunto [i.e., Philip V]." In other words, in 1714 forty-two overdoor and overwindow paintings were transferred from the Torre to the Pardo Palace. This raises the possibility that the memorandum of July 1714 described the paintings in the Torre as they were placed before their removal to the Pardo. It is also interesting that in 1747 the pictures were installed over doors, suggesting that a specific type of painting had been appropriated from the Torre to serve the same function in the Pardo.

If this argument is correct, then it follows that *"El Primo"* and *"Francisco Lezcano"* were executed by Velázquez sometime between the years 1636, when he mentioned that he was working on paintings for the Torre (see chapter IV, note 41, for the document dated 24 October 1636) and late October 1638, when the Torre was visited by the duke of Modena and presumably was completely decorated. It is always possible that these portraits were added later, but arguments to this effect based on style alone should take account of the possibility that the loose brushwork may have been caused by the intention to place the pictures at some height from the floor.

There is one further implication of the proposal to date the pictures *c.* 1636–38. Were it true, then this would constitute conclusive evidence that the "bufón rebestido de Philosopho estudiando" was indeed "El Primo," because Sebastián de Morra, the other candidate for the subject of the portrait, did not arrive in Madrid from Flanders until 1643. The only evidence against this argument is the existence of a copy of *Sebastián de Morra* which was sold in 1690 by the heirs of Gaspar de Haro, VII marquis del Carpio; for this picture see López-Rey, no. 104, pp. 445–6. In the list of the sale, the subject is given as "El Primo." However, as Martín González ("Algunas sugerencias acerca de los 'Bufones' de Velazquez," *V.V.*, I. p. 255) points out, and as López-Rey (1979, p. 445) acknowledges, the 1690 identification of the sitter in the copy is not entirely conclusive.

Finally, it must be noted that the identification of the sitter in the second dwarf portrait from the Torre as Francisco Lezcano is provisional. This name was not applied to the picture until 1794 (see López-Rey, no. 99, p. 430).

APPENDIX B

List of Paintings and Drawings

THE LIST OF PAINTINGS is divided into three categories. The first consists of works which I consider to be entirely by the hand of Velázquez. In the second are paintings executed in part by the master. The third is comprised of paintings often attributed to Velázquez which present unresolvable questions of authenticity or which are damaged beyond the point where reasonable judgments of quality and authorship can be made (the latter are indicated by asterisks). In addition to the title, location, and accession number, each entry includes the reference to López-Rey's catalogue of 1979, given in short form (i.e., L–R 1, etc.).

BY VELÁZQUEZ

Old and New Testament

1. *Adoration of the Magi.* Madrid, Museo del Prado, No. 1166 (L–R 13). Plate 28.
2. *Christ after the Flagellation Contemplated by the Christian Soul.* London, National Gallery, No. 1148 (L–r 35). Plate 81.
3. *Christ in the House of Mary and Martha.* London, National Gallery, No. 1375 (L–R 7). Plate 21.
4. *Christ on the Cross.* Madrid, Museo del Prado, No. 1167 (L–R 59). Plate 179.
5. *Coronation of the Virgin.* Madrid, Museo del Prado, No. 1168 (L–R 105). Plate 202.
6. *Joseph's Bloodied Coat Presented to Jacob.* El Escorial, Nuevos Museos (L–R 43). Plate 88.
7. *Landscape with St. Anthony Abbot and St. Paul the Hermit.* Madrid, Museo del Prado, No. 1169 (L–R 85). Plate 112.
8. *St. Paul.* Barcelona, Museo de Arte de Cataluña, No. 24242 (L–R 14). Plate 36.
9. *St. Thomas.* Orléans, Musée des Beaux-Arts, No. 264 (L–R 10). Plate 35.
10. *Supper at Emmaus.* Blessington, Sir Alfred Beit (L–R 17). Plate 25.
11. *Supper at Emmaus.* New York, Metropolitan Museum of Art, No. 14.40.631 (L–R 42). Plate 62.
12. *Virgin Bestows Chasuble on St. Ildefonso.* Seville, Museo Provincial de Bellas Artes (L–R 22). Plate 30.
13. *Virgin of Immaculate Conception.* London, National Gallery, No. 6424 (L–R 11). Plate 33.
14. *Vision of St. John the Evangelist.* London, National Gallery, No. 6264 (L–R 12). Plate 34.

Mythology and Antiquity

15. *Aesop.* Madrid, Museo del Prado, No. 1206 (L–R 92). Plate 189.
16. *Democritus.* Rouen, Musée des Beaux-Arts (L–R 40). Plate 63.

17. *Fable of Arachne ("Las Hilanderas")*. Madrid, Museo del Prado, No. 1173 (L–R 107). Plate 318.

18. *Feast of Bacchus ("Los Borrachos")*. Madrid, Museo del Prado, No. 1170 (L–R 41). Plate 69.

19. *Forge of Vulcan*. Madrid, Museo del Prado, No. 1171 (L–R 44). Plate 83.

20. *Head of Apollo*. New York, private collection (L–R 45). Plate 87.

21. *Mars*. Madrid, Museo del Prado, No. 1208 (L–R 94). Plate 193.

22. *Menippus*. Madrid, Museo del Prado, No. 1207 (L–R 93). Plate 191.

23. *Mercury and Argus*. Madrid, Museo del Prado, No. 1175 (L–R 127). Plate 313.

24. *Sibyl*. Madrid, Museo del Prado, No. 1197 (L–R 49). Plate 182.

25. *Venus and Cupid ("Rokeby Venus")*. London, National Gallery, No. 2057 (L–R 106). Plate 206.

Historical Subjects

26. *Surrender of Breda*. Madrid, Museo del Prado, No. 1172 (L–R 73). Plate 136.

Genre

27. *Old Woman Cooking*. Edinburgh, National Gallery of Scotland, No. 2180 (L–R 6). Plate 13.

28. *Three Musicians*. Berlin, Gemäldegalerie, No. 413F (L–R 1). Plate 12.

29. *Two Men at Table*. London, Wellington Museum, No. 1593 (L–R 24). Plate 16.

30. *Waterseller*. London, Wellington Museum, No. 1600 (L–R 16). Plate 15.

Portraits of Royalty, Male

31. *Baltasar Carlos*. London, Wallace Collection, No. 12 (L–R 60). Plate 97.

32. *Baltasar Carlos and a Dwarf*. Boston, Museum of Fine Arts, No. 01.104 (L–R 51). Plate 96.

33. *Baltasar Carlos as Hunter*. Madrid, Museo del Prado, No. 1189 (L–R 77). Plate 159.

34. *Baltasar Carlos on Horseback*. Madrid, Museo del Prado, No. 1180 (L–R 72). Plate 135.

35. *Cardinal Infante Ferdinand as Hunter*. Madrid, Museo del Prado, No. 1186 (L–R 64). Plate 157.

36. *Infante Don Carlos*. Madrid, Museo del Prado, No. 1188 (L–R 37). Plate 58.

37. *Infante Felipe Próspero*. Vienna, Kunsthistorisches Museum, No. 319 (L–R 129). Plate 266.

38. *Philip IV* (bust-length). Dallas, Meadows Museum, Southern Methodist University, No. 67.23 (L–R 28). Plate 49.

39. *Philip IV* (bust-length). London, National Gallery, No. 745 (L–R not accepted). Plate 270.

40. *Philip IV* (bust-length). Madrid, Museo del Prado, No. 1185 (L–R 120). Plate 50.

41. *Philip IV* (full-length). Madrid, Museo del Prado, No. 1182 (L–R 36). Plate 268.

42. *Philip IV ("Fraga Philip")*. New York, Frick Collection, No. 138 (L–R 100). Plate 196.

43. *Philip IV as Hunter*. Madrid, Museo del Prado, No. 1184 (L–R 63). Plate 155.

44. *Philip IV in Armor*. Madrid, Museo del Prado, No. 1183 (L–R 38). Plate 54.

45. *Philip IV in Brown and Silver*. London, National Gallery, No. 1129 (L–R 52). Plate 98.

46. *Philip IV on Horseback*. Madrid, Museo del Prado, No. 1178. (L–R 71). Plate 133.

Portraits of Royalty, Female

47. *Infanta Margarita*. Vienna, Kunsthistorisches Museum, No. 321 (L–R 122). Plate 263.

48. *Infanta Margarita*. Vienna, Kunsthistorisches Museum, No. 3691. (L–R 123). Plate 264.

49. *Infanta Margarita*. Vienna, Kunsthistorisches Museum, No. 2130. (L–R 128). Plate 265.

50. *Infanta María Teresa*. New York, Metropolitan Museum of Art, Jules S. Bache Collection (L–R 118). Plate 257.

51. *Infanta María Teresa*. New York, Metropolitan Museum of Art, Robert Lehman Collection (L–R 109). Plate 195.

52. *Infanta María Teresa*. Vienna, Kunsthistorisches Museum, No. 353 (L–R 119). Plate 258.

53. *María of Hungary*. Madrid, Museo del Prado, No. 1187 (L–R 48). Plate 92.

54. *Mariana of Austria*. Dallas, Meadows Museum, Southern Methodist University (L–R 125). Plate 261.

55. *Mariana of Austria*. Madrid, Museo del Prado, No. 1191 (L–R 121). Plate 259.

Male Portraits

56. *Archbishop Fernando de Valdés* (fragment of hand). Madrid, Patrimonio Nacional (L–R 56). Plate 163.

57. *Calabazas*. Madrid, Museo del Prado, No. 1205 (L–R 83). Plate 172.

58. *Cardinal Camillo Astalli-Pamphili*. New York, Hispanic Society of America, No. A 1010 (L–R 117). Plate 233.

59. *Count-Duke of Olivares*. Leningrad, Hermitage, No. 300 (L–R 87). Plate 149.

60. *Count-Duke of Olivares*. New York, Hispanic Society of America, No. A 104 (L–R 32). Plate 57.

61. *Count-Duke of Olivares on Horseback*. Madrid, Museo del Prado, No. 1181 (L–R 66). Plate 146

62. *Cristóbal Castañeda y Pernia ("Barbarroja")*. Madrid, Museo del Prado, No. 1199 (L–R 84). Plate 116.

63. *Cristóbal Suárez de Ribera*. Seville, Museo Provincial de Bellas Artes (L–R 19). Plate 38.

64. *Diego de Acedo, "El Primo"*. Madrid, Museo del Prado, No. 1201 (L–R 102). Plate 174.

65. *Diego de Corral y Arellano*. Madrid, Museo del Prado, No. 1195 (L–R 55). Plate 162.

66. *"Don Juan de Austria."* Madrid, Museo del Prado, No. 1200 (L–R 65). Plate 117.

67. *Francesco d'Este, Duke of Modena*. Modena, Pinacoteca Estense (L–R 89). Plate 166.

68. *"Francisco Lezcano."* Madrid, Museo del Prado, No. 1204 (L–R 99). Plate 175.

69. *Innocent X*. Rome, Galleria Doria-Pamphili (L–R 114). Plate 227.

70. *Innocent X*. London, Wellington Museum, No. 1590 (L–R 115). Plate 230.

71. *Juan de Pareja*. New York, Metropolitan Museum of Art, No. 1971.186 (L–R 212). Plate 234.

72. *Juan Martínez Montañés*. Madrid, Museo del Prado, No. 1194 (L–R 76). Plate 170.

73. *Juan Mateos*. Dresden, Staatliche Gemäldesammlung, No. 697 (L–R 58). Plate 167.

74. *Knight of Santiago*. Dresden, Staatliche Gemäldesammlung, No. 698 (L–R 110). Plate 201.

75. *Luis de Góngora y Argote*. Boston, Museum of Fine Arts, No. 32.79 (L–R 25). Plate 42.

76. *Man with Ruff Collar*. Madrid, Museo del Prado, No. 1209 (L–R 23). Plate 41.

77. *Monsignor Camillo Massimi*. Wimborne, Kingston Lacy, National Trust (L–R 116). Plate 232.

78. *Pablo de Valladolid*. Madrid, Museo del Prado, No. 1198 (L–R 82). Plate 121.

79. *Pedro de Barberana y Aparregui*. Fort Worth, Kimbell Museum of Art (L–R 57). Plate 165.

80. *Portrait of a Man*. London, Wellington Museum, No. 159 (L–R 91). Plate 200.

81. *Portrait of Man.* Munich, Staatsgemäldesammlungen, No. 518 (L–R 50). Plate 59.
82. *Portrait of Man* (the "Pope's Barber"). New York, private collection (L–R 113). Plate 231.
83. *Portrait of Young Man.* Madrid, Museo del Prado, No. 1224 (L–R 27). Plate 61.
84. *Sebastián de Morra.* Madrid, Museo del Prado, No. 1202 (L–R 103). Plate 199.

Female Portraits

85. *Antonia de Ipeñarrieta with Son.* Madrid, Museo del Prado, No. 1196 (L–R 54). Plate 161.
86. *Female Figure.* Dallas, Meadows Museum, Southern Methodist University (L–R 108). Plate 204.
87. *Mother Jerónima de la Fuente.* Madrid, Fernández de Araoz (L–R 21). Plate 39.
88. *Mother Jerónima de la Fuente.* Madrid, Museo del Prado, No. 2873 (L–R 20). Plate 40.
89. *Woman Doing Needlework.* Washington, National Gallery of Art, No. 81 (L–R 81). Plate 178.
90. *Woman with a Fan.* London, Wallace Collection, No. 88 (L–R 79). Plate 176.
91. *Young Girl.* New York, Hispanic Society of America, No. A 108 (L–R 97). Plate 177.

Group Portraits

92. *Baltasar Carlos in the Riding School.* Eccleston, The Grosvenor Estate (L–R 78). Plate 145.
93. *Las Meninas.* Madrid, Museo del Prado, No. 1174 (L–R 124). Plate 323.
94. *Philip IV Hunting Wild Boar* ("*La Tela Real*"). London, National Gallery, No. 197 (L–R not accepted). Plate 151.

Landscape

95. *Villa Medici, Grotto-Loggia Façade.* Madrid, Museo del Prado, No. 1210 (L–R 47). Plate 239.
96. *Villa Medici, Pavilion of Cleopatra-Ariadne.* Madrid, Museo del Prado, No. 1211 (L–R 46). Plate 238.

Animal Subjects

97. *Head of Stag.* Madrid, Museo del Prado (L–R 33). Plate 156.
98. *Rearing Horse.* Madrid, Patrimonio Nacional, (L–R 67). Plate 148.

VELÁZQUEZ AND OTHER ARTISTS

A–1. *Baltasar Carlos.* Vienna, Kunsthistorisches Museum, No. 312 (L–R 90). Plate 194.
A–2. *Isabella of Bourbon.* Switzerland, private collection (L–R 53). Plate 100.
A–3. *Isabella of Bourbon.* Vienna, Kunsthistorisches Museum, No. 731 (L–R 62). Plate 95.
A–4. *Isabella of Bourbon on Horseback.* Madrid, Museo del Prado, No. 1179 (L–R 70). Plate 132.
A–5. *Margarita of Austria on Horseback.* Madrid, Museo del Prado, No. 1177 (L–R 69). Plate 131.
A–6. *Philip III on Horseback.* Madrid, Museo del Prado, No. 1176 (L–R 68). Plate 130.
A–7. *Philip IV.* Vienna, Kunsthistorisches Museum, No. 314 (L–R 61). Plate 94.

Possibly by Velázquez

Q–1.* *A Cleric.* Madrid, Payá (L–R 26). Not illustrated.

Q–2. *Count-Duke of Olivares.* São Paulo, Museo de Arte (L–R 30). Plate 54.

Q–3.* *Head of Man.* Detroit, Institute of Arts, No. 235 (L–R not accepted). Not illustrated.

Q–4. *Head of Young Man.* Leningrad, Hermitage, No. 295 (L–R 8). Not illustrated.

Q–5.* *Kitchen Scene.* Chicago, Art Institute (L–R 18). Plate 26.

Q–6.* *Portrait of Man.* Princeton, N.J., private collection (L–R 34). Not illustrated.

Q–7.* *St. Paul* (?). Madrid, private collection (L–R 15). Not illustrated.

Q–8.* *Self-Portrait.* Valencia, Museo de Bellas Artes (L–R 96). Not illustrated.

Q–9. *Two Men and a Girl at Table.* Budapest, Museum of Fine Art (L–R9). Not illustrated.

Although numerous drawings have been ascribed to Velázquez, only two sheets have an undisputed claim to authenticity. Velázquez certainly made drawings from time to time, but, as explained in the text, his method of composition did not favor the use of this medium. Similarly, his custom of making preparatory portrait studies in oil tended to reduce the number of drawings. The lack of a sizable corpus therefore makes definitive attribution exceptionally difficult.

By Velázquez

D–1. *Cardinal Borja.* Madrid, Real Academia de Bellas Artes de San Fernando (L–R 98). Plate 198.

D–2a. *Study for Surrender of Breda* (recto). Madrid, Biblioteca Nacional (L–R 74). Plate 141.

D–2b. *Study for Surrender of Breda* (verso). Plate 142.

Possibly by Velázquez

D.Q.–1. *Count-Duke of Olivares.* Paris, Ecole des Beaux-Arts (L–R not accepted.) Not illustrated.

D.Q.–2. *Head of Young Woman.* Madrid, Biblioteca Nacional (L–R 5). Not illustrated.

D.Q.–3. *Innocent X.* Toronto, Theodore A. Heinrich. (Plate 228).

D.Q.–4. *Innocent X.* Toronto, Theodore A. Heinrich. (Plate 229).

D.Q–5. *Study of Guardian Angel in Christ after the Flagellation* (destroyed 1936). Formerly Gijón, Instituto Jovellanos (L–R under no. 35). Not illustrated.

D.Q–6. *Young Woman.* Madrid, Biblioteca Nacional (L–R 4). Not illustrated.

LIST OF ABBREVIATIONS

AB	*Art Bulletin*
AE	*Arte español*
AEA	*Archivo español de arte*
AEAA	*Archivo español de arte y arquelogía*
AGS	Archivo General de Simancas
AHP	Archivo Histórico de Protocolos, Madrid
AIEM	*Anales del Instituto de Estudios Madrileños*
AP	Archivo de Palacio, Madrid
BM	*Burlington Magazine*
BMP	*Boletín del Museo del Prado*
BNM	Biblioteca Nacional, Madrid
BRAH	*Boletín de la Real Academia de la Historia*
BSAA	*Boletín del Seminario de Estudios de Arte y Arqueología, Universidad de Valladolid*
BSCE	*Boletín de la Sociedad Castellana de Excursiones*
BSEE	*Boletín de la Sociedad Española de Excursiones*
CODOIN	*Colección de Documentos Inéditos para la Historia de España*
GBA	*Gazette des Beaux-Arts*
JWCI	*Journal of the Warburg and Courtauld Institutes*
MD	*Master Drawings*
RABM	*Revista de Archivos, Bibliotecas y Museos*
VM	*Villa de Madrid*
V.V.	*Varia Velazqueña*

NOTES

CHAPTER I

1. Citations of documents refer to the useful compendium in *Varia Velazqueña*, II (Madrid, 1960), pp. 213–413 (hereafter cited as *V.V.*). For Velázquez' certificate of baptism, see doc. 2, p. 213. A thoughtful account of Velázquez' early years is by Julián Gállego, *Velázquez en Sevilla* (Seville, 1974). Also thought-provoking is the section devoted to the early period by Leo Steinberg, "Review of José López-Rey, *Velázquez. A Catalogue Raisonné of His Oeuvre, with an Introductory Study*," *AB*, 47 (1965), pp. 278–82. Velázquez' name has been given and spelled in various ways, beginning in his own lifetime. I have chosen to use a modified version of the form preferred by the artist in his later years (Diego de Silva Velázquez), which, by use of "de," denotes his noble status.

2. For the social status of painters in seventeenth-century Spain, see Jonathan Brown, *Images and Ideas in Seventeenth-Century Spanish Painting* (Princeton, 1978), pp. 105–7, and Julián Gállego, *El pintor de artesano a artista* (Granada, 1976).

3. This figure is taken from Richard L. Kagan, *Students and Society in Early Modern Spain* (Baltimore and London, 1974), p. 23. For Velázquez' library, see Francisco J. Sánchez Cantón, "La librería de Velázquez," in *Homenaje a Menéndez Pidal*, III (Madrid, 1925), pp. 379–406.

4. *V.V.*, II, doc. 8, pp. 215–16. Palomino supposed that Velázquez spent a short time as the apprentice of Francisco de Herrera the Elder before entering Pacheco's shop, although there is no evidence for the assertion.

5. There is no complete, up-to-date study of Pacheco's life and works. For an outline of his career, see Priscilla E. Muller, "Francisco Pacheco as Painter," *Marsyas*, 10 (1961), pp. 39–44.

6. For the history of Pacheco's academy and its members, see Brown, *Images and Ideas*, pp. 21–83, on which the following is based.

7. Antonio Palomino, *El museo pictórico y escala óptica* (Madrid, 1715–24; ed. cited, Madrid, 1947), p. 892.

8. In March 1610, Pacheco executed a portrait of the count-duke; see Duque de Berwick y Alba et al., *Discursos leídos ante el Real Academia de San Fernando* (Madrid, 1924), pp. 23–4.

9. For Céspedes, see Brown, *Images and Ideas*, pp. 30–2 and 44–8.

10. Francisco Pacheco, *Arte de la pintura*, ed. F. J. Sánchez Cantón (Madrid, 1956). For a discussion, see Brown, *Images and Ideas*, pp. 44–62.

11. See above, note 2.

12. For example, see Vicente Lleó Cañal, *Nueva Roma: mitología y humanismo en el renacimiento sevillano* (Seville, 1979) and Duncan T. Kinkead, "An Analysis of Sevillian Painting Collections of the Mid-17th Century. The Importance of Secular Subject Matter," in *Hispanism as Humanism* (forthcoming).

13. The full range of Charles V's activities as a patron of the arts has never been completely studied. For an introduction, see Hugh Trevor-Roper, *Princes and Artists. Patronage and Ideology at Four Habsburg Courts, 1517–1633* (London, 1976), pp. 11–45.

14. For a recent outline of Philip II as art patron and collector, see Jonathan Brown, "Felipe II como mecenas y coleccionista de arte," in *Ciudades españolas del siglo de oro* (Madrid, 1985).

15. The basic work on the Italian painters at El Escorial, now out-dated but still not superseded, is Julián Zarco Cuevas, *Los pintores italianos en San Lorenzo el Real de El Escorial* (Madrid, 1932). For the importance of these artists in the history of Spanish painting, see Alfonso E. Pérez Sánchez, "Sobre los pintores de El Escorial," *Goya*, 56–7 (1963), pp. 148–53.

16. See Diego Angulo Iñiguez and Alfonso E. Pérez Sánchez, *Historia de la pintura española. Escuela madrileña del primer tercio del siglo XVII* (Madrid, 1969), pp. 14–46.

17. See Angulo Iñiguez and Pérez Sánchez, *Escuela madrileña*, pp. 86–189; Alfonso E. Pérez Sánchez, "Pintura madrileña del siglo XVII: Addenda," *AEA*, 49 (1976), pp. 293–325; Mary C. Volk, *Vicencio Carducho and Seventeenth-Century Castilian Painting* (New York and London, 1977); and Vicente Carducho, *Diálogos de la pintura*, ed. Francisco Calvo Serraller (Madrid, 1979).

18. Of these, only Mohedano has been studied recently; see Rafael González Zubieta, *Vida y obra del artista andaluz Antonio Mohedano de la Gutierra (1563?–1626)* (Córdoba, 1981).

19. For the date, see Alfonso Rodríguez G. de Ceballos, "Alonso Matías, precursor de Cano," in *Centenario de Alonso Cano en Granada*, I (Granada, 1969), p. 169.

20. Pacheco mentions the commission in *Arte*, II, p. 14.

21. See Enrique Valdivieso, *Juan de Roelas* (Seville, 1978).

22. *V.V.*, II, doc. 10, p. 217.

23. *V.V.*, II, doc. 12, p. 218.

24. *V.V.*, II, docs. 13 and 15, pp. 218–19 and 220.

25. *V.V.*, II, doc. 14, pp. 219–20.

26. *V.V.*, II, docs. 16–17, 20, pp. 220–1.

27. The interpretation of this painting as representing the Supper at Emmaus advanced by John F. Moffitt ("Observations on Symbolic Content in Two Early Bodegones by Diego Velázquez," *Boletín del Museo e Instituto Camón Aznar*, 1 [1980], pp. 82–95), seems improbable in the absence of any overt signs that point to a religious subject. Moffitt's assumption that all works of seventeenth-century Spanish painting, regardless of subject, have religious significance, seems to be mistaken. For a more plausible interpretation proposed by Barry Wind, see below p. 15.

28. Following Elizabeth Du Gué Trapier (*Velázquez* [New York, 1948]), who omits it from her book, and Kurt Gerstenberg (*Diego Velázquez* [Berlin, 1957], pp. 27–8), I am inclined to view a related composition in Budapest, Museum of Fine Arts, as the work of an imitator, and perhaps a pastiche of Plate 11 and a lost work which

contained the figure of the woman pouring a glass of wine. The integration of the female figure into the composition is poor and gives the impression that she has been lifted from another scene and deposited into an alien context. However, the picture is accepted by José López-Rey (*Velázquez. The Artist as Maker* [Lausanne–Paris, 1979], no. 9, p. 196). The condition is good.

The *Head of a Boy* in Leningrad has been accepted as a preliminary study for the figure on the right; see José López-Rey, *Velázquez. A Catalogue Raisonné of His Oeuvre* (London, 1963), no. 121, p. 162; Vladimir Kemenov, *Velázquez in Soviet Museums* (Leningrad, 1977), p. 51; and López-Rey, *Velázquez* (1979), no. 8, p. 193. In 1973, it was reported that an X-ray of the picture revealed the image of a head (repr. López-Rey, 1979, fig. 63), which is visible when the picture is turned at right angles to the left. Kemenov and López-Rey believe that the under-image is related to the central figure in *Three Musicians* In my opinion, the authenticity of the painting is uncertain.

29. López-Rey (*Velázquez* [1979], no. 1, p. 177), believes that radiographs of the picture show that the costume of the central figure was originally lighter in color. More likely, the lighter tone is produced by the presence of lead white in the ground, which is visible in other sections of the X-ray.

30. Steinberg ("Review," pp. 279–80), suggests an elaborate interpretation for the painting, which he admits is based on circumstantial evidence. His notion that the painting "has an implicit psychological content which may be described as an awakening . . . on multiple levels: of night into morning, of things into light, and of a boy into consciousness," seems based in part on the tacit assumption that the woman is cooking a breakfast of eggs. Without entering into a discussion of Spanish culinary practices and dietary preferences, not to mention less palatable subjects such as the iconography of food, it can be observed that the woman might just as well be making garlic soup, a traditional peasant dish, which is garnished with eggs.

31. This suggestion was made by John F. Moffitt ("Image and Meaning in Velázquez' *Watercarrier of Seville*," *Traza y Baza*, 7 [1978], p. 9). The clientele for the early genre paintings remains a mystery. The earliest record of ownership in Seville dates from 1655, when three *bodegones* were listed in the inventory of Luis de Medina, a town councillor; see Duncan T. Kinkead, "Tres bodegones de Velázquez en una colección sevillana del siglo XVII," *AEA*, 52 (1979), p. 185.

32. Gállego, *Velázquez en Sevilla*, p. 132, interprets the subject as the Three Ages of Man. Moffitt ("Image and Meaning") accepts and elaborates upon this idea, carrying it to implausible lengths. (He believes that the painting is an allegory of Providence and a "personal emblem of Prudence and Good Counsel." He also suggests that the three figures might be portraits of Pacheco, Velázquez, and Diego Melgar, Velázquez' apprentice.) Neither author acknowledges the article by Leo Steinberg, "The Water Carrier of Seville," *Art News*, 70 (Summer 1971), pp. 54–5, where this interpretation was first proposed. In my view, if the painting has an ulterior or concealed meaning, it has yet to be revealed.

33. The extensive literature is cited and summarized in Halldor Soehner, "Die Herkunft der Bodegones Velázquez," in *V.V.*, I, pp. 233–44.

34. The connection between Velázquez and Caravaggio was first proposed by Roberto Longhi ("Un San Tomasso di Velázquez e le congiunture italo-spagnole tra il '5 e '600," *Vita artistica*, 2 [1927], pp. 4–11), and was given its most detailed formulation by Juan Ainaud de Lasarte ("Ribalta y Caravaggio," *Anales y Boletín de los Museos de Arte de Barcelona*, 5 [1947], pp. 345–413). It has recently been re-stated by Enriqueta Harris (*Velázquez* [Oxford, 1982], pp. 53–4), and Marianne Haraszti-Takacs (*Spanish Genre Painting in the Seventeenth Century* [Budapest, 1983], chapter 3). The "anti-Carravagists," of whom I am one, include José López-Rey (*Velázquez* [1963], p. 26); Alfonso E. Pérez Sánchez (*Caravaggio y el naturalismo*

español [Seville, 1973], Introduction, pp. unnumbered); and Richard E. Spear (*Caravaggio and His Followers* [rev. ed., New York, 1975], pp. 19–20). A link between the picaresque novel and Velázquez' genre paintings has been posited by numerous writers, but I see no specific connection that confirms it.

35. See Christoph L. Frommel, "Caravaggios Frühwerk und der Kardinal Francesco Maria del Monte," *Storia dell'Arte*, 9–10 (1971), p. 7.

36. The connection was first noted in August L. Mayer, "Velázquez und die Niederlandische Kuchenstücke," *Kunstchronik und Kunstmarkt*, 30 (3 January 1919), pp. 236–7. Further examples are presented by Soehner ("Die Herkunft"), who distinguishes as many as five sources for Velázquez' *bodegones*.

For the presence of Flemish genre paintings in Madrid, see Sarah Schroth, "Early Collectors of Still Life Painting in Castile," in *Spanish Still Life in the Golden Age: 1600–1650* (Fort Worth, 1985).

37. For a definition of the type, see Barry Wind, "*Pitture Ridicole:* Some Late Cinquecento Comic Genre Paintings," *Storia dell'Arte*, 20 (1974), pp. 25–35.

38. See Julio Cavestany, *Floreros y bodegones en la pintura española* (Madrid, 1936 and 1940), pp. 36 and 74.

39. This connection is established by Barry Wind in a forthcoming study of Velázquez' *bodegones*, where the naturalist symbolism of the paintings is explained.

40. See note 36.

41. A concise summary of the various opinions about these problematic elements can be found in Neil MacLaren, *The Spanish School*, National Gallery Catalogues, rev. ed., Allan Braham (London, 1970), p. 122.

42. This interpretation is suggested most recently by Allan Braham ("A Second Dated Bodegon by Velázquez," *BM*, 107 [1965], pp. 362–5). López-Rey (*Velázquez* [1979], no. 7, p. 190), asserts that the appearance of the window noted by Braham is the result of tendentious restoration. My examination of the work and the conservation files leads me to disagree with this assertion. To be sure, the wall behind the foreground figures has suffered considerable loss of the original pigment. But the restoration of this section, which does heighten the contrast between the wall and the opening, did not alter the enclosure around the background scene.

Like Braham, I do not believe that either foreground figure represents Martha. In only one instance, Plate 112, did Velázquez paint a picture with consecutive narration, in which the same characters reappear in different parts of the composition, and then he left no doubt about his intentions.

43. For this interpretation of the theme, see Kenneth M. Craig, "*Pars Ergo Marthae Transit:* Pieter Aertsen's 'Inverted' Paintings of Christ in the House of Martha and Mary," *Oud Holland*, 97 (1983), pp. 25–39, which offers a more reliable guide to the iconography of the picture than the recent article by John F. Moffitt, "'Terebat in moratorio': Symbolism in Velázquez' Christ in the House of Martha and Mary," *Arte Cristiana*, 72, fasc. 700 (1984), pp. 13–24. Moffitt seeks to interpret the painting as a complex religious allegory, which is also intended to provide evidence for his thesis that all Spanish art of the seventeenth century, secular or religious, is devoted to explaining the mysteries of Catholicism to the faithful in realistic terms. In addition to specific problems with the argument (for instance, I see no way to prove that the young woman is grinding manna in the mortar), I believe that the author has imposed a set of associations on the picture which are extrinsic to the visual data of the composition. Religious writers of the period could and did bring the full weight of theological exegesis to bear on even the most humble creations of the universe, but this method of interpretation when uncritically applied to works of art implicitly minimizes or eliminates the artist's control over the presentation and perception of his subject matter, and thus his artistry. Furthermore, the reconstruction of the cultural associations of a given motif does not mean that these associations are

automatically to be invoked whenever and wherever they are encountered in a picture. A master-painter deliberately orders his compositions to focus the viewer's attention on matters he considers to be essential.

44. The similarity is noted by Steinberg ("Review," p. 289), who also offers cogent criticisms of the interpretation of the picture proposed by López-Rey.

45. See López-Rey (*Velázquez* (1979), no. 17, p. 216), who notes the loss on the left side of the canvas.

46. See, for example, López-Rey, *Velázquez* (1963), nos. 101–2, 110, 112, 114, 116, 122, 125–7, 130.

47. For the provenance, see Juan Ainaud de Lasarte, "Pinturas de procedencia sevillana," *AEA*, 19 (1946), pp. 54–60.

48. See Enrique Valdivieso and Juan M. Serrera, *La época de Murillo* (Seville, 1982), p. 11, for this phenomenon.

49. A lithograph of the painting by Cayetano Palmaroli, published in 1832, not only "restores" the missing margins, but also subtly corrects the effect of overcrowding. As López-Rey (*Velázquez* [1979], no. 13, p. 206), notes, the print does not prove that the painting was reduced in size only after 1832, because Palmaroli could have decided to "reconstruct the missing parts according to his own idea of Velázquez' sense of composition."

It is not often noted that Velázquez unobtrusively included an allusion to the crown of thorns, and thus to the Passion, in the lower right corner.

50. For the eighteenth-century description, see J. de M. Carriazo, "Correspondencia de don Antonio Ponz con el Conde del Aguila," *AEAA*, 5 (1929), p. 179. The painting was restored in 1960; see Diego Angulo Iñiguez, "'La imposición de la casulla a San Ildefonso,' de Velázquez," *AEA*, 33 (1960), pp. 290–1, for a report of the poor condition.

51. For a complete discussion of these paintings, see MacLaren and Braham, *The Spanish School*, pp. 129–33.

52. For this observation, see Antonio Martínez Ripoll, "El 'San Juan Evangelista en las isla de Patmos,' de Velázquez, y sus fuentes de inspiración iconográfica," *Areas. Revista de Ciencias Sociales*, 3–4 (1983), pp. 201–8.

53. *V.V.*, II, doc. 12, p. 218.

54. Pacheco, *Arte*, II, pp. 208–12.

55. See Martínez Ripoll, "El 'San Juan Evangelista.'"

56. The *Head of a Man* (Madrid, private collection; López-Rey, *Velázquez* [1979], no. 15, p. 210), which somewhat resembles *St. Paul*, is on the borderline of Velázquez' oeuvre.

57. Technical studies of paintings by Velázquez are almost non-existent, although a start is now being made; see María Garrido, José M. Cabrera, Gridley McKim-Smith, and Richard M. Newman, "La Fragua de Vulcano. Estudio técnico y algunas consideraciones sobre los materiales y métodos del XVII," *BMP*, 4 (1983), pp. 79–95, and Gridley McKim-Smith, Greta Anderson, and Richard M. Newman, *Examining Velázquez* (forthcoming).

58. This information is given in José Gestoso y Pérez, *Sevilla monumental y artística*, III (Seville, 1892), pp. 286–91.

59. *V.V.*, II, doc. 4, p. 214.

60. The picture is signed with the monogram "DOVZ," which could be a signature. If so, it would be the only instance of a monogram signature in Velázquez' oeuvre.

61. See López-Rey, *Velázquez* (1979), no. 20, p. 223, and Alfonso E. Pérez Sánchez, *The Golden Age of Spanish Painting* (London, 1976), no. 44, pp. 62–3. The question of which version was done first is impossible to answer.

62. See Juan Ainaud de Lasarte, "Francisco Ribalta. Notas y comentarios," *Goya*, 20 (September–October 1957), p. 88.

63. Although the sitter is often said to be Pacheco, there are no solid grounds for this identification, as López-Rey has pointed out ([1979], no. 23, p. 230).

64. The *Portrait of a Man* (Detroit, Institute of Arts) is in very poor condition. After being accepted provisionally by López-Rey in 1963 (p. 312, no. 556), it was omitted from the 1979 edition of his catalogue.

65. Pacheco, *Arte*, I, p. 156.

66. The drawing of Góngora, however, is not preserved in the manuscript now in the Fundación Lázaro Galdiano, Madrid. See Francisco Pacheco, *Libro de descripción de verdaderos retratos de ilustres y memorables varones*, intr. Diego Angulo (Seville, 1983).

Chapter II

1. This discussion of Madrid's history is based on Jonathan Brown and J. H. Elliott, *A Palace for a King: The Buen Retiro and the Court of Philip IV* (New Haven and London, 1980), pp. 1–7, which lists further references.

2. Luis Cabrera de Córdoba, *Filipe segundo, rey de España*, I (ed. Madrid, 1976), p. 298.

3. Agustín Bustamante García, "En torno a Juan de Herrera y la arquitectura," *BSAA*, 42 (1976), pp. 227–49.

4. This description of the court of Spain is based on J. H. Elliott, "Philip IV of Spain," in *The Courts of Europe*, ed. A. G. Dickens (London, 1977), pp. 169–89; Brown and Elliott, *A Palace*, pp. 31–40; and "Etiquetas generales de la Casa R.l del Rey nro. S.r para el uso y exercicio de los ofizios de sus criados (1647)," *BNM*, sig. 10.666, for which see J. E. Varey, "L'Auditoire du Salón Dorado de l'Alcázar de Madrid," in *Dramaturgie et Société. Rapports entre l'oeuvre theâtrale, son interpretation et son public aux XVIe et XVIIe siècle*, I (Paris, 1968), pp. 77–91.

5. See José M. de Azcárate, "Instrucción para las construcciones reales en el siglo XVII," *BSAA*, 25 (1960), pp. 223–30.

6. The literature on the architectural history of the Alcázar, which was destroyed by fire in 1734, is large and widely-scattered. For a convenient summary and further references, see Véronique Gérard, "Les problèmes artistiques de Alcázar de Madrid (1537–1700)," *Mélanges de las Casa de Velázquez*, 12 (1976) pp. 307–22, and Steven N. Orso, *Philip IV and the Decoration of the Alcázar of Madrid*, chapter 1 (forthcoming at Princeton University Press).

7. See Véronique Gérard, "La fachada del Alcázar de Madrid," *Cuardernos de Investigación Histórica*, 2 (1973), pp. 237–57.

8. This plan was drawn by Juan Gómez de Mora, the court architect, in 1626. See Francisco Iñiguez Almech, *Casas reales y jardines de Felipe II* (Madrid, 1952) pp. 47–8.

9. For a brief account of the country houses and references to the relevant literature, see Brown and Elliott, *A Palace*, p. 55.

10. See George Kubler, *Building the Escorial* (Princeton, 1982), for a history of the construction.

11. There is still no satisfactory biography of Philip IV. The following account is based on Brown and Elliott, *A Palace*, pp. 26–33, 40–54.

12. Ruth S. Magurn, *The Letters of Peter Paul Rubens* (Cambridge, Mass., 1955), letter 180 (2 December 1628), p. 292.

13. See J. H. Elliott and José F. de la Peña, *Memoriales y cartas del Conde Duque de Olivares*, 2 vols. (Madrid, 1978 and 1981); Brown and Elliott, *A Palace*, pp. 13–30; and the forthcoming monograph by Elliott on the count-duke.

14. See Brown and Elliott, *A Palace*, p. 200.

15. For Maino, see Angulo Iñiguez and Pérez Sánchez, *Escuela madrileña*, pp. 299–325; Fernando Marías, "Juan Bautista Maino y su familia," *AEA*, 49 (1976), pp. 468–70; and Juan J. Junquera, "Un retablo de Maino en Pastrana," *AEA*, 50 (1977), pp. 129–40.

16. See above, chapter I, notes 13–14

17. For the document of his appointment, see Juan J. Martín González, "Arte y artistas del siglo XVII en la corte," *AEA*, 32 (1958), pp. 130–1. The crucial distinction between "pintor de cámara" and "pintor del rey" is usually forgotten in the discussion of art at the Habsburg court of Spain, perhaps because of the title of the

otherwise admirable work by Sánchez Cantón, which treats both categories as one — *Los pintores de cámara de los reyes de España* (Madrid. 1916).

For Morán's life and career, about which little is known, see Angulo Iñiguez and Pérez Sánchez. *Escuela madrileña*, pp. 69–73.

18. For Carducho, see above, chapter I. note 17; for Cajés, see Angulo Iñiguez and Pérez Sánchez, *Escuela madrileña*, pp. 212–59.

19. There is no adequate study of González. For his appointment at court, see Sánchez Cantón, *Los pintores de cámara*, pp. 64 and 74.

20. For Villandrando, see José López-Rey, "Muerte de Villandrando y fortuna de Velázquez," *AE*, 26 (1968–69), pp. 1–4. For Francisco López, see Angulo Iñiguez and Pérez Sánchez, *Escuela madrileña*, pp. 47–56.

21. Pacheco, *Arte*, I, p. 156.

22. For Fonseca, see Cayetano Alberto de la Barrera, *Francisco de Rioja* (Madrid, 1867), pp. 292–319, and José López Navío, "Velázquez tasa los cuadros de su protector, D. Juan de Fonseca," *AEA*, 34 (1961), pp. 53–84.

23. *V. V.*, II, doc. 20, p. 221.

24. See López-Rey, "Muerte de Villandrando."

25. This is described by Pacheco, *Arte*, I, pp. 156–7.

26. Gaspar de Bracamonte later had an important career in government service, concluding with the viceregency of Naples. For his activities as an art patron in Naples, see Harold E. Wethey, "The Spanish Viceroy, Luca Giordano and Andrea Vaccaro," *BM*, 109 (1967). pp. 678–87.

27. *V.V.*, II. doc. 22, p. 222.

28. On the basis of the radiograph of the full-length portrait in the Prado (Plate 55), López-Rey (*Velázquez* [1979], p. 31 and no. 36, pp. 264–5) believes that the image partly concealed beneath the overpainted version now visible to the naked eye is the portrait painted by Velázquez on 30 August 1623 which showed the king "with a somewhat flabby face, roundish at the chin, and a very short neck." This image, he believes, although accurate, was found to be too realistic and was therefore replaced by a more idealized version.

This reading of the radiograph is open to question. What López-Rey sees as the "flabby face, " etc. results from the superimposition of the longer head of the second version over the shorter head of the first version. The close overlapping of the two images in the radiograph creates the misleading impression of a single, unattractive portrait of the king. This interpretation has lately been confirmed by McKim-Smith et al. (*Examining Velázquez*). In my opinion, the head of the king in the first version looked as it does in the portrait in Dallas and the copies in New York and Boston.

Priscilla E. Muller ("Mainc, Crayer, Velázquez and a Miniature of Philip IV," *Art Bulletin*, 60 [1978], pp. 87–8) tentatively suggests that the first portrait of Philip IV may be identifiable with a portrait miniature in Munich, Bayerisches Nationalmuseum, which she attributes to Velázquez.

29. For other examples of life studies, see Plates 92, 149, 166, 195, 257, 263, 268, 270.

30. Cited in Enriqueta Harris, "Cassiano dal Pozzo on Diego Velázquez," *BM*, 112 (1970), p. 364.

31. The conservation reports in the files of the museum, dated 10 January and 18 April 1972, specify the full extent of the damaged sections. The hair, the background, and parts of the costume are entirely repainted.

32. The version in the Metropolitan Museum of Art (Plate 51) was part of a documented commission of 1624 (for which, see below, note 34), and has been accepted as an autograph work (for example, López-Rey, *Velázquez* [1979], no. 29, pp. 244–6). In my opinion, the dull, mechanical execution, evident despite the loss of the impasto, suggests the hand of a follower. I am grateful to John Brealey for his assistance in the study of this painting.

33. This image is difficult to interpret because of the extensive reworking. But two important revisions are noted in McKim-Smith et al., *Examining Velázquez*: in the original composition as seen in the radiograph, the left shoulder was broader and the stiff collar originally met the king's face at the level of the lips, not the top of the jaw. In other words, the head and shoulders once looked as they do in the reworked full-length portrait.

The changes in this study may be related to the commission for an equestrian portrait. (For a comparable example of a preliminary study for an equestrian portrait, see below, p. 144). Velázquez executed one and possibly two equestrian portraits in the 1620s. The first, mentioned by Pacheco, was completed in March 1626 and installed in the Salón Nuevo of the Alcázar (see *Arte*, I p. 157, and Harris "Cassiano dal Pozzo," p. 372). The existence of the second equestrian portrait is somewhat circumstantial. On 1 June 1628, Olivares' secretary wrote a request that Velázquez be given access to armor he needed for a portrait he was making of the king. Then, on 3 September 1628, another order was issued to the Royal Armory to give him whatever he needed to execute the portraits of Philip III and Philip IV then in progress. See Pedro Beroqui, "Adiciones y correcciones al catálogo del Museo del Prado," *BSCE*, año 16, 2nd series, II (1918), p. 61. The document does not state that these were to be equestrian portraits, but the possibility cannot be discounted. Hence, the reworking of the full-length standing portrait (Plate 50) could have occurred either in 1625–26 or 1628, with the latter date being more probable.

34. *V.V.*, II, doc. 26, p. 224. A more accurate transcription of the document is given by López-Rey (*Velázquez* [1979], p. 244).

35. It has been doubted that Velázquez had a workshop at this early point in his career at court. However, there are at least two paintings which are generally considered to be contemporary copies of the earliest portraits of the king (Plates 51, 52), and also another of this version of the count-duke (Madrid, Várez-Fisa, the authenticity of which, however, is cautiously defended in Pérez Sánchez, *The Golden Age of Spanish Painting*, no. 47, p. 67). If, as Pacheco says, Velázquez was given the exclusive right to portray the king, then he could have counted on the demand for copies from courtiers, collectors, and foreign ambassadors, and have formed a team of assistants to help with this work.

36. Olivares exchanged his membership in the Order of Calatrava for Alcántara in 1624, which establishes the earliest possible date for this portrait, where he is seen wearing the green cross of Alcántara. See López-Rey, *Velázquez* (1979), no. 30, p. 249, for new details on the exchange of orders.

The timid swag of drapery in the upper right corner does not appear to be original; see Elizabeth Du Gué Trapier, "The Cleaning of Velázquez's *Count-Duke of Olivares*," in *V. V.*, I, pp. 320–2. An inscription on the painting was read as "Año 1625" by Trapier ("Velázquez. New Data on a Group of Portraits," *Notes Hispanic*, 4 [1944], p. 40). However, I believe that López-Rey is correct in interpreting the number as an old inventory number and not a date (*Velázquez' Work and World* [London, 1968], p. 34, note 1).

37. See the letter of James Howell (5 January 1622 or 1623) for this description of the prince: "[Don Carlos] hath neither office, command, dignity, nor title, but is an individual companion to the King, and what clothes soever are provided for the King, he had the very same, and as often from top to toe." *Epistolae Hoelianae*, ed. J. Jacobs (London, 1890), p. 155.

38. Jesús Hernández Perera ("Velázquez y las joyas," *AEA*, 33 [1960], pp. 255–56) notes that the prince had been given a birthday gift of "Una cadena de oro de eslabones grandes sin esmalte alguno" (a golden chain with large links and without any enameling) by his sister, Queen María of Hungary, on 16 September 1628. He identifies the chain in the portrait with this gift and therefore proposes a date of 1628 for the picture. According to Cassiano dal Pozzo, writing in the spring of 1626, the fashion for the gold chain, or *fanfarone*, had

recently been revived in Spain (see Harris, "Cassiano dal Pozzo," p. 371). In fact, golden chains are seen in the 1624 portraits of the king and the count-duke (Plates 51, 54). Hence, in and of itself, the rather vague description of the chain written in the document of 1628 is not conclusive evidence for the date.

More worthy of consideration is Hernández Perera's observation that the prince, in his portrait, appears to be raising a moustache. The king himself began to grow a moustache in late 1628 to early 1629 — Rubens indicates a thin moustache in one of his portraits of the king (Bayonne, Musée Bonnat). If Don Carlos continued to imitate his brother, then the appearance of his moustache would suggest a date of 1628–29 for this portrait.

39. The importance of this practice was first noted in R.A.M. Stevenson, *Velázquez* (2nd ed., London, 1910), pp. 46–7.

40. For the *Portrait of Mariá of Hungary*, sometimes assigned to this period, see below p. 79.

41. The sitter wears a collar known as a *golilla*, which was adopted after the sumptuary laws promulgated in January 1623.

42. See José López-Rey, "Pincelada e imagen en Velázquez," in *V.V.*, I, pp. 200–6. In subsequent works on Velázquez (1963, 1968, and, less emphatically, 1979), López-Rey develops the idea that the artist used a different, more solid and even technique, when painting the faces of the royal family. He explains the difference by imputing to Velázquez the desire to express, via his brushstroke, the "quasi-divine" nature of the king. For the refutation of this interpretation, see Steinberg, "Review of López-Rey," pp. 291–2.

43. For a full discussion of this painting, see Halldor Soehner, *Gemäldekatalog. Bayerische Staatsgemäldesammlungen Alte Pinakothek, München. I, Spanische Meister* (Munich, 1963), pp. 195–9.

44. Portraits which fall into this category are as follows: *Martínez Montañés* (Plate 170; 1.09 × 0.835 m.); *Young Girl* (Plate 177; 0.515 × 0.410 m.); *Knight of Santiago* (Plate 201; 0.665 × 0.560 m.); *Juan Mateos* (Plate 167; 1.08 × 0.895 m.); *Woman Doing Needlework* (Plate 178; 0.740 × 0.600 m.).

45. See Véronique Gérard, "Philip IV's Early Italian Commissions," *Oxford Art Journal*, 5 (1982), pp. 9–14.

46. A man holding a glass of wine is a conventional seventeenth-century symbol for the Sense of Taste. For examples, see Hans Kauffmann, "Die Fünfsinne in der niederlandisch Malerei des 17. Jahrhunderts," in *Kunstgeschichtliche Studien*, ed. Hans Tinteltot (Breslau, 1943), pp. 133–57, and Marielene Putscher, "Die fünf Sinne," *Aachener Kunstblatter*, 41 (1971), pp. 152–73.

For the repainting of the canvas, see "Chroniques du Laboratoire. Notes sur les radiographies de deux tableau appartenant aux Musée de Pau et du Rouen," *Bulletin du Laboratoire du Musée du Louvre*, 9 (1964), pp. 50–3.

For the identification of the subject as Democritus, see Werner Weisbach, "Der sogennante Geograph von Velázquez und die Darstellungen des Demokrit und Heraklit," *Jahrbuch der Preussischen Kunstsammlungen*, 49 (1928), pp. 141–58.

47. For Velázquez' place of residence in February 1625, see María del Carmen González Múñoz, "Datos para un estudio de Madrid en la primera mitad del siglo XVII," *AIEM*, 18 (1981), pp. 159–60.

48. The documents concerning Velázquez' ecclesiastical benefice were discovered by Quintín Aldea, S.J., and published in José Camón Aznar, *Velázquez*, I (Madrid, 1964), p. 330, and partially republished in Enriqueta Harris, "Velázquez and His Ecclesiastical Benefice," *BM*, 123 (1981), pp. 95–6.

49. *V.V.*, II, docs. 31–32, pp. 226–7.

50. Pacheco's presence in Madrid around the year 1625 is implied in his text. However, he seems to have traveled back and forth between Seville and Madrid during 1624–26. According to published documents, his whereabouts can be reconstructed as follows:

5 July 1624 — in Seville (Celestino López Martínez,

Desde Jerónimo Hernández hasta Martínez Montañés [Seville, 1929], p. 184).

20 October 1624 — in Madrid, probably living with Velázquez on the calle de Convalecientes (Celestino López Martínez, *Desde Martínez Montañés hasta Pedro Roldán* [Seville, 1932], p. 190.) His residence with Velázquez is established by González Múñoz ("Datos," p. 179).

4 February 1625 — in Seville (González Múñoz, "Datos," p. 176).

Later 1625 — in Madrid, where he executed a statue a Nra. Sra. de la Expectación for the countess of Olivares, which took four months to complete (*Arte*, II, p. 46).

8 March 1626 — probably in Madrid, when Velázquez petitioned the king to appoint him as *pintor real* in place of the deceased Santiago Morán (*V.V.*, II, doc. 29, p. 225).

8 July 1626 — in Madrid (Francisco Rodríguez Marín, *Francisco Pacheco, maestro de Velázquez* [Madrid, 1923], p. 50).

26 December 1626 — in Seville, apparently for good (López-Rey, *Velázquez* [1979], p. 160, note 72, correcting the erroneous transcription of the date found in *Documentos para la historia del arte en Andalucía*, VIII, [Seville, 1935], p. 67, where the year is given as 1624).

51. Jusepe Martínez, "Discursos practicables del noblíssimo arte de la pintura" (ed. cit., *V.V.*, II, p. 66).

52. The principal source for this competition is Pacheco, *Arte*, I, pp. 157–8. See also Juan J. Martín González, "Sobre las relaciones entre Nardi, Carducho y Velázquez," *AEA*, 31 (1958), pp. 59–66.

53. For the decoration of the Salón Nuevo, see Orso, *Philip IV*, chapter 2.

54. See above, note 15.

55. A growing awareness of Crescenzi's importance is recognized in the recent literature. See Brown and Elliott, *A Palace*, pp. 44–5, for his career and further references. To these should be added the following: Juan J. Martín González, "El Pantéon de El Escorial y la arquitectura barroca," *BSAA*, 47 (1981), pp. 265–84; Maurizio Marini, "Del Signor Giovanni Battista Crescentij, Pittore," *The J. Paul Getty Museum Journal*, 9 (1981), pp. 127–31; and Paul Shakeshaft, "Elsheimer and G. B. Crescenzi (letter to editor)," *BM*, 123 (1981), pp. 550–1, which publishes a letter from Crescenzi to Charles I declining an offer to come to England. Virginia Tovar Martín ("Significación de Juan Bautista Crescenzi en la arquitectura española del siglo XVII," *AEA*, 54 [1981], p. 297–317), answering the ideas proposed by René Taylor ("Juan Bautista Crescencio y la arquitectura cortesana española," *Academia*, 48 [1979], pp. 63–126), seeks to downgrade Crescenzi's importance in the field of architecture. Taylor's case is buttressed by Fernando Marías and Agustin Bustamante García ("La herencia de El Greco, Jorge Manuel Thetocópuli y el debate arquitectónico en torno a 1621," in *El Greco: Italy and Spain*, Studies in the History of Art, 13 [Washington, 1984], pp. 101–11).

56. Carducho's composition is preserved in a drawing in the British Museum; for a reproduction, see Harris, *Velázquez*, plate 56. Unlike Carducho's narrative treatment of the scene, which (unwisely) omits the presence of Philip III, Velázquez' picture, as descibed by Palomino, depicted the king in the center accompanied by a personification of Spain.

57. *V.V.*, II, doc. 30, p. 226 and docs. 36–39, pp. 229–30, dated 18 and 27 September 1628, and 9 February 1629, refer to Velázquez as *pintor de cámara* for the first time and record an unsuccessful attempt by the *Bureo* to assign the obligation for payment of the newly awarded daily ration of twelve reales (one escudo) to the Committee of Works.

58. The standard modern account of the visit is Samuel R. Gardiner, *Prince Charles and the Spanish Marriage* (London, 1869). See also Carl Justi, "Die Spanische Brautfahrt Carl Stuarts," in *Miscellaneen aus Drei Jahrhunderten Spanischen Kunstlebens*, II (Berlin, 1908), pp. 301–46.

59. Carducho, *Diálogos*, p. 435.

60. Pacheco, *Arte*, I, p. 156.

61. See José Simón Díaz, "La estancia del Cardenal Legado Francesco Barberini en Madrid en el año 1626," *AIEM*, 17 (1980), pp. 159–214.

62. The Spanish diary of Cassiano has yet to be completely published. Extracts are found in Harris, "Cassiano dal Pozzo;" Enriqueta Harris and Gregorio de Andrés, "Descripción del Escorial por Cassiano dal Pozzo (1626)," appendix to *AEA*, 45 (1972); and José Simón Díaz, "El arte de las mansiones nobiliarias de 1626," *Goya*, 154 (1980), pp. 200–5.

63. Harris, "Cassiano dal Pozzo," p. 368.

64. The fundamental work on Rubens in Spain is Gregorio Cruzada Villaamil, *Rubens, diplomático español. Sus viajes a España y noticias de sus cuadros* (Madrid, 1874).

65. Harris, "Cassiano del Pozzo." For another drawing possibly related to this commission, see Jonathan Brown, "A Portrait Drawing by Velázquez," *MD*, 14 (1976), pp. 46–51.

66. For the paintings brought by Rubens, see Orso, *Philip IV*, chapter I.

67. The Descalzas tapestries were shipped to Spain in July 1628. See Nora de Poorter, *Corpus Rubenianum Ludwig Burchard. II, The Eucharist Series* (London-Philadelphia, 1978).

68. See Frances Huemer, *Corpus Rubenianum Ludwig Burchard. XIX, Portraits*, I (London, 1977), pp. 62–80 and cat. nos. 24, 30–36.

69. For the portrait, see Huemer, *Portraits*, no. 30, pp. 150–4. It is hard to credit the suggestion of López-Rey (*Velázquez* [1979], no. 101, p. 434) that the head was painted by Velázquez.

70. See Azcárate, "Noticias," p. 361, and above, note 33.

71. See Julius S. Held, "Rubens and Titian," in *Titian: His World and Legacy*, ed. David Rosand (New York, 1982), pp. 282–339.

72. See Martin S. Soria, "La Venus, Los Borrachos y la Coronación de Velázquez," *AEA*, 26 (1953), pp. 278–83; and also Diego Angulo Iñiguez, "La fábula de Vulcano, Venus y Marte y la Fragua de Velázquez," *AEA*, 33 (1960), p. 178.

73. The relationship of Pérez de Moya's text to the picture was pointed out by John F. Moffitt in a paper delivered at the annual meeting of the College Art Association of America, February 1983.

74. The subject was identified by Frédéric Schneider, "Mathias Grünewald et la mystique du moyen age," *Révue de l'art chretien*, 48 (1905), pp. 157–8, who, however, cites no specific textural source. Schneider also points out that peculiar cross-straps worn by the angel symbolize the liturgical star.

75. The painting is exceedingly difficult to date on the basis of style, as a plausible case can be made for either just before or just after Velázquez' trip to Italy. Recent writers have tended to favor a date of *c.* 1628–29 (Trapier, Gudiol, MacLaren and Braham, López-Rey), but Harris has accepted the slightly later date. In general, the technique seems to weigh in favor of 1628–29, although the summary treatment of the hands of all the figures and the feet of Christ is unusual in pre-Italian works. Also, the sophisticated and confident handling of Christ's anatomy is more advanced than the nude figures in the *Feast of Bacchus* (Plate 69), a documented work of these very years. In the end, it is perhaps easier to see the picture as leading into the Italian sojourn than away from it, when Velázquez' technique developed a remarkable sense of touch which is not present in this picture. However, the problem will only be solved by the discovery of a document.

76. *V.V.*, II, doc. 41, pp. 230–1.

77. *V.V.*, II, doc. 43. p. 231, and doc. 44, p. 232.

CHAPTER III

1. Pacheco, *Arte*, I, pp. 158–61.

2. *V.V.*, II, doc. 43. pp. 321–2.

3. *V.V.*, II, doc. 44, p. 232.

4. *V.V.*, II, doc. 45, pp. 232–3.

5. Palomino (*El museo pictórico*, p. 901) mentions that, while in Venice, Velázquez made copies of two paintings by Tintoretto — the *Crucifixion* (presumably Scuola di San Rocco) and the *Last Supper* (presumably also Scuola di San Rocco), the last of which he gave to the king. This picture has been identified as the one now in Madrid, Academia de San Fernando (repr. José Gudiol, *Velázquez*, [London, 1974], fig. 100). A painting of this subject is listed without an attribution in Velázquez' death inventory, but there are no grounds, as far as I can see, for identifying the picture with the one in the Academia de San Fernando.

6. For the relevant documentation, see J. A. F. Orbaan, "Notes on Art in Italy. Velázquez in Rome," *Apollo*, (6 July 1927), pp. 27–9, and Estella Brunetti, "Per il soggiorno fiorentino del Velázquez (Nota d'Archiivo per il Velázquez)," in *V.V.*, I, pp. 296–300, where Orbaan's transcription of the dates is corrected.

7. For the portrait, see below p. 79.

8. For the Sacchetti brothers, see Francis Haskell, *Patrons and Painters*. (New Haven and London, 1980), pp. 38–40.

9. Haskell, *Patrons and Painters*, p. 39.

10. For a useful summary of art in Rome around 1630, see Yves Bonnefoy, *Rome 1630: L'horizon du premier baroque* (Paris, 1970).

11. For Barberini's activities as an art patron, see Haskell, *Patrons and Painters*, pp. 43–6.

12. For the count of Monterrey's biography, and his activities as an art patron, and collector, see Brown and Elliott, *A Palace*, pp. 14, 16–17, 115–16, where additional references are listed.

13. See Haskell, *Patrons and Painters*, p. 136.

14. See J. Domínguez Bordona, "Noticias para la historia del Buen Retiro," *RABM*, 10 (1933), p. 85.

15. López-Rey, *Velázquez* (1979), nos. 43 and 44, pp. 287–91. In their forthcoming study, McKim-Smith et al. (*Examining Velázquez*) revise the conclusions of their earlier study of the painting (see below, note 20) and accept that the three lateral strips on the *Forge of Vulcan* are eighteenth-century additions. Thus, the original dimensions were about 2.23 × 2.57 m. The complete composition of *Joseph's Coat*, which has obviously been cut down on both sides, is preserved in a copy (repr. López-Rey, *Velázquez* [1979], fig. 112). De los Santos (1667) gives the measurements as about 2.09 × 3.34 m.

16. See, for example, John F. Moffitt, "Velázquez's 'Forge of Vulcan.' The Cuckold, the Poets, and the Painter," *Pantheon*, 41 (1983), pp. 322–6, and Santiago Sebastián, "Lectura iconográfico-iconológica de La Fragua de Vulcano," *Traza y Baza*, 8 (1983), pp. 20–7. The premise that all mythological paintings in Spain were understood to have an underlying moralizing message is fallacious, as seen in the abundant number of mythologies in the royal collection. In certain cases, the arrangement of these paintings in a specific and appropriate setting indicates that an ulterior meaning was intended (for instance, the Salón Nuevo, or Hall of Mirrors, of the Alcázar, Madrid, for which see Orso, *Philip IV*, chapter 1). In other cases, the content makes clear that the paintings were regarded simply as illustrations of an antique text (see, for instance, the paintings by Rubens for the Torre de la Parada, for which see Svetlana Alpers, *Corpus Rubenianum Ludwig Burchard. IX, The Decoration of the Torre de la Parada* [London-New York, 1971]).

17. This interpretation is argued in Diego Angulo Iñiguez, "La fábula de Vulcano," pp. 149–81, which also contains an excellent discussion of Velázquez' interpretation of the literary source.

18. See Pierre du Colombier, "La Forge du Vulcain au Chateau d'Effiat." *GBA*, 81 (1939), p. 36.

19. For useful remarks on the development of Velázquez' technique, see Richard Newman and Gridley McKim-Smith, "Observations on the Materials and Painting Technique of Diego Velázquez," *The American Institute for Conservation of Historic and Artistic Works. Preprints of Papers Presented at the Tenth Annual Meeting, Milwaukee, Wisconsin, 26–30 May, 1982*; and Gridley McKim-Smith, "On Velázquez's Working Method," *AB*, 61 (1979), pp. 589–603 and the forthcoming study by McKim-Smith et al.

20. For the radiographs and their interpretation, see Garrido et al., "La fragua de Vulcano."

21. See López-Rey, *Velázquez* (1979), no. 45, p. 294.

22. Garrido et al. ("La fragua de Vulcano," pp. 90–2) suggest that the frequent comparison of the techniques of Velázquez and Titian is misleading and note its origin in a literary topos of sixteenth- and seventeenth-century art theory. This may be true on specifically technical grounds, but there is little reason to doubt that Titian's free manner of painting was a powerful source of inspiration to Velázquez.

23. *V.V.*, II, p. 66.

24. For this painting, see Giuliano Briganti, *Pietro da Cortona, o della pittura barocca* (2nd ed., Florence, 1982), no. 6, pp. 163–4. Velázquez' admiration for Pietro may also be reflected in Philip IV's attempt to bring the Italian to Spain in 1650 (*V.V.*, II, doc. 125, p. 271).

25. See Briganti, *Pietro da Cortona*, no. 33, pp. 185–6, where the date is given after 1626 and before 1631.

26. Enriqueta Harris and John Elliott ("Velázquez and the Queen of Hungary," *BM*, 118 [1976], pp. 24–6) suggest that the portrait could have been commissioned in October 1628 as part of a group of royal portraits intended for the king of Hungary. As López-Rey (*Velázquez* [1979], no. 48, p. 302) points out, it is not known whether Velázquez ever painted the portraits mentioned in the document. However, Harris (*Velázquez*, note regarding p. 68) rightly states that the head was obviously used as the model for the full-length portraits (East Berlin, Staatliche Museum, Gemäldegalerie, and Prague, National Gallery), which suggests that the bust-length portrait was done in Madrid, where presumably it was available to the studio. This idea rests on the tacit assumption that the copies were made before the queen left for Vienna on 29 December 1629. There is no evidence on the date of execution of the copies, and presumably they could have been done after Velázquez returned from Italy. I see nothing in the portrait to support López-Rey's suggestion that the Prado painting may have been part of a larger composition. Like Harris and Gudiol, I am inclined to regard it as a model for use by the workshop.

27. For the document, see *V.V.*, doc. 47, p. 234. For the copies, see López-Rey, *Velázquez* (1963), nos. 247, 248, and 252, and López-Rey, *Velázquez* (1979), no. 61, p. 340, which he believes was originally full-length. *Philip IV in Brown and Silver* (Plate 98), which is usually related to the Vienna version, is assigned a somewhat later date below.

28. José López-Rey ("Review of Enriqueta Harris, *Velázquez*," *Apollo*, 118 [1983], p. 193), following a suggestion made in Camón Aznar, *Velázquez*, I, p. 454, identifies the *juramento* portrait with the picture in the Wallace Collection (Plate 97), and restates his earlier conviction that the Boston portrait was done shortly after Velázquez' return from Italy (early in 1631). I continue to believe that the identification of the Boston portrait with the *juramento* made by myself and Elliott (*A Palace*, pp. 253–4) is correct. First, the symbolism of the portrait, as described below, is appropriate for the occasion. Second, the prince as depicted in the Wallace Collection portrait looks too big and well-developed to be only two years, four months old. Finally, the fragmentary inscription on the Boston portrait, which was misread by López-Rey, gives the prince's age as "[blank]" years, four months. This inscription, in the opinion of Alain Goldrach, Conservator of Paintings, Museum of Fine Arts, Boston, "appears from a purely stylistic point of view not to be by the hand of Velázquez. However, it does seem to be old and even possibly of the period." The prince was in the fourth month of his third year (i.e., two years, four months old) when the *juramento* took place on 7 March 1632. This suggests that the writer of the inscription noted the month so precisely because he associated the portrait with this important state occasion. (Our attempt in *A Palace* to explain the supposed discrepancy in the age cited in the inscription and the date of the *juramento* is unnecessary because the prince would not have turned two years, five months old until ten days after the event.)

29. Antonio de Mendoza, "Forma que se guarda en tener los Cortes el Juramento," *Discursos de don Antonio de Mendoza*, ed. Marqués de Alcedo (Madrid, 1911), p. 26.

30. For this interpretation, see Brown and Elliott, *A Palace*, pp. 253–4. I am grateful to Sam Heath for suggesting certain refinements of our discussion of this picture.

31. Camón Aznar (*Velázquez*, I, p. 437) is probably correct in identifying the dwarf as female, but there is still some room for doubt.

32. According to the entry in *Wallace Collection Catalogues. Pictures and Drawings*, 16th ed. by F. J. B. Watson (London, 1968), pp. 333–4, the background of the painting is unfinished, an observation which seems unwarranted. However, it is apparent that the drapery in the right background is a later addition which destroys the assymetrical balance of the original composition. The catalogue also relates the picture to one of the works sold by Velázquez to Jerónimo de Villanueva in 1633–34. However, as López-Rey (*Velázquez* [1963], pp. 48–9) notes, there are good grounds for believing that this was not an autograph work.

33. For a summary of opinions, see MacLaren and Braham *The Spanish School*, pp. 114–15. López-Rey (*Velázquez* [1979], p. 312) believes that it was "possibly painted over an extended period of time in 1631–2." Harris (*Velázquez*, caption to plate 79, p. 88) also dates it *c*.1631–32. The picture was eventually installed in the library of El Escorial, although there is no evidence that it was painted for this location; see Gregorio de Andrés, "Los cinco retratos reales de la Biblioteca de El Escorial," *AEA*, 40 (1967), pp. 360–3. Perhaps it was moved here in 1656, when Philip made an important donation of manuscripts to the library.

34. MacLaren and Braham (*The Spanish School*, p. 115), who believe that this painting was the model for the version in Vienna, account for these differences by suggesting that Velázquez completed the face and established the pose in 1631–32 and then returned to paint the costume about four years later. The suggestion by Theodore Crombie ("Isabella of Bourbon by Velázquez," *Connoisseur*, 141 [1958], pp. 242–3) that the face had been reworked was not confirmed by radiographs and infrared photographs (see *The Spanish School*, p. 118).

35. The king's interest in having his portrait kept current with his appearance is demonstrated by his order to rework the head of Pietro Tacca's *Equestrian Statue of Philip IV* which, when it arrived in Madrid after a delay of some years, no longer resembled him. See Brown and Elliott, *A Palace*, pp.111–14.

36. Jusepe Martínez ("Discursos practicables," in *V.V.*, II, p. 68) witnessed the rejection of one of Velázquez' portraits for just this reason.

37. For this portrait, see Crombie, "Isabella of Bourbon," pp. 238–44, and the Editor, "Queen Isabella of Bourbon. A 'Lost' Portrait by Velázquez Located," *Connoisseur*, 128 (1951), pp. 3–5. The provenance is reconstructed in López-Rey, *Velázquez* (1979), no. 53, pp. 315–17.

38. *V.V.*, II, doc. 53, p. 236.

39. For this development, see Brown and Elliott, *A Palace*, chapters II and VII.

40. The following account is based on Brown and Elliott, *A Palace*, chapter III.

41. See Hannah E. Bergman, "A Court Entertainment of 1638," *Hispanic Review*, 42 (1974), pp. 67–81.

42. The following account is derived from Brown and Elliott, *A Palace*, chapter V, where references to the relevant bibliography and documentation may be found. I have noted below only studies which have appeared since the publication of this book.

43. See Harold W. Wethey, *The Paintings of Titian*. III, *The Mythological and Historical Paintings* (London, 1975), no. X–13, p. 211.

44. See Jonathan Brown, "Un Ribera encerezado," *AEA*, 52 (1979), pp. 174–8.

45. For a summary biography of this still-unstudied statesman, see Federico Martín Eztala, "Una visita a la colección del Excmo. Sr. Príncipe Pío de Saboya y Marqués de Castell Rodrigo," *BSEE*, 37 (1929), pp. 150–6.

46. For a reconstruction of the Landscape Gallery, see Barbara von Barghahn, "The Pictorial Decoration of the Buen Retiro Palace and Patronage during the Reign of Philip IV," (Ph.D. dissertation, New York University, 1979). Enriqueta Harris ("G. B. Crescenzi, Velázquez and the 'Italian' Landscapes for the Buen Retiro," *BM*, 122 [1980], pp. 562–4) hypothesizes that Crescenzi was responsible for the acquisition of some of the landscape paintings. For a counter-argument, see Brown and Elliott, *A Palace*, pp. 269–70, note 69. Juan J. Luna ("Precisiones sobre las pinturas de Claudio de Lorena en el Museo del Prado," *BMP*, 2 [1981] p. 99) points out that, according to Baldinucci, Gaspar Dughet, another of the artists represented in the Landscape Gallery, also worked for Castel Rodrigo. An excellent account of seventeenth-century Italian landscape painting in Spanish collections is in Juan J. Luna, *Claudio de Lorena y el ideal clásico en el siglo XVII* (Madrid, 1984), pp. 31–43.

47. For a recent discussion of Claude's landscape paintings for the king of Spain, see H. Diane Russell, *Claude Lorrain, 1600–1682* (Washington, 1982), pp. 74–6; Marcel Roethlisberger, *Im Licht von Claude Lorrain. Landschaftsmalerie aus drei Jahrhunderten* (Munich, 1983), nos. 6–8, pp. 68–73; Juan J. Luna, "Claudio de Lorena en las colecciones españolas," *AEA*, 54 (1981), pp. 77–86, and "Un paisajista francés contemporáneo de Calderón: Claudio de Lorena. Obras inéditas en España," *Goya*, 161–2 (1981), pp. 290–7.

48. See Marcel Roethlisberger, *Claude Lorrain. The Paintings* (New Haven, 1961), pp. 180–6.

49. For Domenichino's painting, see Richard E. Spear, *Domenichino* (New Haven and London, 1982), no. 112, pp. 303–6.

50. López-Rey (*Velázquez* [1979], no. 86. p. 402) attributes to Velázquez a rather weak version of the head of St. Anthony Abbot and considers it to be a study for the painting. For the date, see Brown and Elliott, *A Palace*, p. 254.

51. For the visual sources of the composition, see Diego Angulo Iñiguez, "'El San Antonio Abad y San Pablo Ermitaño,' de Velázquez," *AEA*, 19 (1946), pp. 18–26.

52. For the Castelfusano frescoes (1626–29), see Briganti, *Pietro da Cortona*, no. 23, pp. 177–80.

53. For a survey of the subject, see E. Tietze-Conrat, *Dwarfs and Jesters in Art* (London, 1957).

54. For an example of the latter, see Keith P. F. Moxey, "Pieter Bruegel and the *Feast of Fools*," *AB*, 64 (1982), pp. 640–6.

55. For example, in 1628 the French ambassador noted a set of jester portraits in the small gallery leading to Olivares' study in the Alcázar; see Jonathan Brown and J. H. Elliott, "Further Observations on Velázquez' Portraits of Jesters at the Buen Retiro," *GBA*, 98 (1981) pp. 191–2. Another set of jesters hung in a staircase leading to the Galería del Cierzo in the Alcázar (mentioned in José López-Rey, "On Velázquez' Portraits of Jesters at the Buen Retiro," *GBA*, 97 [1981], p. 164.) In addition, there is the set of jesters for the Retiro here under discussion and two pairs of dwarf portraits, one in the Alcázar (added to the jester portraits near the Galería del Cierzo), the other in the Torre de la Parada, discussed in Appendix A.

56. See José Moreno Villa, *Locos, enanos, negros y niños palaciegos. Gente de placer que tuvieron los Austrias en la corte española desde 1563 a 1700* (Mexico City, 1939).

57. See Appendix A for a full discussion of the problem of authenticity.

58. See Brown and Elliott, *A Palace*, pp. 254–5. The proposed identification is disputed in López-Rey, "On Velázquez's Portraits of Jesters," and defended in Brown and Elliott, "Further Observations on Velázquez' Portraits of Jesters," with additional comments by López-Rey. The following discussion takes into account that all the arguments, pro and contra, are based on extrapolation from indirect evidence.

59. For circumstantial evidence that four of the portraits were considered as a group, see below, chapter VII, note 50.

60. Moreno Villa, *Locos, enanos*, pp. 68–9.

61. The cape over the left shoulder was added or completed by another hand.

62. In the present frame, the surrounding space is somewhat larger than was originally intended. The irregular border of about three to four centimeters in width which is now visible was probably originally wrapped around the stretcher. This strip causes the figure to recede from the viewer in a way that slightly reduces its impact.

63. Alfonso E. Pérez Sánchez, *Borgianni, Cavarozzi y Nardi en España* (Madrid, 1964).

64. For these artists, see below pp. 208 and 248. In addition, there was a succession of Italian stage designers at the court, whose impact on the development of painting before 1650 is fairly slight.

65. Francisco Calvo Serraller ed., *La teoría de la pintura en el siglo de oro* (Madrid, 1981).

66. See Mary C. Volk, "On Velázquez and the Liberal Arts," *AB*, 60 (1978), pp. 69–86, and "Addenda: The Madrid Academy," *AB*, 61 (1979), p. 627. For important documentation, see Antonio Matilla Tascón, "La academia madrileña de San Lucás," *Goya*, 161–2 (1981), pp. 260–5, and Alfonso E. Pérez Sánchez, "La academia madrileña de 1603 y sus fundadores," *BSAA*, 48 (1982), pp. 281–90.

67. See González Múñoz, "Datos."

Chapter IV

1. The following discussion of the Hall of Realms is based on Brown and Elliott, *A Palace*, chapter VI, where the essential references can be found. For the fundamental study, see Elías Tormo, "Velázquez, el salón de reinos del Buen Retiro y el poeta del palacio y del pintor," *Pintura, escultura y arquitectura en España. Estudios dispersos* (Madrid, 1949; first published 1911–12), pp. 127–246. The documentation for the paintings was published in María Luisa Caturla, "Cartas de pago de los doce cuadros de batallas para el salón de reinos del Buen Retiro," *AEA*, 33 (1960), pp. 333–55.

2. Cited by Brown and Elliott, *A Palace*, p. 142.

3. For a discussion of this type of palace decoration, see Brown and Elliott, *A Palace*, pp. 147–56, on which this account is based.

4. See Loren W. Partridge, "Divinity and Dynasty at Caprarola. Perfect History in the Room of Farnese Deeds," *AB*, 60 (1978), pp. 494–530.

5. See Catherine Dumont, *Francesco Salviati au Palais Sacchetti de Rome et la décoration mural italienne (1520–1560)* (Rome, 1973), pp. 121–32.

6. See Richard Harprath, *Papst Paul III. als Alexander der Grosse. Das Freskenprogramm der Sala Paolina in der Engelsburg* (Berlin–New York, 1978), and the review by Charles Hope, *BM*, 123 (1981), pp. 104–5.

7. For this phenomenon, see Charles Dempsey, "Review of Malcolm Campbell, *Pietro da Cortona at the Pitti Palace*," *AB*, 161 (1979), pp. 141–4, and Susan Saward, *The Golden Age of Marie de' Medici* (Ann Arbor, 1982), pp. 9–18.

8. See the fundamental work by Frances A. Yates, *Astraea. The Imperial Theme in the Sixteenth Century* (London, 1975).

9. See Hendrik Horn, "Charles V's Conquest of Tunis: Cartoons and Tapestries by Cornelisz Vermeyen" (Ph.D. dissertation, Yale University, 1977); and Orso, *Philip IV*.

10. For the reconstruction of the decoration, see Orso, *Philip IV*, chapter 2.

11. Different authors attribute different sections of the paintings to Velázquez, but there is general agreement that Velázquez was not responsible for the entire execution of these three works. As can be seen with the naked eye, the portraits of Philip III, Margarita of Austria, and Isabella of Bourbon were enlarged by the addition of sizable strips of canvas at the left and right sides. López-Rey (*Velázquez* [1979], no. 68, p. 358), plausibly suggests that the pictures were enlarged when they were installed in the Royal Palace in the later eighteenth century. The *Portrait of Philip IV* was also widened, but apparently by Velázquez himself. For some reason, he did not sign the illusionistic piece of paper painted for the purpose in the lower left corner.

12. The relevant document is published by Azcárate ("Noticias," pp. 361–2), who does not, however, connect the paintings to the works in the Hall of Realms. This association was made by Camón Aznar (*Velázquez*, I, pp. 522–3). As yet, there is no evidence to support this hypothesis, although presumably a radiograph would help decide the matter.

13. Aureliano de Beruete (*Velázquez* [Paris, 1898], pp. 104–8), attributed both *Philip III* and *Margarita of Austria* to González.

14. For this calculation of the dimensions, see Azcárate, "Noticias," p. 361.

15. See above, chapter II, note 32. The document is connected to the paintings by Juan Allende-Salazar and Francisco J. Sánchez Cantón (*Retratos del Museo del Prado. Identificación y rectificaciones* [Madrid, 1919], pp. 163–5), who also believe that the female equestrian portraits were begun at this time.

16. *V.V.*, II, doc. 42, p. 231.

17. See Tormo, "Velázquez," p. 163, who believes that the compositions could only have been invented by Velázquez.

18. Martin Soria ("'Las Lanzas' y los retratos ecuestres de Velázquez," *AEA*, 27 [1954], pp. 93–108), states that the poses of the equestrian portraits are based on engravings of Roman emperors on horseback by Stradanus. The poses, however, are commonplaces in sixteenth-century art and also occur in emblem books and treatises on horsemanship. For this point, see Walter A. Liedtke and John F. Moffitt, "Velázquez, Olivares, and the Baroque Equestrian Portrait," *BM*, 123 (1981), pp. 535–6.

19. For this interpretation, see Liedtke and Moffitt, "Velázquez, Olivares, and the Baroque Equestrian Portrait," pp. 535–6.

20. For an emblematic interpretation of the portrait, which is too specific in its associations, see Martin Warnke, "Das Reiterbildnes des Balthasar Carlos von Velázquez," in *Amici Amico. Festschrift für Werner Gross zu seinem 65. Geburtstag am 25. 11. 1966* (Munich, 1968), pp. 217–27.

21. See López-Rey, *Velázquez* (1979), no. 72, p. 366.

22. For this painting, see Brown and Elliott, *A Palace*, pp. 178–84, where the previous literature is cited. The most recent interpretation by John F. Moffitt ("Diego Velázquez, Andrea Alciati and the Surrender of Breda," *Artibus et Historiae*, 3 [1982], pp. 75–90), omits mention of the discussion of the picture in *A Palace* and is based on inaccurate historical information. Moffitt's attempt to date the picture after 1637 is convenient to his argument but contradicts the testimony of Monanni that a painting of this subject was in place in the Hall of Realms by 28 April 1635. There are no reasonable grounds to assume that this painting was by an artist other than Velázquez.

23. The conclusions of Gridley McKim-Smith in "On Velázquez's Working Method," *AB*, pp. 589–91, are amended in McKim-Smith et al., *Examining Velázquez*.

24. For this painting, see Brown and Elliott, *A Palace*, pp. 184–90.

25. See Michael Levey, *Painting at Court* (New York, 1971), pp. 142–4, and Enriqueta Harris, "Velázquez's Portrait of Prince Baltasar Carlos in the Riding School," *BM*, 118 (1976), pp. 266–75, where the date of execution of 1636 is plausibly suggested.

26. Justi, *Velázquez* (1953), p. 470.

27. The small-scale version of the picture in New York, Metropolitan Museum of Art, is not, in my opinion, by Velázquez. The case against the painting as an autograph work is made in López-Rey, *Velázquez* (1979), no. 66, p. 354, note 1, where it is plausibly attributed to Mazo and associated with an entry in the 1651 inventory of the collection of Gaspar de Haro, marquis of Eliche.

28. Thus, for example, López-Rey, *Velázquez* (1979), no. 66, p. 354.

29. See Liedtke and Moffitt, "Velázquez, Olivares, and the Baroque Equestrian Portrait," p. 531, where all the putative sources are assembled and discussed.

30. This idea originates with Gregorio Cruzada Villaamil, *Anales de la vida y ae las obras de Diego de Silva Velázquez* (Madrid, 1885), pp. 117–20. For the argument against this association and earlier references to the division of opinion on the question, see Liedtke and Moffitt, "Velázquez, Olivares, and the Baroque Equestrian Portrait," p. 531.

31. See Marqués de Lozoya, "El caballo blanco de Velázquez," in *V.V.*, I, pp. 323–7. For the reappearance of the horse in paintings by the Velázquez school, see Camón Aznar, *Velázquez*, I, pp. 520–1.

32. The date is established by the publication of Juan Antonio de Tapia y Robles, *Ilustración del renombre de grande* (Madrid, 1638), which contains an engraving by Hermann Paneels based on Velázquez' portrait. For details and earlier references, see López-Rey, *Velázquez* (1979), no. 87, p. 404.

33. For versions, see López-Rey, *Velázquez* (1963), nos. 509, pp. 512–16.

34. For the Torre de la Parada, see Alpers, *The Torre de la Parada*.

35. Julius S. Held, *The Oil Sketches of Peter Paul Rubens. A Critical Catalogue* (Princeton, 1980), pp. 251–2, establishes that the hunting and animal scenes were executed by Snyders, thus correcting the error of Alpers, who gave them to Peter Snayers. Alpers argues against the existence of a cohesive program for the paintings illustrating Ovid's *Metamorphoses*. For an interesting counter-argument, see Salvador Aldana Fernández, "Rubens en España y el programa iconográfico de la Torre de la Parada," *Archivo de arte valenciano*, 49 (1978), pp. 82–95.

36. See Alpers, *The Torre de la Parada*, pp. 289–301, for the inventory.

37. For the reconstruction of the Galería del Rey, see Alpers, *The Torre de la Parada*, pp. 122–8.

38. Cited by Alpers, *The Torre de la Parada*, p. 102.

39. See Alpers, *The Torre de la Parada*, p. 123.

40. For a complete account of the picture and the defense of its much-disputed authenticity, see MacLaren and Braham, *The Spanish School*, pp. 101–8.

41. Trapier (*Velázquez*, pp. 190–7), followed by López-Rey (*Velázquez* [1979], pp. 79–80), argues that the portraits of the king and his brother were done *c.* 1632. The argument for assigning the *Philip IV as Hunter* to this date rests on the close resemblance of the head to the *Philip IV in Brown and Silver* (Plate 98). I believe that the London portrait and the hunting portrait were done at about the same time and that the approximate date is established by a document of 24 October 1636, in which Velázquez alludes to paintings he is making for the Torre de la Parada, although admittedly no specific works are mentioned.

The relevant part of the document, an autograph letter, is incorrectly transcribed and interpreted by Cruzada (*Anales*, p. 93) and in *V.V.*, II, doc. 66, p. 242, and should read as follows: "Suplica a V. Magd. le haga merced de mandar se le paguen con efecto los dichos 15,803 reales para que pueda mejor acudir al servicio de V. Magd. en esta ocasión que se le a mandado pinte para la Torre de la Parada, que la rᵃ (recibirá) muy grande" (AGS, Casa Real — Obras y Bosques, leg. 309, no. 179). The document, which was graciously transcribed by Amando Represa, Director of the Archivo General de Simancas, is a claim for payment of salary in arrears. In effect, the painter is attempting to apply gentle pressure to the king by associating his ability to complete the commission for the Torre with the payment of his claim. If the king is willing to grant the request, the painter will take it as a great favor — "la recibirá muy grande." Given the sizable amount of money involved, Velázquez must have been working on a number of pictures; otherwise the claim would have seemed implausible.

According to Virginia Tovar Martín (*Arquitectura madrileña del s. XVII* [*Datos para su estudio*] [Madrid, 1983], p. 365), the new construction at the Torre, except for the servants' quarters, was finished by 2 April 1636. This would have been the logical moment for Velázquez to have received the commission for his share of the decoration. However, the inscription on the *Baltasar Carlos as Hunter*, which gives his age as six, if correct, would place the execution of this work between 17 October 1634 and 16 October 1635. The construction contract for the Torre was signed on 25 April 1635, after which time it would also have been feasible to start the execution of the decoration.

As for the *Cardinal Infante Ferdinand as Hunter*, Trapier (but not López-Rey, who relies solely on stylistic arguments) points out that Ferdinand's appearance had changed by 1636, by which time he had been away from Madrid for four years. However, it would have been anachronistic to portray the infante in the Pardo hunting-ground looking as he did in 1636 precisely because he could not have been there at the time.

42. Palomino, *El museo pictórico*, trans. E. Harris, *Velázquez*, p. 205.

43. López-Rey, *Velázquez* (1979), no. 33, pp. 257–8, dates the picture 1626–27. This date is based on an inscription with the date 1626 which was described in the Alcázar inventory of 17 March 1637, as written on a picture of a stag's head by Velázquez. However, it is not certain that this painting is identical with the one listed in 1637. In any case, it is difficult to reconcile the date of 1626–27 to the style of this painting, which is readily comparable in execution to works of the late 1630s and early 1640s.

Like López-Rey, I do not believe that Velázquez is the author of any part of the painting of *Stag's Antlers* published by Diego Angulo Iñiguez ("La cuerna de venado, cuadro de Velázquez," *Reales Sitios*, 4 [1967], pp. 13–25). This attribution is accepted by Alfonso E. Pérez Sánchez (*Pintura española de bodegones y floreros de 1600 a Goya* [Madrid, 1983–84], no. 56, pp. 84–5).

CHAPTER V

1. For biographical information on these two sitters and the provenance of the pictures, see León de Corral y Maestro, *Don Diego de Corral y Arellano y los Corrales de Valladolid. Apuntes históricos* (Madrid, 1905) and José Ramón Mélida, "Un recibo de Velázquez," *RABM*, 10 (1906), pp. 173–98.

2. See Mélida, "Un recibo," p. 193.

3. For the radiograph and the defense of the autograph quality of the child, see López-Rey, *Velázquez* (1979), no. 54, p. 321.

4. See Jonathan Brown, "Un italiano en el taller de Velázquez," *AEA*, 53 (1980), pp. 207–8.

5. The portrait was first published in José López-Rey, "An Unpublished Velázquez; A *Knight of Calatrava*." *GBA*, 80 (1972), pp 61–70. The sitter was identified in Gudiol, *Velázquez*, p. 149. See also William B. Jordan,

"Velázquez's *Portrait of Pedro de Barberana*," *Apollo*, 114 (1981), pp. 378–9.

6. The identification of the fragment on the basis of the full-length copy was made independently in Theodore Crombie, "Archbishop Fernando de Valdés by Velázquez. Some Notes on a Recently-Identified Portrait," *Apollo*, 145 (1960), pp. 102–4, and Juan Ainaud de Lasarte, "Velázquez y los retratos de Don Fernando de Valdés," *V.V.*, I, pp 310–15. For the *Portrait of Archbishop Valdés* in the National Gallery, London, and its relation to this fragment and the copies, see Appendix A.

7. *V.V.*, II, doc. 71, p. 245.

8. The fundamental account of the duke of Modena's visit is in Justi, *Velázquez* (1953), pp. 502–7. Also essential is Adolfo Venturi, "Velázquez e Francesco I d'Este," *Nuova Antologia di Scienze, Lettere ed Arti*, 29 (1881), pp. 44–57.

9. Fulvio Testi, *Lettere*, ed. Maria Luisa Doglio, III (Bari, 1967), pp. 58–113.

10. Testi, *Lettere*, III, pp. 100–1.

11. Testi, *Lettere*, III, p. 113. Documents indicate that Velázquez made portraits in miniature (for example, *V.V.*, doc. 33, p. 227, which seems to refer to Velázquez, although this is not certain). Only one existing miniature has been attributed repeatedly to Velázquez; see López-Rey, *Velázquez* (1979), no. 88, p. 405, which seems at best uncertain. This entry also presents other documentation relating to Velázquez' work as a miniaturist. Arturo Perera, "Velázquez, pintor de miniaturas," *V.V.*, I, pp. 387–81, is not very helpful.

12. Venturi, "Velázquez e Francesco I d'Este," p. 49.

13. *V.V.*, II, doc. 74, p. 246.

14. *V.V.*, II, doc. 209, p. 393, no. 170.

15. See Giuseppe Campori, *Raccolta di Cataloghi ed inventarii di quadri . . . dal secolo XV al secolo XIX* (Modena, 1870), p. 311.

16. Venturi, "Velázquez e Francesco I d'Este," pp. 51–2.

17. Venturi, "Velázquez e Francesco I d'Este," p. 52.

18. Juan Mateos, *Origen y dignidad de la caza*, ed. Manuel Terrón Albarraz (Badajoz, 1978), p. 10–11.

19. A few other lost portraits which probably fell into this category are mentioned in Velázquez' death inventory, including those of *Tomás de Aguiar* (also mentioned in *V.V.*, II, doc. 42, p. 231) and *Carlos Boduquín*, a high-ranking official in the household of Olivares. To these may be added three portraits mentioned in Palomino: *Francisco de Quevedo* (known in several copies, of which the best is in Madrid, Instituto de Valencia de Don Juan); *Nicolás de Cardona Lusigniano*; and a certain *Pereira*, called by Palamino "maestro de cámara de Felipe IV."

20. For Mateos' biography, see the edition of *Origen y dignidad de la caza* cited above, note 18.

21. For the commission, see Brown and Elliott, *A Palace*, pp. 110–14. See also Francisco J. Sánchez Cantón, "Sobre el 'Martínez Montañés' de Velázquez," *AEA*, 34 (1961), pp. 25–30.

22. See Pacheco, *Libro de retratos*, p. 145.

23. See Moreno Villa, *Locos, enanos*, pp. 85–7, for the documents of his life at court.

24. For a discussion of the date and identity of these portraits, see Appendix A.

25. For this portrait, see Enriqueta Harris, "The Wallace Collection. The Cleaning of Velázquez' *Lady with a Fan*," *BM*, 117 (1975), pp. 316–19.

26. These are discussed in López-Rey, *Velázquez* (1979), no. 79, p. 386.

27. The related composition at Chatsworth (López-Rey, *Velázquez* [1979], no. 79, p. 386) is not by Velázquez. See Allan Braham, *El Greco to Goya. The Taste for Spanish Paintings in Britain and Ireland* (London, 1981), no. 27, p. 71.

28. For an evaluation of the various identities proposed for the sitter, see López-Rey, *Velázquez* (1979), no. 81, p. 390.

29. See Francisco J. Sánchez Cantón, "Como vivía Velázquez," *AEA*, 15 (1942), p. 79.

30. For Villanueva and San Plácido, see Mercedes Agulló y Cobo, "El monasterio de San Plácido y su fundador, el madrileño don Jerónimo de Villanueva, Protonotario de Aragon," *Villa de Madrid*, 13, nos. 45–6 (1975), pp. 59–68 and 13, no. 47 (1975), pp. 37–50, and Henry C. Lea, *History of the Inquisition*, II (New York, 1906), pp. 133–58. Another Olivares lieutenant who owned pictures by Velázquez was José González; see Janine Fayard, "José Gonzáles (1583?–1668), 'créature' du comte-duc d'Olivares et conseiller de Philippe IV," in *Homage á Roland Mousnier* (Paris, 1981), pp. 351–68.

31. See J. Domínguez Bordona, "Noticias para la historia del Buen Retiro," *RABM*, 10 (1933), p. 85, and María Luisa Caturla, "Cartas de pago," pp. 343–7.

32. See Julius S. Held (*The Oil Sketches*, no. 319, pp. 442–5), who recognizes the connection of the sketch with San Plácido, but not with Villanueva.

33. Cruzada Villaamil, *Anales*, pp. 114–15, retells a story of uncertain reliability according to which the picture was presented to the convent by the king, who had had relations with an attractive young member of the convent. This story has yet to be verified.

34. See Manuel Gómez-Moreno, "El Cristo de San Plácido," *BSEE*, 24 (1916), pp. 177–88, where the association of the commission with Villanueva's process is also suggested.

35. See, for example, López-Rey (*Velázquez* [1979], no. 49, p. 306) who expresses guarded scepticism about this identification.

36. See Emile Mâle, *L'Art religieux de la fin du moyen age en France* (Paris, 1922), pp. 255–64. Another useful discussion of the iconography is in Edgar Wind, *Michelangelo's Prophets and Sibyls* (London, 1960), pp. 57–66.

37. For these prints, see Arthur M. Hind, *Early Italian Engraving*, I (London, 1948), pp. 153–81. For the currency of this iconography in seventeenth-century Spain, see Paul Guinard, "España, Flandes y Francia en el siglo XVII. Las Sibilas zurbaranescas y sus fuentes grabadas," *AEA*, 43 (1970), pp. 105–116.

38. See Spear, *Domenichino*, pp. 191–2.

39. For this painting of *c*.1650, see Denis Mahon, *Il Guercino (Giovanni Francesco Barbieri, 1591–1666). Catalogo critico dei dipinti* (Bologna, 1968), no. 91, pp. 197–8.

40. The case for the identification of the sitter as Velázquez' wife, for which there is no evidence, is discussed by López-Rey, *Velázquez* (1979), no. 49, p. 306.

41. The most useful discussions of these pictures are as follows: Kurt Gerstenberg, *Diego Velázquez* (Munich-Berlin, 1957), pp. 221–4; Erwin W. Palm, "Diego Velázquez: *Aesop* und *Menipp*," in *Lebende Antike. Symposium für Rudolf Sühnel*, ed. Horst Meller and Hans-Joachim Zimmerman (Berlin, 1967), pp. 207–15; and Alpers, *The Torre de la Parada*, pp. 134–6. As noted in Delphine F. Darby, "Ribera and the Wise Men," *AB*, 44 (1962), p. 282, Aesop was considered to be a philosopher by certain Spanish humanists.

42. See Alpers, *The Torre de la Parada*, p. 134, which nullifies interpretations based on the belief that the four pictures hung together in the same room.

43. See Palm, "Diego Velázquez: *Aesop* und *Menipp*," p. 209.

44. This motif was identified in Gerstenberg, *Diego Velázquez*, p. 224.

45. Aesop's life exists in several versions (as do the *Fables*). This passage is quoted in Lloyd W. Daly, *Aesop Without Morals* (New York-London, 1961), p. 40.

46. Kurt Gerstenberg, *Diego Velázquez*, pp. 221–2.

47. Kurt Gerstenberg ("Velázquez als humanist," in *V.V.*, I, p. 212–13) posits a connection between Porta's porcine type and *Menippus*, which is too loose to be acceptable.

48. It is difficult to trace the origins of this interpretation. Ponz, *Viage de España*, (1794) refers to "*Los Borrachos*" as "the triumph of Bacchus in burlesque," but does not elaborate. Jacinto O. Picón (*Vida y obra de Don Diego Velázquez* [Madrid, 1899]) certainly had a part of play in the process (see p. 54). The diffusion was abetted by José Ortega y Gasset, who popularized the idea that Velázquez' mythological paintings were intended to mock the gods of antiquity. See Ortega's essay, "Tres cuadros de vino," *El Espectador*, 1 (1916). For a convincing refutation of this notion, see Diego Angulo Iñiguez, "Velázquez y la mitología," in *III Centenario de la muerte de Velázquez*, Instituto de España (Madrid, 1961), pp. 47–62, and "Mythology and Seventeenth-Century Spanish Painters," in *Acts of the Twentieth International Congress of the History of Art*, III (Princeton, 1963), pp. 36–40.

49. As far as I can tell, this idea first appeared in Angulo, "La fábula de Vulcano," pp. 176–7, note 12.

50. See Madlyn M. Kahr, *Velázquez. The Art of Painting* (New York, 1976), pp. 91–2.

51. Justi, *Velázquez* (1953), pp. 656–8.

CHAPTER VI

1. Sánchez Cantón, *Los pintores de cámara*, p. 94.

2. See López-Rey, *Velázquez* (1979), no. 90, p. 410. For a convincing case for the collaboration of an assistant, see Trapier, *Velázquez*, pp. 250–3. Justi (*Velázquez* [1953], p. 471) identified the picture with the copy of the *Baltasar Carlos as Hunter* at Ickworth (Plate 160).

3. *V.V.*, II, doc. 76, p. 249.

4. See López-Rey, *Velázquez* (1979), no. 109, p. 460.

5. For the details of this campaign, see José Sanabré, *La acción de Francia en Cataluña en pugna por la hegemonía de Europa (1640–1659)* (Barcelona, 1956), pp. 254–60.

6. For the documentation cited below, see Aureliano de Beruete, *El Velázquez de Parma. Retrato de Felipe IV pintado en Fraga* (Madrid, 1911), pp. 14–15, where the transcription is more accurate than in *V.V.*, II, doc. 91, pp. 255–6.

7. See "Cartas de algunos PP. de la Compañía de Jesús," *Memorial Histórico Español*, V (Madrid, 1863), 17, pp vii–xxiv.

8. For discussions of the portrait, see Fritz Saxl, "Velázquez and Philip IV," *Lectures* (London, 1957), I, pp. 311–24, and López-Rey, *Velázquez* (1979), pp. 93–4 and no. 100, p. 432. The version in the Dulwich College Picture Gallery is now generally held to be a copy. The head of Philip as seen in the Fraga portrait was incorporated into a copy of Rubens' *Equestrian Portrait of Philip IV* (Florence, Uffizi, Plate 76). José López-Rey ("A Head of Philip IV by Velázquez in a Rubens Allegorical Composition," *GBA*, 53 [1959], pp. 35–44) proposes to identify the Uffizi portrait with a painting listed in the 1651 inventory of Gaspar de Haro, marquis of Eliche, in which the work is described as having been done by Mazo, with the head of the king by Velázquez. This attribution is challenged by Harris (*Velázquez*, p. 68) on grounds of style which seem reasonable.

9. This observation is made by Harris, *Velázquez*, p. 113.

10. José Pellicer, *Avisos históricos*, ed. Enrique Tierno Galván (Madrid, 1965), p. 227.

11. See *V.V.*, II, p. 329, for Carreño's testimony.

12. López-Rey, *Velázquez* (1963), nos. 462–8.

13. For this drawing, see Gridley McKim-Smith, "The Problem of Velázquez' Drawings," *MD*, 18 (1980), no. 3, p. 18.

14. See Appendix A for a discussion of the problems of identification raised in López-Rey, *Velázquez* (1979), no. 103, pp. 440–1.

15. See Moreno Villa, *Locos, enanos*, pp. 119–20.

16. For the copy, see López-Rey, *Velázquez* (1979), no. 104, p. 445, where it is catalogued as "Velázquez' replica, possibly with some workshop assistance."

17. Enriqueta Harris, "Velázquez's Apsley House Portrait: An Identification," *BM*, 120 (1978), p. 304.

18. López-Rey, *Velázquez* (1979), no. 110, p. 462. None of the suggestions about the sitter's identity — Gaspar de

Fuensalida or Fernando de Fonseca y Ruiz de Contreras, marquis of Lapilla — has been proven.

19. AHP, prot. 5412, fols, 259–65, 10 October 1647. This reference and the following information on the *Coronation* and the paintings by Vaccaro were generously made available to me by Steven N. Orso. For the oratory, see Véronique Gérard, "Los sitios de devoción de el Alcázar de Madrid: capilla y oratorios," *AEA*, 56 (1983), pp. 275–84.

20. Gudiol, *Velázquez*, no. 96 and pp.151–2.

21. López-Rey, *Velázquez* (1979), no. 105, p. 448. Juan Allende-Salazar, in his edition of Walter Gensel, *Velázquez. Des Meisters Gemälde* (Berlin and Leipzig, 1925), pp. 279–80, notes that a painting of the same subject by Jusepe Martínez (Capilla de Nuestra Señora la Blanca, Seo de Zaragoza), completed at the end of 1644, bears some resemblance to Velázquez' composition and, in his view, establishes a *terminus ante quem* for the *Coronation*. This deduction, which is questioned by López-Rey, is confirmed by the document cited above.

22. Gerstenberg, *Velázquez*. pp. 94–6.

23. See above, pp. 161–2.

24. William B. Jordan, *The Meadows Museum. A Visitor's Guide to the Collection* (Dallas, 1974), pp. 20–1. The work also contains certain attributes of an allegory of Painting, but again essential elements are lacking. For the iconography of this subject, see Mary D. Garrard, "Artemisia Gentileschi's Self-Portrait as Allegory of Painting," *AB*, 62 (1980), pp. 97–112.

López-Rey (*Velázquez* [1979], no. 108, p. 458) identifies the subject as Arachne on the basis of a perceived resemblance to the figure he calls by this name in the *Fable of Arachne* (the figure skeining wool at the far right; see Plate 318). This identification is questionable, first, because the face of the figure in the *Fable of Arachne* is hidden from view, making comparison, except in a generic way, virtually impossible, and second, because, in any event, it is by no means certain that this woman is indeed Arachne.

25. Guy de Tervarent, *Attributs et symboles dans l'art profane, 1460–1600. Dictionnaire d'un langage perdu* (Geneva, 1958), cols. 279–81.

26. López-Rey's date for the Dallas picture is based on his debatable supposition that the *Fable of Arachne* was done *c*.1644–48.

27. See Francisco J. Sánchez Cantón, "La Venus del Espejo," *AEA*, 33 (1960), pp. 137–40.

28. Numerous sources, all more or less plausible, have been suggested for the pose of Venus, proving that it was a well-established artistic convention. For a convenient summary of the leading candidates and the proposal of yet others, see Charles de Tolnay, "La 'Venus au Miroir' de Velázquez," in *V.V.*, I. pp. 339–43. As Tolnay sensibly notes on p. 341, "Toutes ces inspirations sont fondues par Velázquez et completées par l'étude directe d'après nature."

29. Soria ("La Venus, los Borrachos y la Coronación," p. 277) interprets the mirror as a symbol of vanity, in the belief that the reflection shows an older and less beautiful woman than would be suggested by the body. This interpretation seems fanciful.

30. The photograph was kindly provided by Allan Braham, who first reproduced it in *Velázquez. The Rokeby Venus*, Painting in Focus, no. 5, National Gallery (London, 1976).

31. See MacLaren and Braham, *The Spanish School*, pp. 125–6, and José M. Pita Andrade, "Los cuadros de Velázquez y Mazo que poseyó el séptimo Marqués del Carpio," *AEA*, 23 (1952), pp. 223–36.

32. Harris (*Velázquez*, pp. 136–8) cautiously advances the argument that the picture might have been done in Italy and sent back to Madrid by Velázquez before his return. The argument rests principally on the implicit references made in the painting to classical statuary, examples of which Velázquez was collecting while in Rome in 1649–50. This idea is theoretically possible, but needs stronger evidence to support it. The earliest

record of a shipment of works by Velázquez from Italy dates from 23 June 1651, by which time, of course, the "*Rokeby Venus*" had been recorded in the collection of Gaspar de Haro; see Enriqueta Harris, "La misión de Velázquez en Italia," *AEA*, 33 (1960), p. 135, letter XII.

33. For Gaspar de Haro's biography, see Joaquín Ezquerra del Bayo, *El Palacete de Moncloa* (Madrid, 1929), and Gregorio de Andrés, *El Marqués de Liche, bibliófilo y coleccionista de arte* (Madrid, 1975); for his art collection, see José M. Pita Andrade, "Noticias en torno a Velázquez en el Archivo de la Casa de Alba," in *V.V.*, I, pp. 400–18, and Marcus B. Burke, "Private Collections of Italian Art in Seventeenth-Century Spain," (Ph.D. dissertation, New York University, 1984), chapter 4.

34. According to López-Rey (*Velázquez* [1979], no. 106, p. 452), the picture was inventoried in Gaspar de Haro's house in Madrid in 1692 (he died in Naples in 1687), where it was installed on the ceiling of an unidentified room. This unorthodox placement offers some confirmation of its purely erotic significance.

35. Palomino, trans. Harris, *Velázquez*, p. 213.

36. See *V.V.*, II, docs. 74 (Fulvio Testi in 1638, who does not use the word phlegmatic, but states that "he [Velázquez] never finished"); 76 (Cardinal Infante Ferdinand in 1639); and 120 (Philip IV in 1650). Philip IV again applied the term to his artist in an unpublished letter (Washington, D.C., private collection), dated 13 August 1652 (xerox copy in the author's possession).

37. José Martí y Monsó, "Diego Velázquez y Alonso Cano en Castilla," *BSCE*, 2 (1904), pp. 333–7. For Cano's eventful career as a painter, see Harold E. Wethey, *Alonso Cano. Pintor, escultor y arquitecto* (Madrid, 1983). Cano worked at court from 1638 to 1651 (except from 1644 to 1645), part of which time he was painter to the count-duke. His summons to court almost certainly was arranged by Velázquez, whom he had known since his apprenticeship with Pacheco in Seville (1616–21), and may have been in response to the need to form a new team of royal painters as the senior painters grew old and died. (An unsuccessful petitioner for one of the vacant places was Jusepe Leonardo, who applied on 8 December 1638, just a month after Carducho died; see José M. de Azcárate, "Algunas noticias sobre pintores cortesanos del siglo XVII," *AIEM*, 6 [1970], p. 51.) Cano's assignment to Olivares' household was probably done to circumvent the prohibition (1627) against the appointment of additional salaried painters to the royal household; see Martín González, "Sobre las relaciones," pp. 62–3. The friendship of Cano and Velázquez is further confirmed by the fact that Cano was the godfather to two of Velázquez' grandchildren, Inés Manuela (baptized 16 August 1638), and Joseph (18 March 1640); see José López Navío, "Matrimonio de Juan B. del Mazo con le hija de Velázquez," *AEA*, 33 (1960), pp. 392–3.

38. Palomino states that Velázquez was with the king in Aragon in 1642, which is disproved by the document cited below, note 39. Cruzada Villaamil (*Anales*) assumes that Velázquez accompanied the king on the *jornadas* of 1642, 1644, and 1646. Trapier (*Velázquez*, pp. 269–78) suggests that he made the trips to Aragón in 1644, 1645, and 1646. López-Rey (*Velázquez* [1979], p. 448) accepts the possibility that the painter was in Aragon in any or all of these years: 1642, 1644, 1645, and 1646. Only the trip of 1644 is documented.

39. *V.V.*, II, doc. 82, p. 251.

40. The event is described by Juan Francisco Andrés de Uztarroz, *Obelisco histórico i honorario que Zaragoza erigió a la inmortal memoria del Sereníssimo Señor, don Baltasar Carlos de Austria* (Zaragoza, 1646), pp. 58–9, who states that all the servants of the king's household were in attendance.

41. See Mercedes Agulló y Cobo *Noticias sobre pintores madrileños de los siglos XVI y XVII* (Granada, 1978), p. 176.

42. Carducho, *Diálogos*, pp. 440–2.

43. See Matías Fernández García, "Pintores de los siglos

XVI y XVII que fueron filigreses de la parroquía de San Sebastián," *AIEM*, 17 (1980), pp. 109–35.

44. The information on Semín was culled from the following sources: Brown and Elliott, *A Palace*, p. 92; J. J. Martín González, "Arte y artistas del siglo XVII en la corte," *AEA*, 31 (1958), pp. 133 and 138; Azcárate, "Algunas noticias," pp. 57–9, and "Noticias sobre Velázquez," pp. 359–60.

45. Azcárate, "Algunas noticias," p. 46.

46. José Ortega y Gasset, *Velázquez. Six Color Reproductions of Paintings from the Prado Museum* (New York, 1946), pp. 10–11.

47. Julián Gállego, "Datos sobre la calificación profesional de Velázquez," *Actas del XXIII Congreso Internacional de Historia de Arte*, III (Granada, 1976), pp. 95–9.

48. For the above appointments, see chapter II, pp. 44, 57–8.

49. *V.V.*, II, doc. 83, p. 252.

50. *V.V.*, II, doc. 65, p. 242.

51. Cruzada Villaamil, *Anales*, p. 136.

52. This calculation is based on the following data:

Salary as *pintor real* (31 October 1623; *V.V.*, II, doc. 22) — 360 ducats p.a.

Ecclesiastical pension (1627; Camón Aznar, *Velázquez*, I, p. 330) — 300 ducats p.a.

Annual grant for paintings (March 1640; *V.V.*, II, doc. 83) — 500 ducats p.a.

Salary as *superintendente de obras particulares* (9 June 1643; *V.V.*, II, doc. 86) — 720 ducats p.a.

Additional grant for unspecified purposes (27 February 1644; Sánchez Cantón, *Pintores de cámara*, p. 82) — 720 ducats p.a.

Increase in annual grant for paintings (18 May 1648; *V.V.*, II, doc. 106) — 200 ducats p.a.

The annual grants for paintings made in March 1640 and May 1648 were partly intended to cover payments in arrears but, according to the language of the document, were intended also to apply to works done in the future.

For the extraordinary grant of 12 May 1643, see *V.V.*, II, doc. 85, pp. 252–3.

The value of the *casa de aposento* is stated in *V.V.*, II, doc. 83, p. 252.

53. *V.V.*, II, doc. 58, p. 238.

54. Azcárate, "Noticias sobre Velázquez," pp. 384–5.

55. Cited by Brown and Elliott, *A Palace*, p. 115.

56. Max Rooses and Charles Ruelens. *Correspondance de Rubens et documents épistolaires concernant sa vie et ses oeuvres* (Antwerp, 1909), p. 228.

57. 22 June 1639, Cardinal Infante Ferdinand to Philip IV; see Rooses and Ruelens, *Correspondance de Rubens*, p. 231.

58. See Held, *The Oil Sketches*, pp. 305–6. Matías Díaz Padrón ("La Cacería de Venados de Rubens para el Ochavo del Alcázar, en Méjico," *AEA*, 43 [1970], pp. 131–50) suggests that the paintings were done originally for the Pieza Ochavada. The date of commission precludes this possibility because the Pieza Ochavada was not begun until 1643 (see below). Alpers (*The Torre de la Parada*, p. 39) suggests that these paintings were done for the Torre and later moved to Alcázar, which now seems unlikely.

59. For the commission, see Rooses and Ruelens, *Correspondance de Rubens*, pp. 238, 304, 310, 312, and 315–16.

60. Held, *The Oil Sketches*, pp. 379–82.

61. Rooses and Ruelens, *Correspondance de Rubens*, pp. 310 and 316. For the Rubens sale see J. Denucé, *Les Galeries d'art à Anvers aux 16e et 17e siècle. Inventaires. Sources pour l'histoire de l'art flamand*, II (s'Gravenhage, 1932), pp. 74–6.

62. For Philip IV's acquisitions at the Rubens sale, see Jeffrey M. Muller, "Peter Paul Rubens as a Collector of Art," II (Ph.D dissertation, Yale University, 1977) pp. 8–87 and 211–20.

63. See Nora de Poorter, *The Eucharist Series*, II,

pp. 446–7, and María del Carmen Pescador del Hoyo de Yuste, "Los tapices del Convento de Dominicas de Loeches," *AIEM*, 5 (1970), pp. 97–107, for the later history.

64. See Orso, *Philip IV*, chapter 2, for the evolution of the decoration and references to individual works.

65. See Mary C. Volk, "Rubens in Madrid and the Decoration of the King's Summer Apartments," *BM*, 123 (1981), pp. 513–29.

66. For the Salón Dorado, see Juan Vélez de Guevara, *Los celos hacen estrellas*, ed. J. E. Varey and N. D. Shergold (London, 1970) pp. xxxvii–xlii and lv–lxxi, and María L. Caturla, "Los retratos de reyes del Salón Dorado," *AEA*, 20 (1947), pp. 1–10.

67. *V.V.*, II, p. 61.

68. *V.V.*, II, doc. 144, p. 280

69. See Justi, *Velázquez* (ed. 1953), pp. 615–37; Azcárate, "Noticias sobre Velázquez;" Antonio Bonet Correa, "Velázquez, arquitecto y decorador," *AEA*, 33 (1960), pp. 215–49; Francisco Iñiguez Almech, "La Casa del Tesoro, Velázquez y las obras reales," in *V.V.*, I, pp. 649–82, and "Velázquez, arquitecto," *VM*, 3 (1960), pp. 20–6; and Orso, *Philip IV*.

70. *V.V.*, II, doc. 86, p. 253.

71. *V.V.*, II, doc. 95, p. 257 and docs. 100–2, pp. 259–60.

72. See José L. Barrio Moya, "Velázquez y Gómez de Mora juntos en una libranza," *AEA*, 51 (1978), p. 346.

73. See Orso, *Philip IV*, chapter 4, for the construction and decoration of this room.

74. *V.V.*, II, doc. 95, p. 257.

75. See Azcárate, "Noticias sobre Velázquez," pp. 366–73, for this documentation.

76. See Manuel R. Zarco del Valle, *Documentos inéditos para la historia de las bellas artes en España*, LV, *CODOIN* (Madrid, 1870), p. 439.

77. For the authorship of the Planets, see L. Smolderen, "Bacchus et les sept Planètes par Jacques Jonghelinck," *Révue des Archéólogues et des Historiens d'Art de Louvain*, 10 (1977), pp. 102–43; for their installation at the Buen Retiro, see Brown and Elliott, *A Palace*, pp. 109–10; for the transfer to the Alcázar, see Azcárate, "Noticias sobre Velázquez," pp. 371–2.

78. For the pictures in the Octagonal Room, see Orso, *Philip IV*.

79. See Yves Bottineau, "Portrait of Queen Mariana in the National Gallery," *BM*, 97 (1955), pp. 114–16.

80. Yves Bottineau, "L'Alcázar de Madrid et l'inventaire de 1686. Aspects de la cour d'Espagne au XVIIe siècle," *Bulletin Hispanique*, 60 (1958), p. 45. The similarity was noted at the time by the Tuscan ambassador in Madrid; see the dispatch dated 30 August 1651, in Justi, *Velázquez* (1953), pp. 556–7.

81. For the Tribuna, see Francis Haskell and Nicholas Penny, *Taste and the Antique. The Lure of Classical Sculpture* (New Haven and London, 1981), pp. 53–61.

82. See Lorenzo Magalotti, *Viaje de Cosmé de Medicis por España y Portugal (1668–1669)*, ed. Angel Sánchez Rivera (Madrid, n.d.), pp. 121–6, for the visit to the Alcázar.

83. See Iñiguez Almech, "La Casa del Tesoro," p. 674.

84. Azcárate, "Noticias sobre Velázquez," pp. 373–4.

85. For these documents, see Azcárate, "Noticias sobre Velázquez," pp. 379–86.

86. There is reason to believe that the trip to Italy was originally planned for 1646. In a letter to Cassiano dal Pozzo of 29 November 1646, the nuncio, Giulio Rospigliosi, announced Velázquez' forthcoming visit to Rome. See Giacomo Lumbroso, *Notizie sulla vita di Cassiano dal Pozzo, Miscellanea di Storia Italiana*, XV, (Turin, 1874), p. 314.

Chapter VII

1. For general accounts of the second Italian trip, see Palomino, *El museo pictórico*, trans. Harris, *Velázquez*, pp. 208–23; Harris, "La misión," pp. 109–36; and J. M.

Pita Andrade, "El itinerario de Velázquez en su segundo viaje a Italia," *Goya*, 37–8 (1960), pp. 151–2. He left Madrid after 24 November 1648, when he signed a power of attorney in favor of his wife; see Agulló, *Noticias*, pp. 176–7.

2. *V.V.*, II, doc. 114, pp. 266–7.

3. *V.V.*, II, doc. 115, p. 267.

4. *V.V.*, II, doc. 117, pp. 267–8.

5. *V.V.*, II, doc. 113, p. 266, makes clear the purpose of this trip, mentioned in Cardinal de la Cueva's letter of 10 July 1649.

6. Harris, "La misión."

7. For this episode, see Enriqueta Harris, "Velázquez and Charles I: Antique Busts and Modern Paintings from Spain for the Royal Collection," *JWCI*, 30 (1967), pp. 414–20.

8. For the interest in copying antique statues in the seventeenth century, see Haskell and Penny, *Taste and the Antique*, pp. 31–6.

9. See Domingo Martínez de la Peña, "El segundo viaje de Velázquez a Italia: dos cartas inéditas en los Archivos del Vaticano," *AEA*, 44 (1971), pp. 1–7.

10. For a discussion of some of the statues copied on Velázquez' orders, see Haskell and Penny, *Taste and the Antique*, pp. 219–20, 234–6, 260, 308.

11. The trip to Gaeta is referred to in a letter of 21 June 1650, from Fernando Ruiz de Contreras to the duke of Infantado; *V.V.*, II, doc. 124, pp. 270–1. As Harris ("La misión," p. 127, note 56), points out, the trip probably took place in May, when the viceroy was there to meet with Don Juan de Austria.

12. For this commission, see Jacob Hess, "Ein Spätwerk des Bildhauers Alessandro Algardi," *Münchner Jahrbuch der bildenden Kunst*, 8 (1931), pp. 292–303, and Enriqueta Harris, "A Letter from Velázquez to Camillo Massimi," *BM*, 102 (1960), pp. 162–6. Algardi had completed only the statues of *Jupiter* and *Juno* before his death on 10 June 1654. *Neptune* and *Cybele* were made from his models by Domenico Guidi and Ercole Ferrata. For a small-scale copy of Algardi's famous *Meeting of Pope Leo and Attila*, which was given to Philip IV by Cardinal Francesco Barberini in 1658, see Jennifer Montagu, "Un dono del Cardinale Francesco Barberini al Re di Spagna," *Arte Illustrata*, 4 (September–October 1971), pp. 42–51.

13. See Harris, "La misión," pp. 115–16.

14. *V.V.*, II, doc. 171, p. 291.

15. Harris ("La misión," pp. 129–36), publishes the texts of fourteen letters, six from the king, eight from Ruiz de Contreras. López-Rey (*Velázquez* [1979], p. 169, notes 186–7), cites the existence of two more letters in this series.

16. See Jennifer Montagu, "Velázquez Marginalia: His Slave Juan de Pareja and His Illegitimate Son Antonio," *BM*, 125 (1983), pp. 683–5.

17. See Ann Sutherland Harris, *Andrea Sacchi* (Princeton, 1977), nos. 44 and 67–8.

18. Enriqueta Harris ("Velázquez en Roma," *AEA*, 31 [1958], p. 189), notes a passage in Baldinucci's life of Jacopo Cortese which refers to several unfinished portraits by Velázquez in the collection of Baron Jean de Watteville in Milan. Baron de Watteville, called Baron de Batebila in seventeenth-century Spanish documents, became governor of San Sebastián and was there when Velázquez visited the town in 1659 to participate in the marriage ceremonies of Louis XIV and the infanta María Teresa.

19. For Cassiano's portrait by Velázquez, see Francis Haskell and Sheila Rinehart, "Revisiones sexcentistas. Juan de Pareja," *AEA*, 30 (1957), pp. 271–85, and Montagu, "Velázquez Marginalia," where Pareja's status as a slave is documented.

20. The best account of the portrait is still Justi, *Velázquez*

(1953), pp. 579–89. Fundamental for the pope's biography is Ludwig Pastor, *The History of the Popes from the Close of the Middle Ages*, XXX (repr. ed. Consortium Books, 1977), pp. 14–47.

In addition to reasons cited below, another indication of a date in 1649 is the fact that the pope is shown with the satin *mozzetta* worn during the summer months. During the winter months, the pope wears a velvet *mozzetta* trimmed with ermine. (I am grateful to Jennifer Killian for this observation). This suggests that the picture was painted either in the summer of 1649, just after Velázquez arrived in Rome, or in the following summer, just before he left. The former possibility is more plausible than the latter.

21. This idea is proposed by Harris, "Velázquez en Roma," pp. 191–2.

22. Archivio dell'Accademia di San Luca, Rome, vol. 69, fol. 296. According to Anne Sutherland Harris, to whom I owe this reference, the document in question is a small booklet made by order of Bernardino Gagliardi, Principe of the Academy in 1655. It begins with a list of principi and certain academicians, including Velázquez. After Velázquez' name, a line is drawn and a motion made on 17 December 1651, is quoted to the effect that "da qui avanti pro tempore non s'intendi alcuno essere academico se prima non sara dichiarata per tale dalla Congregatione secreta ed accademica." Later in the book, the secretary Ippolito Leone, who made the motion of 1651, describes the irregularities and neglect of the Academy during the tenure of G. B. Soria as Principe (1645–51). The text cited here seems to imply that the academicians did not elect their own membership during the period when Velázquez was admitted.

23. For the drawings, see Mary Cazort Taylor, *European Drawings from Canadian Collections, 1500–1900* (Ottawa, 1976), p. 48, no. 16, and McKim-Smith, "The Problem of Velázquez's Drawings," pp. 7–8, 18–19, no. 4.

24. *V.V.*, II, doc. 137, pp. 276–7. For the portrait and its copies, see López-Rey, *Velázquez* (1963), pp. 272–7, nos. 443–57. Despite the recent discovery of pentimenti in the version in Washington, National Gallery of Art, it still seems likely, on the basis of style, that the picture mentioned by the nuncio is the one in the Wellington Museum. For the arguments, see López-Rey, *Velázquez* (1979), no. 115, pp. 477–8.

25. For the portrait, see Enriqueta Harris, "Velázquez' Portrait of Camillo Massimi," *BM*, 100 (1958), pp. 279–80 and "The Cleaning of Velázquez's Portrait of Camillo Massimi," *BM*, 125 (1983), pp. 410–15. For his biography, see Haskell, *Patrons and Painters*, pp. 114–19, and Harris, "A Letter from Velázquez." As Harris notes in the last-cited article, Massimi owned six portraits by Velázquez of which only his own has survived. Some of these portraits were acquired by Gaspar de Haro upon the death of Massimi; see Enriqueta Harris, "El Marqués de Carpio y sus cuadros de Velázquez," *AEA*, 30 (1957), pp. 136–9.

26. See Trapier, "Velázquez: New Data," pp. 54–60, and Pastor, *The History of the Popes*, XXX, pp. 39–42. For the copy which belonged to Gaspar de Haro, see Harris, *Velázquez*, Plate 157.

27. For the lost portrait of Olimpia Maidalchini, see Harris, *Velázquez*, p. 146.

28. There is no evidence for the identification of the sitter as the Pope's barber, Michel Angelo Augurio, or as any member of the papal court. The suggestion originates with August L. Mayer, *Velázquez* (London, 1936), pl. 82.

29. For Pareja's biography, see Juan A. Gaya Nuño, "Revisiones sexcentistas. Juan de Pareja," *AEA*, 30 (1957), pp. 271–85, and Montagu, "Velázquez Marginalia," where Pareja's status as a slave is documented.

30. J. A. F. Orbaan, "Virtuosi al Pantheon. Archivalische Beiträge zur Römischen Kunstgeschichte," *Repertorium für Kunstwissenschaft*, 37 (1915), p. 45. The activities of the Congregazione are described in Haskell, *Patrons and Painters*, pp. 126–7.

31. For a description of the technique, see the excellent

article by Hubert von Sonnenburg, "The Technique and Conservation of the Portrait [of Juan de Pareja]," *Metropolitan Museum of Art Bulletin*, 29 (1970–71), pp. 476–8.

32. For a summary of a representative sample of opinions on the date, see López-Rey (*Velázquez* [1979], nos. 46–7, pp. 297–300), who himself dates the paintings to the first stay in Rome.

33. Enriqueta Harris, "Velázquez and the Villa Medici," *BM*, 123 (1981), pp. 537–41. For another convincing line of argument for the 1649–50 date, see Luis Díez del Corral, *Velázquez, la monarquía e Italia* (Madrid, 1979), pp. 279–80, note 70, where he observes that the Villa Medici landscapes presume knowledge of the paintings of Claude of the 1640s. See below for further discussion of the possible relationship between Claude (and other northern landscape artists) with Velázquez.

34. For the genesis of this type of drawing, see Marcel Roethlisberger, *Claude Lorrain. The Drawings* (Berkeley and Los Angeles, 1968), pp. 35–44, and Marco Chiarini, *I disegni italiani di paesaggio dal 1600 al 1750* (Rome, 1972), pp. xxxiv–xxxv. For the relationship of Claude's nature drawings to his paintings, see Lawrence Gowing, "Nature and the Ideal in the Art of Claude," *Art Quarterly*, 37 (1974), pp. 91–6.

35. Marcel Roethlisberger, *Bartolomaus Breenberg. Handzeichnungen* (Berlin, 1969), no. 105.

36. Roethlisberger, *Claude Lorrain. The Drawings*, p. 202, no. 480.

37. For the problem of the origin of landscape paintings done out-of-doors, see Gowing, "Nature and the Ideal," pp. 94–5, and Philip Conisbee, "Pre-Romantic *Plein-Air* Painting," *Art History*, 2 (1979), pp. 413–28.

38. See Conisbee, "Pre-Romantic *Plein-Air* Painting," pp. 414–15, for an analysis of Symond's sketch. The descriptions written below the sketch, keyed by the letters A–E, identify the various parts of the box as follows: A — the lid of the box which serves as the easel for the canvas; B — section for the brushes; C and D — compartments for the oil medium and pigments, some of which are concealed by E, the palette. F, which is not described, is the thumb-hole of the palette.

39. One of the few exceptions is the minor painter Pietro Martire Neri (1591–1661), who painted portraits of Innocent X (El Escorial) and Cristoforo Segni, the papal majordomo (Switzerland, private collection), in imitation of Velázquez. See Harris, *Velázquez*, Plates 154 and 155.

40. *V.V.*, II, doc. 131, p. 274. The nuncio reported the performance of the request in a letter of 2 August 1651 (*V.V.*, II, doc. 139, p. 277).

41. Velázquez is last documented in Rome on 23 November; see Montagu, "Velázquez Marginalia," p. 684.

42. *V.V.*, II, doc. 130, p. 273.

43. *V.V.*, II, doc. 143, p. 279.

44. The primary source of knowledge of Velázquez' acquisitions in Venice is Marco Boschini, *La carta del navegar pittoresco* (Venice, 1660; ed. cited *V.V.*, II, pp. 34–6). Boschini is eager to claim Velázquez as an heir to the Venetian tradition, which he was, and an enemy of the Roman tradition, which is not true. Thus, the words he puts in Velázquez' mouth were probably not spoken by the artist.

For the paintings by Veronese acquired by Velázquez, see Manuel Lorente Junquera, "Sobre Veronés en el Prado," *AEA*, 42 (1969), pp. 235–43. The smaller dimensions of *Cephalus and Procris* are the result of the trimming of the picture after the early nineteenth century.

45. *V.V.*, II, doc. 158, pp. 285–6. As López-Rey (*Velázquez* [1979], p. 168, note 177), points out, this painting cannot be identified with Prado 398 or Louvre 1496, both of which are considerably smaller than the picture described by the ambassador.

46. The dates for Velázquez' departure from Genoa and arrival in Valencia and Madrid are established in Harris, "La misión," p. 126.

47. AGS, Estado, leg. 2576, unfoliated. Philip IV to Alonso de Cárdenas, 30 June 1645; cited, through cour-

tesy of Father Albert Loomie, in Oliver Millar, ed., "The Inventories and Valuations of the King's Goods, 1649–51," *The Forty-Third Volume of The Walpole Society* (1970–72), p. xiii, note 5. The king instructs Cárdenas to buy paintings by Titian, Veronese, and "otras pinturas antiguas de opinión."

On 27 September 1645, the king wrote again (AGS, Estado, leg. 2576), instructing Cárdenas to "comprar las (pinturas) que fueren de más insignes y de estimación conforme a los q(ue) os encargue en despacho de 30 de junio."

48. AGS, Estado, leg. 2523, unfoliated. Consulta, 12 May 1646 (cited in Millar, "The Inventories," p. xiii, note 5).

49. For Leganés as collector, see José López Navío, "La gran colección de pinturas del Marqués de Leganés," *Analecta Calasanctiana*, 8 (1962), pp. 260–330, and Mary C. Volk, "New Light on a Seventeenth-Century Collector: The Marqués de Leganés," *AB*, 62 (1980), pp. 256–68.

50. Leganés owned the following paintings attributed to Velázquez: "Calabazas con turbante" (López Navío, no. 549) and "un retrato entero de Pablillos" (no. 553). Also listed without attribution are portraits of the jester "Don Juan de Austria" (no. 545), Pernia (no. 546), and Don Juan de Cárdenas (no. 547). The dimensions are not given but appear to have been about one vara square if they were similar in size to the next preceding entry where measurements are given. There is no way to know whether these versions of the jester portraits (see above, pp. 97–105) were by Velázquez or another artist. They do suggest, however, that the paintings were regarded as forming a series. According to Volk, "New Light," p. 265, the pictures were in the collection by 1642.

51. López Navío, "La gran colección," no. 1030, p. 311.

52. For Monterrey's collection, see Alfonso E. Pérez Sánchez, "Las colecciones de pintura del Conde de Monterrey (1653)," *BRAH*, 174 (1977), pp. 417–59. For the painting, see Harold E. Wethey, *The Paintings of Titian*. I, *The Religious Paintings* (London, 1969), no. 96, pp. 129–30.

53. For the history of this commission, see the following: Antonio García Boiza, *Una fundación de Monterrey: la iglesia y convento de MM. Agustinas de Salamanca* (Salamanca, 1945); Marqués del Saltillo, "Artistas madrileños (1592–1850)," *BSEE*, 57 (1953), p. 179; Ulisse Prota-Giurleo, "Fanzago ignorato," *Il Fuidoro*, 4 (1957), pp. 146–59; Angela Madruga Real, "Cosimo Fanzago en las Agustinas de Salamanca," *Goya*, 125 (1975); Brown and Elliott, *A Palace*, p. 288, note 41; and Angela Madruga Real, *Arquitectura barroca salamantina. Las Agustinas de Monterrey* (Salamanca, 1983).

54. *V.V.*, II, doc. 149, pp. 281–2. José Domínguez Carrascal, *El retrato de la Condesa de Monterrey pintado por Velázquez* (Madrid, n.d.), attempts unconvincingly to identify the portrait with a work then (1920s) in a private collection, although the sitter is undoubtedly the countess of Monterrey. A *Female Portrait* (Berlin, Gemäldegalerie) has also been connected with the portrait mentioned in 1652. It is doubtful, however, that the sitter is the countess of Monterrey. As for the attribution to Velázquez, this was tentatively accepted by López-Rey (*Velázquez* [1963], no. 593, p. 325), but was subsequently, and in my view correctly, omitted from his revised catalogue of 1979.

55. Medina de las Torres is little-studied as a statesman and unstudied as a collector. For the former, see R. A. Stradling, "A Spanish Statesman of Appeasement: Medina de las Torres and Spanish Policy 1639–70," *Historical Journal*, 19 (1976), pp. 1–31. The only sketch of his activities as a collector is found in Elías Tormo, "Al Señor Serrano Fatigati sobre 'Escultura en Madrid' y sobre deudos del Conde Duque (los Felípez de Guzmán)," *BSEE*, 17 (1909), pp. 299–312.

56. For the acquisition of the *Virgin of the Fish*, see Mrs. Horace Roscoe St. John, *The Court of Anna Carafa. An Historical Narrative* (London, 1872), p. 347.

57. For Luis de Haro as collector, see Burke, "Private Collections," chapter 3.

58. Marqués del Saltillo, "Artistas madrileños," pp. 233–4.

59. For a complete transcription of the inventory, discovered by José M. Pita Andrade, "Los cuadros de Velázquez," pp. 233–6, see Burke, "Private Collections," appendix 4.1

60. Much of the following account of Luis de Haro and the Commonwealth sale is based on the documentation in the Archivo de la Casa de Alba which is noted in Burke, "Private Collections," chapter 3.

61. Cárdenas arrived in London in the summer of 1638, having previously served the duke of Alcalá (BNM 9883, f. 273, duke of Alcalá to Cárdenas, 3 June 1635). He was appointed ambassador in July 1649; see J. H. Elliott, "The Year of the Three Ambassadors," in *History and imagination. Essays in Honour of H. R. Trevor-Roper* (London, 1981), pp. 165–81. Cárdenas was the cousin of the gazetteer Jerónimo de Barrionuevo, whose *Avisos* (ed. A. Paz y Mélia, Biblioteca de Autores Espanoles, CCXXI–CCXXII [Madrid, 1968–69]) frequently mention his activities in the 1650s.

62. AGS, Estado 2532, 3 June 1663. Instructions to Patricio Moledi, "Lo que ha de observar por Instrucción la persona que ha de asistir en Inlaterra;" courtesy of Father Albert Loomie.

63. For the conduct of the sale, see Millar, "The Inventories," pp. xviii–xxii, and W. L. F. Nuttall, "King Charles I's Pictures and the Commonwealth Sale," *Apollo*, 82 (1965), pp. 302–9. The literature on the sale is surprisingly exiguous.

64. For the letters from Haro to Cárdenas, see Duquesa de Berwick y de Alba. *Documentos escogidos de la casa de Alba* (Madrid, 1891), pp. 488–97; for references to the letters from Cárdenas to Haro, see Burke, "Private Collections," chapter 3. I am grateful to the duke of Alba for granting permission to read these documents in July 1983.

65. Archivo de la Casa de Alba, caja 182–166. See John Shearman, *Raphael's Cartoons in the Collection of Her Majesty the Queen and Tapestries of the Sistine Chapel* (London, 1972), p. 143, for the history of this set, now destroyed.

66. Archivo de la Casa de Alba, caja 182–173

67. Archivo de la Casa de Alba, caja 182–176.

68. Justi (*Velázquez* [1953], p. 623) publishes a dispatch from the Tuscan ambassador, dated 9 September 1652, which reports the arrival of the Twelve Caesars in Madrid.

69. See H. Léonardon, "Une dépêche diplomatique relative à des tableaux acquis en Angleterre par Philippe IV," *Bulletin Hispanique*, 2 (1900), pp. 24–35. There is a gap in the surviving documentation between 24 November 1651 and 11 August 1653. However, Cárdenas kept buying works of art during this time, as proved by a license granted him on 24 August 1653 to export twenty-four chests containing pictures and hangings; see Shearman, *Raphael's Cartoons*, p. 143. Shearman states that the Acts of Apostles tapestries were in this shipment; however, Cárdenas, in a letter of 29 May 1651 (Archivo de la Casa de Alba, caja 182–170), acknowledges the receipt of a letter from Haro, reporting their safe arrival in Madrid.

70. Archivo de la Casa de Alba, caja 182–195: "Quenta del dinero que se ha remitido a Don Alonso de Cárdenas mi sr para emplearle según las órdenes del exmo sr Don Luis de Haro. . . ."

71. Duquesa de Berwick y de Alba, *Documentos escogidos*, p. 488. This document and the others cited in this publication no longer survive. For a recent discussion of some of this material, see Enriqueta Harris, "Velázquez as Connoisseur," *BM*, 124 (1982), pp. 436–40.

72. Duquesa de Berwick y de Alba, *Documentos escogidos*, p. 491.

73. Duquesa de Berwick y de Alba, *Documentos escogidos*, p. 494.

74. For the identification of the work, see Harris, "Velázquez as Connoisseur," pp. 436–7. The provenance of the Arundel collection is established in an undated document (probably *c.* 1650) in the Archivo de la Casa de Alba, caja 185–195 ("Memoria de las pinturas que se hallan enser y de venta en Londres . . .").

75. Duquesa de Berwick y de Alba, *Documentos escogidos*, p. 493.

76. Archivo de la Casa de Alba, caja 182–185.

CHAPTER VIII

1. *V.V.*, II, doc. 144, pp. 279–80.

2. For the duties of the *aposentador*, see "Etiquetas generales," fols. 123–37. The requirements and emoluments are summarized in Alonso Núñez de Castro, *Solo Madrid es corte* (Madrid, 1675), pp. 204–5, and Antonio Rodríguez Villa, *Etiquetas de la Casa de Austria* (Madrid, n.d.), pp. 45–7.

3. *V.V.*, II, doc. 159, p. 286; doc. 164, pp. 288–9; doc. 169, pp. 290–1.

4. *V.V.*, II, doc. 167, p. 290; doc. 175, p. 293.

5. *V.V.*, II, doc. 162, p. 287.

6. *V.V.*, II, doc. 161, pp. 286–7; doc. 168, p. 290; doc. 176, p. 293.

7. See J. E. Varey, "Velázquez y Heliche en los festejos madrileños de 1657–1658," *BRAH*, 169 (1972), pp. 407–22.

8. For the salary, see "Etiquetas generales," fol. 123. Azcárate ("Noticias sobre Velázquez," p. 375–8) overestimates Velázquez' wealth by treating the annual grants for the expenses of his office as if they were salary payments.

9. *V.V.*, II, doc. 165, p. 289.

10. *V.V.*, II, doc. 163, pp. 287–8.

11. See Jerónimo de Barrionuevo, *Avisos*, II (Madrid, 1892), p. 540.

12. For this episode, see Manuel Espada Burgos, "Velázquez y el abasto de leña a las reales cocinas," *AIEM*, 13 (1976), pp. 123–8.

13. Following Velázquez' death, the *Bureo* began a review of his official accounts, a customary procedure when a court office changed hands. The review was concluded in March-April, 1666. Despite the understandable complaints of Velázquez' heirs about the delay, the process was done expeditiously by the usual standards of the bureaucracy. The information cited in the text below was extracted, with the assistance of J. H. Elliott, from *V.V.*, II, doc. 223, pp. 406–9 and doc. 224, pp. 409–10.

14. The full text of the dispatch, which is partly cited in Justi, *Velázquez* (1953), p. 668, appears in Heinrich Zimmerman, "Zur Ikonographie des Hauses Habsburg. I, Bildnisse der Königen Marianne von Spanien," *Jahrbuch des Kunsthistorisches Sammlungen der Allerhöchsten Kaiserhauses*, 25, no. 4 (1905), p. 185.

15. Justi, *Velázquez* (1903), II, p. 361.

16. Justi, *Velázquez* (1953), pp. 674–6.

17. Justi, *Velázquez* (1953), pp. 676.

18. Justi, *Velázquez* (1953), pp. 676.

19. Justi, *Velázquez* (1953), pp. 676.

20. López-Rey, *Velázquez* (1979), no. 118, p. 484, where the strips added to the canvas are fully discussed.

21. López-Rey, *Velázquez* (1963), nos. 390–1.

22. López-Rey, *Velázquez* (1979), no. 119, p. 486. The painting in Vienna and a replica now in the Museum of Fine Arts, Boston (López-Rey, *Velázquez* [1963], no. 387), but formerly also in the Kunsthistorisches Museum, can be identified with the portraits of the infanta mentioned by Querini, the Venetian ambassador, on 17 December 1653, just after they had been sent to Brussels and Vienna; see Zimmerman, "Zur Ikonographie," p. 186. A third version in a reduced format was sent to France some months later and is now in the Louvre (M.I. 898); see López-Rey, *Velázquez*, 1963, no. 389 (reproduced in pl. 332, not pl. 333). Earlier in the year, on 22 February, the Modenese ambassador noted the dispatch to Flanders of a portrait of the infanta, together with those of the king and queen

(see above, note 14). López-Rey overlooks the notice of the portraits sent in December and therefore mistakenly identifies both the Vienna and Boston portraits with the single portrait mentioned on 22 February. This error leads him to misdate slightly the execution of the Vienna portrait to "late 1652 or early 1653." It is more likely that the portrait was done entirely within the year of 1653. The whereabouts of the portrait sent to Flanders in February is unknown but it is logical to suppose that the portraits sent in December to potential candidates for marriage to the infanta would have been identical and therefore are the ones now in Vienna and Boston and mentioned in Querini's letter of 17 December 1653. The Boston version came to Vienna with the archduke Leopold William, which explains why both the original and the workshop copy eventually passed to the collection of the Kunsthistorisches Museum. According to Zimmerman, "Zur Ikonographie," p. 188, the original by Velázquez was sent to Vienna, not Brussels.

23. López-Rey, *Velázquez* (1979), no. 121, pp. 492–3.

24. López-Rey, *Velázquez* (1979), no. 125, p. 510. The conservation report of M. Grassi, dated 20 May 1978, notes that "there is evidence of a very antique overpainting in the lower area corresponding with the white collar."

25. López-Rey, *Velázquez* (1979), no. 122, p. 498.

26. López-Rey, *Velázquez* (1979), no. 123. p. 500.

27. López-Rey, *Velázquez* (1979), no. 128. p. 516.

28. López-Rey, *Velázquez* (1979), no. 129. p. 518.

29. For the copies, see López-Rey, *Velázquez* (1963), nos. 267–87.

30. López-Rey, *Velázquez* (1963), no. 259, pp. 216–17.

31. The argument against the authenticity is advanced in López-Rey, *Velázquez* (1979), pp. 132–3; the authenticity is defended in MacLaren and Braham, *The Spanish School*. pp. 108–13.

32. See Harris, *Velázquez*, p. 171.

33. For the complete edition of the letters, see *Cartas de Sor María de Jesús de Ágreda y Felipe IV*, ed. Carlos Seco Serrano, Biblioteca de Autores Españoles, CVIII–CIX (Madrid, 1958).

34. The fundamental documentation on the history of the Pantheon was published in Juan J. Martín González, "El Panteón de San Lorenzo de El Escorial," *AEA*, 32 (1959), pp. 199–213. For a polemical interpretation of this documentation, see René Taylor, "Juan Bautista Crescencio," and Juan J. Martín González, "El Panteón de El Escorial," which offers a more balanced assessment of the contributions of the various architects and builders involved in the project.

35. The final phase of the construction is studied in Francisco Iñiguez Almech, "La Casa del Tesoro," pp. 663–70; Federico Navarro Franco, "El Real Panteón de San Lorenzo de El Escorial," in *El Escorial 1563–1963. IV Centenario de la fundación del Monasterio de San Lorenzo el Real*, II (Madrid, 1963), pp. 717–37; and Gregorio de Andrés, "Correspondencia epistolar entre Felipe IV y el P. Nicolás de Madrid sobre la construcción del Panteón de Reyes, 1654," in *Documentos para la historia del Monasterio de San Lorenzo el Real de El Escorial*, VIII (El Escorial, 1965), pp. 159–207.

36. Cited by Navarro Franco, "El Real Panteón," p. 734.

37. The extent of Velázquez' participation in the work of the Pantheon is judiciously evaluated by Iñiguez Almech, "La Casa del Tesoro."

38. *V.V.*, II, doc. 170, p. 291, where the annotation is tentatively dated 1656. However, the Pantheon was inaugurated in March 1654.

39. Fr. Francisco de los Santos, *Descripción breve del Monasterio de San Lorenzo El Real del Escorial*, ed. F. J. Sánchez Cantón, *Fuentes literarias para la historia del arte español*, II (Madrid, 1933), p. 286.

40. De los Santos, *Descripción breve*, pp. 286–7.

41. Iñiguez Almech, "Las Casa del Tesoro," p. 668, for this figure and the information which follows.

42. For the identification of the sculptor, see Elías Tormo, "Los cuatro grandes crucifijos de bronce dorado en El

Escorial," *AEA*, 1 (1925), pp. 117–25. Iñiguez Almech ("La Casa del Tesoro," p. 669i, introduces important modifications of Tormo's account of the statues of the Crucifixion installed in the Pantheon.

43. *Cartas de Sor María de Jesús de Ágreda*, CVIII, p. 343 (letter of 25 March 1654).

44. Julio Chifflet, "Relación de la estancia de Felipe IV en El Escorial (1656) por su capellán Julio Chifflet," in Gregorio de Andrés, ed., *Documentos para la historia del Monasterio de San Lorenzo el Real de El Escorial*, VII (Madrid, 1967), p. 407.

45. Duquesa de Berwick y de Alba, *Documentos escogidos*, p. 492.

46. De los Santos, *Descripción breve*, p. 309.

47. Chifflet, "Relación de la estancia," p. 409.

48. The arrangement of these rooms was described in 1626 by Cassiano dal Pozzo; see Harris and Andrés, "Descripción del Escorial por Cassiano dal Pozzo," pp. 12–15. The fundamental source for the description of the sacristy and ante-sacristy is de los Santos, *Descripción breve*, pp. 232–41. Many of the paintings, which eventually went to the Museo del Prado, are identified in the notes to this edition prepared by Sánchez Cantón. Also important is Gregorio de Andrés, "Relación anónima del siglo XVII sobre los cuadros del Escorial," *AEA*, 44 (1971), pp. 56–62. For the Flemish paintings, Matías Díaz Padrón, *Museo del Prado. Catálogo de pinturas*. I, *Escuela flamenca, siglo XVII* (Madrid, 1975), is very useful. The now-infamous *Memoria* describing the paintings in the sacristy and attributed to Velázquez is universally recognized as a fake. I have also relied on a paper by Elizabeth Nicklas, prepared for my seminar at the Institute of Fine Arts (1980), which contains full information on provenance and bibliography. See also J.M. Morán Turino and F. Checa, "Las colecciones pictóricas del Escorial y el gusto italiano," *Goya*, 179 (1984), pp. 252–61, and Edward J. Sullivan, "Politics and Propaganda in the *Sagrada Forma* by Claudio Coello," *Art Bulletin*, 67 (1985), pp. 255–9. In the interests of convenience and economy, references to individual pictures are given selectively. The inventory numbers of paintings in the Museo del Prado, which houses the majority of works once in El Escorial, are noted in parentheses in the text when the works are not illustrated.

49. For *St. Margaret* and the *Agony in the Garden*, see Wethey, *The Paintings of Titian*, I, nos. 116 and 6 respectively.

50. Wethey, *The Paintings of Titian*, I, no. 91.

51. In addition to the works mentioned in the text, the following were also in the ante-sacristy:

Tintoretto, *Entombment*. El Escorial, Nuevos Museos
Veronese, *Presentation of Christ in the Temple* (lost)
School of Veronese, *St. John Preaching*. El Escorial, Palace
Ribera, *Sts. Peter and Paul*. Paris, private collection?

52. Wethey, *The Paintings of Titian*, I, nos. 53 and X–32.

53. See Maria Küsche, *Juan Pantoja de la Cruz* (Madrid, 1964), pp. 168–71, nos. 43–44.

54. See Matías Díaz Padrón, "Dos nuevos pinturas de Rubens y Van Dyck identificadas en España: *La Santa Cena* y la *Mujer Adúltera*," *AEA*, 40 (1967), pp. 228–37.

55. Wethey, *The Paintings of Titian*, I, nos. 65 and X–9.

56. For the recent re-attribution of the painting to Raphael, see Cecil Gould, "Raphael versus Giulio Romano: the Swing Back," *BM*, 124 (1982), pp. 479–87.

57. Wethey, *The Paintings of Titian*, I, nos. 28 (as with assistance of workshop) and 65.

58. Wethey, *The Paintings of Titian*, I, nos. 148 and 6.

59. See Cecil Gould, *The Paintings of Correggio* (Ithaca, 1976), pp. 224–5.

60. See Donald Posner, *Annibale Carracci: A Study in the Reform of Italian Painting Around 1590*, II (New York, 1971), p. 19, no. 39, and Andrés, "Relación anónima," p. 58, note 70.

61. Wethey, *The Paintings of Titian*, I, nos. 110 and 29.

62. See D. Hannema, *Beschrijvende Catalogus van den Schil-*

derijen uit de Kunstverzammlung Stichtung Willem van der Worm (Rotterdam, 1962), pp. 25–6, no. 22.

63. In addition to the paintings mentioned above, the following works were in the sacristy:

Luca Cambiaso, *Christ at the Column*. El Escorial, Claustro alto principal

Raphael, *Visitation*. Madrid, Prado 300

Andrea Schiavone, *Nativity* (lost)

Sebastiano del Piombo, *Christ in Limbo*. Madrid, Prado 346

Sebastiano del Piombo, *Christ with Cross*. Madrid, Prado 345

Giovanni Serodine, *Miracle of St. Margaret*. Madrid, Prado 246

Tintoretto, *Penitent Magdalene*. El Escorial, Nuevos Museos

Titian, *Madonna and Child*. Munich, Alte Pinakothek

Titian, *Penitent Magdalene*. Formerly London, Bath House

Titian, *St. Sebastian* (lost)

Veronese, *Ecce Homo*. Perhaps El Escorial, Nuevos Museos

Veronese, *Sacrifice of Abraham*. Madrid, Prado 500

64. The drawing was first published by Matilde López Serrano, *Catálogo de dibujos I. Trazas de Juan De Herrera y sus seguidores para el Monasterio del Escorial* (Madrid, 1944), pp. 12–14 and p. 23, pl. 29, no. 33. Her cautious attribution of the plan to Juan Gómez de Mora and of the titles of the pictures to Velázquez is fully accepted by Iñiguez Almech ("La Casa del Tesoro," p. 679).

65. For the reconstruction of the decoration of this room, see de los Santos, *Descripción breve*, pp. 248–9, and Andrés. "Relación anónima," pp. 52–4. I have also used a paper by Sam Heath, written for my seminar at the Institute of Fine Arts.

66. Wethey, *The Paintings of Titian*, I, no. 7.

67. See Matías Díaz Padrón, "Una Piedad de Van Dyck atribuida a Rubens," *AEA*, 47 (1974), pp. 149–56.

68. See Matías Díaz Padrón, "Un nuevo Rubens en el Museo del Prado: La Inmaculada del Marqués de Leganés," *AEA*, 40 (1967), pp. 1–13.

69. In addition to the paintings mentioned above, the following works were in the Chapter Room of the Prior:

Guercino, *St. Jerome in Penitence* (lost)

Daniel Seghers, Four Paintings of Garlands of Flowers (lost)

Van Dyck, *St. Sebastian*. (According to Andrés, this picture is in Munich. However, as Heath points out, the Munich version was acquired in 1806, three years before the Escorial version was removed.)

Veronese (?), *Virgin and Child Enthroned with St. John the Baptist and Two Female Saints* (lost)

70. De los Santos, *Descripción breve*, pp. 254–7. Chifflet, in "Relación de la estancia," p. 421, also mentions the Iglesia Vieja as another sector of El Escorial where Velázquez re-arranged the decoration.

71. Wethey, *The Paintings of Titian*, I, nos. 149 and 38.

72. The other paintings in the Aulilla were as follows:

Titian, *St. Margaret*. El Escorial (Wethey, no. 116)

Titian, *Ecce Homo* (lost)

Palma Giovane, *Penitent St. Jerome* (lost)

Veronese, *Christ in Limbo*. El Escorial, Nuevos Museos

73. De los Santos, *Descripción breve*, p. 257.

74. *V.V.*, II, p. 61.

CHAPTER IX

1. *V.V.*, II, doc. 143, p. 279.

2. Harris, "A Letter from Velázquez," p. 166, note 12.

3. See Alfonso E. Pérez Sánchez, "Una referencia a Velázquez en la obra de Baldinucci," *AEA*, 34 (1961), pp. 89–90.

4. De los Santos, *Descripción breve*, p. 313.

5. Before the move to the prince's quarters, the painter royal's workshop was located in the Galería del Cierzo.

6. See Brown, *Images and Ideas*, pp. 99–100, citing the findings of Steven N. Orso.

7. "Mémoires du Maréchal de Gramont (1659)," *Collection des Mémoires relatifs à l'histoire de France*, ed. A. Pettitot and H. Monmérque, LVII (Paris, 1827), p. 57.

8. This study is based on the annotated publication of the 1686 Alcázar inventory by Bottineau, "L'Alcázar de Madrid," 1956 and 1958, and Orso, *Philip IV*, chapters 2 and 4, for the Hall of Mirrors and the Galería del Mediodía.

9. For the contents of this room, see Bottineau, "L'Alcázar de Madrid," 1958, pp. 149–59, and Orso, *Philip IV*, chapter 4.

10. See Wethey, *The Paintings of Titian*, I, no. L-12.

11. See Harold E. Wethey, *The Paintings of Titian*. II, *The Portraits* (London, 1971), nos. 49, 78, 20, and 53.

12. For the contents of this room, see Bottineau, "L'Alcázar de Madrid," 1958, pp. 172–9. For the start of the re-installation, in July 1652, see Harris, "La misión," p. 128.

13. For the evolution of this type, see the fundamental study of Wolfram Prinz, *Die Entstehung der Galerie im Frankreich und Italien* (Berlin, 1970).

14. For the contents of this room, see Bottineau, "L'Alcázar de Madrid," 1958, pp. 318–25. According to documents discovered by Steven N. Orso, the remodeling of the Bóvedas was accomplished in 1651–52.

15. See Wethey, *The Paintings of Titian*, III, nos. 13, 15, 34, 47, 50.

16. The published sources for Gramont's embassy are his own account, "Mémoires du Maréchal de Gramont (1659)," and Francois Bertaut, *Journal du Voyage en Espagne* (Paris, 1669).

17. The installation and iconography of the Hall of Mirrors are discussed in detail in Orso, *Philip IV*, chapter 2. For the contents, see Bottineau, "L'Alcázar de Madrid," 1958, pp. 34–47.

18. López-Rey, *Velázquez* (1979), no. 127, p. 514.

19. For details on the original placement, see Orso, *Philip IV*, chapter 2, which establishes that the picture was meant to be seen at eye level and not from below, as is sometimes stated.

20. The attribution of the design of the frescoes comes from Palomino, who seems to imply that Velázquez was responsible both for the general distribution of the scenes and the specific composition of each compartment.

21. For the work of Colonna and Mitelli in Spain, see Enriqueta Harris, "Angelo Michele Colonna y la decoración de San Antonio de los Portugueses," *AEA*, 34 (1961), pp. 101–5, and Ebria Feinblatt, "Angelo Michele Colonna: A Profile," *BM*, 121 (1979), pp. 618–30.

22. For the iconography of the ceiling, see Orso, *Philip IV*, chapter 2.

23. Bertaut, *Journal*, pp. 26–7.

24. "Mémoires du Maréchal de Gramont," p. 50.

25. Bertaut, *Journal*, pp. 26–7.

26. "Mémoires du Maréchal de Gramont," p. 51.

27. See *V.V.*, II, docs. 188–201, pp. 378–86, for the documents concerning Velázquez' participation in the *jornada*.

28. The principal source for this event is Leonardo del Castillo, *Viage del Rey Nuestro Señor Don Felipe Quarto El Grande a la frontera de Francia* (Madrid, 1667). For historical studies, see Cruzada, *Anales*, pp. 257–61; Saint René de Taillandier, *Le Mariage de Louis XIV* (Paris, 1928), and *Saint-Jean-de-Luz, Etape Royale, 1660–1960. Exposition Commemorative de Troisième Centenaire du Mariage de Louis XIV avec Marie-Thérèse* (St.-Jean-de-Luz, 1960). I am also indebted to Susanna Schindler for a comprehensive seminar report on the decoration and iconography of the pavilion.

29. Cited in *Saint-Jean-de-Luz, Etape Royale*, p. 89.

30. Palomino, *El museo pictórico*, trans. Harris, *Velázquez*, p. 221.

31. For the *probanza* of Velázquez by the Council of Military Orders, see *V.V.*, doc. 183, pp. 310–77, and Brown, *Images and Ideas*, pp. 107–9.

32. A date of *c.*1657–58 is accepted by most scholars of Velázquez. However, López-Rey (*Velázquez* [1963], no. 56, pp. 139–41 and [1979], pp. 101–6 and no. 107, pp. 454–5) argues that the picture was done *c.*1644–48. This proposal is accepted by Gudiol (*Velázquez*, pp. 262–4). López-Rey bases his argument on his perception of the close stylistic relationship of this picture with the "*Rokeby Venus*" and the *Coronation of the Virgin*, pointing out that many of those who dated the *Fable of Arachne* to the late 1650s did so in the belief that the other two works were done at this time. The discovery of the fact that the "*Rokeby Venus*" was probably in existence before Velázquez left for Rome in November 1648 necessarily compels a change in date for the *Fable of Arachne*, at least for those who find the relationship between the two pictures to be irresistibly close. In addition, it is now also known that the *Coronation of the Virgin* was in existence by 1644 (see above, pp. 177–8).

López-Rey, following Mayer, also believes that the "same model, the same sketch, or just the same idea of a beautiful young woman" appears in all three works as the Virgin, Venus, and the figure he calls Arachne, who skeins the wool at the right of the *Fable of Arachne*. (But see below, note 42, for an argument against this identification.) Without explicitly saying so, he believes that this resemblance reinforces the idea that all three works are contemporary. Finally, he believes that the *Female Figure* (Plate 204) is probably identifiable with the figure with the skein, for which it is a preparatory study. As this work, in his opinion, also dates from the late 1640s, it contributes additional evidence for assigning the *Fable of Arachne* to the same period.

Certain elements of this circular argument rest on debatable suppositions. It is by no means obvious, for instance, that the *Female Figure* is related to the woman with the skein in appearance or pose, especially because the woman with the skein has her face turned completely away from the viewer. Similarly, the resemblance of this figure in the *Fable of Arachne* to the Virgin in the *Coronation of the Virgin* and Venus in the "*Rokeby Venus*" is tenuous. Except for a vaguely similar way of wearing the hair and the youthful appearance, there are no striking similarities between these figures. The comparison is complicated again by the fact that the face of the woman with a skein is hidden. (For similar reservations regarding this line of argument, see Steinburg, "Review," p. 288.) Even granting the supposed similarity between any or all of these figures, it does make a significant difference for the dating of these works whether Velázquez used "the same model, the same sketch or just the same idea of a beautiful young woman." The first possibility might have important consequences for a specific date while the second and third would be much less compelling evidence for any date, inasmuch as either could have been employed well after the initial moment of creation or inspiration. As a matter of fact, this same female type is used for other figures in the *Fable of Arachne* itself. Thus, the use of a specific model or type does not have any implications for dating, which then becomes purely a matter of stylistic analysis.

On this basis, it seems to me that the *Fable of Arachne* is most plausibly related to *Mercury and Argus* and *Las Meninas*, both works of the mid-1650s. The exceptionally loose handling of the brush, the highly allusive manner of treating the figures, especially in the background scene, and the range and subtlety of effects of light and shadow are, in my opinion, closely related to the style of these two late works and suggest that the *Fable of Arachne* was done at the same time.

33. See María L. Caturla, "El coleccionista madrileño Don Pedro de Arce, que poseyó 'Las Hilanderas,' de Velázquez," *AEA*, 21 (1948), pp. 292–304, especially pp. 302–3. For further information on Arce and his important collection, see Burke, "Private Collections," chapter 5.

34. For the history of the painting, see López-Rey, *Velázquez* (1979), no. 107, pp. 454–5. According to a document just discovered by Vicente Lleó (*BMP*, 1985), the painting was ceded to the king by the estate of the IX duke of Medivaceli (died 1711). It is listed in the 1772 inventory of the Royal Palace, by which time, the dimensions had been enlarged to approximately their present size.

35. Madlyn M. Kahr ("Velázquez's *Las Hilanderas*: A New Interpretation," *AB*, 62 [1980], pp. 376–85) argues that the composition and subject alike are explained by reference to Goltzius' engraving of *Lucretia Spinning with Her Maids*. The subject was then given a moralizing twist by Velázquez, who may have relied on a comparable interpretation of the myth propounded by Juan Pérez de Moya, the sixteenth-century Spanish mythographer. This argument, in my opinion, depends on a misreading of the evidence of Arce's inventory. In order to clear the way for the alternative interpretation, Kahr needs to discredit or at least neutralize the description of the subject and dimensions in the inventory, which she attempts to do in a brief appendix to her article. Admitting that "it may well be true that the original dimensions of Velázquez's composition were approximately those of 'la fabula de Aragne' as described in 1664," she nevertheless challenges the evidence by raising a series of questions about the origin of the added strips, questions which, in her opinion, can best be answered by reference to her own hypothesis about the relationship of the painting to Goltzius' print. As has been shown in Gonzalo Menéndez Pidal and Diego Angulo Iñiguez, "Las Hilanderas de Velázquez. Radiografías y fotografías en infrarroja," *AEA*, 38 (1965), pp. 1–12, and as Kahr admits, the central portion of the canvas was at one time attached to a stretcher and thus was presented as a self-standing work. Rather than ignore this evidence, I believe it establishes that the original composition was confined to a canvas that closely coincided with the dimensions of the *Fable of Arachne* in the Arce collection. This view is shared by the international committee of art historians and conservators who studied the picture in 1983; see "Noticias del Prado," *BMP*, 4 (1983), p. 198.

36. Enriqueta Harris (*The Prado. Treasure House of the Spanish Royal Collections* [London and New York, 1940], p. 85) first associated the myth of Arachne with the painting, although she mistakenly believed that the figures of Arachne and Minerva were part of the tapestry and that the composition as a whole was a genre scene set in a tapestry factory. The correct identification of the subject was made independently by Charles de Tolnay ("Velázquez' *Las Hilanderas* and *Las Meninas* (An Interpretation)," *GBA*, 35 [1949], pp. 21–38) and Diego Angulo Iñiguez ("Las Hilanderas," *AEA*, 21 [1948], pp. 1–19).

37. Trapier (*Velázquez*, p. 350) pointed out that the helmeted figure and the woman directly in front of the tapestry were intended to be seen as standing in the space with the other three women and not as part of the hanging.

38. See Diego Angulo Iñiguez, "Las Hilanderas. Sobre la iconografía de Aracne," *AEA*, 25 (1952), pp. 67–84, for the history of the scene in illustrated editions of Ovid.

39. The identification was first made by Charles Ricketts (*The Art of the Prado* [Edinburgh, 1903], p. 86). It was also noticed by Philip Hendy (*Spanish Painting* [London, 1946], pp. 23–4) just before it entered into general circulation in the Velázquez literature. Kahr ("Velázquez's *Las Hilanderas*," p. 384) regards the tapestry as a marginal element in the composition, despite the fact that the Rape of Europa was one of the subjects woven by Arachne in the contest with Minerva. She believes (p. 380) that this scene shows the faithless wives of the Roman officers "at a luxurious banquet" (Livy), when they are discovered by Sextus Tarquinius!

40. For this idea, see Tolnay, "Velázquez' *Las Hilanderas*," pp. 26–32. Recent intepretations of the painting have been based on emblematic literature. José M. de Azcárate ("La alegoría de 'Las Hilanderas,'" in *V.V.*, I, pp. 344–51), in a mechanical application of emblems to

disparate motifs in the picture, concludes that it is a political allegory designed to express the idea of obedience as the cornerstone of civic harmony among the diverse kingdoms of the Spanish monarchy. Taking a similar approach, but applying a different set of emblems, is the article by Santiago Sebastián, "Nueva lectura de 'Las Hilanderas,' La emblemática como clave de su interpretación," *Revista "Fragmentos"* 1 (1984), pp. 45–51. Here the meaning is identified as a didactic allegory on the vices of the prince. Bartolomé Mestre Fiol ("'El cuadro en el cuadro' en la pintura de Velázquez: Las Hilanderas," *Traza y Baza*, 4 [1974], pp. 77–101) tries to prove that the entire background, including the additional strip above, represents a tapestry.

On the shaky foundations of Kahr's article, Angel del Campo has built an elaborate mathematical construction designed to prove that the "plot (or weft) of the *Spinners* is an harmonious play of pentagonal compositions;" see "La trama de 'Las Hilanderas,'" *Boletín de Información. Colegio Oficial de Ingenieros de Caminos, Canales y Puertos*, 67 (April 1983), pp. 22–31 (also in *Traza y Baza* [March 1983]).

41. This connection was proposed by Mary C. Volk in a paper delivered at the Annual Meeting of the College Art Association of America, February 1977.

42. Angulo ("Las Hilanderas" [1948], p. 15) was the first to identify, if hesitatingly, the woman at the wheel as Minerva and the woman at the skein as Arachne. Kahr ("Velázquez's *Las Hilanderas*," p. 378, note 15) offers valid objections to these identifications. Also, following Tolnay's reading of the composition, I believe that Velázquez was seeking to differentiate the assistants from the master weaver.

43. The following discussion is an extension of my earlier essay, "On the Meaning of *Las Meninas*," in *Images and Ideas*, pp. 87–110, where the literature up to 1977 is reviewed. Since then, writing on the picture has continued apace, much of it inspired by the introductory chapter of Michel Foucault, *Les mots et les choses* (Paris, 1966), translated into English as *The Order of Things: An Archaeology of the Human Sciences* (New York, 1970). See, for example, John R. Searle, "*Las Meninas* and the Paradoxes of Pictorial Representation," *Critical Inquiry*, 6 (1980), pp. 177–88, and Svetlana Alpers, "Interpretation Without Representation, or the Viewing of *Las Meninas*," *Representations*, 1 (February 1983), pp. 31–42, where Foucault's ideas are blended with the author's debatable definition of the nature of representation in seventeenth-century Dutch painting. Leo Steinberg ("Velázquez' *Las Meninas*," *October*, 19 [1981], pp. 45–54) is also concerned with the interaction of spectators and picture, and with the picture as a complex essay on the relationship of representation and reality. However, his reading of the picture does not take into account that the picture was addressed to the king, as indicated by the evidence; see below, pp. 259–60. Searle's convoluted article is effectively challenged in Joel Snyder and Ted Cohen, "Critical Response. Reflexions on *Las Meninas*: Paradox Lost," *Critical Inquiry*, 7 (1980), pp. 129–47.

The approach to the painting through the application of post-structuralist and critical theory is intrinsically interesting, especially where it shows how contemporary ideas about art can be applied to works created in earlier periods. But its value for understanding the picture within an historical framework is intentionally limited. Other recent contributions to the literature will be mentioned below as they touch on the points under discussion below.

The painting was meticulously cleaned in 1984 by John Brealey; see Manuela Mena Marqués, "La restauración de Las Meninas de Velazquez," *BMP*, 5 (1984), pp. 87–107.

44. For Palomino's biography, see Juan Antonio Gaya Nuño, *Vida de Acisclo Antonio Palomino* (Córdoba, 1931).

45. Palomino, *El museo pictórico*, p. 767.

46. *V.V.*, II, p. 329.

47. Palomino, *El museo pictórico*, pp. 1024–30.

48. See Eric Young, "A Signed and Dated Portrait by Juan de Alfaro," *BM*, 136 (1984), pp. 151–2.

49. Palomino, *El museo pictórico*, pp. 999–1005.

50. Palomino, *El museo pictórico*, p. 1002.

51. For the biographies of those portrayed in *Las Meninas*, see Francisco J. Sánchez Cantón, *Las Meninas y sus personajes* (Barcelona, 1943), and Marqués del Saltillo, "En torno a 'Las Meninas' y sus personajes," *AEA*, 15 (1944), pp. 125–33.

52. Bottineau, "L'Alcázar de Madrid" (1958), pp. 450–3.

53. See above, note 6.

54. See above, note 51.

55. Palomino. *El museo pictórico*, trans. Harris, *Velázquez*, p. 214.

56. For further comments on this point, see Brown, *Images and Ideas*, pp. 92–4

57. For another instance of this interpretation of the picture by a seventeenth-century writer, see Felix da Costa, *The Antiquity of the Art of Painting*, ed. George Kubler (New Haven and London, 1967), p. 458. Kubler dates the composition of the manuscript between 1685 and 1696.

58. For a description of the action, see Brown, *Images and Ideas*. pp. 90–2. Hermann U. Asemissen, *Las Meninas von Diego Velázquez*, Kasseler Hefte für Kunstwissenschaft und Kunstpädogogik, Heft 2 (Cassel, 1981), seeks to prove that the painting represents the scene as reflected in a large-scale mirror. Thus, the figures are not looking at the king and queen, but at themselves.

George Kubler ("The 'Mirror' in *Las Meninas*," *Art Bulletin*, 67 [1985], p. 316) suggests that the mirror is intended to be a "painting of what is seen in a mirror" rather than a mirror which reflects the presence of the king and the queen in front of the picture plane.

59. Among the recent attempts to reconstruct the perspective are the following: Angel del Campo y Francés, *La magía de Las Meninas. Una iconología velazqueña* (Madrid, 1978), who bases his interpretation on a complicated numerology appropriate to his profession of engineer; Joel Snyder and Ted Cohen, "Critical Response;" and John F. Moffitt, "Velázquez in the Alcázar Palace in 1656: the Meaning of the Mise-en-scène of *Las Meninas*," *Art History*, 6 (1983), pp. 271–300, the most assiduous attempt at the reconstruction of the perspective to date. I am grateful to Martin Kemp for his help in understanding Velázquez' use of perspective in this picture, and for his help in general in understanding Velázquez' considerable interest in perspective and mathematics.

60. For analysis of the minimal changes in the composition, see McKim-Smith et al., *Examining Velázquez*.

61. Bottineau, "L'Alcázar de Madrid," 1958, p. 297. According to this author, the picture is also listed in this location in the inventory of 1666.

62. In this sense, the picture is structured like a representation of a court play which was attended by many, but intended for the king, who was present both as spectator and participant in the drama. See Bartolomé Mestre Fiol, "Los tres personajes invisibles de *Las Meninas*," *Mayurqa*, 8 (1972), pp. 5–20, and J. E. Varey, "The Audience and the Play at Court Spectacles: The Role of the King," *Bulletin of Hispanic Studies*, 61 (1984), pp. 399–406. Bo Vahlne ("Velázquez' *Las Meninas*. Remarks on the Staging of a Royal Portrait," *Konsthistorisk Tidskrift*, 51 [1982], pp. 21–8) also argues that the picture was intended for a specific royal person. However, he believes that this was the queen rather than the king. Given the importance of Philip IV to Velázquez, it seems more likely that, if the painting was indeed painted with a single person in mind, this person would have been the king.

63. For an example of a double royal portrait which was also regarded as a mirror when the king and queen appeared before it, see the passage in Calderón's *Hado y divisa de Leonido y de Marfisa* (1680), quoted in Varey, "The Role of the King," p. 403.

64. For a stimulating discussion of Velázquez' ideas on the relationship of art and nature and their place in the context of seventeenth-century thought, see José A. Maravall, *Velázquez y el espíritu de la modernidad* (Madrid, 1960), pp. 69–107.

65. Palomino, *El museo pictórico*, trans. Harris, *Velázquez*, p. 214.

66. Palomino, *El museo pictórico*, trans. Harris, *Velázquez*, p. 214.

CHAPTER X

1. *V.V.*, II, doc. 195, pp. 382–3.

2. *V.V.*, II, doc. 198, p. 384.

3. See Mercedes Agulló and Alfonso E. Pérez Sánchez, "Juan Bautista Moreli," *AEA*, 49 (1976), pp. 109–20.

4. See the account of Palomino in Harris, *Velázquez*, pp. 222–3.

5. *V.V.*, II, doc. 205, pp. 388–9.

6. *V.V.*, II, doc. 209, pp. 391–400.

7. *V.V.*, II, doc. 206, p. 390.

8. See Francisco J. Sánchez Cantón, "Como vivía Velázquez," for a full description of the artist's *modus vivendi*.

9. See José L. Barrio Moya, "Un documento sobre adquisiciones de Velázquez," *AEA*, 49 (1976), pp. 327–8, for Velázquez' purchases at the 1636 sale of the effects of the inquisitor Alonso de Salazar y Frías.

10. For the identification of the titles and analysis of the collection, see Francisco J. Sánchez Cantón, "La librería de Velázquez," in *Homenaje a Menéndez Pidal*, III (Madrid, 1925), pp. 379–406, and "Los libros españoles que poseyó Velázquez," in *V.V.*, I, pp. 640–8. For purposes of comparison, it can be noted that Vicente Carducho owned about 313 books at his death; see María L. Caturla, "Documentos en torno a Vicencio Carducho," *AE*, 26 (1968–9), pp. 145–221.

11. The connections of Velázquez' art to some of the major developments in seventeenth-century thought are outlined in Maravall, *Velázquez y el espíritu de la modernidad*.

12. For a discussion of Velázquez' influence on painters of Madrid in the later seventeenth century, see Jonathan Brown, "Velázquez and the Evolution of High Baroque Painting in Madrid," *Record of The Art Museum, Princeton University*, 41 (1982), pp. 4–11.

13. The history of Velázquez' critical fortunes is yet to be written, despite its importance to the understanding of the artist and of nineteenth-century art and taste. The following lines are intended only to indicate some of the milestones in the process.

14. Palomino was translated with abridgements into English in 1739, French in 1749, and German in 1781. The accounts of A. J. Dézallier D'Argenville, *Abregé de la vie des plus fameux peintres* (Paris, 1762) and Richard Cumberland, *Anecdotes of Eminent Painters in Spain* (London, 1787) are heavily indebted to Palomino.

15. Quoted in *Velázquez. Homenaje en el tercer centenario de su muerte* (Madrid, 1960), pp. 219–21.

16. For Le Brun's career, see Jeannine Baticle, "Récherches sur la connaissance du Velázquez en France," *V.V.*, I, pp. 532–52, and Francis Haskell, *Rediscoveries in Art: Some Aspects of Taste, Fashion and Collecting in England and France* (Ithaca, 1976), pp. 18–23. Buchanan speaks for himself in *Memoirs of Painting* (London, 1824); see also Hugh Brigstocke, *William Buchanan and the 19th-Century Art Trade: 100 Letters to His Agents in London and Italy* (London, 1983).

17. For British collecting of Spanish painting in the nineteenth century, see Braham, *El Greco to Goya*. I am also indebted to Carolyn Logan for her paper on the taste for Velázquez in nineteenth-century England, which was presented in the Velázquez seminar at the Institute of Fine Arts in 1983.

18. See Jeannine Baticle and Cristina Marinas, *La Galerie Espagnole de Louis-Philippe au Louvre, 1838–1848* (Paris, 1981).

19. Quoted in Buchanan, *Memoirs*, p. 203.

20. Quoted in Allen Cunningham, *Life of Wilkie*, II (London, 1843), p. 486.

21. *Journal de Eugène Delacroix*, I (Paris, 1932), entry of 11 April 1824, p. 74. For a general discussion of Velázquez and nineteenth-century French painting, see Louis Réau, "Velázquez et son influence sur les peintres français du XIXeme siècle," in *Velázquez, son temps et son influence* (Paris, 1960), pp. 95–103.

22. See Paul Guinard, *Dauzarts et Blanchard, peintres de l'Espagne romantique* (Paris, 1967), p. 413.

23. Gabriel Séailles, *Alfred Dehodencq: L'homme et l'artiste* (Paris, 1910), p. 32, letter to M. Dubois, 22 December 1850.

24. See Paul Guinard, "Velázquez et les Romantiques français," in *V.V.*, I, pp. 561–73, and Ilse H. Lipschutz, *Spanish Painting and the French Romantics* (Cambridge, Mass., 1972), part 1.

25. See Braham, *El Greco to Goya*, pp. 28–30.

26. Quoted in Etienne Moreau-Nelaton, *Manet, raconté par lui-même*, I (Paris, 1926), pp. 71–2.

BIBLIOGRAPHICAL ESSAY

INTRODUCTION

This section, devoted to the bibliography of writings on Velázquez, has an unusual format in which a bibliographical essay is combined with a select bibliography. The essay is confined to three classes of writings: sources and documents; catalogues and monographs; and interpretations. Studies of particular aspects of Velázquez' life and art are cited and often evaluated in the text and notes and are therefore omitted from the essay.

Although a bibliographical essay normally supplants a bibliography proper, I have adopted this hybrid format in order to give the reader a sense of how the study and interpretation of Velázquez have evolved since the middle of the nineteenth century, as well as to indicate the principal works devoted to the artist. To avoid repetition, only the name of the author and date of publication are cited in the essay. Full information will be found in the Select Bibliography.

For other guides to the Velázquez literature, see the following: Halldor Soehner, "El estado actual de la investigación sobre Velázquez," *Clavileño*, 9 (May-June, 1951), pp. 23–9; J. A. Gaya Nuño, "Después de Justi. Medio siglo de estudios velazquistas," in C. Justi, *Velázquez y su siglo* (Madrid, 1953), pp. 799–865; Theodore Crombie, "Velázquez Research since Stevenson (1900–1960)," in R. A. M. Stevenson, *Velázquez* (London, 1962), pp. 165–72; and J. A. Gaya Nuño, *Bibliografía crítica y antológica de Velázquez* (Madrid, 1963), which lists 1814 books and articles, with short comments.

SOURCES AND DOCUMENTS

No Spanish artist of the seventeenth century was better served by contemporary biographers than Velázquez. The information provided by Francisco Pacheco (Eng. trans., Harris, *Velázquez*, pp. 191–5), if fragmentary, is valuable for the early years and especially the beginnings of his career at court. Velázquez' friend, the court musician Lazáro Díaz del Valle (or Díez del Valle), prepared a series of panegyric notes which are primarily useful for gauging the artist's reputation in the final years of his life (*V.V.*, II, pp. 59–62). The Aragonese painter Jusepe Martínez, who had met Velázquez and followed his career from Zaragoza, dedicated several paragraphs to the artist in a treatise written in the 1670s, but not published until 1852 (*V.V.*, II, pp. 65–8). Although necessarily schematic, Martínez' remarks provide a reasonably accurate sketch of the highpoints of Velázquez' career and offer a few pieces of information not recorded elsewhere.

Palomino's biography of Velázquez is in a class by itself (Eng. trans. Harris, *Velázquez* pp. 196–224). Although published in 1724, it was probably begun soon after Palomino arrived in Madrid in 1678. By drawing on the reminiscences of Velázquez' younger contemporaries who were still alive, on a biography prepared by his pupil, Juan de

Alfaro (now lost), and documents in the royal archive, Palomino compiled a detailed version of the master's career which is remarkably accurate and reliable. It is and will remain the basis of all Velázquez studies.

Modern archival research on Velázquez has been very productive. Although information on the Seville years is still spotty, there is abundant documentation of his career at court. Most of the documents are preserved in the Archivo de Palacio, Madrid, and the Archivo General de Simancas. Valuable material has also been found in the Archivo Histórico de Protocolos, Madrid, and the Archivo Histórico Nacional, Madrid.

First to tap the riches of the Archivo de Palacio was its archivist, Manuel Zarco del Valle, who published a group of documents in 1870 (CODOIN, LV). But no one has ever surpassed the contribution of Cruzada Villaamil (1885), who discovered a wealth of documents in the Archivo de Palacio and Simancas, on which is founded the modern study of the artist. Important documents, although fewer in number, also appear in Justi's famous study of the artist (1888 and 1903). Since the turn of the century, new documents have appeared with considerable frequency. Among the most significant of these are the death inventory of Velázquez, discovered by Francisco Rodríguez Marín and published in its entirety by Sánchez Cantón (1942), the information on the dwarfs and court jesters published by Moreno Villa (1939), and the series of documents on the Hall of Realms of the Buen Retiro, published by Caturla (1960). Most, but not all, of the documents known prior to 1960 were compiled by Antonio Gallego Burín (*V.V.*, II), where the author and original place of publication are noted. Since that date, important documentary discoveries have been published by Enriqueta Harris (1960, 1967, 1970, 1981). Also noteworthy is the article by Azcárate (1960).

The most serious gap in the documentation are personal letters and communications. If Velázquez wrote letters to friends touching on his work, life, and thought, they have disappeared. This fact, and the failure of his contemporaries to record details of Velázquez' private life, make it difficult to understand the artist's personality and to define explicitly his goals as a painter.

CATALOGUES AND MONOGRAPHS

The first catalogue of Velázquez' works appeared as an appendix to Stirling-Maxwell's *Annals of the Artists of Spain* (1848) and contained 226 entries. Since then, eleven more catalogues of Velázquez' paintings have appeared. In general, the number of authentic pictures has drifted downward, until settling around the figure of 120 to 125. However, the tendency to reduce the oeuvre has not been entirely consistent.

The highpoint was reached in Curtis' catalogue of 1883, which has 274 entries. Nowadays, its value is considered to be limited to the information about provenance. Cruzada Villaamil (1888) listed 240 paintings, but cast doubt on about eighty attributions. The turning point in the definition of the oeuvre was reached in the reductionist catalogue of Beruete who, in the first edition of his book (1898), dismissed all but eighty-three of the existing attributions. By the time the German edition of the text appeared (1909), the number had risen to ninety-four, partly as the result of the discovery of new pictures. This number was revised upward in the edition of the Klassiker der Kunst volume prepared by Allende-Salazar (1925), which included 114 paintings as authentic. Eleven years later, August L. Mayer published his sizable catalogue of paintings by Velázquez and his followers and imitators. Mayer accepted 164 paintings as authentic, many of which have since been excised from the oeuvre. The chief value of the book is as an illustrated encyclopedia of "Velázquez y lo velazqueño." Lafuente's summary catalogue of 1943 provided an antidote to Mayer and listed 128 paintings by the master. In 1955, Pantorba included 123 entries in his oeuvre catalogue but had considerable doubts about the authenticity of around half-a-dozen.

The catalogue now in widest use is the one by José López-Rey, which first appeared in 1963 and was revised in 1979. In the first edition the author accepted 120 paintings;

in the second, 123, although the number in the second edition was arrived at by dropping certain pictures in the first edition and adding others which had come to light in the interim. The 1979 edition includes only pictures regarded as fully or partly autograph, whereas the 1963 edition lists and reproduces originals, versions, copies, and incorrect attributions. Students of Velázquez, therefore, will need to consult both versions of the catalogue.

Other recent catalogues include those of Camón Aznar (1964) and Gudiol (1973), both of which are too permissive in their definition of the oeuvre.

As yet, there is no comprehensive catalogue raisonné of Velázquez' works which fully satisfies the requirements of present-day scholarship. The two versions of López-Rey's catalogue, used collectively, come closest to the ideal. However, the entries are not always complete. Discussions of attribution, chronology, provenance, and condition are often satisfactory. But questions of iconography and the visual and literary sources, which the author believes to be of secondary importance to understanding the artist, are not fully examined in some instances. There is also a tendency to dismiss without discussion ideas which the author judges to be "derivative or trifling" (see, for example, 1979, p. 167, note 163).

Numerous monographic studies of the artist, without catalogue, have been written over the years, of which a few deserve mention. In a class by itself is Justi's *Velázquez und sein Jahrhundert*, first published in 1888. A revised edition with important changes appeared in 1903 and should be regarded as the definitive text. Although inevitably out-of-date in certain respects, this book felicitously combines a wide perspective on the artist with a wealth of factual information, much of it unknown before the publication of the book. Elizabeth Trapier's study of 1948 is also excellent. Although dry in style, it pays scrupulous attention to the facts and sheds light on numerous paintings, primarily through a careful investigation of contemporary historical and literary sources. It also contains the most complete bibliography up to the date of publication. The study of Kurt Gerstenberg (1957) is arranged in a somewhat arbitrary manner in keeping with the author's thematic approach. But it is important for the attempt to integrate the artist into the literary and visual traditions of the seventeenth century. López-Rey's *Velázquez' Work and World* (1968) is a revision of the introduction of his catalogue of 1963 and will be discussed in the section on interpretations. The best of the recent books is Harris' *Velázquez* (1982). Although intended primarily for a general readership, it contains much of interest to the specialist. This objective, accurate account of Velázquez will be of use for many years to come. Finally, the short book by Julián Gállego (1983) offers a spirited interpretation of Velázquez, and is the best general study now available in Spanish.

INTERPRETATION

Since the re-emergence of Velázquez as a universally admired painter around 1850, the interpretation of his art and its place in the history of art has gone through several stages. At each stage, the prevailing view has reflected the artistic and critical concerns of the day.

During the last half of the nineteenth century, Velázquez was regarded as the supreme realist and the father of modern art, ideas promoted by the most influential writers of the day, including Stirling-Maxwell, Justi, and Paul Lefort (1888). Toward the end of the century, this approach was supplemented, but not supplanted, by the interpretation of Velázquez as a proto-Impressionist. The protagonist of this viewpoint was the English painter and critic, R. A. M. Stevenson (1899), who had studied in Paris with Carolus-Duran. Stevenson looked at the pictures with the keen eye of a painter and saw numerous connections between the technique of Velázquez and contemporary artists in France. Despite the plea by Beruete for a less-biased approach, the links with Impressionism have proved to be durable.

For the first quarter of this century, most writing on Velázquez interpreted him as a precursor of one or another of the styles of modern painting. But in 1925, a revolutionary document came to light — the inventory of Velázquez' library, discovered in 1923 by F. Rodríguez Marín and published in 1925 by Sánchez Cantón. The significance of the collection transcended the mere contents because it demonstrated that Velázquez had used his eyes to read as well as to study nature. Thus, his art could be connected to several branches of Renaissance learning.

The full impact of this discovery was not felt for another twenty-five years. But in the early 1940s, three Spanish writers began to question the notion that Velázquez could be understood solely in formal terms. Sánchez Cantón (1943) drew attention to Velázquez' spiritual treatment of religious subjects, while Lafuente Ferrari (1943) based his interpretation on what he called the "special coloring given by the national soul of Spain to the Velázquez version of the Baroque." Most influential of all were the brilliant, idiosyncratic writings of the philosopher, José Ortega y Gasset. Velázquez had long fascinated Ortega, who wrote his first study of the artist in 1912. In 1943, he published a long essay which was translated into several languages and frequently reprinted. Although difficult to summarize, Ortega's essay was primarily devoted to Velázquez' mental world and particularly to his conception and depiction of reality, which Ortega defined by means of paradoxes. By lifting Velázquez from the history of style and placing him in the center of a complex intellectual universe, Ortega opened the way to a philosophical interpretation of the artist.

By the later years of the decade, scholars began to base their approaches to Velázquez on the contents of his library. De Tolnay's interpretation of *Las Meninas* and the *Fable of Arachne* (1949) assumed the artist's familiarity with certain ideas promulgated in sixteenth-century art theory. Diego Angulo (1947) drew attention to putative sources in works of other artists for certain of Velázquez' compositions, not all of them plausible, which indicated that the artist had a broad visual culture and was not solely inspired by looking at nature.

Thus, by 1950 the ground had been laid for a thorough revision of the art of Velázquez. Without denying his genius as a pure painter, it was now possible to perceive an intellectual dimension to his art, the definition of which has become the major enterprise of Velázquez scholarship during the last thirty-five years. Several distinct branches of this inquiry can be identified.

The first is the iconographical interpretation, which uses evidence from literary sources and emblem books, examples of which were included in Velázquez' library. The writings of Gerstenberg (1957 and 1960), Emmens (1961), Moffitt (1980, 1983), and Sebastián (1983, 1984), show the possibilities and pitfalls inherent in this approach, which sometimes seems to discover a more complex significance in the pictures than is warranted by the visual evidence.

One of the more puzzling lines of approach is through the application of geometry to certain works, notably *Las Meninas*. The number and variety of diagrams applied to this picture and also the *Fable of Arachne* constitute a unique case in the history of seventeenth-century art, in which an easel painter's mastery of linear perspective, and a willingness to apply its rules intuitively, is taken for granted by most students of the period. It remains to be seen whether great pictures will yield their secrets to quantitative analysis from which subjective conclusions tend to be drawn. For elaborate examples of this approach, see Campo y Francés (1978) and Cavallius (1972).

Another recent approach to Velázquez involves the application of social, political, and intellectual history to the study of his art and career. One of the pioneering examples is Fritz Saxl's lecture, "Velázquez and Philip IV," delivered in 1942 and published in 1957. Much of this work is concerned with establishing Velázquez' artistic response to the events, ideas, personalities, and institutions of his time. Considerable attention has been paid to defining the social status of the artist in Spain and its possible implications on Velázquez' career (see Brown [1978]; Volk [1978]). Velázquez as a creator of political imagery is discussed by Díez del Corral (1978) and Brown and Elliott (1980).

The most successful study of Velázquez' place in the intellectual world of the seventeenth century is the somewhat neglected, but stimulating book by Maravall (1960), which could be read with profit by all students of the artist. For Velázquez as court artist, Levey (1971) is excellent.

The paintings of Velázquez, especially *Las Meninas*, have also been used as the springboard for ideas about the nature of artistic representation. One approach (Birkmeyer [1958] and Steinberg [1981]) views certain of the paintings as statements about the real, the represented, and the reflected which require the viewer to consider the nature of art and reality alike. Through the use of analysis by paradox, reminiscent of Ortega, but yet more complex, Michel Foucault (1966) understands *Las Meninas* as a visual disquisition on the essence and limits of what he calls "classical representation." The brilliance of this analysis has inspired imitations (Searle [1980] and Alpers [1983]). However, the concepts and language of this type of approach belong distinctly to the later twentieth century.

A reaction against the application of historical and conceptual constructs to Velázquez is found in the formalist approach of López-Rey. As stated in the preface to his book of 1968, his interpretation is based principally on his analysis of the paintings, all of which were studied in the original, "unhurriedly, with leisure enough to answer my own questions, and even to verify the validity of my answers before the very works that provoked them" (p. 11). By definition more subjective than empirical, this method relies principally on the intuition of the author to interpret the objectives of Velázquez' art. His belief in the primacy of artistic considerations in Velázquez' creative process, if not always clearly explained, offers a corrective to the tendency to approach the artist by studying the subject matter and sources of his paintings.

One of the most promising developments in recent Velázquez scholarship is the collaboration of art historians, conservators, and conservation scientists in the technical examination and analysis of individual paintings. The new information about Velázquez' technique and working methods is already helping to correct the interpretation of existing data and is providing new information on the genesis and elaboration of certain pictures. See Garrido et al. (1983), as well as the forthcoming book by McKim-Smith and her collaborators.

SELECT BIBLIOGRAPHY

This bibliography is confined to works on Velázquez cited in the text.

Agulló y Cobo, Mercedes. *Noticias sobre pintores madrileños de los siglos XVI y XVII*. Granada, 1978.

Ainaud de Lasarte, Juan. "Pinturas de procedencia sevillana," *Archivo español de arte*, 18 (1946), pp. 54–60.

——. "Ribalta y Caravaggio," *Anales y Boletín de los Museos de Arte de Barcelona*, 5 (1947), pp. 345–413.

——. "Francisco Ribalta. Notas y comentarios," *Goya*, 20 (September–October 1957), pp. 86–9.

——. "Velázquez y los retratos de Don Fernando de Valdés," in *Varia Velazqueña*, I, pp. 310–15.

Allende-Salazar, Juan. See Gensel, Walter, *Velázquez. Des Meisters Gemälde*.

Allende-Salazar, Juan and Francisco J. Sánchez-Cantón. *Retratos del Museo de Prado. Identificación y rectificaciones*. Madrid, 1919.

Alpers, Svetlana. *Corpus Rubenianum Ludwig Burchard*. IX, *The Decoration of the Torre de la Parada*. London–New York, 1971.

——. "Interpretation without Representation, or the Viewing of *Las Meninas*," *Representations*, 1 (February 1983), pp. 31–42.

Andrés Martínez, Gregorio de (ed.). "Relación de la estancia de Felipe IV en El Escorial (1656) por su capellán Julio Chifflet," in *Documentos para la historia del Monasterio de San Lorenzo el Real de El Escorial*, VII. Madrid, 1964, pp. 403–31.

——. "Correspondencia epistolar entre Felipe IV y el P. Nicolás de Madrid sobre la construcción del Panteón de Reyes, 1654," in *Documentos para la historia del Monasterio de San Lorenzo el Real de El Escorial*, VIII. El Escorial, 1965, pp. 159–207.

——. "Los cinco retratos reales de la Biblioteca de El Escorial," *Archivo español de arte*, 40 (1967), pp. 360–3.

Angulo Iñiguez, Diego. "'El San Antonio Abad y San Pablo Ermitaño,' de Velázquez," *Archivo español de arte*, 19 (1946), pp. 18–26.

——. *Velázquez. Como compuso sus cuadros principales*. Seville, 1947.

——. "Las Hilanderas," *Archivo español de arte*, 21 (1948), pp. 1–19.

——. "Las Hilanderas. Sobre la iconografía de Aracne," *Archivo español de arte*, 25 (1952), pp. 67–84.

——. "La Fábula de Vulcano, Venus y Marte y la Fragua de Velázquez," *Archivo español de arte*, 33 (1960), pp. 149–81.

——. "'La imposición de la casulla a San Ildefonso,' de Velázquez," *Archivo español de arte*, 33 (1960), pp. 290–1.

——. "Velázquez y la mitología," *III Centenario de la muerte de Velázquez*. Instituto de España, Madrid, 1961, pp. 47–62.

——. "Mythology and Seventeenth-Century Spanish Painters," in *Acts of the Twentieth International Congress of the History of Art*, III. Princeton, 1963, pp. 36–40.

——. "La cuerna de venado, cuadro de Velázquez," *Reales Sitios*, 4 (1967), pp. 13–25.

Asemissen, Hermann U. *Las Meninas von Diego Velázquez*. Kasseler Hefte für Kunstwissenschaft und Kunstpädogogik, II. Cassel, 1981.

Azcárate, José M. de. "La alegoría de 'Las Hilanderas,'" in *Varia Velazqueña*, I, pp. 344–51.

——. "Noticias sobre Velázquez en la corte," *Archivo español de arte*, 33 (1960), pp. 357–85.

Baticle, Jeannine. "Recherches sur la connaissance de Velázquez en France," in *Varia Velazqueña*, I, pp. 532–52.

Barrio Moya, José L. "Un documento sobre adquisiciones de Velázquez," *Archivo español de arte*, 49 (1976), pp. 327–8.

——. "Velázquez y Gómez de Mora juntos en una libranza," *Archivo español de arte*, 51 (1978), p. 346.

Barghahn, Barbara von. "The Pictorial Decoration of the Buen Retiro Palace and Patronage during the Reign of Philip IV." Ph.D. dissertation, New York University, 1979.

Bergman, Hannah E. "A Court Entertainment of 1638," *Hispanic Review*, 42 (1974), pp. 67–81.

Beroqui, Pedro. "Adiciones y correcciones al Catálogo del Museo del Prado," *Boletín de la Sociedad Castellana de Excursiones*, año 16, 2nd series, II (1918), p. 61.

Beruete, Aureliano de. *Velázquez*. Paris, 1898.

——. *El Velázquez de Parma. Retrato de Felipe IV pintado en Fraga*. Madrid, 1911.

Berwick y de Alba, Duquesa de. *Documentos escogidos de la Casa de Alba.* Madrid, 1891.

Birkmeyer, Karl M. "Realism and Realities in the Paintings of Velázquez," *Gazette des Beaux-Arts*, 52 (1958), pp. 63–77.

Bonet Correa, Antonio. "Velázquez, arquitecto y decorador," *Archivo español de arte*, 33 (1960), pp. 215–49.

Bottineau, Yves. "'L'Alcázar de Madrid et l'inventaire de 1686. Aspects de la cour d'Espagne au XVIIe siècle," *Bulletin Hispanique*, 58 (1956), pp. 421–52; 69 (1958), pp. 30–61, 145–79, 289–326, 450–83.

Braham, Allan. "A Second Dated Bodegón by Velázquez," *Burlington Magazine*, 197 (1965), pp. 362–5.

——. *Velázquez. The Rokeby Venus.* Painting in Focus, no. 5. National Gallery, London, 1976.

——. *From El Greco to Goya. The Taste for Spanish Paintings in Britain and Ireland.* London, 1981.

Brown, Jonathan. "A Portrait Drawing by Velázquez," *Master Drawings*, 14 (1976), pp. 46–51

——. *Images and Ideas in Seventeenth-Century Spanish Painting.* Princeton, 1978.

——. "Un italiano en el taller de Velázquez," *Archivo español de arte*, 53 (1980), pp. 207–8.

——. "Velázquez and the Evolution of High Baroque Painting in Madrid," *Record of The Art Museum, Princeton University*, 41 (1982), pp. 4–11.

Brown, Jonathan and J. H. Elliot. *A Palace for a King: The Buen Retiro and the Court of Philip IV.* New Haven and London, 1980.

——. "Further Observations on Velázquez' Portraits of Jesters at the Buen Retiro," *Gazette des Beaux-Arts*, 97 (1981), pp. 191–2.

Brunetti, Estella. "Per il soggiorno fiorentino del Velázquez (Nota d'Archivio per il Velázquez)," in *Varia Velazqueña*, I, pp. 296–300.

Burke, Marcus B. "Private Collections of Italian Art in Seventeenth-Century Spain." Ph.D. dissertation, New York University, 1984.

Camón Aznar, José. *Velázquez*, 2 vols. Madrid, 1964.

Campo y Francés, Angel del. *La magía de Las Meninas. Una iconología velazqueña.* Madrid, 1978.

——. "La trama de 'Las Hilanderas,'" *Boletín de Información. Colegio Oficial de Ingenieros de Caminos, Canales y Puertos*, 67 (April 1983), pp. 22–31.

Carducho, Vicente. *Diálogos de la pintura.* Ed. Francisco Calvo Serraller. Madrid, 1979.

Caturla, María L. "El coleccionista madrileño Don Pedro de Arce, que poseyó 'Las Hilanderas,' de Velázquez," *Archivo español de arte*, 21 (1948), pp. 292–304.

——. "Cartas de pago de los doce cuadros de batallas para el salón de reinos del Buen Retiro," *Archivo español de arte*, 33 (1960), pp. 333–55.

Cavallius, Gustaf. *Velázquez' Las Hilanderas. An Explication of a Picture Regarding Structure and Associations.* Uppsala, 1972.

Cavestany, Julio. *Floreros y bodegones en la pintura española.* Madrid, 1940.

Chifflet, Julio. "Relación de la estancia de Felipe IV en El Escorial (1656)," in Gregorio de Andrés (ed.), *Documentos para la historia del Monasterio de San Lorenzo el Real de El Escorial*, VII. Madrid, 1964, pp. 403–31.

"Chroniques du Laboratoire. Notes sur les radiographes de deux tableaux appartenant aux Musée de Pau et de Rouen," *Bulletin du Laboratoire du Musée du Louvre*, 9 (1964), pp. 50–3.

Colombier, Pierre du. "La Forge de Vulcain au Chateau d'Effiat," *Gazette des Beaux-Arts*, 81 (1939), pp. 30–8.

Conisbee, Philip. "Pre-Romantic *Plein-Air* Painting." *Art History*, 2 (1979), pp. 413–28.

Crombie, Theodore. "Isabella of Bourbon by Velázquez," *Connoisseur*, 141 (1958), pp. 238–44.

——. "Archbishop Fernando de Valdés by Velázquez. Some Notes on a Recently-Identified Portrait," *Apollo*, 145 (1960), pp. 102–4.

Cruzada Villaamil, Gregorio. *Anales de la vida y de las obras de Diego de Silva Velázquez.* Madrid, 1885.

Curtis, Charles B. *Velázquez and Murillo. A Descriptive and Historical Catalogue.* New York, 1883.

Díaz (or Díez) del Valle, Lázaro. "Epílogo y nomenclatura de algunos artífices," in *Varia Velazqueña*, II, pp. 59–62.

Díez del Corral, Luis. *Velázquez, la monarquía e Italia.* Madrid, 1979.

Domínguez Bordona, Jesús. "Noticias para la historia del Buen Retiro," *Revista de Archivos, Bibliotecas y Museos*, 10 (1933), pp. 83–90.

Elliott, J. H. See Brown, Jonathan and Harris, Enriqueta.

Emmens, J. A. "Las Ménines de Velasquez. Miroir des Princes pour Philippe IV," *Nederlands Kunsthistorisch Jaarboek*, 12 (1961), pp. 51–79.

Espada Burgos, Manuel. "Velázquez y el abasto de leña a las reales cocinas," *Anales del Instituto de Estudios Madrileños*, 13 (1976), pp. 123–8.

Foucault, Michel. *Les mots et les choses.* Paris, 1966.

Gállego, Julián. *Velázquez en Sevilla.* Seville, 1974.

——. "Datos sobre la calificación profesional de Velázquez," in *Actas del XXIII Congreso Internacional de Historia de Arte*, III. Granada, 1976, pp. 95–9.

——. *El pintor de artesano a artista.* Granada, 1976.

——. *Velázquez.* Madrid, 1983.

Garrido, María del C., José M. Cabrera, Gridley McKim-Smith, and Richard Newman. "La Fragua de Vulcano. Estudio técnico y algunas consideraciones sobre los materiales y métodos del XVII," *Boletín del Museo del Prado*, 4 (1983), pp. 79–95.

Gaya Nuño, Juan A. "Después de Justi. Medio siglo de estudios velazquistas," in C. Justi, *Velázquez y su siglo.* Madrid, 1953, pp. 799–865.

——. *Bibliografía crítica y antológia de Velázquez.* Madrid, 1963.

Gensel, Walter. *Velázquez. Des Meisters Gemälde*. Rev. ed. Juan Allende-Salazar. Berlin and Leipzig, 1925.

Gérard, Véronique. "Los sitios de devoción en el Alcázar de Madrid: capilla y oratorios," *Archivo español de arte*, 56 (1983), pp. 275–84.

Gerstenberg, Kurt. *Diego Velázquez*. Munich–Berlin, 1957.

———. "Velázquez als humanist," in *Varia Velazqueña*, I, pp. 207–16.

Gómez-Moreno, Manuel. "El Cristo de San Plácido. Pacheco se cobra de un descubierto que tenían con el Velázquez, Cano y Zurbarán," *Boletín de la Sociedad Española de Excursiones*, 24 (1916), pp. 177–88.

———. "'Los Borrachos' y otras notas velazqueñas," in *Varia Velazqueña*, I, pp. 688–91.

González Muñoz, Carmen. "Datos para un estudio de Madrid en la primera mitad del siglo XVII," *Anales del Instituto de Estudios Madrileños*, 18 (1981), pp. 149–91.

Gudiol, José. *Velázquez*. London, 1974.

Guinard, Paul. "Velázquez et les Romantiques Français," in *Varia Velazqueña*, I, pp. 561–73.

Haraszti-Takács, Marianna. *Spanish Genre Painting in the Seventeenth Century*. Budapest, 1983.

Harris, Enriqueta. "El Marqués de Carpio y sus cuadros de Velázquez," *Archivo español de arte*, 30 (1957), pp. 136–9.

———. "Velázquez en Roma," *Archivo español de arte*, 31 (1958), pp. 185–92.

———. "Velázquez's Portrait of Camillo Massimi," *Burlington Magazine*, 100 (1958), pp. 279–80.

———. "A Letter from Velázquez to Camillo Massimi," *Burlington Magazine*, 102 (1960), pp. 162–6.

———. "La misión de Velázquez en Italia," *Archivo español de arte*, 33 (1960), pp. 109–36.

———. "Velázquez and Charles I: Antique Busts and Modern Paintings from Spain in the Royal Collection," *Journal of the Warburg and Courtauld Institutes*, 30 (1967), pp. 414–20.

———. "Cassiano dal Pozzo on Diego Velázquez," *Burlington Magazine*, 112 (1970), pp. 364–73.

———. "The Wallace Collection. The Cleaning of Velázquez' *Lady with a Fan*," *Burlington Magazine*, 117 (1975), pp. 316–19.

———. "Velázquez's Portrait of Prince Baltasar Carlos in the Riding School," *Burlington Magazine*, 118 (1976), pp. 266–75.

———. "Velázquez's Apsley House Portrait: An Identification," *Burlington Magazine*, 120 (1978), p. 304.

———. "G. B. Crescenzi, Velázquez and the 'Italian' Landscapes for the Buen Retiro," *Burlington Magazine*, 122 (1980), pp. 562–4.

———. "Review of José López-Rey, *Velázquez. The Artist as Maker*," *Burlington Magazine*, 123 (1981), pp. 555–6.

———. "Velázquez and His Ecclesiastical Benefice," *Burlington Magazine*, 123 (1981), pp. 95–6.

———. "Velázquez and the Villa Medici," *Burlington Magazine*, 123 (1981), pp. 537–41.

———. *Velázquez*. Oxford, 1982.

———. "The Cleaning of Velázquez's Portrait of Camillo Massimi," *Burlington Magazine*, 125 (1983), pp. 410–15.

Harris, Enriqueta and John Elliott. "Velázquez and the Queen of Hungary," *Burlington Magazine*, 118 (1976), pp. 24–6.

Haskell, Francis. *Rediscoveries in Art: Some Aspects of Taste, Fashion and Collecting in England and France*. Ithaca, 1976.

———. *Patrons and Painters. A Study in the Relations between Italian Art and Society in the Age of the Baroque*. New Haven and London, 1980.

Haskell, Francis and Nicholas Penny. *Taste and the Antique. The Lure of Classical Sculpture, 1500–1900*. New Haven and London, 1981.

Haskell, Francis and Sheila Rinehart. "The Dal Pozzo Collection, Some New Evidence," *Burlington Magazine*, 102 (1960), pp. 318–26.

Hernández Perera, Jesús. "Velázquez y las joyas," *Archivo español de arte*, 33 (1960), pp. 251–86.

Huemer, Frances. *Corpus Rubenianum Ludwig Burchard*. XIX, *Portraits*, I. London, 1977.

Iñiguez Almech, Francisco. "La Casa del Tesoro, Velázquez y las obras reales," in *Varia Velazqueña*, I, pp. 649–82.

———. "Velázquez, arquitecto," *Villa de Madrid*, 3 (1960), pp. 20–6.

Jordan, William B. "Velázquez's *Portrait of Pedro de Barberana*," *Apollo*, 114 (1981), pp. 378–9.

Justi, Carl. *Diego Velázquez und sein Jahrhundert*, 2nd ed. Bonn, 1903; Spanish ed., *Velázquez y su siglo*. Madrid, 1953.

Kahr, Madlyn M. *Velázquez. The Art of Painting*. New York, 1976.

———. "Velázquez's *Las Hilanderas*: A New Interpretation," *Art Bulletin*, 62 (1980), pp. 376–85.

Kemenov, Vladimir. *Velázquez in Soviet Museums*. Leningrad, 1977.

Kinkead, Duncan T. "Tres bodegones en una colección sevillana del siglo XVII," *Archivo español de arte*, 52 (1979), p. 185.

Kubler, George. "The 'Mirror' in *Las Meninas*," *Art Bulletin*, 67 (1985), p. 316.

Lafuente Ferrari, Enrique. *Velázquez. Complete Edition*. London and New York, 1943.

Lefort, Paul. *Velázquez*. Paris, 1888.

Levey, Michael. *Painting at Court*. New York, 1971.

Liedtke, Walter A. and John F. Moffitt. "Velázquez, Olivares, and the Baroque Equestrian Portrait," *Burlington Magazine*, 123 (1981), pp. 529–37.

Longhi, Robert. "Un San Tomasso di Velázquez e le congiunture italo-spagnole tra il '5 e '600," *Vita artistica*, 2 (1927), pp. 4–11.

López Martínez, Celestino. *Arquitectos, escultores y pintores vecinos de Sevilla*. Seville, 1928.

———. *Retablos y esculturas de traza sevillana*. Seville, 1928.

———. *Desde Martínez Montañés hasta Pedro Roldán*. Seville, 1932.

López Navío, José. "Matrimonio de Juan B. del Mazo con la hija de Velázquez," *Archivo español de arte*, 33 (1960), pp. 387–419.

———. "Velázquez tasa los cuadros de su protector, D. Juan de Fonseca." *Archivo español de arte*, 34 (1961) pp. 53–84.

López-Rey, José. "A Head of Philip IV in a Rubens Allegorical Composition," *Gazette des Beaux-Arts*, 53 (1959), pp. 35–44.

———. "Pincelada e imagen en Velázquez," in *Varia Velazqueña*, I, pp. 200–6.

———. *Velázquez. A Catalogue Raisonné of His Oeuvre, with an Introductory Study*. London, 1963.

———. *Velázquez' Work and World*. London, 1968.

———. "Muerte de Villandrando y fortuna de Velázquez," *Arte español*, 26 (1968–69), pp. 1–4.

———. "An Unpublished Velázquez: A Knight of Calatrava," *Gazette des Beaux-Arts*, 80 (1971), pp. 61–70.

———. *Velázquez. The Artist as Maker*. Lausanne–Paris, 1979.

———. "On Velázquez's Portraits of Jesters at the Buen Retiro," *Gazette des Beaux-Arts*, 97 (1981), pp. 163–6.

———. "Review of Enriqueta Harris, *Velázquez*." *Apollo*, 118 (1983): pp. 192–3.

López Serrano, Matilde. *Catálogo de dibujos I. Trazas de Juan de Herrera y sus seguidores para el Monasterio del Escorial*. Madrid, 1944.

Lorente Junquera, Manuel. "Sobre Veronés en el Prado," *Archivo español de arte*, 42 (1969), pp. 235–43.

Lozoya, Marqués de. "El caballo blanco de Velázquez," in *Varia Velazqueña*, I, pp. 323–7.

MacLaren, Neil. *The Spanish School*. National Gallery Catalogue. Rev. ed. Allan Braham. London, 1970. (Cited as MacLaren and Braham.)

McKim-Smith, Gridley. "On Velázquez's Working Method," *Art Bulletin*, 61 (1979), pp. 589–603.

———. "The Problem of Velázquez's Drawings," *Master Drawings*, 18 (1980), pp. 3–24.

McKim-Smith, Gridley, Greta Anderson, and Richard Newman. *Examining Velázquez*. Forthcoming.

Maravall, José A. *Velázquez y el espíritu de la modernidad*. Madrid, 1960.

Martí y Monsó, José. "Diego Velázquez y Alonso Cano en Castilla," *Boletín de la Sociedad Castellana de Excursiones*, 2 (1904), pp. 333–7.

Martínez de la Peña, Domingo. "El segundo viaje de Velázquez a Italia: dos cartas inéditas en los Archivos del Vaticano," *Archivo español de arte*, 44 (1971), pp. 1–7.

Martín González, Juan J. "Arte y artistas del siglo XVII en la corte," *Archivo español de arte*, 32 (1958), pp. 125–42.

———. "Sobre las relaciones entre Nardi, Carducho y Velázquez," *Archivo español de arte*, 31 (1958), pp. 59–66.

———. "Algunas sugerencias acerca de los 'Bufones' de Velázquez," in *Varia Velazqueña*, I, pp. 250–6.

———. "El Pantéon de El Escorial y la arquitectura barroca," *Boletín del Seminario de Estudios de Arte y Arqueología, Universidad de Valladolid*, 47 (1981), pp. 265–84.

Martínez, Jusepe. "Discursos practicables del noblíssimo arte de la pintura," in *Varia Velazqueña*, II, pp. 65–8.

Martínez Ripoll, Antonio. "El 'San Juan Evangelista en la isla de Patmos,' de Velázquez, y sus fuentes de inspiración iconográfica," *Areas. Revista de Ciencas Sociales*, 3–4 (1983), pp. 201–8.

Mayer, August L. "Velázquez und die Niederlandische Kuchenstücke," *Kunstchronik und Kunstmarkt*, 30 (3 January, 1919), pp. 236–7.

———. *Velázquez. A Catalogue Raisonné of the Pictures and Drawings*. London, 1936.

Mélida, José R. "Un recibo de Velázquez," *Revista de Archivos, Bibliotecas y Museos*, 19 (1906), pp. 173–98.

Mena Marqués, Manuela, "La restauración de Las Meninas de Velazquez," *Boletin del Museo del Prado*, 5 (1984), pp. 87–107.

Menéndez Pidal, Gonzalo and Diego Angulo Iñiguez. "'Las Hilanderas,' de Velázquez. Radiografías en infrarroja," *Archivo español de arte*, 38 (1965), pp. 1–12.

Mestre Fiol, Bartolomé. "'El cuadro en el cuadro' en la pintura de Velázquez: Las Hilanderas," *Traza y Baza*, 4 (1974), pp. 77–101.

Moffitt, John F. "Image and Meaning in Velázquez' *Watercarrier of Seville*," *Traza y Baza*, 7 (1978), pp. 5–23.

———. "Observations on Symbolic Content in Two Early Bodegones by Diego Velázquez," *Boletín del Museo e Instituto Camón Aznar*, 1 (1980), pp. 82–95.

———. "Diego Velázquez, Andrea Alciati and the Surrender of Breda," *Artibus et Historiae*, 3 (1982), pp. 75–90.

———. "Velázquez in the Alcázar Palace in 1656: the Meaning of the Mise-en-Scène of *Las Meninas*," *Art History*, 6 (1983), pp. 271–300.

———. "Velázquez's 'Forge of Vulcan,' The Cuckold, the Poets, and the Painter," *Pantheon*, 41 (1983), pp. 322–6.

———. "'Terebat in moratorio:' Symbolism in Velasquez's Christ in the House of Martha and Mary," *Arte Cristiana*, 72, fasc. 700 (1984), pp. 13–14.

Montagu, Jennifer. "Velázquez Marginalia: His Slave Juan de Pareja and His Illegitimate Son Antonio," *Burlington Magazine*, 125 (1983), pp. 683–5.

Morán Turino, J.M., and Fernando Checa. "Las coleccions pictóricas del Escorial y el gusto italiano," *Goya*, 179 (1984), pp. 252–61.

Moreno Villa, José. *Locos, enanos, negros y niños palaciegos. Gente de placer que tuvieron los Austrias en la corte española desde 1563 a 1700*. Mexico City, 1939.

Muller, Priscilla E. "Maino, Crayer, Velazquez and a Miniature of Philip IV," *Art Bulletin*, 60 (1978), pp. 87–8.

Navarro Franco, Federico. "El Real Panteón de San Lorenzo de El Escorial," in *El Escorial 1563–1963. IV Centenario de la Fundación del Monasterio de San Lorenzo el Real*, II. Madrid, 1963, pp. 717–37.

Newman, Richard and Gridley McKim-Smith, "Observations on the Materials and Painting Technique of Diego Velázquez," *The American Institute for Conservation of Historic and Artistic Works. Preprints of Papers Presented at the Tenth Annual Meeting*, Milwaukee, Wisconsin, 26–30 May, 1982.

Orbaan, J. A. F. "Virtuosi al Pantheon. Archivalische Beiträge zur römischen Kunstgeschichte," *Repertorium für Kunstwissenschaft*, 37 (1915), pp. 17–52.

——. "Notes on Art in Italy. Velázquez in Rome," *Apollo*, 6 (July 1927), pp. 27–9.

Orso, Steven N. *Philip IV and the Decoration of the Alcázar of Madrid*. Princeton, forthcoming.

Ortega y Gasset, José. *Velázquez. Sechs Farbige Wiedergaben nach Gemälden aus dem Prado Museum*. Bern, 1943; English ed., Oxford, 1946.

Pacheco, Francisco. *Arte de la pintura*. Ed. Francisco J. Sánchez Cantón. 2 vols. Madrid, 1956.

Palm, Erwin W. "Diego Velázquez: *Aesop* und *Menipp*," in *Lebende Antike. Symposium für Hans-Joachim Zimmerman*. Berlin, 1967, pp. 207–15.

Palomíno, Antonio. *El museo pictórico y escala óptica*. Madrid, 1947.

Pantorba, Bernardino de. *La vida y la obra de Velázquez. Estudio biográfico y crítico*. Madrid, 1955.

Perera, Arturo. "Velázquez, pintor de miniaturas," in *Varia Velazqueña*, I, pp. 378–81.

Pérez Sánchez, Alfonso E. "Una referencia a Velázquez en la obra de Baldinucci," *Archivo español de arte*, 34 (1961), pp. 89–90.

——. *Caravaggio y el naturalismo español*. Seville, 1973.

Pita Andrade, José M. "Los cuadros de Velázquez y Mazo que poseyó el séptimo Marqués de Carpio," *Archivo español de arte*, 23 (1952), pp. 223–36.

——. "El itinerario de Velázquez en su segundo viaje a Italia," *Goya*, 37–8 (1960), pp. 151–2.

——. "Noticias en torno a Velázquez en el Archivo de la Casa de Alba," in *Varia Velazqueña*, I, pp. 400–13.

"Queen Isabella of Bourbon. A 'Lost' Portrait by Velázquez Located," *Connoisseur*, 128 (1951), pp. 3–5.

Réau, Louis. "Velázquez et son influence sur les peintres français du XIXeme siècle," in *Velázquez, son temps et son influence*. Paris, 1960, pp. 95–103.

Rodríguez Marín, Francisco. *Francisco Pacheco, maestro de Velázquez*. Madrid, 1923.

Saltillo, Marqués del. "En torno a 'Las Meninas' y sus personajes," *Arte español*, 15 (1944), pp. 125–33.

Sánchez Cantón, Francisco de. *Los pintores de cámara de los reyes de España*. Madrid, 1916.

——. "La librería de Velázquez," in *Homenaje a Menéndez Pidal*, III. Madrid, 1925, pp. 379–406.

——. "Como vivía Velázquez," *Archivo español de arte*, 15 (1942), pp. 69–91.

——. "La espiritualidad de Velázquez," *Revista de la Universidad Literaria de Oviedo*, 1943.

——. *Las Meninas y sus personajes*. Barcelona, 1943.

——. "La Venus del espejo," *Archivo español de arte*, 33 (1960), pp. 137–40.

——. "Los libros españoles que poseyó Velázquez," in *Varia Velázqueña*, I, pp. 640–8.

——. "Sobre el 'Martínez Montañés de Velázquez," *Archivo español de arte*, 34 (1961), pp. 25–30.

Santos, Francisco de los. *Descripción breve del Monasterio de San Lorenzo El Real del Escorial*. Ed. F. J. Sánchez Cantón, *Fuentes literarias para la historia del arte español*, II. Madrid, 1933.

Saxl, Fritz. "Velázquez and Philip IV," *Lectures*, I. London, 1957, pp. 311–24.

Searle, John R. "*Las Meninas* and the Paradoxes of Pictorial Representation," *Critical Inquiry*, 6 (1980), pp. 177–88.

Sebastián, Santiago. "Lectura iconográfico-iconológica de 'La Fragua de Vulcano,'" *Traza y Baza*, 8 (1983), pp. 20–7.

——. "Nueva lectura de 'Las Hilanderas.' La emblemática como clave de su interpretación," *Revista Fragmentos*, 1 (1984), pp. 45–51.

Snyder, Joel and Ted Cohen. "Critical Response. Reflexions on *Las Meninas*: Paradox Lost," *Critical Inquiry*, 7 (1980), pp. 129–47.

Soehner, Halldor. "El estado actual de la investigación sobre Velázquez," *Clavileño*, no. 9 (May–June 1951), pp. 23–9.

——. "Die Herkunft der Bodegones Velázquez," in *Varia Velazqueña*, I, pp. 233–44.

Sonnenburg, Hubert von. "The Technique and Conservation of the Portrait (of Juan de Pareja)," *Metropolitan Museum of Art Bulletin*, 29 (1970–71), pp. 476–8.

Soria, Martin S. "La Venus, Los Borrachos y La Coronación de Velázquez," *Archivo español de arte*, 26 (1953), pp. 269–84.

——. "'Las Lanzas' y los retratos ecuestres de Velázquez," *Archivo español de arte*, 27 (1954), pp. 93–108.

Spear, Richard E. *Caravaggio and His Followers*. New York, 1975.

Steinberg, Leo. "Review of José López-Rey, *Velázquez. A Catalogue Raisonné of His Oeuvre, with an Introductory Study*." *Art Bulletin*, 47 (1965), pp. 274–94.

——. "The Water Carrier of Seville," *Art News*, 70 (Summer, 1971), pp. 54–5.

——. "Velázquez' *Las Meninas*," *October*, 19 (1981), pp. 45–54.

Stevenson, R. A. M. *Velázquez*. London, 1910.

Stirling-Maxwell, William. *Annals of the Artists of Spain*. London, 1848.

——. *Velázquez and His Works*. London, 1855.

Taylor, Mary Cazort. *European Drawings from Canadian Collections, 1500–1900*. Ottawa, 1976.

Taylor, René. "Juan Bautista Crescencio y la arquitectura cortesana española," *Academia*, 48 (1979), pp. 63–126.

Tolnay, Charles de. "Velázquez' *Las Hilanderas* and *Las Meninas* (An Interpretation)," *Gazette des Beaux-Arts*, 35 (1949), pp. 21–38.

——. "La 'Venus au Miroir' de Velázquez," in *Varia Velazqueña*, I. pp. 339–43.

Tormo, Elías. "Velázquez, el salón de reinos del Buen Retiro y el poeta del palacio y del pintor," in *Pintura, escultura y arquitectura en España. Estudios dispersos*. Madrid, 1949 (first published 1911–12).

Trapier, Elizabeth Du Gué. "Velázquez. New Data on a Group of Portraits," *Notes Hispanic*, 4 (1944), pp. 37–63.

——. *Velázquez*. New York, 1948

——. "The Cleaning of Velázquez's *Count-Duke of Olivares*," in *Varia Velazqueña*, I, pp. 320–22.

Vahlne, Bo. "Velázquez' *Las Meninas*. Remarks on the Staging of Royal Portrait," *Konsthistorisk Tidskrift*, 51 (1982), pp. 21–8.

Varey, John E. "Velázquez y Heliche en los festejos madrileños de 1657–1658," *Boletín de la Real Academia de la Historia*, 169 (1972), pp. 407–22.

Varia Velazqueña. Homenaje a Velázquez en el III centenario de su muerte, 2 vols. Madrid, 1960.

Velázquez. Homenaje en el tercer centenario du su muerte. Madrid, 1960.

Venturi, Adolfo. "Velázquez e Francesco I d'Este," *Nuova Antologia di Scienze, Lettere ed Arti*, 29 (1881), pp. 44–57.

Volk, Mary C. "On Velázquez and the Liberal Arts," *Art Bulletin*, 60 (1978), pp. 69–86.

Warnke, Martin. "Das Reiterbildnes des Balthasar Carlos von Velázquez," in *Amici Amico. Festschrift für Werner Gross zu seinem 65 Geburtstag am 25.11.1966*. Munich, 1968, pp. 217–27.

Weisbach, Werner. "Der sogennarte Geograph von Velázquez und die Darstellungen des Demokrit und Heraklit," *Jahrbuch der Preuszischen Kunstsammlungen*, 49 (1928), pp. 141–58.

Wind, Barry. *Velázquez's Bodegones: A Study in Seventeenth-Century Genre Painting*, Forthcoming.

Zarco del Valle, Manuel R. "Documentos inéditos para la historia de las bellas artes en España," in *Colección de documentos inéditos para la historia de España*, IV. Madrid, 1870.

Zimmerman, Heinrich. "Zur Ikonographie des Hauses Habsburg. I, Bildnisse der Königen Marianne von Spanien," *Jahrbuch des Kunsthistorisches Sammlungen der Ailerhöchsten Kaiserhauses*, 25 (1905), pp. 173–218.

PHOTOGRAPHIC ACKNOWLEDGMENTS

Photographs have been supplied by the owners of the works reproduced except for the following plates:

Mas   9, 11, 25, 30, 31, 39, 66, 118, 164, 181, 244.
Alinari   76, 126, 127
Royal Academy of Art   90
Gavin Ashworth   208
Philip Evola   115, 123, 124, 125, 168, 169, 187
Ron Vickers   218, 219
Los Angeles County Museum   240
Art Resource   305

INDEX